1989

Nuclear deterrence and moral

This unusual collection of essays brings together the work of prominent philosophers, political scientists, policy analysts, and defense consultants. It moves beyond the stalemated debate between mutual assured destruction (MAD) and nuclear utilization target selection (NUTS) to propose ethical and strategic assessments of the fundamental underlying tendencies as well as the current options for deterrence. These tightly integrated essays vigorously debate the moral and the military aspects of current U.S. policies and of leading alternatives recently added to the agenda of policy options, ranging from forms of strategic defenses less ambitious than SDI, to competing varieties of finite deterrence, to conventional deterrence for Europe. Contributors: C. A. J. Coady, Harold A. Feiveson, Robert E. Foelber, Steven Lee, David Lewis, George H. Quester, Henry Shue, Leon Sloss, Lutz Unterseher.

Nuclear deterrence and moral restraint

Critical choices for American strategy

Edited by
HENRY SHUE

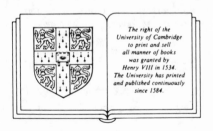

The right of the
University of Cambridge
to print and sell
all manner of books
was granted by
Henry VIII in 1534.
The University has printed
and published continuously
since 1584.

CAMBRIDGE UNIVERSITY PRESS

CAMBRIDGE

NEW YORK   PORT CHESTER   MELBOURNE   SYDNEY

Published by the Press Syndicate of the University of Cambridge
The Pitt Building, Trumpington Street, Cambridge CB2 1RP
40 West 20th Street, New York, NY 10011, USA
10 Stamford Road, Oakleigh, Melbourne 3166, Australia

First published 1989

Printed in the United States of America

Library of Congress Cataloging-in-Publication Data

Nuclear deterrence and moral restraint : critical choices for
American strategy / edited by Henry Shue.
p. cm.
ISBN 0-521-38063-4. – ISBN 0-521-38967-4 (pbk.)
1. Nuclear arms control – United States – Moral and ethical aspects.
2. Nuclear arms control – Soviet Union – Moral and ethical aspects.
3. Deterrence (Strategy) – Moral and ethical aspects.   I. Shue, Henry.
JX1974.7.N8133   1989
172'.422 – dc20   89-32209

British Library Cataloguing in Publication Data

Nuclear deterrence and moral restraint: critical
choices for American strategy.
1. Nuclear warfare. Policies of United States
government
I. Shue, Henry
355'.0217

ISBN 0-521-38063-4 hard covers
ISBN 0-521-38967-4 paperback

Contents

Contents

Preface

From start to finish this book has been a product of the Institute for Philosophy and Public Policy at the University of Maryland, College Park. Under the Institute's aegis the need for a book of this unusual kind was understood, the plans for it gradually evolved, thorough discussions of the issues were repeatedly held, and the results were revised – and revised. Loyal colleagues with other agendas of their own – Robert K. Fullinwider, Judith Lichtenberg, David Luban, Douglas MacLean, Claudia Mills, Mark Sagoff, Jerome Segal, and Robert Wachbroit – as well as visiting fellows – C. A. J. Coady, Amy Gutmann, Steven Lee, Richard Mohr, Thomas Pogge, and Ferdinand Schoeman – listened and responded to worried musings about nuclear weapons systems month after month, until "no more nukes" acquired a whole new meaning. Invaluable advice during the initial planning for the research came from Bob Fullinwider and Doug MacLean, as well as from other Maryland colleagues with deep understandings of international security, George H. Quester in the Department of Government and Politics and Catherine McArdle Kelleher in the School of Public Affairs.

All the authors of chapters in this volume except Steven Lee were members of the Institute's multiyear Working Group on Nuclear Policy and Morality, and Lee wrote his own chapter at the Institute as a Rockefeller Fellow during the year after the Working Group's initial meetings. The meetings of the Working Group were also enriched by the contributions of insightful members who did not provide chapters for this book: Catherine McArdle Kelleher, Michael Nacht, Terumasa Nakanishi, and Richard Wasserstrom. The meetings of the Working Group, in which such different people with such diverse views from four different nations tested each other's reasoning while respecting each other's integrity, pushed all of us who were writing chapters well beyond where we began. Participation in these intensive and extensive discussions was certainly one of the richest educational experiences of my life.

The meticulous care of Louise Collins combined with the boundless energy of Carroll Linkins produced the many versions of the manuscript. Along the way extensive correspondence, elaborate meetings, complicated budgets, and happier times than one might have expected at any other research institute all flowed from the various delightful combinations of Louise and Carroll with Lyndal Andrews, Susan Mann, Lori Owen, Mary Ellen Stevens, and Kate Wiersema.

The international interdisciplinary working group and this collection of extensive studies were made possible by a grant (No. 850-0088) to the Institute from the Division of International Affairs Programs of the Ford Foundation. All the authors are grateful for Ford's support for everything the project needed, and the editor especially benefited from the good counsel – and patience – of Enid C. B. Schoettle, program officer in charge of the International Division. We are also grateful for the suggestions of two anonymous reviewers for Cambridge University Press. I appreciated as well the informal hospitality of Michael Walzer and the School of Social Science of the Institute for Advanced Study in Princeton during portions of one year of my background research. Tony Coady and I would also like to thank the Strategic Air Command for briefings we received (as well as for the only up-close and personal in-flight refueling we ever hope to witness). The authors of individual chapters are, of course, entirely responsible for the views expressed in their own chapters.

As the work on this book ended, so did my formal association with the Institute for Philosophy and Public Policy – "the Center," as we knew it for the first decade. I would like to think the book is almost good enough to be worthy of the Maryland home in which it was nurtured.

Berkshire, New York
March 1989

Notes on Contributors

C. A. J. Coady is Reader in Philosophy at the University of Melbourne and has held visiting fellowships at Oxford and Cambridge as well as visiting positions at American universities. He has published extensively in leading philosophical journals on topics including epistemology and philosophy of language and has a particular interest in philosophical problems of political violence.

Harold A. Feiveson is a member of the Senior Research Staff of the Center for Energy and Environmental Studies, as well as a member of the Center of International Studies, at Princeton University. He has contributed to the development of the technical bases for arms control agreements, including a proposal for a low-threshold nuclear test ban and studies of plutonium recycling and nuclear proliferation.

Robert E. Foelber is a Research Fellow at the Logistics Management Institute studying wartime logistics. In earlier research positions at the Congressional Research Service of the Library of Congress and the Heritage Foundation he has written on a variety of national security issues including strategic forces modernization, arms control, and U.S. and Soviet defense spending and force readiness.

Contributors

Steven Lee is Associate Professor of Philosophy, and Chair of the Department, at Hobart and William Smith Colleges and has been a Rockefeller Fellow at the Institute for Philosophy and Public Policy. He has published several articles on ethical issues raised by nuclear weapons policy and has co-edited *Nuclear Weapons and the Future of Humanity* (1986).

David Lewis is Professor of Philosophy at Princeton University. He is the author of *Convention: A Philosophical Study* (1969), *Counterfactuals* (1973), and *On the Plurality of Worlds* (1986).

George H. Quester is Chairman of the Department of Government and Politics at the University of Maryland and formerly Chairman of the Department of Government at Cornell University. Author of a number of books and articles on international politics and international security issues, he is a member of the International Institute for Strategic Studies and the Council on Foreign Relations.

Henry Shue is the first Director of the Program on Ethics & Public Life, and Professor of Philosophy, at Cornell University. During a decade at the Institute for Philosophy and Public Policy at the University of Maryland he served as Director, conducted interdisciplinary research projects on ethical issues concerning world hunger and human rights as well as national security, and wrote *Basic Rights* (1980).

Leon Sloss is a consultant on defense strategy and foreign affairs, based in Washington. He has served in the Department of State, the Department of Defense, the Arms Control and Disarmament Agency, and other government agencies, as well as in private research and consulting organizations providing guidance on defense policy to government and industry.

Contributors

Lutz Unterseher is Chairman of the European Study Group on Alternative Security Policy (SAS) and a partner in the private social research institute SALSS, both based in Bonn. In addition to conducting research on intraorganizational communication, he has been a visiting lecturer at Konstanz University and for the British Army, and is an advisor on security policy to the Social Democratic Party of West Germany.

Introduction

Henry Shue

At least in the West nuclear "strategy" is in chaos. This is nothing new. Already in 1981 Lawrence Freedman had concluded his magisterial *The Evolution of Nuclear Strategy:*

> The position we have reached is one where stability depends on something that is more the antithesis of strategy than its apotheosis – on threats that things will get out of hand, that we might act irrationally, that possibly through inadvertence we could set in motion a process that in its development and conclusion would be beyond human control and comprehension.[1]

Others as different as Robert Jervis and Robert McNamara have continued to point out that, in McNamara's words, "The fact is, the Emperor has no clothes. Our present nuclear policy is bankrupt."[2]

What is new is that we have now reached a historic juncture where the incoherence of the existing rationales for nuclear deterrence in general and for specific nuclear weapons systems in particular is more likely than ever to lead to mistaken policies that could cost hundreds of billions of dollars and hundreds of millions of lives. The Soviet Union has agreed in the Intermediate Nuclear Forces Treaty to asymmetrical reductions in nuclear weapons. It has also volunteered asymmetrical and unilateral reductions in conventional weapons and forces. The United States must decide, in the face of this, whether to spend tens of billions on the production of Stealth bombers *and* tens of billions on the development of strategic defenses *and* tens of billions on the development of a new small land-based missile *and* tens of billions on production of a new submarine-launched missile, among other weapons systems. We need to know what form of deterrence the United States is attempting to implement in order to decide which, if any, additional weapons systems its implementation would take. The accustomed luxury of simply borrowing enough to go ahead with everything, and thereby evading all the hard choices, appears to have slipped away from the United States just as it has from the Soviet Union. If the no-longer-evadable decisions are to be made with some semblance of rationality, we need to know whether there is some specific form of nuclear deterrence that is both militarily and morally acceptable. This is the subject of this book: If there is a form of nuclear deterrence that can be justified in current circumstances, what is it?

This is a book that no one person could have written, and the nine of us have teamed together to accomplish something that is rarely achieved. A great deal has been written to assess specific forms of nuclear deterrence in strategic terms, and increasingly a considerable amount is being written to assess nuclear deterrence in ethical terms. The ethical discussions tend, however, to ignore the full range of strategic choices and to concentrate upon the simplest and most manageable – and therefore purely abstract – cases. For example, most discussions of the ethics of deterrence are written as if there were simply two nuclear powers attempting to deter attacks upon each other – as if, in the jargon, all deterrence were central deterrence. The facts could not be more different. From the beginning the main concern of the United States has always been what is called extended deterrence, the deterrence of attacks not upon itself, but upon allies like West Germany and Japan. And extended deterrence has always been aimed, since before the Soviet Union even had nuclear weapons, at deterring conventional attacks upon allies – hence NATO's policy of the first use of nuclear weapons against conventional attack. Such facts as that U.S. nuclear deterrence has been intended to prevent attacks upon allies, as well as attacks upon the U.S. homeland, and that U.S. nuclear deterrence was first and foremost intended to deter conventional attacks upon those allies, are not details that can be added into an ethical assessment later when it is otherwise almost finished. The philosophers who have written for this volume have therefore tried to assess deterrence as it actually is, not as it might have been in some world of rational games. However much we have challenged reality, we have tried to be sure that it is reality that we have challenged. This has required all the philosophers (Coady, Lee, Lewis, and Shue) to wade into the strategic debates.

And the strategists – not all the non-philosophers who have contributed would think of themselves primarily as strategists, so I use the term loosely – have borne in mind the relevant ethical considerations as they have argued that deterrence should now move in one direction rather than another. Some defend forms of deterrence that are relatively close to current policy (insofar as it is possible to say what current policy is). Others defend more or less sharp departures in one direction or another, from the incorporation of strategic defenses without abandoning offensive missiles (Sloss) to considerably deeper cuts in offensive missiles than are currently being contemplated (Feiveson) to deterring attack in Europe without relying upon either nuclear forces or the kind of conventional forces currently favored by NATO (Unterseher). Some of the strategists (especially Foelber and Quester) have waded explicitly into the ethical debates.

Thus, in this volume the strategic analysis is done with a relatively high level of ethical awareness, and the ethical analysis is done with a relatively high level of strategic awareness. The combined level of strategic and ethical sophistication is, I think, far beyond what any one person could have hoped to achieve. Best of all, in spite of the wide range of views represented – among both strategists and philosophers are both supporters and critics of nuclear deterrence – the amount and depth of direct debate among chapters gives the book as a whole an unusual degree of unity. Over the years during which we debated these issues with each other most chapters came to respond directly to several other chapters – some of the running battles spill out of the text and on into the notes, where they will stop only when the print is cold (if then). Therefore, although the book is not the expression of any one point of view, the reader is given much guidance in seeing how the various positions stack up against each other.

AN OVERVIEW

My opening chapter, like the second chapter by David Lewis, offers a fresh characterization of the fundamental choices in nuclear strategy. Yet, while Lewis constructs a powerful defense of a carefully defined form of "modest counterforce," I conclude that the pursuit of "countervailing counterforce," which I take to be the current policy of both superpowers, must either be pointless or encourage preemption. My chapter analyzes the internal logic of the two fundamental tendencies in nuclear strategy, the tendency to welcome and rely upon the mutual vulnerability of the two populations held hostage by nuclear weapons and the tendency to seek militarily decisive targets for nuclear weapons rather than targeting the cities and the general population. On the one hand, mutual vulnerability is best seen, I suggest, as a bizarre kind of utopianism, because its goal is the abolition of all war between nuclear powers. This boundless goal is what seems to justify the grotesquely disproportionate means, the disproportionate threat to the adversary's population and the disproportionate risk to one's own, in spite of a long history of the moral requirement of proportionality. On the other hand, the countervailing strategy tries to have it both ways by retaining the utopian goal of the prevention of all war between nuclear powers while purporting to eliminate, through flexible response, the disproportionality of the threat

4

to others, and to eliminate, through damage limitation, the disproportionality of the risk to ourselves. This creates, I argue, a militarily unstable and theoretically incoherent position that in the end makes no sense even in its own terms.

While the first chapter has worked inside the orthodox assumptions about nuclear strategy in an effort to show them incoherent or dangerous, David Lewis's chapter radically challenges orthodox combinations and imaginatively creates new ones on the way to formulating a strategy of "modest counterforce" that, he argues, is morally and strategically justified. Adopting what McGeorge Bundy has called "existential deterrence," Lewis carries this conception of deterrence to its logical conclusion by challenging the generally unquestioned assumption that weapon employment policy must dictate weapon procurement policy and suggesting instead that one could, as a first approximation of a better strategy, "buy like a MADman, use like a NUT." MAD (Mutual Assured Destruction) and NUTS (Nuclear Utilization Target Selection) are logical extremes, and each is a package consisting of a policy for procuring nuclear weapons dictated by a plan for using weapons if deterrence fails. MAD's plan for using weapons is to commit vast massacres, which are utterly unacceptable, but its policy for procuring weapons is relatively sane. In contrast, the NUT's plan for using weapons is relatively restrained, but his procurement policy easily becomes dangerously ambitious. Lewis's heretical suggestion is that one could "buy like a MADman" through accepting as one's quantitative benchmark the size of forces that MAD would require but, since one would in the case of deterrence failure "use like a NUT," select the kind of counterforce weapons useful against military, not civilian targets. This produces "modest counterforce," which should both effectively deter war and provide military options that are not immoral to use if deterrence fails. In the process of working out his original strategic proposal in thorough detail and dealing systematically with eleven possible objections to it, Lewis explains why what philosophers have called the "paradox of deterrence" need not arise and constructs by far the most complete account to date of a version of existential deterrence.

Like Lewis, Robert Foelber chooses not to evade, as so many defenders of nuclear deterrence do, the crucial issue of whether, if deterrence fails, the actual use of nuclear forces can ever be justified. Defending thoroughly a position he calls "Nuclear Protectionism," Foelber specifies two particular sets of circumstances – a "high" and a "low" case – in which he believes the defense of shared values would require a nuclear response to attack. Grounded in the arguments for these two types of nuclear retaliation is a defense of "a 'cautious' nuclear damage-limiting strategy that, with some notable exceptions, is roughly consistent with declared U.S. nuclear strategy" but that stops short of a full-blown countervailing strategy. Foelber directly takes on both critiques of offense-dominated damage-limiting strategies focused upon morality, especially the Just War tradition as invoked by the U.S. Catholic bishops and developed in this volume by Coady, and critiques focused upon stability, which appeal either to the logic of preemption or to the psychology of preemption, like my own chapter. Maintaining that "deterrence cannot be had on the moral cheap," Foelber unequivocally and forcefully formulates some of the rock-bottom choices, and makes and forthrightly defends his judgments against leading criticisms of nuclear deterrence. If Foelber is correct on the moral issues, we do not face the dilemma explored in a later chapter by Quester and assumed in mine.

C. A. J. Coady's chapter, like my own, is a critique of nuclear deterrence in general and of the kinds of counterforce strategies, in particular, put forward by Lewis and Foelber (and, in a later chapter focusing upon the role of defense, Sloss). Coady, however, presents the specifically moral case against nuclear deterrence, carrying forward the current debates among philosophers in the first half of his chapter and, in the second half, launching a fascinating and critical new debate about what he calls "extrication morality," the ethical considerations that should guide the transition out of an initial situation in which one is already doing wrong (as he concludes, in the first half, we are in maintaining nuclear deterrence). Coady pursues not "consequentialist" morality, or arguments based entirely on the consequences of actions, but "internalist" morality, which gives a central place to the nature of actions themselves and the kinds of persons who will perform them. In direct contradiction of Lewis and Foelber, he argues, first, that all uses of nuclear weapons as they would in fact occur are immoral, even where the use would be retaliatory. He then argues, replying to objections as he goes, that nuclear deterrence itself cannot be morally justified. Other philosophers who have reached this negative assessment of deterrence have often then instantly leapt to the conclusion that the way out is unilateral nuclear disarmament. Without in any way qualifying his condemnation of nuclear deterrence, Coady at this point sensitively explores what he suggests are the partly independent moral considerations that govern prudent disengagement from what is wrong and thus opens the promising and largely uncharted area of the morality of extrication, ending with specific implications for nuclear strategy.

In defending assured destruction as the best available nuclear strategy, George Quester provides a critique of moral critiques like Coady's (and the U.S. bishops') as likely to do more harm than good, as well as a challenge to the various forms of counterforce strategy defended by others in the volume, including Lewis's "modest counterforce." While acknowledging the strangeness of the strategy of assured destruction, and our consequent difficulty in accepting it morally or psychologically, Quester portrays what he sees as the current tendency to claim to be employing counterforce strategy while actually also relying heavily upon countervalue effects (harm to civilians) as the current chapter in the long history of a two-part phenomenon of exaggerating the counterforce effects of military operations and hypocritically concealing the countervalue effects. The naval blockades employed before the invention of the airplane were, Quester argues, much less a matter of counterforce and much more a matter of countervalue – of hurting the general population – than their

7

proponents would have us believe. So too were the aerial bombardments even as early as World War I, when the young Winston Churchill accepted the "terrorization of the civil population" as "incidental and inevitable." Believing that in nuclear deterrence tendencies toward counterforce are in fact dangerous, Quester makes the provocative suggestion that if we cannot revolutionize our morality to make the much safer strategy of assured destruction acceptable – and he considers that moral revolution most unlikely – the less said the better (by, for example, most of the philosophers in this volume) about the unacceptability by traditional moral standards of the targeting of civilians. Better to live with hypocrisy than to die from moralism.

Harold Feiveson's position in his chapter presents both sharp contrasts and natural complementarities with other positions defended in the volume. While Lewis too considers the form of deterrence he favors to be finite, Feiveson has long advocated nuclear forces considerably smaller than those Lewis recommends and only one-tenth the size of current Soviet and American forces. These deep reductions could leave more than enough survivable retaliatory capability to maintain the mutual hostage relationship – 2,000 strategic warheads on each side – and the pursuit of any other goals by means of nuclear weapons is argued to be illusory. Earlier versions of finite deterrence have been criticized as lacking the credibility necessary for extended deterrence because of the vast destruction the use of their forces would cause, compared to some supposedly less destructive form of counterforce. Feiveson argues, citing recent careful projections, that this contrast depends on baseless notions of the effects of counterforce in Europe. This leads Feiveson to an interpretation of existential deterrence (which Lewis has challenged) on which one need have no firm plans about what to do if deterrence fails: "One answer is to target nothing or, rather, to the extent possible, to design the retaliatory force to allow time after a nuclear attack for the political authorities to decide what to do in the real context of a nuclear war rather than having them rely on some prepackaged contingency plans designed during peacetime." The only realistic goal if nuclear war begins would be to limit and end the war.

The implementation of the Intermediate Nuclear Forces (INF) Treaty between the Soviet Union and the United States has swung the spotlight onto conventional military forces and their role in deterring war in Europe. Lutz Unterseher presents a detailed illustration of a militarily effective form of what might be called unconventional conventional defenses for Europe. The "interactive forward defense" developed by the European Study Group on Alternative Security Policy with headquarters in Bonn, and presented in this chapter, is conventional in that it does not rely at all on nuclear weapons for the deterrence of attack and "unconventional" in that it differs sharply from the mainstream NATO thinking of recent decades. Unterseher maintains that NATO's current unhappy mix of nuclear deterrence and conventional deterrence weakens both kinds of deterrence and has produced the "de facto no first use" of nuclear weapons. Showing why he believes that NATO's notion of threatening penetration eastward as the retaliatory punishment for a Warsaw Pact invasion is provocative, he recommends the reestablishment of denial, rather than punishment, as the basic concept of NATO defense. The conventional forces capable of denying success to an invading force through interactive forward defense, with its reliance upon highly resistant complexity in organization and tactics rather than the high technology relied upon by NATO, would also satisfy, as NATO fails to do, the two fundamental principles central to the various versions of alternative defense formulated in the Federal Republic of Germany: no-provocation (creation of an unambiguously defensive posture) and no-target (avoidance of an invitation to attack by presenting only a multitude of individually unimportant targets). The alternative form of conventional defense detailed by Unterseher could be adopted unilaterally by NATO prior to, and creating better conditions for, negotiated mutual conventional reductions. Interactive forward defense would also permit the Europeanization of the conventional deterrence and defense of Europe, leaving the United States to be concerned only with strategic nuclear deterrence, which Unterseher believes should be the finite deterrence advocated by Feiveson.

No issue is more central and controversial than whether active defenses against nuclear missiles contribute to or detract from deterrence. The final two chapters present respectively the strongest available arguments for and against strategic defenses. Leon Sloss, writing with the authority of an architect of the current countervailing strategy, sums up the dominant U.S. thinking about national security and the role of nuclear weapons in it. Against that background he presents the case for a planned natural evolution from current strategy to a careful mix of nuclear offense and nuclear defense. Sloss recommends, then, not the visionary, near-perfect defenses of Ronald Reagan's SDI, but the "incremental incorporation of intermediate, less-than-perfect defenses" as a complementary component of the countervailing strategy. Sloss's far more sophisticated and qualified proposal seeks to supplement offenses, not to supplant them – to reinforce offensive missiles, not to replace them. After a critique of five alternative approaches to strengthening deterrence, including SDI and NATO's preferred forms of conventional defense, Sloss presents a clear rationale for the addition of active missile defenses. The goal of the countervailing strategy for the use of offensive missiles is already "to deny an adversary confidence in achieving his military objectives." Defenses against attacking missiles can reduce the potential attacker's confidence to a still lower level, further complicating his calculations about which targets his attack is likely to destroy and making it considerably more uncertain that the attack could be worth launching than it would be in the absence of defenses. "The deployment of limited active defenses . . . is perfectly consistent with our traditional nuclear strategy, enhancing the denial component of deterrence while working to preserve retaliatory forces." Sloss thus sees not a revolutionary, but a nevertheless potentially vital, role for defenses in the most credible form of nuclear deterrence.

Steven Lee conceptualizes defenses against ballistic missiles as a new means to a long-cherished goal: the capability to fight a limited nuclear war. He distinguishes as "SDI-1" the leakproof defenses envisioned by Ronald Reagan and as "SDI-2" the only moderately effective, or leaky, defenses endorsed as nevertheless highly valuable by Leon Sloss. The moral argument for SDI-1 had been that once our defenses had made us safe we could abandon our morally questionable offensive missiles; when their missiles were impotent, ours would be obsolete. The quite different, and much more significant, moral case for SDI-2 made here by Leon Sloss (and to some extent also by Robert Foelber) has two elements. Damage limitation, as a form of the avoidance of great harm, is in itself of moral value; so too is the war avoidance that might result if Sloss is correct that additional uncertainty created by defenses yields enhanced deterrence. Taking seriously the fact that SDI-2 defenses are intended as a means of counterforce warfare in the form of a countervailing or warfighting strategy, Lee maintains that while damage limitation and war avoidance are each in themselves of moral value, "war avoidance is more important morally than damage limitation." He then offers several challenges to the rationale for defenses that is based on increasing the uncertainty of success for the potential attacker. Lee suggests, first, that we have no good reason to believe that existing levels of uncertainty are not already high enough for a more-than-adequate level of deterrence. Then, using the notion of attack price, defined as "the number of warheads that would have to be launched at a target to achieve a high level of assurance of its destruction," Lee argues that defenses cannot increase the level of uncertainty about success but can only increase the attack price for any given level of confidence. Contending further that defenses in earth orbit present what Paul Nitze has called "tempting targets," Lee concludes that defenses not only would not decrease the likelihood of war but would positively increase it.

NOTES

1. Lawrence Freedman, *The Evolution of Nuclear Strategy* (New York: St. Martin's, 1981), p. 400.
2. Robert S. McNamara, *Blundering into Disaster: Surviving the First Century of the Nuclear Age* (New York: Pantheon, 1986), p. 138. Also see Robert Jervis, *The Illogic of American Nuclear Strategy*, Cornell Studies in Security Affairs (Ithaca: Cornell University Press, 1984).

Chapter 1

Having it both ways: the gradual wrong turn in American strategy

Henry Shue

To domesticate or not to domesticate is, I think, the question about nuclear weapons. To deter attack upon your nation and its allies by possessing nuclear weapons has been much like protecting your house and neighborhood against a rival neighborhood by keeping a wild and ferocious beast chained in your basement.[1] The wildness and ferocity of the beast may either persuade potential attackers to keep their distance or convince them that you will never actually unchain the beast for fear he will destroy you before, while, or after destroying your attackers.

Picture the beast as a hungry tiger. The initial credibility problem is made worse by two additional factors. Now, the people in the rival neighborhood also have wild tigers – perhaps even bears – chained in their basements, and it seems likely that if we ever unchained our tigers against them they would unleash theirs against us. The increased imprudence of releasing our tigers raises further doubts about whether we would do it. The other factor is that, as far as anyone can tell, a lot of the tigers are basically man-eaters. One might have hoped that if both sides released their tigers, the tigers would just fight each other. It seems more likely, however, that the tigers will largely ignore each other and rampage through one or the other neighborhood, slaughtering whoever is at home.

What seems to be needed, then, are smart tigers. The tigers need to be domesticated to the extent of learning to obey a few commands. Then they can be taught that, when released, they are not to roar through the streets killing people, but are to engage the enemy tigers. This will be better not only because it is pointless just to kill a bunch of people in the other neighborhood but primarily because our threat to unleash our tigers will be much more believable if everyone knows that our tigers are smart and reliable.

There are problems, however. If the domestication effort works, we are no longer guarded by wild beasts but only by big strong cats – serious cats, no doubt, but nothing wild, unpredictable, and terrifying – and our rivals can train their tigers too. If the domestication effort does not work, the likely imprudence and cruelty of actual release may continue to undermine the credibility of threats to do so. Of course, no one will be sure whether the attempts at domestication have worked or not, although doubters and believers will feel strongly. Meanwhile, tigers are cheaper than armed guards.

The most fundamental criticisms of nuclear deterrence may well be "external" to the "system" of deterrence. International affairs have not always been dominated by a small number of nuclear-armed powers attempting to prevent change through military force by threatening to turn any skirmish into a holocaust. Perhaps international politics need not always be conducted this way throughout all time. It may at least be worth stepping (mentally) outside the whole regime of mutual nuclear deterrence and asking basic questions about it. Is a system of nuclear deterrence in fact the most effective means of war prevention available? Do the desires of the nuclear powers to avoid war among themselves justify their imposition of extraordinary risks upon the peasants and tradesmen, the parents and children, of other societies to whom the major powers are of no use and no interest – how do you justify risking a nuclear winter, if we are risking one, to a Bolivian homemaker or a Kenyan herder? These are, I think, hard and important questions, but I will not pursue them.[2]

I want instead to look at a difficulty "internal" to nuclear deterrence, that is, a problem about the overall coherence of the explanations available for what is now being done. Nuclear deterrence seems to me to be coming unstuck from the inside. Such incoherence is as fatal an objection as any external critique, and it has the persuasive advantage of not resting upon alien premises.

VULNERABILITY, CONTAINMENT, AND THE ABOLITION OF WAR

From almost any point of view the policy of mutual assured destruction would look strange indeed – "weird" is not too strong a description. Consider separately the means and the end.

The means employed for the prevention of war in a regime of mutual assured destruction would consist of two complementary elements, one considerably stranger than the other: first, an incentive for the adversary not to attack you, and, second, an assurance to the adversary against being attacked by you.

The incentive for the adversary not to attack is the defender's capability and will to wreak destruction upon the adversary's society. Massacres themselves are not at all strange, but it is fairly unusual, even if not unprecedented, to have premeditated massacre as an announced policy. The nearest precursors may have been the practices of those tribes – it is hard to avoid adding "of primitive people" – who made a point of establishing an unequivocal track record, so to speak, that made abundantly clear what failing attackers could expect to have happen to their homes and families. Certainly there was no tradition prior to the nuclear age of planning the massacres in advance of the conditions that would provoke them and posting the conditions. Of late we have, as George Quester shows below, tended to package our massacres as either collateral damage or counterforce targets.[3]

Yet stranger still is the other element in mutual vulnerability – to switch to a name for MAD not coined by a critic in

15

order to provide an embarrassing acronym – as a means of deterring war: an assurance to the adversary against his being attacked by you, in the form of the equal vulnerability of your own society.[4] This assurance is, like the first element, a kind of incentive not to attack, or, more precisely, it is the elimination of an incentive to attack. You need not attack us, it says, for fear we will attack you – that is, you need not attack preemptively – because we would not attack you when we ourselves are so thoroughly vulnerable to your retaliation: We offer you our entire society as hostage to the sincerity of our pledge not to attack first.

It is this second, stranger element that there has been some tendency to forget in recent years. The emphasis in the first element on intentional direct countervalue attack is certainly unusual, but general attempts to prevent war by saying, in effect, "If you mess with me I'll smash you" are hardly a new idea. What is radical as a move in big-power international politics is the second element: "You need not attack me because I lie bare before your retaliation (and you can therefore rest assured I will not attack you, however much I hate you)."

This is not politics as usual. Einstein was at least partly wrong (how often do we get to say that?) when he declared that "the unleashed power of the atom has changed everything save our modes of thinking." He was presumably talking about allowing nation-states to continue to be the main effective political units, which has not changed. Mutual vulnerability, however, is a new idea about the means of conducting big-power international affairs. "New," of course, does not imply better, and nothing said herein is intended as an absolute defense of mutual vulnerability as a policy.

What is the end sought through mutual vulnerability? The end, or purpose, also is two-part: the containment of communism without direct military conflict. Nuclear deterrence was from the beginning – see National Security Council Directive 68 – intended to stop the Soviet Union where it was in 1950 without having to fight a war to do it.[5] As declaratory doctrines of general nuclear deterrence became declaratory doctrines specifically of mutual vulnerability, the duality of purpose remained. It is vital to accurate understanding to remember that the concept of nuclear deterrence and the concept of containment – and their summary concept of national security – all evolved together: Try explaining the contemporary American concept of national security without making essential and central reference to the deterrence of nuclear war and the containment of communism.[6] The policy was never conflict avoidance at any cost – specifically, never conflict avoidance at the cost of ceding additional territory and people.

When has one of two great empires – evil empires or good empires is not my concern here – ever said to the other: "We will not attempt to take by military force anything that you have, because we will always allow you to be able to destroy us, and you must not attempt to take by military force anything that we have, because we will always remain able to destroy you"? The containment half of the package of goals was not especially new. Great empires have normally attempted to check each other's expansion, at the very least – genuine renunciation of any attempt at a rollback of the other would be more remarkable. What is truly revolutionary, however, is the attempt to combine containment with what amounts to the abolition of war between the two camps concerned. Nuclear deterrence in the form of mutual vulnerability is supposed to make any direct military conflict between the two sides, nuclear or conventional, as unlikely as is humanly possible. *All* war between these two parties is to be abolished – successful conventional attack runs the same ultimate risk of assured nuclear destruction as nuclear attack. Nuclear attack is to be outright suicide, conventional attack is to be suicide on the installment plan. George Quester once described the proposed sharing of the technology for ballistic missile defenses as mutual disarmament by national technical means. Mutual vulnerability is intended, it seems to me, to be the abolition of direct major conflict among the nuclear powers by national technical means, namely by means of your guaranteeing both their and your own vulnerability.

This gallows humor about national technical means veils

an important point: Mutual vulnerability is a game that one can play alone. It is often breathlessly announced that the Soviet Union has never accepted "MAD logic," or the doctrine of mutual vulnerability. As far as I can understand it, this is (a) true, (b) unfortunately expensive for both sides, but (c) not vitally important. It is possible for one side successfully to maintain mutual vulnerability simply by taking effective measures to guarantee the vulnerability of both sides. (Whether it is smart or ethical are, of course, the questions.) Maintaining your own vulnerability is simple enough – it is primarily a matter of not going to great lengths to build adequate defenses. Maintaining the other side's vulnerability means maintaining an invulnerable second-strike force capable of assured destruction (a very small force, in the absence of defenses, as argued below by Harold Feiveson)[7] and developing penetration aids faster than the other side develops defenses, if it is developing general defenses. Obviously, such unilaterally maintained mutual vulnerability is not guaranteed to succeed, but a technologically superior state needs no cooperation from the adversary state – it needs only to maintain technological superiority.

I am not asserting that the unilateral abolition of major direct war among the nuclear powers, which is the promise of mutual vulnerability, can be attained. That would be to say that mutual vulnerability will in fact deter war – I make no such claim. I am noting only that, with superior technology, mutual vulnerability itself can be unilaterally maintained: It is possible to keep both your own and your adversary's societies vulnerable without your adversary's cooperation.

On the other hand, mutual vulnerability actually allows for cooperation between the adversaries. That a "balance of terror," correctly so called, also could be a cooperative endeavor may be the strangest feature of all. (Emphasis on "could be," of course, since it is not now very cooperative.) Cooperative behavior is possible on both offenses and defenses. On offenses, cooperating with mutual vulnerability means either not building weapons capable of destroying hardened counterforce targets at all or building at most a number of hard-target-counterforce weapons far too small to appear to threaten the adversary's second-strike force – keeping your forces "finite," or limited. On defenses, it means basically, not building them, unless they defend only second-strike forces rather than population. In both instances you would be cooperating in the maintenance of your own vulnerability.

The preceding point was that if one side is technologically superior such cooperation is not necessary. The cooperation is nevertheless, possible. Whether such cooperation in your own potential destruction is as crazy as it sounds, or is an exceedingly clever way to prevent wars, is of course the issue about the wisdom of mutual vulnerability. I have only come to lay out the alleged dynamics, not, at this point, to praise them or to condemn them.

One final point, for now, about this characterization of mutual vulnerability. It should be obvious that I consider the second element of the means used – your own society's vulnerability to destruction as the assurance to the adversary that he is safe from attack – essential to the doctrine of mutual vulnerability in its finished form. There is, however, no denying, but no need to deny, the fact that this element was a later addition. During the American monopoly of nuclear weapons, as well as the significant period of clear American superiority, which we now know lasted longer than we then thought, there was no mutuality in fact or in doctrine. The doctrine of *mutual* vulnerability is the clearest case one could ever hope to see of making a virtue of necessity. Still, this is merely another reminder that military doctrine tends to follow military technology. That the doctrine of mutual vulnerability welcomes a development that in any case advocates of the doctrine could hardly have prevented tells us only that we would be well advised to give the doctrine a critical look. It does not tell us that it is not appropriate to the situation that did develop. Doctrinal genesis does not determine doctrinal adequacy.

How could anyone possibly believe that the cultivation of mutual social vulnerability, the maintenance of balance of civilian terror, mutual hostage-taking and hostage-giving on a mass scale, is the way to prevent war among the nuclear powers? The answer, in a word, is disproportionality, which also explains why the doctrine has been the despair of most people for whom a necessary condition of a Just War is proportionality. The genius – evil genius, perhaps – of the doctrine of mutual vulnerability is the absurdity of the ratio, the wild disproportion, between the potential gains to be expected from, say, an invasion of Western Europe and the promised costs from the retaliatory holocaust. Who would risk losing virtually everything he already has for the sake of trying to gain a small, or even a large, amount more? The key to any effectiveness that the policy described by the doctrine may have is precisely that the retaliatory punishment is not proportionate to the crime, but is so extremely disproportionate as to deter, it is hoped, even the reckless. The key to its apparent immorality is the same: What by strategic standards are disproportionate costs seem by moral standards to be disproportionate harms. These costs are not mere costs, they are the severest of human harms: dead children, incinerated neighborhoods, irradiated environments, mangled genes. The justification offered for such extraordinary means is an extraordinary end: the abolition of major war among the nuclear powers.

I will not now take up the deep moral issues about risking the undergoing and, especially, the commission of such great harms even to prevent all war between the superpowers. The only crucial points so far about mutual vulnerability are two: first, that its most essential element is an intentionally grotesque disproportion between expected gains and expected losses/harms from starting a conflict; and, second, that the extraordinariness of the means employed was matched by, and justified by, the grandeur of the end, which was no less than the abolition of all war, conventional as well as nuclear, among the nuclear powers. The prospect of social annihilation is to produce the abolition of war. Mutual vulnerability is a weird form of utopianism.

COUNTERFORCE AND THE PURSUIT OF PROPORTIONATE THREAT

The policy of maintaining mutual vulnerability has been crit-icized as so wrong in itself, because of the harms one must be willing to allow one's own society to suffer and be willing to inflict on another society in retaliation for an attack, that it is to be condemned irrespective of its effectiveness at pre-venting war.[8] I leave that line of criticism aside in order to consider the criticism that the policy, if implemented in its pure form, would have been ineffective anyway, and the ef-fects of the criticism of ineffectiveness. The policy would have been ineffective, it is said, because it lacks credibility: The threat would not have been believed. The charge of lack of credibility can be filled out in more than one way, the most convincing of which rests upon an appeal to prudence.

Suppose a fairly measured military attack has occurred in a way that has left American cities relatively undamaged, strongly suggesting that the attacker had genuinely at-tempted to do the least civilian damage to Americans com-patible with his military objective. This could be an attack, conventional or nuclear, only against American allies, or it could, in theory at least, be as purely as possible a counter-force nuclear attack upon American missile silos and bomber bases that held civilian damage as low as possible (which is, of course, not very low in absolute terms). Would it be sen-sible – forget, for now, moral – to retaliate against Soviet cities? The counsel of prudence is: No, because the destruc-tion of Soviet cities would strongly invite the retaliatory de-struction of American cities, which had so far been largely spared (doubly pointless though that return retaliation might be). Why at this stage – after the war we had hoped to deter was under way but with *relatively* small social destruction – launch mutual assured destruction of a good part of the ur-ban areas of the Northern Hemisphere? Surely not merely in order to establish that we are as good as our word. It is too late to inflict (and to provoke the reciprocal infliction of) so

21

much harm. Yet any sooner would have been before the first attack on us and thus would have been too early. It turns out, then, that it could be prudent to destroy their cities only after they had destroyed yours, which is one good reason why whoever starts a war will not begin it by attacking your cities. The destruction of the cities on the other side could be prudent only after it is pointless – only after your own cities are in ruins. No time is the right time for assured destruction.[9] How credible, then, is a threat to do what can only be colossally imprudent or utterly pointless?

Actually, it is hard to say, since governments regularly do colossally imprudent and utterly pointless things. The stupidity and the improbability of government policies do not, unfortunately, correlate very highly, although the stupidities usually cannot reach the magnitudes made possible by nuclear weapons. The critique of the potential effectiveness of mutual vulnerability has, then, yielded conflicting responses. On the one hand, it is certainly not obvious that there is no deterrent value in threatening foolish actions. Indeed, there is the well-known crazy-man gambit: Convince your adversary that you are unpredictable when provoked, and your adversary may give you a very wide berth. It is even possible to plan to lose control of yourself if certain infuriating circumstances arise. A demonstration that the execution of a threat would be imprudent, pointless, stupid, or even crazy goes only so far in the direction of demonstrating that the making of the threat will not be effective. It all depends on whether your adversary believes you capable of imprudence, stupidity, blind rage, or any of a number of other traits that would lead you to launch missiles in the face of all the good reasons why you should not. The mere possibility that you might do it inserts an awesome uncertainty into the calculations of the adversary who, for whatever gain he might seek, risks losses of virtually unlimited magnitude, however low their probability. Do not domesticate the beasts chained in the basement – it is only because they are wild that they are terrifying.

On the other hand, presumably threats are not in some simple black-and-white way just either credible or not credible; a threat may lack credibility on sunny days and gain it on gloomy days. Whatever the absolute degree of credibility of the threats of social destruction that energize mutual vulnerability, more credible forms of deterrence may be available. Rather than defending the pure form of mutual vulnerability, one can alternatively respond to the criticisms of its credibility by modifying the policy of mutual vulnerability to a lesser or a greater degree. This is the path that leads, I will argue, to trying to have it both ways. This is the path of the domestication of the nuclear beasts. But it is not necessary to take this route all the way to its end – it has an intermediate stopping-place, which, however, has its own problems. One can, in effect, go halfway to having it both ways or all the way to having it both ways.

These two stages in the modification of mutual vulnerability constitute, respectively, changes in each of the two essential means that would be employed by a pure policy of mutual vulnerability: The first stage is to modify the incentive not to attack, and the second is to modify the assurance against being attacked. By "stages" I primarily mean analytically separable moves, not necessarily a chronological sequence. I will, however, analyze them in the order in which they have in fact been occurring.

First, one can try, in effect, to provide credibility through proportionality. (This will also, according to Albert Wohlstetter, provide morality through proportionality, but here I leave the more strictly moral arguments aside.)[10] Enemy force will be met with decisively but not excessively superior force, whenever and wherever possible. Here there is no threat that an attack will bring the apocalypse, only that the attack will be denied its objective. A wide range of capabilities will be developed so that responses can be flexible. Small attacks will be met with relatively small, but superior, counterattacks. Larger attacks will be met with relatively larger, and superior, counterattacks. This is deterrence by (threatened)

23

denial rather than deterrence by (threatened) punishment. There is no threat now to bring down the whole temple on all our heads, only the assurance that none shall pass.

Historically, of course, the Doctrine of Flexible Response was one thing, the Countervailing Strategy is another, and the Doctrine of Deterrence by Denial was yet a third. However, what I am suggesting, at considerable risk of oversimplification, is that the essential core of all these doctrines is the attempt to attain enhanced credibility through greater proportionality. Whatever the variations in doctrinal detail, the central thrust is to make the incentive for the adversary not to attack – the first means of deterrence – more effective by making it more measured, less disproportionate, more believable – and thus more genuinely threatening.

The spirit of this countervailing strategy (to give it its current name) is captured in Robert Goodin's quip that "in essence deterrence is a scheme for making nuclear war less probable by making it more probable."[11] That is, you develop capabilities that you are in fact more likely to implement, if provoked, in order to bring your adversary to believe that you are more likely to implement them, if provoked, so that he will be less likely to provoke.

In what sense is this halfway to having it both ways? It is halfway, not all the way, because it affects only the first of the two means of deterrence. In what sense both ways? Mutual vulnerability had promised, in effect: We will deliver an extraordinary result, the abolition of war among the nuclear powers, but the price is the employment of an extraordinary means, the threat of disproportionate destruction as the deterrent to war. The countervailing strategy says, in effect: We do not need the extraordinary means, and we will deliver the extraordinary result anyway. This is one respect in which it is an attempt to have it both ways. Is this not too good a deal to be true? So much for so little?

The question I want to raise about this second response to the critique of the credibility of mutual vulnerability is whether, purely in terms of effectiveness, we have good reason to believe that the gain in the probability that we would respond outweighs the loss in the magnitude of the response. Is a more probable more proportionate (lower-magnitude) response a better deterrent than a less probable less proportionate (higher-magnitude) response? Two quick qualifications need to be made. First, all discussions of the effectiveness of nuclear deterrence are appallingly speculative. Deterrence "theory" is genuinely tennis without a net. Never has so much hinged on so little. Unfortunately, the speculative character of discussions of effectiveness is a no-edged sword: It does not cut either way. We still have to muddle through, if we are going to continue with policies of deterrence – the point is only that we should step with the appropriate tentativeness.

Second, the question as I have phrased it (is a more probable more proportionate response actually a better deterrent than a less probable less proportionate response? or is proportionality a virtue when judged for effectiveness?) is certainly too abstract for any thorough discussion. Deterrence of whom, by whom, when, where, with which interests at stake, in the shadow of what previous history – all these and many other features need filling in sooner or later. Still, a few useful observations can be made even at this level of generality about the plausibility of the claim to greater effectiveness for the countervailing strategy.

However wicked or insane mutual vulnerability may be, it was a novel approach to the prevention of war. Before the development of nuclear weapons it was impossible to threaten to turn an entire nation into "a smoking, radiating ruin at the end of two hours."[12] The threat on which the effectiveness, if any, of mutual vulnerability rests is the prospect of national annihilation. It is, however, merely the prospect of military defeat on which rests the effectiveness, if any, of the countervailing strategy – insofar as the countervailing strategy can in fact be operated in sharp distinction from the policy of mutual vulnerability, a complication to which we will return later. And I think that history has taught us something about this very familiar threat of military defeat, namely that it is a poor deterrent.

134,745

25

Henry Shue

First, it is very difficult to convince the other side in advance that you can deny them victory, even if you can. Especially if they believe that they have history on their side, it is difficult for them not to believe that they can prevail if they are braver and more willing to sacrifice. Second, nations frequently start wars that they do not really believe they are likely to win. Besides simply hoping against hope that they might win, although they do not actually expect to, other deep motivations regularly serve to outweigh prudent calculations of expected results: National honor demands glorious defeat rather than craven surrender, it is too late to back down now, and so forth.

History is rife with examples of nations not deterred from war solely by the clear prospect of military defeat. The more purely counterforce the deterrent, the more thorough the return to the old rules and the old game. There are reasons for choosing to try to back off from mutual vulnerability, but the proven effectiveness of counterforce deterrents is not one of them. We have no particular evidence that a disproportionate threat will deter, but we have plenty of evidence that a proportionate threat alone will not. The extraordinary goal of the abolition of war among the nuclear powers may or may not be attainable by the extraordinary means involved in mutual vulnerability, but if the simple prospect of military defeat could deter war, surely it would have worked more often in the past. "Si vis pacem, para bellum" is a venerable saying, but where is the beef? The absence of any convincing demonstration from the historical record of a correlation between threat proportionality and deterrent effectiveness is, as far as I know, a gaping hole in the case for the countervailing strategy.

COUNTERFORCE AND THE PURSUIT OF PROPORTIONATE RISK

The second and third difficulties for the countervailing strategy and its reliance on counterforce, which will be discussed in this section and the next, are complementary to each other, but each is an independent problem. The pursuit of proportionate risk involves, I will suggest, going the second half of the distance to having it both ways by adding the renunciation of the second means of implementing mutual vulnerability to the abandonment of the first, discussed in the preceding section, while keeping the extraordinary goal. It is impossible to overstate the bizarre character of the second element of the means employed under the doctrine of mutual vulnerability: assurance to the adversary against being attacked, in the form of undefended vulnerability. It is not at all strange that people are troubled by the absence of any direct defenses, active or passive. Deterrence can be viewed as an indirect form of defense, of course, but the indirect route makes a very significant detour through the decision processes of the adversary one hopes to deter. There is no denying that your safety depends upon choices made by your worst enemy, a situation no one could be expected to tolerate with much ease. Nevertheless, this late addition to the doctrine, which initially came as a cool embrace of the unavoidable, is an essential element of the full-blown position.

The countervailing strategy is said to do better for you, on some variant of the general principle that the best defense is a good offense – at least, until it is possible actually to have a good defense.[13] What evidence there is for thinking that the countervailing strategy can deliver this gain I have already queried in the preceding section. The loss involved, by contrast, is clear. The countervailing strategy renounces in principle any intentional preservation of one's own society's vulnerability. I say "renounces in principle" because, as proponents readily admit, if the countervailing strategy is to be run in the foreseeable future, it will have to be run without the relevant defenses, because there are no population defenses. Yet proponents are emphatic that even if, as Robert Jervis says, the situation is mutual assured destruction, the policy is assured destruction only of the adversary's society – when the mutuality of the vulnerability can be ended, it will be ended.[14] As I have already once promised, I will confront presently the thesis of the inseparability in practice of mutual vulnerability and the countervailing strategy.

Giving up the mutuality of the vulnerability when and if you can is also giving up the major advantage of a regime of mutual vulnerability. Importantly, it is to withdraw the tangible assurance that you will not attack first. Verbal assurance can, and undoubtedly will, continue to be given. The issue, however, is not whether the leadership of the United States has the intention of attacking the Soviet Union or can truthfully issue verbal assurances that it will not. The issue is what objective evidence the Soviet Union has that the United States will not attack (and vice versa). If you are fully confident in your own mind of your own good intentions, it is difficult to appreciate the value for others of objective corroboration of your verbal assurances. Yet what we know about Russian history should make it apparent why Soviet leaders are unlikely to rely completely on verbal assurances or even nonaggression pacts. The objective vulnerability of U.S. society still cannot be completely reassuring to the Soviets, precisely because governments can launch suicidal attacks – several regimes have launched them against Russia – but it is presumably more effective than mere words.

What more effective assurance for the Soviet leadership does for us is to weaken one of the most persuasive rationales for a Soviet attack: fear that the United States is about to attack them. We may be confident that they have nothing to fear from us in any case, but our safety from preemptive attack depends upon their confidence that they have nothing to fear from us in the form of a preemptive attack. They could, if they were already determined for other reasons to attack the United States or its allies, pretend that they feared a U.S. attack anyhow. The pretense of fear as an excuse is ineliminable, but real fear as the motivating reason can be, at least, reduced. How significant this is depends upon how strong the temptation to preempt is. For reasons I give in the section on preemption below, I think the incentives are being created to make preemption an ever stronger temptation.

The net effect on safety, then, of the change from reliance upon mutual vulnerability to reliance upon the countervailing strategy depends on whether more is lost through the abandonment of the objective assurance that we will not attack than is gained through any increase in deterrent effectiveness resulting from a more proportionate and more credible threat. This balancing judgment is unavoidably highly speculative. However, since I see no historical basis for expecting a more proportionate threat to be more effective, whereas I do see how the abandonment of objective assurance against attack feeds the temptation to preempt, I have to think that we face a net loss in safety from attempting to achieve comprehensive proportionality by complementing a reduced (and allegedly more credible) threat to the adversary with a reduced risk to ourselves. We are once again trying to have it both ways by scaling down the means without scaling down the end, which remains the abolition of war.

The situation is, however, worse than that. To this point in this section we have seen the disadvantage of attempting to limit the vulnerability of your own society, irrespective of how the attempt to limit damage is implemented. This general disadvantage would result even from the most purely defensive measures one could possibly take. However, if what is done is in accord with the dictum that the best (available) defense is a good offense, matters deteriorate further. This happens if the renunciation of your own vulnerability takes the form of what aficionados call "damage limitation." Like many paradox-inviting terms of the nuclear art, "damage limitation" in practice means roughly the opposite of what it first appears to mean. You do indeed attempt in the end to limit damage to yourself, but the means by which you do so is to damage the forces of the adversary as much as possible – in order to limit their capacity to damage you. The guiding principle is the Mafia version of the Golden Rule: Do unto others before they do unto you.

Joking about the Mafia is not, however, intended to operate as a slur on damage limitation, which has much to be said for it.[15] From the point of view of the principle of discrimination, or noncombatant immunity, in the doctrine of Just War, for example, damage limitation is doubly compliant: It is a form of counterforce attack (you limit damage to yourself by eliminating adversary forces, not by killing civilians), and it serves to reduce the potential for "damage" to your own civilians as well as to your own forces. And from the point of view of Clausewitzian military principles nothing is more rational than the destruction of enemy forces before they can inflict damage upon either your forces or your society.

The only problem is the "before": destruction of enemy forces before they can inflict damage. Damage limitation involves destroying enemy forces before they are used, which must mean using your forces before the forces on which they are targeted are used. They must be struck before they can strike – they must be struck first. To adopt the goal of damage limitation is to create for yourself a powerful temptation to preemption, and for your adversary a strong fear of preemption – and a resultant temptation to preempt, which you must fear.

Before we consider preemption itself in a later section, I want to be as clear as possible about the two separate tributary tendencies that feed into preemption's vicious circle of temptations and fears. By using the imagery of the distinction between going only halfway and going all the way to the point of having things both ways, as well as the distinction between the two elements of the means required to implement mutual vulnerability, I have tried to make it unmistakably clear that, to use the jargon of nuclear insiders, flexible response and damage limitation are conceptually distinct,[16] even though they have a natural complementarity. One could adopt either without the other, or, in my terms, one could reject either element of the means of maintaining mutual vulnerability and keep the other.

I believe, although this factual thesis is not a premise of my argument, that under the countervailing strategy that the United States is now following it is creating a significant objective capability for damage limitation, and that the Soviet Union is doing the same. I say this because of the preoccupation with *prompt* hard-target-kill-capable counterforce. What I want to establish in this paper, however, is the double thesis that the pursuit of proportionate threat (flexible response, etc.) and the pursuit of proportionate risk (damage limitation) are at one and the same time both separable and naturally complementary. They are naturally complementary because they both involve the attempted restoration of proportionality to war threatened in the nuclear age.

Having indicated in this section the strong connection between proportionate risk and the temptations and fears of preemption, I want now to go back and pick up the other somewhat weaker but, I think, still significant thread that leads from proportionate threat to preemption.

COUNTERFORCE AND THE DEMANDS
OF SUPERIORITY

The countervailing strategy is an endeavor to gain political effect – namely, prevention of any decision by an adversary to go to war, combined with containment – from military preparedness. In spite of some of the silliness that has been written, by some who are confident they are the prophets of peace, about the dastardly character of "warfighting" strategies, the general idea of preventing war by being so well prepared for war that no opponent will start one is not in the least new and is not particularly sinister. Indeed, what is wrong with the countervailing strategy and other strategies for "warfighting" – not a particularly helpful category – is not that they introduce some creatively diabolical notion but that they rely on a very familiar type of deterrence by (capacity for) denial on the battlefield, a type of deterrence that often failed before the nuclear age and seems to me especially likely to fail again in the nuclear age. The strategy is not diabolical; it is ineffectual.

What we mainly need to do is to catalogue thoroughly the reasons for the unreliability of countervailing strategies. I am doing this under the three general headings of proportionate threat, proportionate risk, and superiority. Under proportionate threat I have suggested that it is very unclear that more proportionate threats produce gains in deterrent effectiveness. Under proportionate risk I indicated that it is quite clear that the abandonment of objective assurance to the adversary yields a loss in the incentives working against preemption by the adversary and creates incentives to preempt oneself. To this point the net effect is already negative. Now I want to show why the proportionate threats make no sense without the pursuit of a certain kind of superiority, and why that pursuit positively and independently creates additional incentives for preemption, which greatly deepen the overall negative balance for the countervailing strategy.

The claim to greater credibility on behalf of the countervailing strategy rests upon its military plausibility. Unlike assured destruction, it is not "overkill" – not too terrible to use. On the other hand, it has to be terrible enough. This is precisely why I say it is intended to be proportionate: It is to be neither too much nor too little. Not too little for what? Not too little to be able to deny military victory to an attacker. The attacker is to be deterred by his poor prospects for military success.[17]

Now, the line of reasoning that leads in this case toward preparations for preemption is not undeniable, and it is certainly not independent of context. If a nation had such an evident excess of the weapons considered to be needed to deny victory to an attacker and such a robust system of command, control, and communications that it could simply ride out a counterforce/countercommand first strike on itself, or if the adversary had not chosen to develop major capability for attack on counterforce/countercommand facilities so that such an attack was not to be feared, the pressures toward adopting options for preemption might not be especially strong. Obviously much depends on how much capability is thought to be needed to deny victory and, obviously, on how the goal of the denial of victory is itself construed. In general, however, the pressures toward military conservatism – worst-case thinking, if you like – are powerful, and this will be even more decisively so when the deterrence of nuclear war is what is at stake. On any deterrence policy one is talking perceived capability, not just objective capability. One will not unreasonably want one's objective capability to be at least a little in excess, whatever exactly that means, lest it be underestimated.

Therefore, in order to consider oneself to be in the position simply to ride out a counterforce/countercommand first strike and then later calmly consider whether to retaliate – when one is relying not upon assured destruction but upon military defeat as one's deterring capability – one would have to consider oneself already to have nuclear capabilities greatly superior to what would be needed to deny victory. This creates a dilemma for adherents to the countervailing strategy. Someone who is willing to say that we have more than enough offensive weapons can also consistently renounce preemption. For, if we will have plenty of weapons left over after a first strike, we also have plenty of time and no need to preempt. But one who believes more offensive weapons are needed cannot intelligibly claim that preemption can now be forgone. He can of course argue that we need more weapons just so that we need not always stand ready to preempt. The question is simply: How likely is it that adherents of a countervailing strategy will ever actually conclude that we have enough offensive weapons for the foreseeable future and therefore can, for the foreseeable future, drop the option of preempting? Until that day I do not see how under a countervailing strategy – even one committed only to deterrence by denial and not to damage limitation – preemption can fail to be a ready option. What, then, is so bad about preemption?

PREEMPTION: FEAR AND TEMPTATION

Preemption is not a "sneak attack" – on the contrary, it is conceived as closer to the prevention of a sneak attack, although preemption will in fact be impossible when the adversary is stealthy enough. Naturally we all have some tendency to view sneak attacks as what our adversaries do and surprise attacks, which are perfectly permissible even under the principles of Just War (provided certain conditions, including the formal declaration of war, have been met), as what we do. Some useful distinctions can, however, be drawn with adequate clarity.

Consider the conception of preemption actually used in the Operation Plan for the U.S. Commander-in-Chief Europe that was in effect at the time of the Cuban Missile Crisis: A preemptive attack is one "in response to unequivocal strategic warning of impending major Sino-Soviet Bloc attack upon the U.S. or its allies."[18] Apart from noting that there was no Sino-Soviet bloc in 1962, the Sino-Soviet rupture having occurred two to three years earlier,[19] I want for now to omit concrete references and concentrate upon the essential features of this otherwise clear definition. Here are the abstracted essentials:

> A preemptive attack is a response to (2) unequivocal warning of (1) impending attack.

I have numbered the two essential features in reverse order simply to flag the fact that the primary condition for an attack's being preemptive is what we might call the reality condition: An attack by the adversary is in fact imminent. The secondary, but also essential, condition we might call the evidence condition: Compelling evidence is available that the adversary's attack is imminent. Quite simply, the adversary really is about to attack and we can tell it. I will say, for short, that attack is *imminent* and *evident*. If it is not evident, we will not react in time to preempt – it will turn out to have been a surprise attack, and we will be left to decide whether to retaliate. If the adversary's attack is not imminent, that is, if our belief that it is coming is mistaken, we will have panicked, not preempted, and we may have started an unnecessary nuclear war.

Now, I do not think that there is anything especially mysterious about the condition of imminence. Sometimes before the point at which something happens an earlier point is passed after which it is going to happen. Sometimes, not always, before a couple divorces, matters reach a state after which they are going to divorce – the fighting and making-up between that point and the divorce change nothing fundamental and, as far as the ultimate outcome is concerned, might just as well have been skipped, not that they could have been. Historians debate whether, if the German Chancellor Bethmann-Hollweg, during his panic in the night of July 29–30, 1914, had telephoned Berchtold in Vienna instead of merely cabling, and had thereby communicated unequivocally his belated desperation over British nonneutrality, the Austrians could have been persuaded to halt their bombardment of Belgrade and World War I could at that point still have been averted.[20] It is, of course, difficult to say whether at, for example, midnight on July 29 World War I was imminent, or impending, in the sense that it was then too late to stop it; but the question is certainly meaningful. Either the war could still have been avoided or it could not.

Nor is there any special difficulty in principle about the condition of evidence: The adversary's attack is imminent and evidently so. Of course, there are many ways to be mistaken. It is perfectly clear, however, what some forms of "unequivocal warning" would look like. For example, an attack upon the satellites that the other side uses to watch for attacks upon its forces is understood by all to be so provocative a step that it would never be taken without the firm commitment to take further steps. We know, in other words, what an unequivocal warning of an imminent attack might look like. In conception, then, preemptive attack is relatively clear.

A preemptive strike is a very specific kind of attack. It is at least technically speaking a first strike, especially if it is successful at preempting – preempting means getting to them before they get to you, which in the case of missiles means before launch. Perhaps a preemptive strike is also morally speaking merely a first strike; that is, perhaps it deserves a moral condemnation not one whit less strong than the condemnation appropriate to any other type of first strike, any other initiation of nuclear war. That is a moral issue I want briefly to consider, however, because in some respects a preemptive strike appears to be a classic case of self-defense. Compared to the retaliation that the policy of mutual vulnerability promises to execute after deterrence has already failed and you have already suffered whatever the adversary has chosen to inflict, preemption seems eminently defensive, especially insofar as it is designed for "damage limitation," that is, for the reduction of possible damage to yourself by destruction of enemy forces before they are used.

The clearest case of preemption – its very purity makes it disanalogous, of course – comes from the cowboy stories that are deep in the psyches of many Americans. The Good Guy sees the Bad Guy reaching for his six-shooter. Happily the Good Guy is faster on the draw (he doesn't drink and he practices faithfully), and he shoots the pistol from the hand of the Bad Guy, who is left disarmed – and unharmed (or shot through the heart – when does it matter?). The Good Guy shot first and talked, if at all, later.

The Good Guy used preemptive counterforce: He used his weapon to eliminate the adversary's weapon before it could be used to do the harm intended. Does the Good Guy's having shot first make him an aggressor? Surely not – that he struck first shows only that his eye is clear and his reflexes quick. He didn't start first – he just finished first. Does morality require that you be slow on the draw? If so, this is a perverse morality: If a Good Guy may fire only after the Bad Guy's bullet has left the barrel, morality appears to tilt in favor of Bad Guys. This is a morality for suckers.[21]

Now, it is not even very good sport to point out all the disanalogies between dueling with pistols and exchanging nuclear missiles, so I will not tediously rehearse them. The only lesson I want to derive from the cowboy example is, to switch the metaphor, that the person who lands the first blow need not be the person who threw the first punch. Even more clearly, he need not be the one who picked the fight. Which is to say: He may fundamentally be simply defending himself and just doing it very well. His action is defensive because it is the disruption of an attack in motion.[22] An offen-

36

sive weapon can be used for a defensive purpose (just as –
supporters of SDI take note – a defensive weapon can be
used for offensive purposes). It is, to put it archaically, as if
the Good Guy's hand is faster than the Bad Guy's will: The
Bad Guy had willed to strike first. This, I think, is why his
being struck first seems, at the very least, to be fair.

The case against having preemptive options in the operational plan cannot, I think, be made in terms of the aggres-
siveness of a true act of preempting, because genuine
preemption is not at all aggressive in the morally relevant
sense. It may be militarily aggressive in the sense that it is
an urgently energetic effort to prevent the seizure of the initiative by the other side, but there is nothing inherently objectionable about a militarily aggressive stance, which can
more favorably be called taking the initiative.

What is wrong is not fundamentally the act of preemption,
given the situation that has by then been created, but the
creation of that situation by the implementation of a countervailing strategy. The situation requires a heroic level of restraint in order for the evidence condition for preemption to
be fulfilled. As Schelling and Halperin put it some two decades ago, "Hardly anything would be as tragically ironic as
a war that both sides started, each in the belief that the other
was about to, each compelled by its expectations to confirm
the other's belief that attack was imminent."[23] Once you have
a countervailing strategy, it becomes instrumentally rational
at some point to seize the initiative before it is lost irretriev-
ably. When you switch from threatening to prevail (in order
to deter) to fighting (in order to prevail), you need to switch
fast and hard (in a world of counterforce capabilities). This,
however, makes the countervailing strategy likely to self-
destruct in any severe crisis in which an attack appears imminent or seems evident. As Betts has observed, preemption
"is the only situation in which the initiator would have reason to believe that starting a nuclear war could cost less than
waiting to try other options."[24] This is especially true if you
are serious about prevailing in battle – it makes no military
sense to sit still while your forces are reduced by a damage-

limiting attack by the other side. If deterrence has already failed – attack is imminent – you must switch from deterrence logic to military logic.

Mutual countervailing strategies, which I take to be the current Soviet and American postures, may well have the initial and intermediate effect of tending to hold down the temperature of an impending crisis. (We can only speculate – the strategy in its current form has never been severely tested.) We have every reason to expect, however, that once the political temperature of a crisis rises above some unspecifiable point, its rate of rise will increase sharply. Even in this superheated atmosphere absolutely cool heads could remember "(1) imminent and (2) evident" – unless I have unequivocal warning of impending attack, I will be not preempting but launching a nuclear aggression. But to rely, as a matter of policy, on this degree of cool in so hot a situation is surely to tempt fate. Rousseau, in arguing against what he took to be an overly pure form of democracy, said that it was a politics for angels and that what we need is politics for ordinary shmucks like ourselves: We need a system that will still work when some people do not care and other people mess up. In this sense the countervailing strategy seems to me to be nuclear policy for angels. It is the apocalyptic snafu waiting to happen when the severe crisis comes.

In the circumstances it would still be possible to wait long enough to carry out a pure act of preemption: The adversary's attack might really be imminent, and this might really become evident to you. But the pressure in these circumstances to go too soon rather than too late – pressure on both sides: temptation and fear, fear and temptation – will be enormous. It is the circumstances that have to be avoided, and this means avoiding strategies that place an extra premium on preemption. Otherwise our nuclear policy is like the rhythm method of birth control. In theory the right action can be specified, and in practice the right thing can be done – but how likely is it that, in the circumstances, it will be done? Is this a probability to bet the fate of the earth on?

The superiority of the countervailing strategy is supposed

to lie in its greater capacity (compared to mutual vulnerability) to prevent – deter – war. Yet it seems likely to deter war only when war does not seem imminent. It is a roof for sunny days. When a war comes to seem imminent, the strategy dictates a rush into action. A built-in change of gears – as if we were accelerating an automatic, not a stick-shift, war machine – occurs: Suddenly, the only rational thing left to do is to attack with full seriousness. That is what is bad, very bad.

Am I not exaggerating the practical significance of a merely theoretical danger of preemption? After all, no matter how hard anyone tries to have a policy of countermilitary warfare, like the countervailing strategy, the situation remains – "objectively," as the Soviets like to say – mutual vulnerability. Countervailing strategy has not been substituted for, or replaced, mutual vulnerability – it has been added on top of it (barring the possibility of population defenses like the "Astrodome" version of SDI). But the ineradicability of vulnerability provides a basis for rejecting my criticism that the countervailing strategy encourages preemption within crises. This is the answer to my criticism: No one will preempt, because whatever the military benefits of landing the first blow, the social costs of being involved in a nuclear war at all can, in the end, be utter destruction of your society, perhaps even of your way of life. You might be ahead after landing the first blow, but after the last blow both sides have lost.

Two possibilities are apparent: Either the ultimate prospect of social destruction will constrain leaders from attempting preemption, or it will not. This means, however, either that the countervailing strategy is no better but no worse than mutual vulnerability, or that it is worse. What it cannot be is better. Consider the first alternative: that awareness of ineluctable vulnerability will constrain preemption. The *relative initial* military advantage of striking first will be outweighed by the *absolute ultimate* social costs of being involved in a nuclear war. If this is correct – and I insist again that this too is speculation – I have to admit that the countervailing strategy is no worse; at least, it is not worse for the reason that it makes the outbreak of war in a crisis more likely. If, however, it is to be constrained by the same fears of social destruction that allegedly undermine the credibility of mutual vulnerability, it is more difficult than ever to see what makes the countervailing strategy superior in credibility. And if it is not superior in credibility and not superior in morality – since it runs the same risk of mutual destruction – in what is it superior? I shall return to this question presently.

The second alternative is the one already much discussed here: that in spite of the acknowledged situation of ineradicable vulnerability, the temptation to preempt either in order to seize the military advantage or to prevent the adversary from succeeding in seizing it – as you will think he is already doing if you are genuinely preempting – is much stronger than it would be if mutual vulnerability were our policy (as of course it is not and never was). Here is why I do not think the belief that mutual vulnerability always lurks in the background can block the impetus toward preemption.

The prospect of the assured destruction of the society supposedly being defended is said to remind anyone contemplating preemption that the advantages of preemption may be relative and temporary, while the ultimate costs of involvement in nuclear war are absolute and enduring. Ultimate costs will, we are assured, outweigh relative benefits, especially temporary ones. Who, it is asked, would choose to bring about a large absolute loss in pursuit of a temporary relative military advantage that might not translate into any reduction in the size of that final absolute loss? Any decision maker can see, we are told, that unless his preemption will completely disarm the opponent of his second-strike capability he will still lose his society in the end.

My reply is that to argue against the likelihood of preemption in this way is to fail to understand the real meaning of preemption. To attempt to preempt is to (counter)attack when you believe that an attack upon you *is already coming*. The crucial significance of the perceived imminence of the attack is that all consideration of any fixed costs of becoming involved in nuclear war drops out of the calculations. You believe you *are* becoming involved in a nuclear war – you *are* being attacked with nuclear weapons. You believe that whatever are the minimum fixed costs of involvement in nuclear war, you *will* pay. You can only change the amount of the destruction beyond the fixed minimum, and you can affect it only by gaining the military advantage. And you can gain the military advantage, now that nuclear war is coming in any case, only through preemption.

As Steven Lee puts it, the alternative to which one compares a potential preemption changes radically when one believes that a nuclear attack is already coming whatever one does.[25] In normal circumstances one's strategic question is whether attacking the other side, and then suffering the retaliation of which the other side still remains capable after absorbing one's attack, is preferable to remaining in a state of peace. When, however, one sincerely believes one is being attacked whatever one does, the strategic question becomes whether attacking – first if possible – and then suffering retaliation is preferable to suffering an assault by an unhindered and undamaged adversary. This is, as Lee notes, "a very different question."

Preemption might, however, reduce only the extent of overkill in the adversary's attack, without actually reducing the amount of damage to one's society. Why disregard the possibility that your belief that nuclear war has become inevitable is in fact false by launching what is intended as a preemption, when any temporary military advantage may simply evaporate in the end even if your belief is true? If, once deterrence has failed, fighting may be pointless, why fight, either sooner or later? This is to ask whether the relative military advantage that comes from preempting can actually affect the final level of social destruction. I shall not speculate further but simply pose one last dilemma: Either fighting back as quickly as possible is pointless, or it is not.

If it is pointless, it is pointless. Having a countervailing strategy that depends upon the credibility of doing something pointless is an improvement over mutual vulnerability only to the extent that planning to do something pointless is an improvement over planning to do something suicidal.

41

Pointless, I have to admit, is *much* better than suicidal. We may at last have found the superiority of the countervailing strategy: It may require the pointless but *possibly* not the suicidal.

If, on the other hand, fighting back as quickly as possible is not pointless but has instead some hope of affecting the ultimate outcome, reducing the final social destruction, then it should be done to maximum effect. If there is advantage in preempting, one should preempt. But if there is an advantage in preempting, there is an advantage in preempting, which is my main complaint against the strategy.

In sum, then, the countervailing strategy seems to me to depend either upon the credibility of doing something pointless or upon being sure to preempt.

HAVING IT BOTH WAYS THE WRONG WAY

I have been criticizing the countervailing strategy for trying to have it both ways by retaining the extraordinary goal of abolishing war but eliminating the extraordinary threat and the extraordinary risk that constitute the complementary means under mutual vulnerability. Often I have alluded to a completely different sense in which we may have it both ways willy-nilly, namely that regardless of whether our policy embraces or renounces mutual assured destruction, the fact remains that for the foreseeable future the capabilities for mutual destruction continue. However fully each side develops the capability to implement the countervailing strategy, the capability for assured destruction also remains in the background. Countervailing capabilities are added on, not substituted. (This fact would, obviously, change if one or both sides developed the capacity for a disarming counterforce strike, or if one or both sides developed population defenses.)

If it is true, as I have just argued in the preceding section, that the countervailing strategy creates circumstances that greatly increase the probability of preemption once a severe crisis has developed, the intermediate-term inescapability of mutual vulnerability means that the magnitude of the destruction risked is no less than it would have been with the pure policy of mutual vulnerability. Raising the probability (once severe crisis has arisen) without reducing the magnitude does not sound like a good approach to a catastrophic risk. This is a very familiar point, and I will not labor it. But it means that the pursuit of proportionality comes up empty.

A second feature is perhaps less apparent. Although we cannot soon eliminate the capabilities for mutual assured destruction, the replacement of mutual vulnerability as chosen policy with the countervailing strategy does incur the loss of one odd political benefit of mutual vulnerability. Within a regime of mutual vulnerability the two adversaries can cooperate in a manner that not only is compatible with the regime but helps to maintain it. As I have indicated earlier, this kind of regime can be maintained unilaterally, and cooperation is not necessary. Nor is cooperation now occurring to any great extent, so it is difficult to know how much weight to assign to the loss of the possibility of its expansion.

Still, the loss of even the possibility of such cooperation between the two adversaries on nuclear matters is of some significance. And the loss is clear. The countervailing strategy produces a kind of military competition that is relentless in the sense that it has no specifiable end. The countervailing strategy requires the capacity to deny victory to the adversary (even without the goal of damage limitation). To be able to deny victory one's forces must be better than the adversary's forces. Adequacy, then, must mean superiority: Your forces are not adequate to the execution of the countervailing strategy unless they are superior to the adversary's forces.

What is sauce for the goose is sauce for the gander: The same applies to the adversary. For him too adequacy means being superior. Unlike mutual vulnerability, which can be cooperative, mutual countervailing policies require endless competition, because the minimum for each is superiority over the other. The need for superiority, which is built into the strategy, requires never being the first to relax in the arms race.

I do not suggest that arms reductions more significant than

those in the Intermediate Nuclear Forces Treaty are impossible under mutual countervailing strategies, but neither side can, consistent with its strategy, agree to any reductions that fail to maintain its superiority. With asymmetrically triadic force structures, it is not even inconceivable to have reductions that allow each side the respective kind of superiority its kind of triad needs. The point, however, is simply that reductions are made maximally difficult in such a relentlessly competitive atmosphere.

THE GRADUAL WRONG TURN IN AMERICAN STRATEGY

The last firm step on the slippery slope is not usually the one noticed, but it is the one we need to be able to identify. We can lose our way gradually, which makes it harder to recover direction than if an easily identifiable sharp turn had been taken. The three most articulate defenders of the countervailing strategy – Harold Brown, Walter Slocombe, and Leon Sloss – have all emphasized the continuity in U.S. operational nuclear policy for virtually the entire period from 1945 to 1985, certainly from 1965 to 1985. Thus, Walter Slocombe:

> It is worth restating what the countervailing strategy is *not*. It is *not* a new strategic doctrine; it is *not* a radical departure from U.S. strategic policy over the past decade or so. It *is*, rather, an evolutionary refinement and a recodification of the U.S. strategic policy from which it flows . . .[26]

This thesis of the absence of abrupt or radical change in operational policy, which appears to me to be correct, has been further corroborated by the prodigious documentary analysis of David Alan Rosenberg and the comprehensive policy analysis of Michael Nacht.[27]

Yet methinks the lady doth protest too much. The much-stressed continuity of operational policy does indeed seem to lie beneath the rhetorical vagaries of declaratory policy. Continuity, however, need not mean the absence of change but may instead mean simply that change has been gradual. Accumulated small changes, especially if their tendency has been continuously in the same direction, can add up to a major shift in direction. I have tried to suggest that in at least one fundamental respect U.S. policy has changed very nearly 180 degrees, even if it has happened one degree at a time. What I am not suggesting is that the change has been carried out deceptively – or even fully consciously, which would have been a precondition for doing it deceptively. On the contrary, I am hoping that even some initiators of current policy have not yet realized how far we have come and will themselves want to turn back when they see where we are now headed.

We have tried, bit by bit, to domesticate our ferocious nuclear weapons. We have tried to turn from "blowing up buildings and killing people," which is surely not a military strategy, to meeting enemy force with force sufficient to deny it gain. We have tried to design proportionate nuclear forces, moral but intimidating. We have tried, I am suggesting, to have it both ways. We have tried, but I fear we were bound to fail because the strategy is incoherent.

Some recent actions, like the decision to ratify the Intermediate Nuclear Forces Treaty, may well appear not to fit announced strategy. So much the better for the recent actions. Since what passes for strategy is incoherent, we might try relying instead upon common sense.

NOTES

1. I would like to thank my dog, Dragon, for suggesting this image to me.
2. Moral challenges to the whole system of deterrence are raised in this volume by C. A. J. Coady (Chapter 4, "Escaping from the Bomb"), concentrating upon offenses, and Steven Lee (Chapter 9, "Morality, the SDI, and Limited Nuclear War"), concentrating upon defenses. Five different forms of nuclear deterrence are defended, with widely varying degrees of enthusiasm, in five different ways by, respectively, David Lewis,

Robert E. Foelber, George H. Quester, Harold A. Feiveson, and Leon Sloss.

3. George H. Quester, "The Necessary Moral Hypocrisy of the Slide into Mutual Assured Destruction," Chapter 5 of this volume.

4. The acronym MAD was invented, not surprisingly, by one of the policy's doubters, the penetrating strategic thinker Donald G. Brennan, who thereby performed one of the most brilliant acts of persuasive labeling ever (ranking right up there with "forced bussing" as labels that oblige the supporters of the policy so named to start by apologizing for what they are defending). Since I am not a supporter of mutual vulnerability, my main objection to the acronym MAD is that I think it tends better to reflect the first half of the complementary means, the readiness to destroy the other side, than it does the second half, the readiness to be destroyed if you yourself attack first. It is now often said as well that the *situation* may be mutual assured destruction, but the *policy* is simply assured destruction (of the other side). That, however, is only one policy, which we shall be discussing. A policy that intentionally preserves the second element, assurance through one's own vulnerability, is a policy of *mutual* vulnerability to destruction.

   The other objection to "MAD" is that it builds the failure of the policy into its name as if the failure were its goal. The policy is mutual *vulnerability*, which is, rightly or wrongly, intended to deter destruction. Naturally, someone who believes that mutual vulnerability will in fact result in mutual destruction may well prefer to call it MAD. Brennan's acronym is, in any case, deeply entrenched.

5. "NSC 68: United States Objectives and Programs for National Security," April 14, 1950. First published in *Naval War College Review* 27, no. 6/Sequence No. 255 (May–June 1975), 51–108; readily accessible in the valuable collection *Containment: Documents on American Policy and Strategy, 1945–1950,* edited by Thomas H. Etzold and John Lewis Gaddis (New York: Columbia University Press, 1978), pp. 385–442.

6. I think the best single discussion of national security remains Daniel Yergin, *Shattered Peace: The Origins of the Cold War and the National Security State* (Boston: Houghton Mifflin, 1977), ch. 8, "The Gospel of National Security."

7. Harold A. Feiveson, "Finite Deterrence," Chapter 6 of this volume.

8. See the first half of Chapter 4 below, by Coady, and the works cited there.

9. See Richard Wasserstrom, "War, Nuclear War, and Nuclear Deterrence: Some Conceptual and Moral Issues," *Ethics* 95, no. 3 (April 1985), 424–44, at 433; rpt. in Russell Hardin, et al., *Nuclear Deterrence: Ethics and Strategy* (Chicago: University of Chicago Press, 1985), pp. 15–35.

10. See Albert Wohlstetter, "Bishops, Statesmen, and Other Strategists on the Bombing of Innocents," *Commentary* 75, no. 6 (June 1983), 15–35. For a critique, see Henry Shue, "Conflicting Conceptions of Deterrence," *Social Philosophy & Policy* 3, no. 1 (Fall 1985), 43–73.

11. Robert Goodin, "Nuclear Disarmament as a Moral Certainty," *Ethics* 95, no. 3 (April 1985), 641–58, at 642; rpt. in Hardin, *Nuclear Deterrence*, pp. 267–84.

12. See David Alan Rosenberg, " 'A Smoking Radiating Ruin at the End of Two Hours': Documents of American Plans for Nuclear War with the Soviet Union, 1954–1955," *International Security* 6, no. 3 (Winter 1981–82), 3–38. This speaker, of course, had more in mind than assured destruction in McNamara's sense.

13. I have discussed SDI in "Morality of Offense Determines Morality of Defense," *Philosophical Forum* 18, no. 1 (Fall 1986), 8–14; rpt. in Douglas P. Lackey, ed., *Ethics and Strategic Defense: American Philosophers Debate Star Wars and the Future of Nuclear Deterrence* (Belmont, Calif.: Wadsworth, 1989), pp. 84–90; and earlier in "Are Nuclear Defenses Morally Superior?" *QQ: Report from the Institute for Philosophy and Public Policy* 5, no. 2 (Spring 1985), 6–8; rpt. in Zbigniew Brzezinski et al., ed., *Promise or Peril: The Strategic Defense Initiative* (Washington: Ethics and Public Policy Center, 1986), pp. 411–17. In this volume, see Chapters 8 ("The Case for Deploying Strategic Defenses") by Leon Sloss and 9 ("Morality, the SDI, and Limited Nuclear War") by Steven Lee.

14. Robert Jervis, *The Illogic of American Nuclear Strategy*, Cornell Studies in Security Affairs (Ithaca and London: Cornell University Press, 1984).

15. Robert E. Foelber and Steven Lee, each in a very different

47

way, present some of the arguments for damage limitation in Chapters 3 and 9 of this volume.

16. The full significance of this distinction was first made clear to me by my then-colleague Robert K. Fullinwider.

17. If one accepts, as David Lewis does, the hypothesis of existential deterrence, one can believe that forces insufficient to deny victory may nevertheless deter. For a striking alternative to the standard view, which I am analyzing here and which does not accept existential deterrence, see "Finite Counterforce" by Lewis, Chapter 2 of this volume.

18. Operation Plan USCINCEUR NR 100-6, June 15, 1962, p. 1, quoted in Desmond Ball, "U.S. Strategic Forces: How Would They Be Used?" in Steven E. Miller, ed., *Strategy and Nuclear Deterrence: An "International Security" Reader* (Princeton: Princeton University Press, 1984), pp. 215–44, at 218 n. 9; also in *International Security*, 7, no. 3 (Winter 1982/83), 31–60.

19. The phenomenon of bureaucratic inertia is not a recent discovery, but one of the more chilling facts about U.S. policy during the nuclear age is that under the Single Integrated Operational Plan in effect in 1962 (during the Cuban Missile Crisis) the options for responding to aggression by the Soviet Union included nuclear attack upon the major cities of *China*. Execution of one of these options including China would have constituted one of the largest senseless massacres in human history – if not the largest.

20. See the fascinating account, and psychological analysis, in Richard Ned Lebow, *Between Peace and War: The Nature of International Crisis* (Baltimore: Johns Hopkins University Press, 1981), pp. 119–47; for the telephone call that was not made, see pp. 135–39.

21. I am grateful to my then-colleague Douglas MacLean for emphasizing the importance of the tendency for moral criticisms of nuclear deterrence to take this perverse twist.

22. I do not assume that as long as an attack is defensive it is morally permissible. On the contrary, even self-defense is subject to additional moral constraints. I simply want to pursue a different line of criticism. This line of argument has already been nicely laid out in Thomas Donaldson, "Nuclear Deterrence and Self-Defense," *Ethics* 95, no. 3 (April 1985), 537–48; rpt. in Hardin, *Nuclear Deterrence*.

23. Thomas C. Schelling and Morton H. Halperin, "Preemptive,

Having it both ways

- Premeditated, and Accidental War," in Dean G. Pruitt and Richard C. Snyder, ed., *Theory and Research on the Causes of War* (Englewood Cliffs, N.J.: Prentice-Hall, 1969), pp. 43–48, at pp. 43–44.
24. Richard K. Betts, "Surprise Attack and Preemption," in Graham T. Allison, Albert Carnesale, and Joseph S. Nye, Jr., ed., *Hawks, Doves, and Owls: An Agenda for Avoiding Nuclear War* (New York: W. W. Norton, 1985), pp. 54–79, at p. 57.
25. See Lee, Chapter 9 of this volume.
26. Walter Slocombe, "The Countervailing Strategy," in Miller, *Strategy and Nuclear Deterrence*, pp. 245–54, at p. 251 (emphasis in original); also in *International Security* 5, no. 4 (Spring 1981), 18–27. Also see Leon Sloss and Marc Dean Millot, "U.S. Nuclear Strategy in Evolution," *Strategic Review* 12, no. 1 (Winter 1984), 19–28.
27. David Alan Rosenberg, "The Origins of Overkill: Nuclear Weapons and American Strategy, 1945–1960," in Miller, *Strategy and Nuclear Deterrence*, pp. 113–81; also in *International Security* 7, no. 4 (Spring 1983), 3–71; and Michael Nacht, *The Age of Vulnerability: Threats to the Nuclear Stalemate* (Washington: Brookings Institution, 1985).

49

Chapter 2

Finite counterforce

David Lewis

INTRODUCTION

When theoreticians like ourselves think about nuclear deterrence, often we focus on a nasty choice between two rival package deals. The two have gone by various names over the years, but let me take the paired epithets: It's MAD versus NUTS.[1] Each package is a bundle of policies: centrally, policies for the procurement of strategic nuclear forces, conditional intentions about how to use those forces in case of

Note: The up-to-date reader may wonder why I refer to the Soviet Union throughout as "the enemy." The reason is that my chapter was completed in February 1986, to meet a deadline of the University of Maryland Working Group on Nuclear Policy and Morality. I've mostly withstood temptation to tinker afterward.

Much has changed in the three years since. I applaud those changes, and do not at all mean to belittle them. It seems reasonable to hope, though foolhardy to assume, that the name "enemy" is no longer right – anyhow not today, 20 January 1989. As for tomorrow, who knows? The most important lesson we're learning is that the Soviet Union can change course unforeseeably. We can imagine all too many alternative future Soviet Unions – some benign, some not. The same goes for other powers that have the wherewithal to menace us. We cannot yet bid good riddance to nuclear deterrence and its moral dilemmas.

David Lewis

war, war plans, declaratory policy. Each package also carries implications about military research and development, arms control, conventional preparedness, relations with our allies, and foreign policy generally.

In a debate between MAD and NUTS, each side may say that the other's policies involve a twofold risk: a grave moral risk of committing massacres and a grave prudential risk of inviting and undergoing like massacres.[2] If they say so, they are right: Both MAD and NUTS are morally questionable, to put it mildly, and imprudent as well. (Imprudence is itself immoral, if it is the imprudence of a statesman who bungles the task of protecting his countrymen.) The contest between these two repugnant alternatives gives nuclear deterrence itself a bad name, and winds up making a strong case for a third package deal: nuclear pacifism, renunciation of all the risks and all the benefits of nuclear deterrence. Of course this third package carries its own grave moral and prudential risks.

No alternative looks good. How does the very idea of nuclear deterrence turn into the nasty choice between MAD and NUTS? Does it have to happen? Is there no way around it?

It happened for a reason, to be sure. The fundamental premise was that if we are to practice nuclear deterrence we have to solve the credibility problem. Not many solutions can be found. One leads to MAD. Another leads to NUTS. The rest – automated retaliation, in various forms – are worse still. The premise of the credibility problem is the adhesive that binds together the repugnant packages.

The solvent that dissolves the adhesive is the hypothesis of *existential deterrence* (for short, *existentialism*).[3] Existentialism says that the credibility problem more or less solves itself – deterrence is easy. If that is true, then the packages fall apart. We can practice nuclear deterrence in a much safer way – safer both morally and prudentially. We can borrow ideas from the MADman and the NUT, and have the best of both.[4] But we can leave behind the parts of their reasoning that require us to run grave risks in order to solve the credibility problem.

As a philosopher, my business is with the coherence of

positions and the range of logical possibilities – not with the truth of empirical hypotheses. (I dare say many a strategist ought to say the same.) I had better leave it to others, far more expert than I about the details of current history, to determine how well the evidence supports existentialism. I see that some of these experts have become convinced existentialists.[5] What they say has the ring of truth, but I myself cannot muster additional evidence. My task will not be to argue for existentialism, but to argue from it.

Caveat: the MADman and the NUT, as I shall portray them, are ideal types. Those real people who endorse deterrence but reject counterforce will seldom agree fully with my MADman. Likewise, the friends of counterforce will seldom go all the way with my ideal NUT. The importance of the ideal MADman and NUT is that they are logical in the derogatory sense – they follow the argument relentlessly wherever it may lead. All statesmen, and even most theoreticians, have better sense. The evils of pure MADness and NUTtery are plain to see. When we face the nasty choice, we long for compromise. But the question is: Can compromise make sense?[6] It's no good just hopping aboard a premise when it's going your way and hopping off again when you think it's gone too far. I mean that it's no good as honest theory – it may be safe enough. Or it may not. We must earn the right to compromise, by faulting the reasoning that drives us MAD or NUTS. We can do that, I say, if we embrace existentialism and don't fuss much about credibility.

MAD: IF YOU CAN'T BE CREDIBLE, BE DREADFUL

To trace the reasoning that drives us MAD, start with a simple conception of nuclear deterrence. We deter the enemy from doing x by threatening that if he does, then we will punish him by doing y; y is bad enough to offset anything he might gain by doing x; we hope he will reckon that doing x cannot be worthwhile, and so will not do it.

But the enemy might notice that if he does x, we will then have no good reason to do y. What's more, he may be able to give us a reason not to: He may threaten that if we do y, then he will punish us by doing z. Just as we had hoped to deter him from doing x, so he might hope to deter us from retaliating if he does x. Then he might hope to do x and go unpunished. Of course we may threaten that if he does z then we will . . . but he might doubt that as well. In short, we have a credibility problem: Our deterrence is apt to fail because our threats are not believed.

How to solve it? One way is to make the threatened retaliation very, very severe. Then even if the enemy thinks we would have excellent reason not to retaliate, and even if he concludes that most likely we would not do what we have excellent reason not to do, still he would not dare to call our bluff. If he evaluates risks as he should, multiplying the magnitude of the harm by the probability, we can make up in the first factor for what is lacking in the second. We can threaten a vast nuclear massacre, on an altogether different scale from the ordinary horrors of war: "It seems reasonable to assume the destruction of, say, one-quarter to one-third of its population and about two-thirds of its industrial capacity . . . would certainly represent intolerable punishment to any industrialized nation and thus should serve as an effective deterrent."[7] Destruction on this dreadful scale needn't be credible to deter. Although it could serve no good purpose to fulfill the threat, the risk that we might do so in blind anger suffices.

We can, at any rate, dispel any doubts about our ability to fulfill the threat, no matter what may have been done to try to stop us. For it takes only a small remnant of our many nuclear weapons, launched in ragged fashion by rudimentary surviving command and control, to assure the destruction of many of the enemy's cities and the murder of much of his urban population.

It is the same in reverse, of course; the enemy can rest assured that our cities also will remain vulnerable, and that it would take only some small remnant of his nuclear weapons to devastate them. The vulnerability is mutual. Nothing much can be done about it. Only the starry-eyed dreamer hopes to render the cities invulnerable, and even he doesn't hope to do it soon. It might be possible to limit damage to a limited extent by counterforce warfare or by defense, or to protect populations to a limited extent by teaching them how to shelter from fallout. Such measures might well save enough lives (or enough resources for recovery) to be worthwhile. Or they might instead turn out to accomplish very little. But even if they live up to our highest hopes, the cities remain subject to vast and intolerable destruction.

It has been rightly said that "mutual assured destruction exists as a fact, irrespective of policy."[8] To be sure; but how to cope with this fact is a question of policy. The fact is that we can threaten the cities; the question is whether we should.

The MADman says we should. He sees the credibility problem as a fundamental difficulty for deterrence. He doubts that any threat can be made very credible, given that we too are deterred. To this predicament he knows one solution, and one only: We must make our threat so dreadful that it doesn't need to be credible. The most dreadful threat is the threat to destroy the cities. Therefore this threat must be the centerpiece of our nuclear deterrence.

It needn't be our only threat – that would be MADness in an especially pure form. But lesser threats have no life of their own; they serve mainly as a not-too-incredible way of bringing the ultimate threat to bear against less-than-ultimate provocations. "If you do x, we will do y, which might be enough to provoke you to do z, which might provoke us to destroy your cities." Dreadfulness is not enough to overcome any amount of incredibility; if x is a minor provocation, the threat to respond straightway by destroying cities might be just too incredible to work. But each of the steps of escalation might be somewhat credible, and together they amount to a somewhat credible threat to impose a risk: "If you do x, we start something that might end in the destruction of your cities."[9]

The MADman thinks it obvious that deterrence requires a solution to the credibility problem, and obvious that the only solution is to find a threat so dreadful that it needn't be credible; and he expects the enemy not to overlook the obvious. Therefore he thinks that for the enemy, as for us, an assured capacity to destroy cities will be seen as the sine qua non of nuclear deterrence. Further, he thinks it would take no great effort for the enemy to counteract any steps we might take to protect our cities. Therefore he thinks such steps would be, at best, costly and futile. We buy the means to reduce the enemy's strategic forces by counterforce warfare; the enemy buys enough more missiles to assure himself that enough of them will survive. We buy expensive defenses; the enemy buys more missiles to assure himself that enough of them will get through. We buy shelters, he buys bigger bombs and relies on fire. (Or he buys extra-dirty bombs, or he switches to groundburst even against cities.) We spend money, he spends money. Afterward, there are many more nuclear weapons in the world, and each of them is one more place where an accident could happen. In case of war, not only does the world get fallout and smoke from the destroyed cities, but also it gets fallout (and smoke and dust) from preliminary counterforce attacks and intercepted warheads. And still our cities are subject to vast and intolerable destruction. What have we gained? How much can we limit the damage? If the enemy agrees with the MADman that deterrence requires a certain standard of assured destruction – say, one-quarter to one-third of the population and two-thirds of the industrial capacity – then we can count on his having what it takes to meet that standard. The most we can do is to prevent him from exceeding it.

The MADman boasts that his goals for deterrence are "finite."[10] You might reply that even a finite quantity may be too big; but in fact he has a point. What the MADman thinks we need for deterrence is easily compatible with what he thinks the enemy needs. If each side can count on having enough surviving weapons to meet the standard of assured destruction, that is all that either side has reason to want. So long as they are well hardened, the strategic forces on either side could be small by present-day standards, and still they would suffice.[11] Further, there is no particular need for the forces to be even approximately equal, so long as each is sufficient. Given due attention to hardening, the balance of terror is by no means delicate. Neither side has an incentive to expand or improve its forces, for all that would happen is that the balance would be reestablished at increased cost, increased risk, and increased danger to the rest of the world.

Thus the MADman's policy for procurement of nuclear weapons is as moderate and benign as can be, short of renouncing nuclear deterrence altogether. But his policy for conduct of nuclear war is quite the opposite. What is the commander-in-chief – the president, or his successor de jure or de facto – supposed to do if deterrence fails? If deterrence is on the way to failing, he is supposed to attempt to restore it by frightening maneuvers on the lower rungs of the ladder of escalation, and that is all very well. But what is he supposed to do in the last resort, if deterrence fails decisively? He is not supposed to do anything to protect the country entrusted to his care; because he cannot, since it was thought futile to provide the means for limiting damage. Rather he is supposed to fulfill the threat to destroy enemy cities – a vast massacre, serving no good purpose whatever. There is nothing else he can do.

Then he ought to do nothing. The MADman may say, if he says it quietly among theoreticians, that it would be best if the ultimate threat were just an enormous bluff. But he cannot condone such remarks in public, least of all by the very men who might some day face the decision. For even if a threat is so dreadful that it needn't be very credible, still the MADman thinks it needs all the credibility it can get. What we need are demonstrations of resolve, not of reason and humanity.

If the commander-in-chief were a good man, he might do the right thing – nothing – despite all temptation. But the situation would do a lot to tempt him into wickedness. He would be angry, frightened, and rushed. He and those around him would be accustomed to talk as though it were a matter of course that the threat would be fulfilled. In peacetime, when it mattered less, he might have found it easy to take

57

retaliation for granted also in his secret thoughts. He might think of himself as retaliating against the enemy, and forget that most of his victims would be those who have the misfortune to live under the enemy's rule. Sophistries can be found which purport to show that it would be right after all to fulfill a threat of useless destruction, and he might find it comforting to recall or concoct one of them.[12] And, worst of all, he would have no honorable alternative to retaliation. Doing nothing would be tantamount to surrender, and surrender would be treason.

All this is as the MADman would wish it to be; for if credibility is badly needed and hard to get, then anything that can be seen to raise the chance of retaliation is all to the good. All to the good for deterrence, that is; but all to the bad if deterrence fails, for what is raised is the chance of the most wicked act that it is possible for anyone in our time to perform.

Thus, MADness carries a grave moral risk. It also carries grave prudential risks. One is that we decline to do what we can to protect our cities; and even imperfect protection might save tens of millions. Another is that if we burn cities, we and all the world may freeze in the dark beneath their smoke. (Maybe and maybe not – who knows?) A third is that we may teach the enemy to go MAD along with us, so that if deterrence failed his aim would be not to protect himself but to destroy us – let us hope he is a slow learner!

NUTS: THE CREDIBLE WARNING

To trace the reasoning that drives us NUTS, we start as before: The simple conception of nuclear deterrence encounters the credibility problem. The NUT agrees with the MADman that it is essential and difficult to solve the credibility problem, but he favors a different solution. His plan is to find some sort of nuclear attack that would not only be a retaliation, but also would serve some vital purpose. Our threat would be credible because we would have, and we would be seen to have, a compelling reason to fulfill it. In Schelling's terms, it would not be a threat at all, but rather a warning.[13] "Be warned that by doing x, you would thereby give us reason to do y"; or perhaps "you would thereby take away the reason that now stops us from doing y."

The response we could have compelling reason to deliver is counterforce warfare. The enemy's forces – especially, but not only, his strategic nuclear weapons – are his means of harming us and our allies. Of course we would prefer it if he had less of them. It is worthwhile to destroy weapons that could destroy our cities, and shorter-range weapons that could destroy our allies' cities. It is worthwhile to destroy weapons that could destroy our weapons, if those weapons continue to exert some sort of deterrence even during a war, or if they could be used beneficially in a second wave of counterforce warfare. It is worthwhile to destroy tanks and planes and troops that menace our allies, or to cripple them by destroying the transport and fuel and munitions on which they depend. It is worthwhile to destroy forces that hold captive the unwilling subjects of the enemy's empire, so that he must withdraw forces from foreign adventure to restore his internal security.[14] All these are ways to reduce the risk to ourselves and our allies if war continues. They might also serve to persuade the enemy that whatever hopes he may have had for the war will be unfulfilled, and that he would do best to seek a cease-fire without delay.

The MADman argued that attempts to limit damage, by counterforce warfare or any other way, would be costly and futile. The NUT plainly disagrees. The reason is that he rejects the MADman's premise. The MADman said that since one can't be credible, one must be dreadful; the enemy understands this; therefore he will at all costs maintain an assured capacity to destroy our cities, that being the sine qua non of his deterrence; therefore he will counter all preparations we make to limit damage. The NUT replies that it is not so necessary after all to be dreadful, because credibility can be had after all. The enemy too might reasonably be a NUT.

If he is, he may take more interest in limiting the damage we can do to him than in making sure, at all costs, that we cannot reduce the damage that he could to do us.

Of course, we must deplete our own forces to attack the enemy's. It's a bilateral force reduction, unilaterally imposed. But if the terms of trade are favorable, or not too unfavorable; and if we have weapons enough; and if there is no other good use for our weapons except for counterforce warfare (except perhaps for a small reserve to threaten cities, if our NUTtiness is not of the purest sort); then the bilateral reduction will seem advantageous. We can warn that we will find it so, if war makes force reductions seem more beneficial than they did in peacetime. Even when force reductions now seem beneficial, we do not pursue them by national technical means. We have an excellent reason not to, being well deterred from going to war. But we can warn that if war begins, or if it even seems imminent, that reason will disappear. Whatever assets we still have left to lose, the prospect of peace will no longer be one of them. There is still deterrence after deterrence fails, but it is a lesser deterrence. It relies on the uncertain hope that the enemy might reciprocate restraint in the way we fight, and that he might be willing and able to accept an early cease-fire. We can warn that this lesser deterrence will not seem to outweigh the benefits of counterforce warfare.

Thus we solve the credibility problem, and thereby we make it possible to succeed in nuclear deterrence – so says the NUT. But note a consequence of his argument: It has to be ambitious counterforce. If we want a highly credible warning that we would resort to counterforce warfare, there has to be little doubt that we expect its gains to be worth its risks. It wouldn't be much use to say (or to be seen to believe) something more like this: "We think counterforce warfare would have a moderately good probability of moderately reducing the vast damage that we and our allies may suffer. We acknowledge a grave risk that it might not work very well, or that it might invite further attacks on us, or that it might postpone or prevent a cease-fire. Still, we are inclined to think that on balance it would be worthwhile." Whatever a halfhearted and modest counterforce warrior may be doing, he is certainly not providing that highly credible warning that was supposedly needed if deterrence was to succeed.

What the NUT requires to solve the credibility problem is an excellent counterforce capacity. We need a force that offers assured destruction of some very large part of the enemy's forces, so that using it will be obviously the inevitable choice. And at first sight that seems a fine thing, quite apart from its effect on the credibility of deterrence. For if force reduction is good, more of it is better. The more enemy missiles we hit, the fewer are left to hit us.

But we know the drawbacks. First, and worst, an excellent counterforce capability demands preemption. A former aide to McNamara, faulting his Ann Arbor no-cities speech, said "he should have known there could be no such thing as primary retaliation against military targets after an enemy attack. If you're going to shoot at missiles, you're talking first strike."[15] I question this as it stands; but if you're going to shoot at missiles *and hope to get almost all of them,* you most certainly are talking first strike. If our excellent counterforce capacity has been attacked, it may still be some sort of counterforce capacity, but it will no longer be excellent. (Here I have in mind the loss not only of missiles but also of the softer parts of their command and control.)[16] More simply, we cannot hit those birds that have flown; at best we can fight them with defenses, and that is one kind of counterforce warfare that does not double as retaliation. So *if* we are talking about the ambitious counterforce that solves the credibility problem by affording the highly credible warning, *then* we are talking first strike. The highly credible warning is, alas, not a warning of retaliation but of preemption. Further, it gives the enemy his own incentive to preempt. His forces are under the gun: Use them or lose them. Whatever use he may have in mind had better be done before it is too late. Beyond a certain point, prophecies of war become self-fulfilling.

If no prophecies could pass that point except those which would have come true without benefit of self-fulfillment, then incentives to preempt might be no bad thing – at least, for whichever side is quicker on the draw.[17] But there is no reason to suppose anything of the kind. Rather we must fear the war that nobody wants, brought on by fears that would otherwise have proved groundless. And here the very success of deterrence – never mind just how it works – turns into a danger. Well-deterred people fear crisis, because they fear that somehow it could lead to war. So whenever someone gets just a little more daring than usual, even if everyone wants as much as ever to avoid war and even if things are still fairly well under control, well-deterred people start telling one another that they are on the brink of war.[18] If that gives them reason to back out of crisis, well and good. If that gives them reason to preempt, not good.

This pressure to preempt is an excellent reason to shun ambitious counterforce. It is probably the gravest risk – prudential and moral both – that the NUT embraces in his quest for credibility.

But it is not the only one. Besides short-term instability in times of crisis, also there is a second, long-term instability. The MADman could boast that his goals for deterrence are finite, in the sense that what he thinks we need is easily compatible with what he thinks the enemy needs. Not so for the NUT. If we need enough capacity for counterforce warfare that we can credibly warn of our strong incentive to undertake it, then what is needed is an increasing function of what the enemy has. In fact, the increase is more than linear.[19] We need superiority. If we and the enemy both pursue credibility by the NUT's method, one of us will be disappointed; and if credibility is desperately needed then it might be pursued by desperate means. If one side pursues credibility by the NUT's method, while the other side MADly pursues dreadfulness instead, then again their goals are incompatible. In this case MADland's goals are more easily fulfilled, and

NUTland is likely to find itself permanently disappointed until such time as it changes its goals.

What's wrong with arms racing, so long as we can win? Is it that weapons exert some malign influence on the brain, turning those who spend time among them into lovers of death and destruction? Some of our dislike of arms races looks like mere superstition. But there are some good reasons to be found among the bad. The MADman has already listed three drawbacks of increased arsenals. There is cost; more weapons present more opportunities for accidents; more weapons used in war, even if for counterforce only, give the world more fallout (and smoke and dust). A fourth danger, if we race for ambitious counterforce, comes from the combination of long- and short-term instability. In races, it sometimes seems to one side that the other is overtaking. (It may seem that way to both sides at once.) If you already have some incentive to preempt, it will not help if you also think that war next year would go worse for you than war today. Nor will it help if the other side thinks you think that; or if you think they think so; or. . . . So for several reasons (even if not for all the reasons that have been offered) it seems that a risk of arms racing is indeed a grave risk, both moral and prudential.

The third grave risk, this one primarily a moral risk, concerns the collateral damage from ambitious counterforce warfare. Consider an example.[20] There are missile fields near Kozelsk, about 140 miles southwest of Moscow; Teykovo, about 135 miles northeast; Kostroma, about 190 miles northeast; and Yedrovo, about 215 miles northwest (and a similar distance southeast of Leningrad). Because these fields (with the possible exception of Yedrovo) fall in the protective range of Moscow's Galosh system of missile defense, a thorough attack on them might have to be more than usually redundant; then if the Galoshes leaked, or were saved to fight direct attacks on the city, the delivered attack also would be more than usually redundant. A thorough attack on a field of hardened missiles requires at least one groundburst per silo, and spreads a many-times-lethal dose of local fallout for several hundred miles downwind.[21] Unless the wind were just right, Moscow would be downwind from one or two of the four. An ambitious counterforce attack – ambitious enough that we could credibly warn of our strong incentive to undertake it – could not very well spare an entire missile field. (Or rather four fields, since it probably is not practical to vary the attack depending on the wind direction.) In short: If we go in for ambitious counterforce, it makes little difference whether we target the population of Moscow per se. To take credit for "sparing" them would be hypocrisy.[22,23]

The NUT runs a grave moral risk of committing vast massacres, just as the MADman does. Not an equally grave risk: The MADman's attack is useless, whereas the NUT's is meant to destroy weapons that menace us. Further, the NUT's attack kills many fewer people. Too many people live downwind from the enemy's hardened missiles, but not as many as live in the enemy's cities. The numbers do count; they are not infinite, and not incomparable. One vast massacre differs from five side by side more than none differs from one. The people who live in cities but not downwind from missiles matter no less than the people who are doomed in either case. Yet though the numbers do count, and though the numbers that measure the NUT's moral risk are much better than those that measure the MADman's, still even the better numbers are far from good.

(A fourth risk is the risk of failure. An ambitious counterforce attack, even as a first strike by an undamaged force, is a technically difficult and untried military operation. It could go wrong in ever so many expected or unexpected ways. But this is not to be counted as a flaw in the NUT's position. He acknowledges the risk of failure. What he takes to be worthwhile, and so obviously worthwhile that it provides the highly credible warning, is the expected value: the gain properly discounted by the risk of failure, and also by the risk of provoking retaliation that might otherwise be avoided. And insofar as the NUT's main goal is credible deterrence, with damage limitation a bonus, it matters not at all whether the counterforce attack would really work. What matters is that he can be seen to expect success.)

The MADman proposes to run grave moral and prudential risks so that a none-too-credible threat can be made very dreadful. The NUT proposes instead to run grave risks so that a somewhat less dreadful threat can be made very credible. His risks are different – most important, lesser massacres but more chance of inadvertent war – but no less grave overall.

EXISTENTIAL DETERRENCE

But what else can we do? How could the enemy be very powerfully deterred by a none-too-credible threat of a none-too-dreadful outcome? If he has really compelling reasons why he has to do x, why should he stop because we might then do y – when y is something he knows we know would mean uncertain and limited gains and serious risks for us, and something he could, in the last resort, survive? How can there possibly not be a serious credibility problem?

This is how. Let us suppose, first, that the enemy we seek to deter is – like many of us – averse to risk. His deliberations are skewed a bit away from ideal rationality. When faced with the prospect of an outcome that he takes to be very bad although very improbable, he discounts it by its improbability, but he doesn't discount it enough. Even if he gets the losses and probabilities right, he still shuns a one-in-a-thousand risk of losing 1,000 much more than he shuns a one-in-ten risk of losing 10.

Let us suppose, second, that he is pessimistic. He finds the world frightening, and if there are two contingencies that might seem equally probable to some disinterested bystander, he will assign higher probability to the one that would be worse for him.

Let us suppose, third, that he is skeptical. He tries as best he can to foresee the consequences of alternative actions, but never puts great confidence in his predictions. He mistrusts his experts, always thinking they have overlooked the weak spots in their schemes. Even if he cannot spot any loopholes himself, that does not much reassure him that none are there. He is like those among us who say that Murphy was an optimist.

Let us suppose, fourth, that he is conservative. He thinks there is no substitute for experience. He much prefers the devil he knows to the devil he doesn't. He never has much faith that he can predict and control the course of events, but when it comes to the prospect of success by new and untried methods, then he is even more skeptical than usual.

Let us suppose, fifth, that he is not too doctrinaire. He is ready enough to mouth the party line, perhaps without conscious cynicism, but he will not let it do his thinking for him. If there are passages in scripture that counsel bold action and assure him that history is on his side, he will make sure to find also the passages that counsel prudence and patience.

Let us suppose, finally, that he is not too hard pressed. While he sees that adventure, if successful, might offer him gains – might even enhance his safety – he is not so pressed by danger that he finds himself forced to be daring. His back is not to the wall.

(What I do not suppose is that he is at all restrained by humanity or honor. If he were, that would be a bonus; but I am not relying on it. I only imagine him to have the low but useful virtues of a competent *mafioso*. And for somewhat the same reasons – those virtues help one to survive and rise amid ruthless competition.)

If the enemy is as I have portrayed him, then it matters little what we say we will do, whether we threaten or whether we warn. He can do his best to figure out our incentives to respond to his actions in one way or another, but he will put little faith in his best guess. He may conclude that we would have no good reason to retaliate – and still fear vividly that we might retaliate for no good reason, or for some reason that he had overlooked. He will not rely on us to do as we have threatened or warned, but he certainly will not neglect the risk that we might. Nor will he rely on us not to do as we have not threatened; so it will not matter much if we have

66

neglected to threaten. And if he does not trust his predictions about how we will respond to one move of his, still less can he rely on any scenario for a chain of several moves and countermoves in crisis or in war.

What he can do, with some degree of confidence, is think about worst cases. The worst case is given by what we could do if we chose, regardless of all speculations about whether we would or wouldn't have sufficient reason to do it. It is our military capacities that matter, not our intentions or incentives or declarations. If we have the weapons, the worst case is that somehow – and never mind why – we use them in whatever way he likes least. Of course he is not at all sure that the worst case will come about. But he mistrusts arguments to the contrary, being skeptical; and he magnifies the probability of the worst case, being pessimistic; and he weighs it in deliberation out of proportion to the probability he gives it, being averse to risk.

Finding the worst case is not just a matter of supposing that we somehow choose to do our worst. There is plenty of room for skeptical pessimism about what the worst is that we could do. Doubtless he knows very well what we have in our arsenal. He may hope to reduce our forces by counterforce warfare and by defense, and he may hope to save people by sheltering them; but here he is hoping for success in a complex and untried technical task, and that is not the sort of hope he puts much faith in. He may hope that the delivered weapons will do the bulk of their destruction directly, by blast and fire and fallout; but he will have heard warnings that the indirect effects might be even worse, and he will not disregard these just because he knows they are somewhat speculative.

In short: He will be deterred by the *existence of* weapons that are *capable* of inflicting great destruction. He will not be much released from deterrence by the thought that maybe we will be deterred from using our weapons, and maybe we will have reason not to do our worst, and maybe he will succeed in blunting our attack, and maybe the more speculative horrors of war will not come true.

67

Compare two ways a burglar might be deterred from trying his luck at the house of a man who keeps a tiger.[24] The burglar might think: "I could do *this*, and then the tiger would do *that*, and then I could do *so-and-so*, and the tiger would do *such-and-such*, and then. . . ." If all such plans turn out too low in their expected payoff, then he will be deterred. But if he is a somewhat sensible burglar – or even a none-too-sensible burglar, but not downright daft – his thoughts will take a different turn. *"You don't tangle with tigers* – it's that simple. Especially when you've never tried it before. Not even if someone (someone you don't trust) claims that these tigers have somehow been tamed. Not even if you carry what the salesman claimed was a surefire tiger-stopper. You just never know what might happen." I suppose it to be through thoughts like these that our nuclear arsenal deters our somewhat sensible enemy.[25]

That is the hypothesis of existential deterrence as it applies to the enemy. The other half of the hypothesis of existentialism, not so important for my present argument, is that we too are averse to risk, skeptical, conservative, not too doctrinaire, not too hard pressed; and so are thoroughly deterred just by the existence of weapons capable of inflicting great destruction on us. We may calculate that the enemy would have no good reason to do his worst. But such calculations do not make us any less deterred.[26]

Existentialism is an empirical hypothesis, as I said; and so are the suppositions about the enemy's character (and ours) that underlie it. If they seem to "stand to reason," as I think they do, that does not mean that they hold *a priori*. Rather, it means that they cohere with our abundant but inchoate experience of human nature around us and of current events. Read current history, or live through it, imagining all the while that the enemy leadership (and ours) are averse to risk, pessimistic, . . . , and easily deterred by the prospect of worst cases; and it will all seem to fit. Seldom will we be too baffled by what is going on. That, I take it, is the sort of empirical investigation that has persuaded Bundy et al. that existentialism is true.

The reason is inconclusive, I grant. Maybe current history, even seen close up, is a sort of Rorschach blot: Any of many organizing hypotheses could seem to fit, if not perfectly, at least well enough to impress and persuade. And certainly there is at least one rival hypothesis, an alarming one, that fits. If the enemy were a daring gambler, and farsighted and fiendishly clever, and knew very well how to lull us, then would we not see just what we are seeing? Would we not expect existentialists to come forward urging that the enemy is easily deterred? Would we not expect him to take great care not to upset their preconceptions? – As with other hypotheses that we are fooled by a demon no less powerful than deceitful, decisive counterevidence is impossible. We just have to decide what seems plausible and what seems absurd.

Three objections to existentialism demand replies. First, you may object that existentialism is all very well for the enemy of today, but Hitler might rise again. I reply mainly by granting the point, and saying that we may cross that bridge if we come to it. It would be splendid to find a morally acceptable method of nuclear deterrence that works against all manner of enemies, under all manner of circumstances, . . . But if we can find no such splendid thing – as very likely we can't – that does not mean that deterrence here and now is bankrupt. It is enough to solve the problem of deterrence we actually face. We are not required to solve hypothetical problems as well.

But also I doubt that there are as many potential new Hitlers around as meet the eye. If someone sees fit to rant and rave, that does not mean that he is a genuine new Hitler. He might be crazy like a fox. He might know that in a very well-deterred world, where everyone is afraid of crisis, making a little bit of crisis is an effective means of getting one's way. And he might know that in a well-deterred world it is not a very risky thing for him to do.

Second, you may object that existential deterrence is all very well for every day, but not good enough for a really severe crisis. When the enemy's back is to the wall, when he has no choice but to be daring, then it takes more to deter him. That is when we have a credibility problem to solve.[27] I reply that I do not understand how the "really severe crisis" is supposed to undermine deterrence. It certainly doesn't make the dangers of nuclear war look less horrible or less unpredictable! I can see how the enemy might have his back to the wall, say by a chain of revolts in many parts of his empire at once. I see how he could imagine gains if he would dare to run the risk of nuclear war with us. What I don't see is the connection. He may fear that we will press him hard some day, but we will not – he has us too well deterred. If he finds his back to the wall it will not be we who put him there, and attacking us will not offer him any way out of his danger.

If striking first offers not only a great and obvious advantage, but also the prospect of getting off very lightly, *then* it is plain to see how a really severe crisis might undermine deterrence and lead to nuclear war. But only then. The case is relevant only if we and the enemy make it so – if one side pursues overambitious counterforce, and the other side allows him to succeed. It would be a pity if we were worried about the temptation to preempt, and therefore we doubted that existential deterrence would work in a severe crisis, and therefore we decided that we had to solve the credibility problem, and therefore we required a very credible warning, and therefore we bought an excellent counterforce capacity, and thereby we created the temptation to preempt!

Even without much temptation to preempt, we would still fear crisis. We think that somehow crisis can very easily lead to war. *Somehow* – but we have no clear notion how, no scenario that shows incentives for every step of escalation. We settle for loose talk of "brinks" or "powder kegs" or "war fever." We are pessimistic and skeptical. So even if we cannot figure out how existential deterrence might break down under the strain of severe crisis (absent the deadly temptation to preempt), still we do not put faith in reassuring predictions about the unknown.

This is exactly how we ought to think, if existentialism is

true. We as theoreticians cannot help thinking somewhat as our statesmen do, and well-deterred statesmen should have an exaggerated fear of crisis. Existentialism itself predicts that we should find existentialism too good to be true!

Even if the statesmen's fear of crisis is unreasonably magnified, still it protects us well (absent the temptation to preempt) in times of crisis. We ought to cherish that fear, not undermine it just for the sake of better theory. But if this same fear also endangers us when we think about the buying and using of nuclear weapons, because it provides the crucial premise supporting MAD or NUTty policies, then we had better challenge it after all. Let's hope it is a very robust fear, so that by challenging it in one context we will not lose its benefits in another.

If you must live among tigers, not tangling with them is only the beginning. You also try not to startle or confuse or excite them. And you try not to cause anyone else to startle or confuse or excite them. Even if all you want to do is to pick on some friendless weakling, still you do it very carefully – because who knows what might somehow happen? The tigers are a generally calming influence. Likewise, if our fear of crisis is not so much fear of some predictable scenario of escalation as fear that things will get out of hand somehow, who knows how, then it is an unspecific fear. Any kind of crisis, anywhere, looks dangerous. To that extent, nuclear deterrence extends itself willy-nilly, whether or not we make any effort to extend it. It is not up to us to say who may shelter under our nuclear umbrella; nor is it up to those who accept or disdain to be sheltered. The calming effect of nuclear deterrence protects our friends and foes alike.

I do not mean that there is nothing at all we can do to enhance or to undermine extended deterrence; any potential crisis looks dangerous whatever we do, but we can make it look somewhat more dangerous or somewhat less. Unfortunately, the way we make a crisis *look* more dangerous is to make it *be* more dangerous. The art of extending deterrence is the art of increasing the seeming danger a lot by increasing the real danger only a little. We have many techniques at our disposal: We can arrange a path for escalation in easy stages, we can pledge our credibility, we can put our troops or weapons in harm's way. The biggest thing we could do to make crises look more dangerous is to destabilize nuclear deterrence itself – if we create a temptation to preempt, that will make crises very dangerous indeed, and they will seem to be at least as dangerous as they really are, and that will enhance extended deterrence. This is a NUT's plan. The existentialist will disagree, thinking that even if we try to make crises as safe as we can they will still look quite dangerous enough. The enemy will not be calmed entirely, he may engage in cautious adventures, but he will not try any really daring mischief.

Here you may make a third objection against existentialism: You may insist that the enemy has in fact proved daring. He blockaded Berlin, he put missiles in Cuba, he invaded Afghanistan. . . . I reply by doubting that those adventures were as daring as they seemed. Again, if existentialism is true and we are well deterred, we will exaggerate the risk that crisis may somehow lead to war. Then adventures will seem more daring than they are, because we will exaggerate the risks that the adventurer chose to run. (And sometimes the adventurer also will come to see his risks as more serious than he first thought, and back down in great haste.) If there is some normal range of severity of crises, then some crises will fall at the top of that range. Those ones will be seen as very dangerous, just because they are worse than the rest. And he who creates them will seem daring. But this could happen almost *no matter where* the limits of the normal range might be. If, with no knowledge of the history of the nuclear era, someone tried to imagine possible provocations and rank them on a scale from less dangerous to more, I do not think anything that has actually been done, either by the enemy or by us, would have ranked very high.

Still, when all is said and done, I do concede that we run some risk if we rely on existential deterrence. If we neglect to provide a threat that is either very dreadful or very credible, and if it turns out that the enemy is more daring than we thought, then he will not be well deterred. Then we'll be sorry. But we have yet to hear of any policy that is free of all risk. If existentialism is false, so that there really is a serious credibility problem then I think we're left with MAD versus NUTS – halfway houses make little sense, since they offer threats that are neither as dreadful nor as credible as the supposed problem demands. We have reviewed the risks the MADman runs to make his threat dreadful, and the risks the NUT runs to make his credible. The risks of pursuing credibility through automated retaliation and the risks of nuclear pacifism are still more obvious. The risks of relying on existential deterrence are, I submit, a very much better choice than these.

BUY LIKE A MADman, USE LIKE A NUT

The MADman's policy for procurement of nuclear weapons is as moderate and benign as can be. The forces he requires are comparatively small and cheap. He creates no temptation to preempt. His standards of adequacy are finite, in the sense that both sides at once can meet them. We could be well content – if it were not for his abominable policy about what to do in case of war. But if existentialism is true, the package deal comes apart. We can buy like a MADman, if we like, but that implies nothing about what we ought to do in case of war, or what we ought to intend beforehand. We needn't strive to give some credibility to our dreadful threat to destroy the enemy's cities. We needn't threaten it at all. We have weapons that give us the assured capacity to do it, and their very existence is deterrent enough.

So far, so good; but a big question remains. What if we buy the MADman's finite deterrent, but it lets us down? What if deterrence fails after all, and in a big way? In particular, suppose we come under a major nuclear attack. What ought we to do then? And what ought we to do beforehand? What intentions should we cultivate, and what should we habitually assume in discussions that include those who might be in command after an attack? What war plans would we prepare? What should we declare publicly about our policy for fighting nuclear war?

The key question is the first: What ought we to do? Intentions and assumptions can simply fall into line. Whatever it is that would be right to do, *that* is what we should intend to do, and *that* is what we should habitually assume we would do. If existentialism is true, and it is not intentions but capacities that deter, then deterrence does not require us to cultivate intentions to do anything except what would at the time be right. The "paradox of deterrence", in which supposedly it is intentions that deter, and intentions to do the right thing would deter inadequately, and therefore it is right to form intentions that it would be wrong to fulfill, does not arise.[28]

A qualification. We should intend to do the right thing – *if* we can succeed in so intending, and firmly enough to withstand temptation. But if the right thing is repellent and the worst is tempting, then it may be safest to aim for second best. The worst, surely, is wicked destruction of the enemy's cities. I shall argue below that the best is counterforce warfare; if I am right, then doubtless any potential commander-in-chief should have the strength of character to intend the best. But suppose I am wrong: Suppose instead that surrender is best, counterforce warfare is only second best. If so, what should a potential commander-in-chief aim for? If he is uncommonly strong-willed and has the courage to face dishonor, he may still intend the best. But if he is weaker he had better not try it, lest his good intentions give way when the time comes and leave him in confusion and panic. He needs an honorable alternative to surrender, or who knows what he might do. For him it is best to intend the second best.[29] Although in fact I favor intending counterforce warfare because I think it the best thing to do, I might still favor intending it even if I thought it only second best.

The question of war plans is harder. We should have two war plans, at least: one for whatever it would be right to do (or right to intend to do), and one for destroying the enemy's cities. Why the second? Because our war plans are part of our capacities, even when they are not part of our intentions.[30] If capacities are all it takes to deter, still we need genuine capacities, not sham. A genuine capacity to destroy the cities in retaliation takes one of two things: a plan prepared in advance, or else the capacity to improvise a plan and carry it out. A capacity to improvise takes several things. We would need an atlas of principal cities; we also would need time to work out which missiles to aim at which coordinates, channels to communicate this allocation to the centers that launch. the missiles, further time to load the coordinates into the missiles. We might have the atlas; we are unlikely to have the rest, unless wartime command and control can be made much less vulnerable. So without the plan, the missiles probably can't work. They are little better than missiles with no warheads or fuel tanks inside, or plywood mock-ups. They are sham capacity, and it would not take much espionage to reveal the fact. So we need the plan for destroying cities. Of course we need not intend to carry out that plan – not so, we ought to fully intend to do something better, or nothing. But the plan must at least be there, just as the warheads and fuel tanks must be there.

(I set aside the question whether it is also a good idea to have advance plans for small nuclear attacks to rock the boat in times of severe crisis. If we make a crisis seem more dangerous than before, that should make all concerned want more than before to back out of it. Making crises seem dangerous is the way we extend deterrence. Existentialism predicts that it is easy to make a crisis seem very dangerous, but hard [absent the temptation to preempt] to make it be as dangerous as it seems. A small nuclear attack would provide some genuine danger and a great deal of seeming danger – you never know what might happen if you tangle with tigers – and, again, the advance plan is part of the capacity. But the capacity might tempt us to use it. So I don't know whether "limited nuclear options" are on balance a good idea. But in any case, I am here concerned with our ultimate options: What options should we have for big attacks, and which of them, if any, would it ever be right to carry out?)

The question of declaratory policy also is not settled just by deciding what it would in fact be right to do in case of war. There seem to be three alternatives: lying, truth, and obfuscation. Suppose we had decided (as we should) that it would be wicked and useless to retaliate by destroying the cities; suppose our firm intention was to deliver some other sort of attack, or perhaps none. Then should we nevertheless threaten vigorously that we would destroy the cities? Or should we explain, clearly and truthfully, what we think we would do and why? Or should we simply boast of our flexibility, declining to say anything about which of our many options we might prefer?

So far as deterrence goes, it should scarcely matter.[31] We deter by what we have, not by what we say. If we have the capacity to destroy cities, and we have evident reasons not to, and we say we will, the pessimistic and skeptical enemy will think we maybe will and maybe won't, and he will fear the worst. If we say we won't, but we keep the capacity, then too he will think we maybe will and maybe won't. The one thing we cannot do is keep him guessing by obfuscation – *we* cannot keep him guessing, because he is sure to keep guessing no matter what we say. If we threaten or if we decline to threaten, that might make some marginal difference to the enemy's expectations. But if existentialism is true, he is not at all sensitive to marginal differences in expectations.

The proposal to deter by lying is a staple of philosophical writing about the morality of deterrence.[32] Scarcely anyone supports it; but critics of deterrence feel obliged to knock it down. The straw man proposes that if we threaten a wicked retaliation yet secretly intend to do nothing, our intentions are innocent and yet we deter. The critic's rejoinder is that the secret of the innocent intentions would soon leak out (which I take to be true) and deterrence would thereupon collapse (which I take to be false). But the critic has a point; it is that declaratory policy is mainly a question of politics. If the truth about our intentions is acceptable to those whose assent is required if our policies are to be legitimate and feasible – Congress, the voters, our allies – then it may be told plainly. If the truth would be disturbing, then we can count on some seeking political advantage by revealing it and others seeking advantage by denying it; the result will be obfuscation. The big lie is a bogus option; the choice is between the plain truth (if palatable) and obfuscation (otherwise).

Now back to the main question: What should we do? What is the right response if we have bought like a MADman, and then deterrence fails in a big way? In particular, what should be our ultimate response to a major nuclear attack? In that case, I say, we ought to use like a NUT. We ought to engage in counterforce warfare with what remains of our forces, hoping thereby to limit further damage to us and to our allies. We should not retaliate by destroying cities; on the contrary, we should compromise the efficacy of our attacks so as to reduce collateral death and destruction. We should be scrupulous in our targeting: Prevention of future harm should be our only goal; reciprocation of past harm should be no part of our goal.[33] We should proceed as if we valued the lives of the enemy's civilians and soldiers – simply because we *should* value those lives – but less than we value the lives of those on whose behalf we are fighting.

If we use like a NUT, but with nothing more than what remains of a MADman's forces, then our aims in counterforce warfare cannot be too ambitious. In particular, we cannot hope to reduce the enemy's remaining forces to the point where he no longer has the capacity to do dreadful damage to whatever remains of our population and our resources for recovery. But there is dreadful damage and there is dreadful damage; outcomes that deserve the same adjectives may nevertheless be unequal. The numbers count. If tens of millions are already dead, doubtless that is quite enough to exhaust our stock of adjectives and saturate our capacity to feel horror. But that is no reason why it is not worthwhile to save the lives of tens of millions more. To cease to care about the further tens of millions, just because the prospect of losing them makes no impact on our overloaded emotions, would be self-centered and irresponsible and frivolous. A private person might be forgiven if he just gave up, overwhelmed and past all caring. But one who has accepted a high position in government, or a commission in the armed forces, is not allowed the same self-indulgence.

The MADman argued that attempts to limit damage would be futile. Thinking as he does that MADness is the way to go, he expects the enemy to go properly MAD; if the enemy sees a certain standard of assured destruction as the sine qua non of his deterrence, he will do whatever he must to meet that standard despite our efforts; therefore the most we can do is to prevent him from exceeding that standard; and if the MAD enemy attacks us, he will most likely fulfill his dreadful threat for lack of anything worthwhile to do instead. To this the NUT replied that MADness is not the way to go and so the enemy might well not go MAD. We existentialists can agree with that, and hope to accomplish something worthwhile in damage limitation in case the enemy does not see fit to do his worst. But that is not our only goal. Even if the MADman turns out exactly right, and the enemy does fulfill the dreadful threat he had thought essential for deterrence, it is still worthwhile to see to it that he does only that much harm and not even more. If we can limit the enemy to killing one-quarter to one-third of us, when otherwise he would have killed one-half to two-thirds, that is not a goal to inspire enthusiasm. Nevertheless it saves tens of millions. The MADman's indifference to those tens of millions is not the least of his moral failings.

It is worthwhile to limit damage. Counterforce warfare, even of a modest sort, is a way to limit damage. It is not as effective as we might wish, but it is somewhat effective and we have no better way. Therefore using our remaining nuclear weapons for counterforce warfare is the right thing to do. It is, of course, a better thing to do than destroying the enemy's cities. That alternative is easy to beat. But also, I say, it is a better choice than doing nothing and waiting to see what sort of follow-on attack we suffer from the enemy's remaining forces.

Several objections demand replies. First, you may object that there is a better way to limit damage: make no counter-attack of any kind, and propose an immediate cease-fire on acceptable terms. Even if the enemy imposed draconian terms, and even if the enemy's follow-on attacks could be blunted by our counterforce warfare, is it not clear that we would suffer less harm from the cease-fire than from the follow-on attacks?

I think, for one thing, that it is not *perfectly* clear. We can imagine a great variety of postwar conditions on terms acceptable to the enemy; we can imagine a great variety of follow-up nuclear attacks. Some of the former may well be worse than some of the latter. Which would you prefer: The fate of the Afghans? Or a few tens of warheads, airburst, against military targets far from our cities? This particular comparison, of course, is shamelessly rigged: an especially harsh cease-fire versus an especially mild follow-on attack, two extreme cases, neither one especially believable. We need some idea which cases, both of cease-fire and of war, are the believable ones. The trouble is that we are already supposing something unbelievable: that a nuclear war is under way. Suspend disbelief that far, and what premises do you have left? Which of our actual beliefs about the enemy do you hold fixed, which do you abandon? All is guesswork, whether about the cease-fire or about the continued war. For what it is worth, I join the objector in guessing that the cease-fire would do us far less harm than the enemy's follow-on nuclear attacks. So if we were given that choice, I too would choose the cease-fire.

But I insist that we would not be given that choice. Or rather, we might be, but we couldn't know it. It is indeed quite possible that the enemy might reciprocate our restraint, withholding his follow-on attacks if and only if we did not attack him. But there are other possibilities as well.

The enemy might be willing to accept a cease-fire if, but only if, we had disarmed him to the point where he could not complete his intended plan of attack against us. Or he might be unwilling to consider a cease-fire in any case. He might believe, as many among us do, that nuclear war would be destined to go on to the bitter end. He might think the cease-fire would last only as long as it took us to assess our damage, get our airborne command posts into position, and retarget our remaining missiles. Or his attack might have damaged communications to the point where he could not hear our offer, could not tell whether we were firing or not, or could not countermand his own firing orders for the second wave.[34]

Counterforce warfare does give away all hope for an immediate cease-fire, and that must be counted among its costs. But it is not clear whether it is more likely to cause follow-on attacks or to prevent them; and it is likely that there will be follow-on attacks no matter what we do. Therefore it seems well worth doing what we can to blunt them.

Second, you may object that the best way to limit damage is to inflict limited countervalue retaliation, punishing the enemy a little at a time, and prove by demonstration that we will keep it up until the enemy stops attacking. At the same time, we offer generous terms for a cease-fire. We do harm, but we hope to prevent greater harm.[35]

I reply that whether we succeed depends on what harm the enemy expected to suffer. When he decided to attack us, he surely did not expect to get away unscathed! If he is skeptical and pessimistic, and disinclined to put faith in untried theories about how to engage in nuclear war safely, he probably expected to suffer quite a lot of harm. Even so, he decided to attack us. He was willing to pay the price. Then if we prove to him that he must indeed pay the price, how is that going to change his mind? (If we show him that the price is less than he thought, we might even encourage him to continue. And if his main fear was that things might somehow get out of control in the end, it might not be a good

idea to show him just how careful and restrained we can be.)
To dissuade him, we must show him that he will suffer more
harm than he expected. If he is skeptical and pessimistic,
and therefore expected a lot of harm, that will be no easy
thing to do. A demonstration shot against some economic
target in the wilderness will not suffice. It will be necessary
to shoot at cities – and not just one at a time, and not just
the very smallest ones. If it takes some time to convince him
that we will keep up the punishment, we may very soon
exceed the amount of harm we would have done by scrupulous counterforce warfare. And if that is still not enough
to dissuade, it is all in vain.

I take it the objector imagines a scenario something like
this. The enemy calculates that if he attacks us in just the
right way – as it might be, a "surgical" counterforce first
strike, accompanied by threats of what he will do to us if we
strike back – we will not dare to retaliate, and he will be in a
safer position to cope with some desperate situation he is in.
Trusting his calculation, he attacks. Our limited retaliation
proves to him that he has miscalculated. The war ends there.
– I say we shouldn't believe the part of the story where the
enemy trusts the calculation.

You may reply that it's all very well to believe *now* that the
enemy is skeptical and pessimistic, and not about to believe
any calculation that says he could attack us and not suffer
much harm. Existentialism fits our present evidence. But existentialism predicts that the enemy will be well deterred and
not attack at all. Yet we are asking what to do if, nevertheless, he does attack. The attack will be strong evidence that
the enemy was not so skeptical and pessimistic as we thought.
Once attacked, we should change our mind about how the
enemy thinks. We should infer that he did not after all expect to pay a high price, and therefore that it will be easy to
show him that the price is more than he expected. – I agree
that the attack should change our mind about the enemy.
But it should not leave us thinking that he is a confident
calculator who has calculated that the price will be low. Rather,
it should leave us not knowing what to think. We should

learn that we did not understand the enemy as well as we thought we did; we should not abandon one hypothesis only to embrace another. We should modestly conclude that we have very little idea whether the price he is prepared to pay is high or low, and hence very little idea whether limited retaliation will have any effect.

Limited countervalue retaliation is a gambler's strategy. If it works to stop follow-on attacks altogether, and if it works quickly, and if the smoke from the cities we burn does not prove deadly, then it may protect us better than any blunting of follow-on attacks possibly could. If it fails, it accomplishes nothing at all. But whether it works or whether it fails, we kill vast numbers of people in the cities we attack. And the cities burn, and the smoke rises.

An additional problem is that if we are to inflict punishment a little at a time, we need to remain in control of our forces until we are done. If the enemy stops, we need to know it. If the enemy doesn't stop, we need to launch yet another limited attack, and for that we need to know which of our weapons are still there that could do the job. If we seek to avoid escalation by a policy of less-than-equal response,[36] then also we need to know in some detail what kind of attacks we are receiving. And if we want to explain to the enemy what we are doing and what we propose to continue doing, and what we are not doing, and what terms we propose for a cease-fire, then we need communication with him. All this may be a tall order. Partly, that depends on whether the enemy has chosen to target our command and control, as he well might. Partly, it depends on the severity of weapons effects whereby an attack might damage communications whether the enemy intended it or not.

You might counter this with a *tu quoque:* Damage limitation by counterforce warfare also would benefit from adequate post-attack command and control. It would help if we could adjust our targeting in the light of information about the state of our forces and the enemy's. It might help to break our attack into several waves, using information gained between one wave and the next. So how can the vulnerability of command and control be a reason to favor counterforce warfare over limited countervalue retaliation? Rather, is it not a problem for both methods of damage limitation alike? – Yes, it is a problem for both alike, but not to the same degree. Without adequate command and control, counterforce warfare becomes less effective; but limited retaliation probably fails altogether and turns out to be worse than useless. If our countervalue attacks peter out before the enemy is persuaded to accept a cease-fire, the harm they do is all in vain. (And if they go on after the enemy does accept a ceasefire – say, because we have ordered submarine captains to fire until further notice and then cannot countermand our order – that is worse still.) Suppose the last words of the commander-in-chief before he is killed or communication collapses are "Execute option 4." We will be better served if this option 4 is a large preplanned counterforce attack, badly executed though it would be, than if it is the first of a series of small countervalue attacks that we cannot then continue (or worse, cannot discontinue).

I have no difference of moral principle with the objector who advocates limited countervalue retaliation. He and I agree that we must weigh the harm done against the prospect of harm prevented. How the balance tilts is a difficult job of guesswork, and it is only there that we disagree. I think the harm done is disproportionate, given the slim chance of success. I think that counterforce warfare affords a somewhat more favorable balance.

(To avoid misunderstanding, we must remember which case we have in mind. My question was: What to do if deterrence fails in a big way? What should be our ultimate response to a major nuclear attack? There, I say, limited countervalue retaliation is out of place. But lesser crises and provocations are quite another story. There, if we resort to limited nuclear options of any kind, our aim is to enhance deterrence by making the crisis look dangerous. We raise the perceived risk of escalation, preferably without equally raising the genuine risk. We want to frighten; any punishment or any force reduction we actually inflict is of secondary importance. There is a premium on drama. Further, in responding to lesser crises, we are not dealing with an enemy who ex hypothesi has already chosen to attack us and pay the price. And we still have peacetime command and control. Under these different conditions, the balance of advantages between countervalue and counterforce options may look very different. [Which is not to say that the balance tips the other way. But if some sort of counterforce is preferable in this case too, as I rather think it is, it will be for different reasons.] Also, some very limited options, altogether too mild to make sense as ultimate responses, may come into their own: countervalue against the economic target in the wilderness, counterforce directed exclusively against conventional forces, maybe even the harmless demonstration shot.)

Third, you may object that it is futile to limit further damage, because if we have suffered a major nuclear attack, all of us are doomed in any case. Those who survived the initial blast and fire will die over the next months from fallout, or they will freeze in the shadow of the smoke, or they will starve because the crops have been destroyed, or they will starve because the economy is destroyed, or they will die in epidemics, or they will die when desperate survivors fight over what little food is left. I reply that all of this may be so, or it may not. Nobody doubts that the indirect effects of nuclear war would be serious.[37] But nobody knows how serious. Fortunately we lack direct evidence, and the questions are far beyond our powers of analysis. Also, the indirect effects presumably depend on the direct effects. So even if, *per impossibile*, we understood them perfectly, still we could not tell whether we were doomed unless we knew what sort of attack we had suffered. But that would be a hard thing to know. Before the attack hit, we could see only roughly where the warheads were going; afterward, our means of gathering information would be badly damaged. The country might be doomed by indirect effects, but we could not know it at the time. In considering the costs and benefits of counterforce warfare, we must somewhat discount the benefits because we know they would vanish in case the indirect effects proved sufficiently deadly. But it would be the height of irresponsibility to assume this case and dismiss all others.

Further, the indirect effects count on both sides of the question. If our worst guesses about indirect effects are true, then indeed the initial attack dooms us all and damage limitation is futile. But if the next-to-worst guesses are true, it may rather be the indirect effects of the follow-on attack that doom us, unless we blunt it by counterforce warfare. Then the benefits of counterforce warfare turn out greater than we would have thought. Suppose, as now seems plausible, that far the most deadly indirect effect is shadow of smoke and dust; that the initial attack hits missile fields in open country; that the follow-on attack would burn cities; and that smoke from burning cities casts a darker shadow than dust from groundbursts.[38] Then whatever protects cities from fire saves lives far away from the cities themselves. Or suppose that economic and political chaos is indeed a very serious effect, but that it takes only a very few intact cities to alleviate it greatly.

Further, if the benefits of counterforce warfare are lost to indirect effects, the costs may also be lost. One cost is that we give away all hope for an immediate cease-fire; but if we are already doomed, no cease-fire could save us and the loss of it is no cost. Another cost is the collateral death and destruction that our counterattack would inflict. But at present, it is the shadow of smoke that seems most dangerous among all the indirect effects that have been suggested. If indeed we are doomed by some indirect effect of the enemy's attack, most likely that is how. And in that case, the enemy's subjects will very soon freeze along with us, for the smoke does not take long to spread around the hemisphere. Then it scarcely matters if we kill the doomed a little sooner.

Fourth, you may object that it is futile to limit further damage even if there are lives to be saved, because the survivors' lives will not be worth living. I reply that if so, they are free to kill themselves afterward. The decision that they would be better off dead is not one that someone else should take for them, least of all someone who has undertaken a responsibility to protect them. Anyhow it seems – or it has seemed hitherto – that people who survive the worst that nature or malice can do to them can somehow find their way back into our lives that are far from worthless. It may be hard for the fortunate to imagine how they do it, but that is no reason to assume that they cannot.

Fifth, you may object that second-strike counterforce warfare is futile because the enemy's remaining weapons will be few and widely scattered. Our attack would mostly hit the empty holes where missiles used to be, doing no good and inflicting collateral death and destruction to no good purpose. Or, sixth, you may object that second-strike counterforce warfare is futile for the opposite reason: The enemy will have kept a reserve force that is much more than enough for a devastating follow-on attack against us. What is left of our MADman's arsenal might somewhat reduce the enemy's reserve force. But if that force is redundant, reducing it somewhat will do nothing much to limit the damage it can do. It is one or the other of these objections that McNamara's aide must have had in mind when he said that "if you're going to shoot at missiles, you're talking first strike."

I take both these objections very seriously, and it is small comfort that at least they cannot both be right. I reply, first, by repeating that damage limitation does not have to succeed extremely well to be worthwhile; and, second, by listing reasons why the enemy would hold back some of his weapons, not too few and not too many.

Here are some reasons why he would hold back not too few. First come four reasons why he would have a reserve force whether he wanted it or not. (1) Some of his weapons would not be in working order. Aircraft and missiles need maintenance; submarines need time in port. Unless he could wait until everything was ready – unlikely, and not just to the extent that any scenario for outbreak of nuclear war is unlikely – his unready weapons would be left out of the first attack, and when made ready would become part of the reserve force. (2) Missiles are imperfectly reliable. Substantial numbers would not launch when they were supposed to. Those that failed, but not beyond repair, would become part of the reserve force. (3) Safety precautions meant to prevent unauthorized firing tend also to impede authorized firing.[39] Missiles unlaunched because their safety devices work too well would become part of the reserve force. (4) For reasons best known to himself, the enemy has built more missiles than he has launchers. Some of his launchers are meant to be reloaded after use, and he keeps reload missiles available.[40] These reloads are part of the reserve force. So long as the enemy persists in his folly – which may not be long – his reloads make an ideal target for second-strike counterforce. We know where they are. They may even be unhardened, at least until he puts them into the holes.

I continue the list with four reasons why he might want a reserve force. (5) If the enemy has (or hopes he has) adequate command and control, he can do a more efficient job if he fires in several waves, with retargeting between.[41] Whether the efficiency seems worthwhile will depend, of course, on how well he thinks we will be able to reduce the forces he keeps back; and on how important it is to hit the targets in question as soon as possible. (6) He may believe, as many of us do, that deterrence does not automatically end when war begins. He may keep a reserve force, and tell us so, to dissuade us from attacking his cities. Even if he once claimed to believe that restraint in nuclear war is absurd, imminent danger might give him reason to change his tune. (7) While he seems to appreciate the horrors of nuclear war as well as we could wish, he is not in the habit of telling himself that it would be the end of the world. He may think that after the war he will be weaker, he will still have enemies, he will still need nuclear deterrence, and he will not be able to rebuild his forces in a hurry. (8) He might possibly use some of his weapons as targets to draw our fire, so that we will have fewer warheads left to shoot at other targets. We are not necessarily making a mistake if we shoot at the targets he wants us to shoot at.[42]

The reasons why he would hold back not too many are simpler. (1) If he thinks we may respond to his attack by counterforce warfare, he will have more weapons to use if he uses them at once. Those he has not held back will not be caught on the ground. (2) To the extent that he is attacking our missiles (or bombers), his chances of catching them on the ground are best if he does not delay. If he is going to take the risk of a major nuclear attack on us he may as well accomplish all he can by it.

What about the enemy's invulnerable submarine-launched missiles? Are these enough of a reserve force, all by themselves, to guarantee that second-strike counterforce is futile? Possibly; but (1) just how invulnerable are they? We are prepared to hunt submarines. How good a job can we do? (2) Some possible futures include defenses (doubtless mediocre) and submarine-launched missiles may be comparatively easy to intercept. (3) We think of these missiles as an ideal reserve, but they also have an opposite role: as weapons for the most urgent targets in the first wave of an attack, taking advantage of the short flight time from a nearby submarine. In particular, they can hit fast enough to stop bombers from taking off after longer-range missiles have been seen launching. (4) If they are held in reserve, are they reserved for use late in the war? Or are they meant to be the enemy's postwar nuclear force? (5) I repeat, finally, that my goals for counterforce are modest. Even if we don't stop a final strike by the submarine-launched missiles, we may cut the damage enough to be worthwhile. A cut from 120 million to 80 million fatalities (to pick numbers out of thin air) would be nothing to rejoice about – still, 40 million lives are not to be ignored.

These considerations end in a standoff. If you claim that second-strike counterforce cannot succeed (even by unambitious standards of success) because the enemy would have too few or too many remaining weapons, I think I have shown that you have no easy way to prove your case. But neither do I have any easy way to prove the opposite: that the number of remaining weapons will be right, not too few and not too many. The question is a hard one. The answer must depend on matters of detail about the capacities of the opposing forces and about the enemy's strategic doctrines.

Then the answer depends partly on things that are not known to philosophers but are known to practical strategists. It would be worth knowing exactly what we have to assume about the opposing forces and the enemy's strategic doctrines in order to find cases in which second-strike counterforce can accomplish some moderately worthwhile limitation of damage. I hope that somebody well informed, and without an axe to grind, will work through some hypothetical wars in detail to find out what such cases look like, and how far they overlap with possible present or future realities. If it turns out that they are not at all realistic, then my position is untenable.

I think it much more likely that, despite our best investigations, the question will remain very hard. Although the answer depends partly on things we can know, it depends a lot on things we cannot. We know what the enemy says about his strategic doctrines, but that's a far cry from knowing what he'd really do. We know something about the realities and accuracies of weapons as tested under peacetime conditions, but it would be no surprise to find that we were seriously off. Most likely, the alleged futility of second-strike counterforce because of too few or too many remaining weapons will remain in the same boat as its alleged futility because we are already doomed. That is, it will be a possibility that we cannot dismiss and cannot assume; all we can do is to take it into account by somewhat discounting our hopes of success. But if we hope to destroy the weapons that might kill many tens of millions of us, those hopes can stand a lot of discounting before they fade away! Absent calculations more decisive than I expect to see, I still think the right response to a major nuclear attack is to try our luck at counterforce warfare.

Seventh, you may object that if it is our policy never to attack cities, then we have given the enemy an excellent way to protect his weapons from our attack: He has only to put them in his cities. Then what can we do?

I reply that if the enemy does such a peculiar and foolhardy thing, then he is by no means the enemy I have assumed. If he relies on our declared policy to this extent, he is by no means skeptical; rather, he is gullible. If he chooses to risk losing his weapons and cities all at once, he is by no means risk-averse and pessimistic; rather, he is a go-for-broke gambler. If he stakes his safety on this one novel scheme, he is by no means conservative. He is a theoretician, in love with artificially clearcut cases. We may well wonder how he managed to leave his institute and reach a position of power.

My position on deterrence and nuclear use is not held *a priori*. It is premised on existentialism. If existentialism turns out false, my position is untenable. If the enemy puts his weapons in his cities, existentialism stands refuted. What I have to say about the case is not that we should do this or do that if it arises; rather, I say it will never arise.

Eighth, you may object that, try as we will to avoid it, our counterforce warfare would cause a lot of collateral death and destruction. We would kill great numbers of civilians who have the misfortune to live under the enemy's rule and near his weapons. What we do to limit damage to ourselves does too much damage to others. No effective nuclear counterattack could satisfy established standards of justice in warfare, because the harm done would be out of proportion to the expected benefits.[43]

I reply that second-strike counterforce would indeed do a great deal of harm. But the harm done would not be out of proportion to the good purpose served – or not unless we had independent reasons to expect our efforts to prove futile.

Suppose that hijackers are holding 70 hostages, and we consider a rescue. Unfortunately a crowd has gathered. We estimate that about 7 bystanders, foolish and ghoulish but otherwise innocent, would be killed by the rescuers' stray bullets. We think it likely that the rescue will succeed; and that the hijackers may well kill the hostages soon if there is no rescue; and that no safer method of rescue or of settlement can succeed. But we are far from certain of any of these things. Should we try our luck? Yes. The harm done, though indeed it matters very much, is not out of proportion to the good purpose served, even when we discount it as we should to take account of the many uncertainties.

Now let it be 70 million hostages versus 7 million spectators. This comparison of dreadful alternatives exhausts our adjectives and saturates our emotions, but the proportion is the same as before. What is right once is right a million times over, and why should it matter that a million little cases are lumped into one big case?

If we are shooting at missiles that menace cities, and if we compromise the efficacy of our attack somewhat to reduce collateral damage, then the numbers just mentioned – 70 million versus 7 million – might fall somewhere within the range of reasonable guesses. Change each of them up or down by a factor of two and they might be no less reasonable. But even if it's 35 million versus 14 million, and even with the 35 million duly discounted, it still does not seem that the harm done is disproportionate to the good.

When we remember the missile fields at Kozelsk, Teykovo, Kostroma, and Yedrovo, it may seem hard to believe that collateral damage could possibly be limited to a few million deaths. (Moscow alone has a population well over eight million.) I said earlier, in berating the NUT, that a counterforce attack could not be very effective if it failed to do a thorough job on these four missile fields. But if our aims are not so ambitious as the NUT's – if we do not seek the very effective damage limitation that offers the compelling incentive that supports the credible warning, but if we only seek damage limitation for its own sake – then we can better afford to compromise the efficacy of our attack. We can better afford to limit groundburst yield against targets near cities, to attack less redundantly than we might, or to pass up some targets altogether. Indeed, if we mount a modest counter-force attack with what remains of a MADman's forces, we may simply have too few warheads left for all the targets we'd like to hit. If we are forced to pass up some targets anyway, then it costs us little if the ones we choose to pass up are the ones near cities.

It's a bit less clear that the harm is proportionate if, instead of shooting at the enemy's missiles that menace our cities, we are shooting rather at his missiles that menace our missiles that menace his missiles that menace our cities. (Our cities have to enter into it in the end; if we were defending our missiles just for their own sakes, of course the harm done would be disproportionate.) This is a somewhat artificial distinction, since any missile he has can menace both, and we cannot tell with confidence how he will use them. But suppose our best guess is that, although he may attack cities in the end, what he will do next is carry on with counterforce warfare against us. So there will be missiles shooting at missiles. There will be bilateral force reductions, unilaterally imposed, whether we fire at his missiles or whether we wait for him to fire at ours. Our only choice is which way it will happen. That matters for two reasons. First, because the terms of trade depend on whether we fire or wait. (The terms if we fire are not necessarily better; they would not be, for instance, if the missiles on both sides were well hardened and unMIRVed.) Second, because it matters whether the explosions, with their fallout and other collateral damage, take place on the enemy's territory or on ours. Now it's a question of doing harm to avoid suffering roughly equal harm. Maybe the harm we would do if we fired is less than the harm we would suffer if we waited, either because of the characteristics and locations of the weapons or because we would take more trouble than the enemy would to avoid collateral damage. Then again the harm is proportionate, though less clearly so than in the previous case.

Alternatively, maybe the harm we would do if we fired is somewhat more than the harm we would suffer if we waited.

I am inclined to think we should fire even then. My answer depends on the moral judgment that it would be right for a commander-in-chief to proceed as if he valued the lives of the enemy's subjects somewhat, but less than the lives of those on whose behalf he is fighting. That judgment has two parts: first, the judgment that it is permissible to undertake a responsibility to serve the interests of some people more than others; and second, the judgment that one who has done so is permitted, indeed required, to be partial toward those he has undertaken to serve. Whoever the commander-in-chief may be, he will have accepted either a high position in government or a commission in the armed forces. Either way, he has undertaken a special responsibility to his countrymen. (And to those they have taken on as allies.) He betrays his obligation if he chooses no longer to serve his country, but rather to become an impartial servant of mankind at large. When he deliberates between alternative courses of action, such as waging counterforce warfare or not, he is entitled and required to weigh the consequences – but with a finger on the scale.

Ninth, you may object that much of the collateral death and destruction from counterforce warfare would fall not on the enemy's soldiers but on his civilians. No effective nuclear counterattack could satisfy established standards of justice in warfare, because those standards require that noncombatants must be immune from attack.

I reply in two parts. First, I deny that it matters whether those who die in war are soldiers or civilians. Some say this because they doubt the innocence of civilians, claiming that all the populace is caught up in total war. (Infants too?) But I do not doubt the innocence of the enemy's civilians. They live as best they can under his iron rule, and his misdeeds are not of their making. It is too much to ask that they rise up in revolt when they have no hope of success. It is rather that I doubt the guilt of the enemy's conscript soldiers. It is absurd to say that they have chosen to wage war against us, if all that is true is that they would rather wage war than be shot as mutineers. Most of them would be innocent not only in the everyday sense but also in the special usage of Just War theory: not *nocentes*, not engaged in harming us.[44] The question is what to do if we have come under a major nuclear attack. At that point, the *nocentes* are the soldiers who launch the enemy's strategic nuclear weapons. The rest, whatever fighting they may have done before and whatever their role might be in various possible futures, are for the moment bystanders.

But in the second place, it is not exactly true that counterforce warfare puts noncombatants under attack. The dubious principle that noncombatants must be immune keeps company with the dubious principle of double effect. The latter principle rests on a distinction between three kinds of foreseen effect of an action – as it might be, the foreseen death of victims of nuclear attack. The effect might be intended as an end: We want them dead because we hate them. Or the effect might be intended as a means to some other end: We want them dead because we think their death will weaken the enemy's resolve to continue attacking us. Or the effect might be foreseen but not intended either as an end or as a means: We want to destroy the enemy's missiles, and we know that a side effect will be the death from fallout of many victims who live downwind. But we do not want them dead, either as an end or as a means to some other end. We would prefer it if somehow they survived. Far from designing our attack to kill them, we design it to spare all we can, given our main goal of destroying the weapons. The principle of double effect says that harm done as a foreseen but unintended side effect of an action matters less than harm intended as an end or as a means. What matters is not so much the harm itself as the intending of it!

So the immunity of noncombatants turns out to mean immunity from attacks in which their death is intended either as an end or as a means. It does not extend to immunity from attacks in which their death is merely a foreseen consequence, intended neither as an end nor as a means. This standard of justice in warfare grants protection to noncombatants with one hand and takes much of it back with the other. And it is well for it that it does. Noncombatant immunity without the principle of double effect would face a reductio ad absurdum. It would tell us that an enemy who shelters his soldiers and weapons among unwilling civilians may not be fought in any feasible way, no matter how many lives would be saved by fighting him and no matter how much the lives saved might outnumber the lives lost![45]

The theory of justice in warfare is another package deal much in need of breaking up. One part is broadly consequentialist: It requires that warfare must be undertaken only in the service of good ends, and only if there is sufficient chance of success at achieving the good ends, and only if the harm done is not out of proportion to the good that is pursued. This part deserves our firm adherence. A second part is self-regarding: It has to do with the state of the warrior's heart and soul. To intend someone's death, whether as an end or as a means, and not because he has undertaken to attack you but for some more devious reason, is to have murder in your heart. We may doubt whether this is the correct way to delineate what it is to have a murderous heart; and we may ask whether some murderous hearts may not be preferable to the heart of one who cares more for the state of his own heart than he does for the lives of his countrymen. But the simplest thing to say (for those of us who do not accept the contrary as an article of faith) is that other things at stake in warfare are just much more important than the state of the warrior's heart and soul. The self-regarding part of the theory of justice in warfare deserves rejection.

But in the present case it makes no difference, because the dubious companion principles of incombatant immunity and of double effect cancel out. It is true, though I say it makes no difference, that those who live downwind from hardened missiles are for the most part civilians. It is also true, though again I say it makes no difference, that their death from fallout would be a foreseen consequence of an attack on the missiles, but in no way intended either as an end or as a means. They would therefore not be under attack in the sense that is relevant to their supposed immunity.

Tenth, you – doubtless not the same "you" who made the previous two objections – may object that I have understated the commander-in-chief's obligation of loyalty. He should serve his countrymen (and allies) wholeheartedly. He betrays them if he does *anything* to protect the lives of the enemy's subjects at their expense. If counterforce warfare protects those it is his duty to protect, he should wage it as effectively as he can. It would be wrong to compromise the efficacy of our attacks so as to reduce collateral damage. When weighed against damage to us, collateral damage should be a matter of indifference.

The objection is hard to answer, once I have granted that it is legitimate for the commander-in-chief to weigh consequences with a finger on the scale. I cannot stand on principle and insist that all lives have equal worth; therefore I am badly placed to resist the rival principle of wholehearted loyalty. Each of the two uncompromising principles appeals to our moral sensibilities; compromise does not. To see this more plainly, imagine that the terms of compromise are spelled out exactly: The right thing is to proceed as if one of them is worth 58 percent as much as one of us. This particular compromise is arbitrary. It has no appeal at all. An argument that 58 is exactly the right percentage would be a bit of black comedy. The same could be said, of course, if the percentage had been 59, 97, 23, or anything else. Only the extremes, 0 percent and 100 percent, are principled. The pure ideals of loyalty and of impartial benevolence are incommensurable. No attempt to compromise them can be right, whatever the terms. Compromise betrays both.

I reply that we must nevertheless strike a compromise, however unsatisfying and arbitrary any particular terms of compromise may be. For the claims of benevolence are compelling, unless we harden our hearts and close our minds; and so are the claims of loyalty. What must go is neither benevolence nor loyalty, but rather purity of principle.[46]

FINITE COUNTERFORCE

Finally, you may object that it seems senseless to build forces designed for one mission when all the while we intend to use them only for another. If we buy like a MADman, we buy a force that is just right for retaliating against cities; but if the time comes to use like a NUT, we will wish the forces had been made more suitable for their only truly intended use. To be sure, they had another use: They were supposed to sit there looking dangerous. But wouldn't they have done that perfectly well, even if they had been properly designed for counterforce warfare?

I do not reply to this objection; instead I endorse it. *If* we have bought like a MADman, and deterrence fails in a big way, *then* I say we ought to use like a NUT. But I agree that it would be better to buy forces especially suited for modest, second-strike counterforce warfare with avoidance of collateral damage.[47]

Now it is the NUT's turn to have his package deal broken up. His policy about what to do in case of war – counterforce warfare meant to limit damage – is comparatively moderate and benign, at any rate compared to the MADman's. We could be well content – if it were not for his dangerous policy for procurement of weapons. Because he wants damage limitation not only for its own sake but for the sake of credibility, he requires weapons capable of meeting ambitious goals. Then the very same strength that supports the credible warning also makes dangerous incentives to preemption in the short term and arms racing in the long term. Should we not avoid these dangers as the MADman does, by shunning weapons that are well suited to counterforce?

No. We should indeed avoid those dangers. To do so, we must keep our capacity for counterforce warfare within modest limits. But not as the MADman does, by insisting on unsuitable weapons. Rather, we should buy suitable weapons but limit their numbers. Counterforce capacity is accused of undermining stability. I say that *ambitious* counterforce capacity is guilty as charged. But *modest* counterforce capacity is innocent.

The modest counterforce capacity I have in mind is still supposed to be good enough to accomplish something worthwhile even in a second strike. Any counterforce capacity, modest or ambitious, will accomplish more if it is used in a preemptive first strike. Isn't that enough to tempt us into preemption and make prophecies of war fulfill themselves? – I think not. A cold-blooded gambler might be tempted into preemption just by the advantage of striking first; but for a real-life statesman, an effective lure would have to consist of two parts. There would have to be not only the first-strike advantage, but also the prospect of getting off very lightly. (Lightly compared to other possible nuclear wars – of course that would still be an immense catastrophe.) Ambitious counterforce capacity presents both parts of the temptation; modest capacity presents the first part, sure enough, but not the second.

Any counterforce capacity, modest or ambitious, will accomplish more if the enemy's forces are smaller. Success depends on the balance of forces. Isn't that enough to tempt us into arms racing to improve the balance? We do have some incentive to tilt the balance in our favor, so that we could do better at limiting damage in case of war. But this is not an urgent incentive. Damage limitation is not our primary goal in procurement – deterrence is. The NUT said that damage limitation and deterrence are linked: Deterrence requires the credible warning, which requires an excellent capacity for damage limitation, which requires superiority. If he were right, then we would indeed have an urgent incentive to race, lest we lose the sine qua non of deterrence. But if existentialism is right and credibility is not a problem, then deterrence and damage limitation are separate goals. Both are part of the protection we gain from our nuclear arsenal, but deterrence is by far the greater part. If we race and lose, or if we decline to race, we are not in a desperate predicament. We still have our existential deterrence; we still have some worthwhile capacity to limit damage by counterforce warfare, though perhaps not as much as we would prefer. Our goals of deterrence and damage limitation, *un*linked, are finite, in the same sense that the MADman's goals for deterrence are finite and the NUT's are not. They can be satisfied, not perfectly but well enough, for both sides simultaneously. There is a balance of forces that both sides can live with, thinking it not ideal but good enough.

Even a MADman's finite deterrent gives some significant capacity for first-strike counterforce; indeed, it gives some worthwhile capacity even for second-strike counterforce, as I urged in the previous section. But all agree that the MADman's forces create little temptation to preemption or arms racing. They are not yet above the danger line. Then let them set a benchmark; let us have forces suited for counterforce warfare, but let us have only enough of them to match the first-strike counterforce capacity of the MADman's finite deterrent. In that case, they should be no more destabilizing. All who have agreed that finite deterrence is admirably stable ought to agree that this finite counterforce capacity is safe as well.

(Maybe this standard of safety is too conservative. I do not assert that if we exceed it, straightway there is a deadly temptation to preempt or to race. More likely, the danger becomes severe only at some much higher level. But for the sake of argument, I will rest content with a standard that seems to be uncontroversial.)

Within the safe limit on first-strike counterforce capacity, we want all the second-strike counterforce capacity we can get. Whatever enhances second-strike capacity without enhancing first-strike capacity is all to the good. If we buy more weapons, we enhance both together. Likewise if we improve our weapons so as to increase their chance of destroying their targets. So those are not wanted, at least not if we are near the safe limit and want to stay below it. But improvements in hardened command and control are another story. Second-strike counterforce means putting together an effective attack out of what remains of our partly destroyed forces, against what remains of the enemy's partly expended forces. The more information we can gather about the state of our forces and his (the latter being the more difficult job), and the more we can retarget our weapons to make good use of whatever information can be had, the better we can do. Excellent post-attack command and control would be very advantageous. But it would not increase first-strike counterforce capacity in the least – because pre-attack command and control is already excellent. So one difference between the MADman's finite deterrence and my finite counterforce is that the latter includes going all out for hardened command and control.[48]

Another difference arises because the intended mission is not counterforce warfare *simpliciter;* it is counterforce warfare that scrupulously avoids collateral death and destruction. For any given level of capacity, any improvement which holds the capacity fixed while reducing collateral damage is all to the good. Therefore we should pursue accuracy of aim. Not accuracy of aim by itself; that increases counterforce capacity, and so might take us above the safe limit. But if we aim our warheads more accurately and reduce their explosive yield (a trend that is already well under way), we hold capacity fixed while we reduce the fallout, both local and global. Likewise if improved accuracy means that we need fewer warheads altogether. And if very accurate aim makes it possible to attack hard targets in new ways, without digging craters and raising the dust that brings down local fallout, so much the better.[49] The MADman has no use for accuracy; cities are soft and large. But finite counterforce should go all out for accuracy if, but only if, it takes the place of yield or numbers.

If we trade yield or numbers for accuracy, that reduces our capacity to destroy cities. Of course we have no reason to want to destroy cities, but we do want the enemy to be deterred by the thought that somehow we might anyway. If the capacity is what deters, dare we reduce the capacity? I suggest that we can reduce it a lot without making existential deterrence any less robust. For remember our benchmark:

the MADman's finite deterrent, capable on a second strike of assuring the destruction of, say, one-quarter to one-third of the enemy's population and about two-thirds of his industrial capacity. We used to think that much lower levels of destruction would do for deterrence. We would think so still if higher levels had proved unfeasible. The required level of assured destruction went up over the years because our capacity to destroy went up – not because the enemy turned out to be less easily deterred than we thought at first. Any second-strike force that could accomplish something worthwhile in counterforce warfare, even with lower yields than we use today, would *a fortiori* be capable of enormous destruction.

I suspend judgment about the question whether finite counterforce should include defense. The question is not what sort of weapons give us our capacity to limit damage; the question is how much of that capacity we have altogether. Overambition is bad, lest it tempt preemption; but within safe limits, the more the better. Defense is not destabilizing just because it is defense. It might, however, turn out to be destabilizing for special reasons. If a system of defense works badly against a first strike, but well against a ragged retaliation after our first strike, then it adds to the first-strike advantage and helps tempt preemption. If the defense works best when it's alert, but it can't stay alert for long, then it might pressure us into preemption in much the same way that an airborne bomber fleet could; we must use it or lose it. Even if defense does not pose these dangers, it might simply turn out to cost too much, compared with alternative methods of damage limitation. Probably it does cost too much compared with a modest civil defense program; but if civil defense is politically impossible, it is not a genuine alternative.

At any rate, defense had better not take over too much of the job of damage limitation – not unless we get the system of our dreams, so good that we can abandon deterrence. If existential deterrence requires it, some substantial part of our counterforce capacity must double as our deterrent capacity to attack cities. Missiles have the double capacity; defensive weapons have little or none of it. It would be bad to have different weapons for damage limitation and for deterrence. In that case the commander-in-chief would have to choose whether to use his city-destroying weapons or leave them idle. It is better if he must choose whether to use the same weapons one way or the other, knowing that if he destroys cities he wastes the ammunition he could use to blunt a follow-on attack. He is less likely to go wrong if he faces the second choice than if he faces the first.

TO CHANGE THE WORLD? OR TO UNDERSTAND IT?

Doubtless it will seem that I have been advocating a changed way to conduct nuclear deterrence, more moral and more prudent than our present arrangements. Maybe to some extent that is right. But consider: What if we lived in a world where deterrence *was* conducted strictly according to the principles of finite counterforce? What would that world look like?

First, the weapons. They would provide an assured capacity to destroy cities, even after suffering attack. They would also have some capacity for second-strike counterforce, but a modest capacity. As a consequence, they would have some capacity for preemptive counterforce. But not an excellent capacity; not enough to give us too much hope of getting off lightly if we preempt, therefore not enough to make prophecies of war fulfill themselves.

Second, the intentions for use. These we could not see. We could only hope that they were right. If indeed we lived in a world of finite counterforce, they would be as we hoped.

Third, the declaratory policy. Many members of Congress, voters, and allies believe in a credibility problem; they would want to see threats of some retaliation more dreadful than mere counterforce warfare to limit damage. Therefore we would expect not clarity and truth, but rather obfuscation. We would expect much talk of flexibility and options. When government officials did say anything about which options should be preferred, we would expect different ones to say different things. We would expect empty phrases, and controversy even over those.

Fourth, the war plans. Whatever other options might turn up, we would expect at least two: the option of destroying cities (whether as population per se or as economic targets matters little) and the option of counterforce warfare, with avoidance of collateral damage.

That is what we would see; and it seems very like what we do see. Is it reasonable to think, then, that we really do live in just the sort of world I have been advocating? Surely not. The hypothesis that our present arrangements have been designed strictly according to the principles of finite counterforce conforms, more or less, to the direct evidence of weapons, declaratory policy, and war plans. But it conforms not at all to what we know about the politics of defense policy. Finite counterforce is mediocre counterforce, and who can rise in this world by advocating mediocrity? When mediocrity triumphs, it is as an unprincipled compromise between the advocates of too much and the advocates of none. What we see is the proverbial horse designed by a committee. It has been bodged together by many hands, guided by many different theories of deterrence, some coherent, some not. But what we should understand, I think, is that we have come out not too far away from where we should want to be.

If I am right about how we ought to be conducting our nuclear deterrence, what is needed is not a radical new start, but piecemeal change in the right directions. We want to make sure we have well-planned attack options for second-strike counterforce with avoidance. We want the command and control needed to carry out such options. We want lower yields and higher accuracies. We want the right size of arsenal – preferably not too small, but more urgently not too large. In all probability we want substantial force reductions, preferably bilateral. Maybe we want defense. Probably we want civil defense, but probably that is a lost cause.

David Lewis

We do *not* want too much counterforce capacity. Especially, we do not want counterforce capacity that is good only in a first strike – too many warheads in a single silo, or dependence on pre-attack command and control. We do not want defense if it works well only as part of a first strike.

As theoreticians, we want an understanding of nuclear deterrence that is neither MAD nor NUTS. We don't want to be committed to wickedness, and we don't want to invent specious reasons why retaliation against cities would be less wicked than it seems. We don't want to regard death and destruction as a "bonus" in counterforce warfare, or as a matter of indifference. We don't want to fuss over credibility. We don't want deterrence through damage limitation – we want damage limitation for its own sake, and deterrence can look after itself. We don't want to think that damage limitation is worthless unless it is wonderful. We don't want to put adjectives in place of numbers, shirking the responsibility to save tens of millions of lives just because the outcome is dreadful either way.[50]

NOTES

1. See Spurgeon M. Keeny, Jr., and Wolfgang K. H. Panofsky, "MAD versus NUTS," *Foreign Affairs* 60 (Winter 1981–82), 287–304. "MAD" stands for "Mutual Assured Destruction"; "NUT" stands for "Nuclear Use Theorist," or "NUTS" for "Nuclear Utilization Target Selection."

2. In emphasizing the moral risk of doing wrong, rather than the unconditional corruption of holding wrongful conditional intentions, I follow the lead of Jeff McMahan, "Deterrence and Deontology," *Ethics* 95, no. 3 (April 1985), 517–36. The idea of moral risk is puzzling: Two of us are disposed alike to do wrong if put to a test; it happens by luck that one goes untested whereas the other is put to the test and does wrong; we fault the second far more than we fault the first, although the difference is entirely in their luck and not at all in their moral fiber. Puzzling or not, this discrimination is built into our ordinary moral thinking, and it would be rash to challenge it on philosophical grounds. For general discussion of

moral luck and moral risk, see Bernard Williams, "Moral Luck," and Thomas Nagel, "Moral Luck," both in *Proceedings of the Aristotelian Society,* Supplementary Volume 50 (1976), 115–51.

3. No relation to other doctrines of the same name. See Alvin Plantinga, "On Existentialism," *Philosophical Studies* 44 (1983), 1–20.

4. *Pace* Henry Shue, "Having it Both Ways," Chapter 1 of this volume.

5. McGeorge Bundy, "Existential Deterrence and Its Consequences," in Douglas MacLean, ed., *The Security Gamble: Deterrence Dilemmas in the Nuclear Age,* Maryland Studies in Public Philosophy (Totowa, N.J.: Rowman and Allanheld, 1984), pp. 3–13; Kenneth N. Waltz, "Will the Future Be Like the Past?" in Nissan Oren, ed., *When Patterns Change: Turning Points in International Politics* (New York: St. Martin's, and Jerusalem: Magnes, 1984), pp. 16–36; Robert Jervis, *The Illogic of American Nuclear Strategy,* Cornell Studies in Security Affairs (Ithaca and London: Cornell University Press, 1984).

6. See Jervis, *The Illogic of American Nuclear Strategy.*

7. From McNamara's budget statement for Fiscal Year 1966; cited in Desmond Ball, *Targeting for Strategic Deterrence,* Adelphi Paper No. 185 (London: International Institute for Strategic Studies, 1983), p. 14. In later budget statements, McNamara lowered the number somewhat. If the numbers already seem unexpectedly low, remember that they are meant to measure only the *assured* part of the destruction; that is, the prompt destruction by blast, that being the part that can be estimated with the greatest certainty.

8. Jervis, *The Illogic of American Nuclear Strategy,* p. 146.

9. See Thomas C. Schelling, *The Strategy of Conflict* (Cambridge, Mass.: Harvard University Press, 1960) on "the threat that leaves something to chance"; Jervis, *The Illogic of American Nuclear Strategy,* pp. 130–46; and Herman Kahn, *On Escalation: Metaphors and Scenarios* (New York: Praeger, 1965).

10. Terminology is elastic. Sometimes (especially, perhaps, by detractors) the term "finite deterrence" is used broadly, to mean the entire package deal that I call "MADness." But often it is used more narrowly to mean, simply, the doctrine that we would be wise to keep our strategic forces fairly small, and that (within limits) we need not match the size of the enemy's forces. Finite deterrence, in this narrow sense, has to do purely

with the procurement of weapons. It implies no particular hypothesis about how deterrence works and no particular doctrine about what to do if deterrence fails. I reject finite deterrence in the broad sense, that is MADness; I support some sort of fairly finite deterrence in the narrow sense. Just how finite? Just how many warheads should we ideally have? – On that question I have no very precise opinion.

11. As "present-day standards" rise with the years, the numbers proposed for finite deterrence also rise. Harold A. Feiveson, "Finite Deterrence," Chapter 6 of this volume, proposes a finite deterrent force of 2,000 warheads on each side, small by present-day standards but large by the standards of, say, 1961. In 1961, however, some of Feiveson's counterparts had in mind 500 warheads on each side in the first stage of a bilateral force reduction, to be reduced soon after to 300 and then below 200. See Louis B. Sohn and David H. Frisch, "Arms Reduction in the 1960's," in David H. Frisch, ed., *Arms Reduction: Programs and Issues* (New York: Twentieth Century Fund, 1961).

12. See for instance, David Gauthier, "Deterrence, Maximization, and Rationality," in MacLean, *The Security Gamble*, pp. 101–22.

13. *The Strategy of Conflict*, pp. 123–34.

14. Whenever the enemy values his military forces, or values what they can do for him, an attack upon them counts both as counterforce and countervalue. Since the enemy values the cohesion of his empire and needs the means to suppress revolt, a counterforce attack against his internal security forces is a punishment to him, as well as a way to protect ourselves by drawing his forces away from elsewhere. If one fears that the enemy may find the NUT's warning of counterforce warfare sufficiently credible, but not sufficiently dreadful, one might wish to play up this aspect of it. See Arthur Lee Burns, *Ethics and Deterrence: A Nuclear Balance Without Hostage Cities?* Adelphi Paper No. 69 (London: International Institute for Strategic Studies, 1970); Bruce Russett, "Assured Destruction of What? A Countercombatant Alternative to Nuclear MADness," *Public Policy* 22 (1974), 121–38.

I myself think that punishment should be no part of our goal in responding to a major attack. However, if it proved possible to target the enemy's means of ruling without disproportionate harm to those he rules, and to do so effectively, that would be a form of punishment less unsatisfactory than any other. But here we must take care, for it would be all too easy to target the means of ruling in ways that *would* do disproportionate harm to the ruled. That is not to be condoned: 50 kilotons aimed at a city is an attack on the city – whether it is aimed at the KGB building or at an orphanage is of no importance whatsoever.

15. Henry L. Trewhitt, *McNamara* (New York: Harper & Row, 1971), p. 115.

16. On the vulnerability of command and control, see Desmond Ball, *Can Nuclear War Be Controlled?* Adelphi Paper No. 169 (London: International Institute for Strategic Studies, 1981); Bruce G. Blair, *Strategic Command and Control: Redefining the Nuclear Threat* (Washington: Brookings Institution, 1985); and Paul Bracken, *The Command and Control of Nuclear Forces* (New Haven and London: Yale University Press, 1983).

17. See Shue, Chapter 1 above.

18. See Robert F. Kennedy, *Thirteen Days: A Memoir of the Cuban Missile Crisis* (New York: W. W. Norton, 1969); and Theodore Sorensen, *Kennedy* (New York: Harper & Row, 1965), p. 705: "the odds that the Soviets would go all the way to war, [Kennedy] later said, seemed to him then 'somewhere between one out of three and even.' "

19. See Schelling, *Strategy of Conflict*, pp. 236–37.

20. Desmond Ball, "Research Note: Soviet ICBM Deployment," *Survival* 22 (1980), 167–70. I have taken the distances from atlases. They are not to the missile fields themselves, which of course are not shown, but to the towns of Kozelsk, Teykovo, Kostroma, and Yedrovo.

21. Compare the fallout patterns shown for attacks on American missile fields in William Daugherty, Barbara Levi, and Frank von Hippel, "The Consequences of 'Limited' Nuclear Attacks on the United States," *International Security* 10, no. 4 (Spring 1986), 3–45. The cases aren't perfectly comparable, since even a more than usually redundant attack on the missile fields around Moscow might involve fewer and smaller warheads than the 0.5-megation groundburst (plus 0.5-megaton airburst) per silo and per launch control center assumed by Daugherty, Levi, and von Hippel. But since their pattern shows 3,500-rad contours many hundreds of miles long, adjustment for a somewhat lighter attack would not make much difference to the fate of someone within 135–215 miles. What might

make a difference is excellent fallout protection, with food and water enough for many weeks.

22. See George H. Quester, "The Necessary Moral Hypocrisy of the Slide into Mutual Assured Destruction," Chapter 5 of this volume. However, I don't see why a friend of counterforce warfare must *necessarily* be hypocritical about collateral damage. Suppose his firm policy is to confine himself, come what may, to counterforce attacks meant to serve a good purpose in protecting us; suppose he acknowledges and warns that such attacks will cause a lot of collateral damage; suppose he acknowledges also that the prospect of collateral damage augments deterrence, and he doesn't mind if it does; but suppose he never compromises the efficacy of his attacks to increase the damage, or suppose he does the opposite. Whether this is a morally acceptable policy depends on how well it serves its purposes and what risks it imposes, and in particular on the likely level of collateral damage. But at least it is honest.

23. Why not prove the moral risk of collateral damage more easily? There are 22,000 miscellaneous military targets listed in our war plan; see Ball, *Targeting for Strategic Deterrence*, pp. 25–29. Many of these must be in or near cities. For instance, a battery of anti-aircraft missiles defending a city from bomber attack is a military target in or near that city. So if counterforce warfare meant attacking all "military targets," that would well and truly destroy the cities. This argument, though dramatic, is specious. The war plan includes a vast gazetteer of "targets," more indeed than we have warheads. Ball suggests that ever since 1945 "target lists have been generated in order to provide an argument for larger strategic forces" (p. 40). Lists of military targets in cities also may be meant "to avoid moral guilt and thoughts of future war-crimes indictments," as Quester suggests in this volume. Be that as it may, what counts is not the long list of 22,000 military targets, but rather the short list of *important* military targets – for instance, missile silos – that would be hard to leave out of serious attack options for counterforce warfare. The long list is a red herring; the moral risk of collateral damage arises because targets on the short list are sometimes too near the cities.

24. See Shue, Chapter 1 above.

25. It is ironic when critics claim that theories of successful deterrence depend on unrealistic assumptions of hyperrationality.

The opposite is true: Hyperrationality would make deterrence harder. The best theoreticians have always understood this. See, for instance, Herman Kahn, *On Thermonuclear War* (Princeton: Princeton University Press, 1960), pp. 198–99, for an imaginative sketch of a skeptical, pessimistic, and far-from-hyperrational Khrushchev.

26. Those of you who believe that the enemy poses a Present Danger may at least accept the second half of existentialism. My picture of the well-deterred enemy is your picture of *us*, at least during a Democratic presidency. But in that case, I ask you: What do you think causes us to be that way? Is it plausible that the principal causes of aversion to risk, pessimism, skepticism, and so forth should be factors that do their work only here? Why shouldn't the same causes work also on the enemy?

27. Herman Kahn takes this view in *Thinking about the Unthinkable* (New York: Horizon, 1962), pp. 55–56.

28. For discussion of the alleged paradox, see Gregory S. Kavka, "Some Paradoxes of Deterrence," *Journal of Philosophy* 75 (June 1978), 285–302, and Gauthier, "Deterrence, Maximization, and Rationality"; and for discussion of why it does not arise, see my "Devil's Bargains and the Real World," in MacLean, *The Security Gamble*, pp. 141–54.

29. On the general question of aiming for second best to allow for one's own weakness, see Frank Jackson and Robert Pargetter, "Oughts, Options, and Actualism," *The Philosophical Review* 95 (1986), 233–55.

30. The word "plan" is ambiguous. Imagine that I want to persuade you to spend more money on precautions against sabotage. I make a plan for sabotage, just to show you how easy it would be. I do not at all plan to commit the sabotage I have planned. It is even true to say it this way: I never planned to do what I planned to do. This ambiguity may cause some needless alarm among those who read of our "plans" for nuclear war – though genuine cause for alarm may be found there as well.

31. Gregory S. Kavka considers a "no-retaliation policy" in his "Nuclear Deterrence: Some Moral Perplexities" in MacLean, *The Security Gamble*, pp. 123–40. This would be a policy of promising never to retaliate, yet keeping our weapons. He judges that it would have "considerable deterrent value" but

would make deterrence "considerably less reliable than it is now." I disagree with the second part: When we promise no retaliation, why should the enemy heed our words at all? He sees that we keep the weapons! Kavka goes on to say that the no-retaliation policy "would be a domestic political impossibility," and with that I agree completely.

32. See, for instance, Anthony Kenny, *The Logic of Deterrence* (London: Waterstone, 1985; Chicago: University of Chicago Press, 1985), pp. 45–56; and C. A. J. Coady, "Escaping from the Bomb: Immoral Deterrence and the Problem of Extrication," Chapter 4 of this volume.

33. Thus my position is something like the Scrupulous Retaliation policy considered (and rejected) in Gregory S. Kavka, *Moral Paradoxes of Nuclear Deterrence* (New York: Cambridge University Press, 1987), pp. 48–51. But not quite: Kavka's scrupulous retaliator would respond to a nuclear attack by limited strikes against military and economic assets located far from population centers. I support the strikes against military assets; and I note that some economic assets, such as petroleum supplies and civilian airfields, are short-term military assets as well. But why the strikes against other economic assets? These reciprocate past harm, but they do nothing – anyway, nothing very direct and certain – to prevent future harm. Therefore I regard them as gratuitous harm, and also as a waste of weapons. The counterattack I would favor is "scrupulous," sure enough; but not, strictly speaking, "retaliation."

34. Why should his attack damage his own communications? He may have little choice if he wants to damage ours. A thorough attack on our reconnaisance and communication satellites, for instance, might well require high explosions over his own territory.

35. In considering this objection, I am indebted to discussion with Donald Baxter.

36. See McGeorge Bundy's remarks at an *Ad Hoc* Hearing on Nuclear Danger, House of Representatives, November 22, 1983: "Let me suggest, not as a binding rule but merely as an indicator of an approach that may avoid escalating to oblivion, that it should be a guideline for any second use of nuclear weapons that the response be clearly and substantially *smaller* than the original attack."

37. Some critics of nuclear deterrence keep pointing this out as

though it were controversial. This is not because they have
met with doubters, I think. Rather, they say it in order to
portray their opponents as fools and knaves.

38. See R. P. Turco, O. B. Toon, T. P. Ackerman, J. B. Pollack,
and C. Sagan, "The Climatic Effects of Nuclear War," *Scientific American* 251 (1984), 33–43. However, these authors note
that "nuclear explosions over forests and grasslands could also
ignite large fires, but this situation is more difficult to evaluate." The question is not only how much smoke a counterforce attack would produce, but also whether it would go high
enough to stay up for a long time. It just might turn out that
the indirect effects of counterforce warfare are worse than we
think, and would unavoidably produce death and destruction
of the same order as direct attacks on cities. If so, my position
becomes untenable.

39. See Blair, *Strategic Command and Control*, pp. 216–18.

40. *Soviet Military Power*, fifth edition (Washington: U.S. Government Printing Office, 1986), p. 24.

41. Example. He wants to destroy fifty soft targets using missiles
with 80 percent reliability. If he fires one big salvo of one
hundred warheads, two on one, his expectation is that two of
the targets survive. Whereas if he fires a first wave of fifty
warheads, one on one, his expectation is that ten of the targets survive the first wave; and if he can then retarget and fire
a second wave of ten warheads, one on one, his expectation
is that two of the targets survive the second wave. So sixty
warheads in two waves do as well as a hundred warheads in
one wave. If he were shooting at hard targets with warheads
that not only could fail to launch but also could miss, or if he
were shooting through defenses, then retargeting becomes
much more advantageous. But also it becomes much more
difficult: He would need to know not only which of his warheads had departed but also which had arrived on target, so
he would need excellent reconnaisance.

42. Example. After a certain amount of counterforce warfare, the
enemy has 150 warheads left and we have 250. Each side has
100 cities, so far undamaged; and each side still can't guess
whether the other will end by shooting at cities. If we then
destroy 100 of his warheads with 200 of ours, we have spent
those warheads well – we have made sure that 50 of our cities
will be spared. But also *he* has spent his 100 warheads well in

having them attacked – he has made sure that 50 of his cities will be spared. He might have held them back exactly to spend them in this way, knowing that he had no better way to use them. Had we not seized the opportunity, he might have done well to call it to our attention. Apart from collateral damage, the effect is as if the two sides had agreed to keep 50 warheads each and fire the rest into the sea, except that it takes no mutual trust to do the deal.

43.   In Chapter 4 of this volume Coady writes: "No doubt there are some purely military targets that could be destroyed by an accurate nuclear weapon having virtually no disproportionate side effects . . . [but] it is fanciful to suppose that the present war plans of the Eastern and Western powers can find moral comfort in such a fact." ("Virtually no disproportionate side effects" is an odd phrase. Surely the relevant proportionality is between total harm done and total good accomplished, and it makes no sense to ask whether some particular effect is proportionate.) I claim that a missile in a silo is a military target which could be destroyed, not without very harmful side effects, but without disproportionate side effects. Counterforce warfare of this kind has a great deal to do with the present war plans of both East and West. We put great emphasis on flexibility and options, including options for counterforce warfare, and we obfuscate about which option would be chosen. I think it fanciful to be confident, but not unreasonable to hope, that counterforce warfare would be our ultimate response to nuclear attack – the worst we would ever do, come what may. I think that it safely could be, and should be; and making it so, if it were a change in direction at all, would not be a radical step.

44.   See Kenny, *The Logic of Deterrence*, p. 10.

45.   A previous objection said that we should limit damage not by counterforce warfare, but rather by limited countervalue retaliation, a little at a time, to dissuade the enemy from persisting in his attack. This would be the present-day counterpart of terror bombing in World War II – surely the very thing that noncombatant immunity is meant to forbid! – But no. Here again a standard of justice in warfare that tempers immunity with double effect takes back with one hand the protection it grants with the other. However else we may fault it, the strategy of limited countervalue retaliation does not in-

volve intending evil as a means. For consider how the causal chain running from our launch of a missile to the dissuasion of the enemy commander is meant to work. How do we think the enemy will first get the dissuading news? Only when he gets reports of death and destruction? – Not likely! More likely he will track a warhead on course toward his city, and he will detect the fireball from a satellite sensor, and then already he will know that death and destruction must inevitably follow. If confirming reports follow later, they will tell him only what he already knew and so will make no relevant difference to his state of mind. The visible flight of the warhead and the visible fireball are means to our good end of dissuading the enemy, sure enough; but these things per se are not evil. The death and destruction are evil, sure enough; but these things are not intended as means to our end. The causal chain we intend is one in which the detection of the warhead and the fireball causes the enemy to infer the death and destruction, and thereby causes the enemy to stop attacking us. The death and destruction themselves are not links on that chain; they are merely foreseen and inevitable side effects – exactly on a par with the collateral death and destruction from counter-force warfare. In that case, we are back to the same old question: Is the harm done by limited countervalue retaliation disproportionate to the prospect of harm prevented? (And the same old answer: Probably yes.) Given double effect, plus reasonable assumptions about the flow of information, noncombatant immunity turns out to be irrelevant to the question whether we may attack noncombatants.

46. It is not only in desperate situations, but in everyday life, that we must strike unsatisfying compromises between incommensurable ideals. For a good discussion, see Susan Wolf, "Above and Below the Line of Duty," *Philosophical Topics* 14 (1986), 131–48.

47. Even the policy of buying like a MADman and using like a NUT requires us to buy something extra. Even if we buy just like a MADman so far as the weapons themselves are concerned, we must at least buy an extra war plan for second-strike counterforce. Again, plans are as much part of a genuine capacity as warheads or fuel tanks.

48. It is one thing to provide enough post-attack command and control to put together one big effective counterforce second

strike; it is a much more difficult thing to provide command and control that can last long enough to permit slow-motion counterforce warfare. I advocate the former; I suspend judgment about the latter. Slow motion has advantages and drawbacks. It allows time to try for a cease-fire, if communication and the enemy's frame of mind permit it. And as already noted, attacks can be more efficient if they come in several waves with retargeting between. On the other hand, slow motion means missed opportunities as both our weapons and their targets disappear. The restraint of slow motion is a different thing from the restraint I principally advocate, which consists of avoiding collateral damage and never attacking cities.

49. Given very precise aim, we might for instance be able to use warheads fused to explode underground, deep enough that the fission products would be largely contained and a hard target could be destroyed by shock waves in the earth. See T. B. Cochran, W. M. Arkin, and M. M. Hoenig, ed., *Nuclear Weapons Databook* (Cambridge, Mass.: Ballinger, 1984), vol. I, p. 311.

50. I am grateful for comments from D. M. Armstrong, Donald Baxter, Michael Doyle, Mark Johnston, Gregory Kavka, and the members of the University of Maryland Working Group.

Chapter 3

Deterrence and the moral use of nuclear weapons

Robert E. Foelber

A fundamental underlying assumption of America's nuclear deterrence doctrine throughout its evolution over the past forty years is that deterrence is a function of both capability and resolve. For nuclear deterrence to work, it is held, the United States must not only have the capability to make nuclear warfare "a totally unacceptable and unrewarding proposition for the Soviet leadership": U.S. leaders must also be perceived as willing to inflict unacceptable nuclear destruction on the Soviet Union in response to a Soviet nuclear attack on the United States or its allies.[1] This assumption about the critical role of resolve in deterrence lies behind the concern for "credible" response options so prevalent in U.S. strategic nuclear doctrine and was a major motivating factor in the development of America's "countervailing" nuclear warfighting strategy, adopted in 1979 and reaffirmed by the Reagan Administration.[2]

The familiar logic of the countervailing strategy is that for deterrence to work the United States needs, first of all, the capability to destroy "those assets which are essential to Soviet warmaking capability and political control" (such as strategic and general-purpose forces, hardened command and control centers, and leadership cadres) because this is what Soviet leaders value most – not the general Soviet population and civilian economy. But, to make nuclear threats cred-

115

ible, the United States also needs the capability to minimize damage in a nuclear war to itself and its allies primarily through options for limited, controlled counter–military/political attacks ("to defeat Soviet military objectives without necessarily triggering a massive nuclear exchange") but also through civil defenses (to provide some limited protection for the U.S. population).[3]

For decades now, Western strategists have been debating the merits of offense-dominated damage-limiting deterrence postures and their two chief rivals: finite deterrence and defense-based deterrence. With the Reagan Administration's high-level commitment to the Strategic Defense Initiative (SDI) and the development of what some view as promising new defense technologies, dissatisfaction among defense enthusiasts with the comparatively modest damage-limiting capability of a countervailing strategy has intensified, although the Reagan Administration in the end viewed strategic defenses as enhancing, not replacing, deterrence through offensive victory denial.[4] At the same time, finite deterrence theorists have become increasingly anxious as official U.S. nuclear doctrine has expanded requirements for damage-limiting capabilities, especially for hard-target counterforce weapons and strategic defenses, to maintain parity with improvements in Soviet strategic offensive and defensive capabilities. Some were especially disturbed by what they saw as a conscious shift during the early years of the Reagan Administration toward a more aggressive warfighting strategy that aims at winning a nuclear war, although the extent to which the Administration actually adopted such a posture is a matter of dispute.[5] In any case, opposition to America's nuclear strategy has broadened since 1981 to include a significant portion of the Western public, which rejects nuclear warfighting strategies as needlessly dangerous and provocative and, as Robert W. Tucker has pointed out, may be losing faith in nuclear deterrence in general.[6] The fear is that deterrence cannot last forever; that no matter how hard nations try to prevent a nuclear war, deterrence is bound to fail, and that when – not if – it does, Western civilization, and possibly the entire human species, will become extinct.

The critique of America's damage-limiting countervailing strategy is manyfold. But one of the most serious challenges to the strategy is the view that the military use of nuclear weapons cannot be morally or strategically justified. As former Defense Secretary Robert S. McNamara has recently proclaimed: "Nuclear weapons serve no military purpose whatsoever. They are totally useless – except only to deter one's opponent from using them."[7] Other thoughtful individuals, including a majority of the U.S. Catholic bishops, have reached this same conclusion after contemplating the effects of a nuclear war. Focusing on the moral dimension of nuclear warfare, the bishops in their widely discussed 1983 pastoral letter concluded that any use of nuclear weapons is likely to cause – either immediately or through an uncontrolled escalation process – the deaths of millions of innocent human beings that can in no way be justified by Just War standards.[8]

From a narrower strategic perspective, nuclear war cannot be defended either, it is claimed. The vast destructive power of nuclear weapons precludes their use as a tool of rational state policy, for it is a virtual certainty that any use of nuclear weapons will escalate to an all-out nuclear exchange that would lead to the destruction of the very national interests that are to be defended. If the "nuclear winter" hypothesis is true, all human interests could be at risk as well in a nuclear war.

What is not clear, however, is how Soviet aggression could be deterred if the United States were in fact firmly committed to a genuine "deterrence only" stance. On the other hand, if the orthodox theory of deterrence is correct and deterrence can succeed only if the United States is perceived by Soviet leaders as willing, or at least not unwilling, to retaliate for Soviet nuclear aggression, then the United States needs a strategy for using nuclear weapons that not only is effective in the eyes of Soviet leaders but also is not obviously immoral or strategically absurd in the eyes of the American public. Whether America's countervailing nuclear strategy or indeed any nuclear strategy is morally and strategically defensible may be the fundamental issue in the nuclear debate in the West.

The argument of this paper is fourfold: (1) Deterrence can work over the long haul only if the West is resolved to use nuclear weapons in its defense. (2) Although the case against using nuclear weapons – under any circumstances – is impressive, it is not decisive. There are moral perspectives falling within the broad Western moral tradition, one of which I will call "Nuclear Protectionism," that would sanction the use of nuclear weapons under certain conditions. Whether these essential conditions obtain is a matter of considerable debate. But a plausible case can be constructed for the proposition that, in extreme circumstances, the United States would be morally and strategically justified in implementing a "cautious" nuclear damage-limiting strategy that, with some notable exceptions, is roughly consistent with declared U.S. nuclear strategy. (3) A Nuclear Protectionist force posture is not obviously destabilizing, either logically or psychologically. (4) On the other hand, given Nuclear Protectionist assumptions, deterrence may not require all the damage-limiting capability of a countervailing strategy.

The case for a nuclear-use policy sketched out here can only be tentative, given the many empirical and philosophical uncertainties relating to the morality of nuclear weapons use. In light of further evidence and analysis, Nuclear Protectionism may have to be severely modified or abandoned altogether. As it stands, however, Nuclear Protectionism has implications for U.S. nuclear force deployments, U.S.–allied relations, and arms control that challenge the traditional thinking of both defenders and critics of U.S. nuclear policy.

RESOLVE AND DETERRENCE

Before considering the case for a nuclear-use policy, more needs to be said about the role of resolve in deterrence. It is one thing to contend that first use of nuclear weapons cannot be morally or strategically justified and quite another to assert the same about second use. A "no first use" strategy does not obviously undermine deterrence if supported by strong conventional forces clearly capable of defeating a Warsaw Pact conventional attack, although there may be some deterrent value in not making "no first use" official NATO policy, in order to complicate Soviet planning. To oppose the second use of nuclear weapons, however, both limited and large-scale, raises serious questions about the future of deterrence. According to the late Bernard Brodie, one of America's pioneering nuclear strategists, "It is precisely the fact that one finds it difficult if not impossible to find a valid political objective that would justify the destruction inevitable in a strategic nuclear exchange that makes the whole concept of nuclear deterrence credible."[9] Other nuclear strategists, though, would draw the opposite conclusion: The fact that it is difficult to justify the destruction of a nuclear war could lead the West to adopt a "no use" stance, which would undercut the credibility of the American nuclear deterrent. Indeed, in 1946 Brodie himself wrote, in a seminal work on nuclear strategy (*The Absolute Weapon*), that nuclear weapons can deter aggression only if it is "as nearly certain as possible that the aggressor who uses the bomb will have it used against him."[10]

Some look to strategic defenses as a way to compensate for uncertain resolve in maintaining deterrence. At the current stage of hardware (and software) research, though, it is an open question whether the United States can design an affordable strategic defense system that can assure national survival against nuclear attack if the Soviets are determined to place U.S. values at risk. Strategic defenses might have greater success in a more constrained strategic nuclear threat environment.[11] And, in fact, both Ronald Reagan and Jonathan Schell have proposed deployment of strategic defenses against missiles and bombers as part of a grand arms control agreement culminating in the dismantling of all nuclear weapons.[12] Under this new regime, strategic defenses would function as a hedge against cheating; if one side breaks out of the treaty, it would provide some temporary protection until the other side can build up its offensive retaliatory force. A fatal flaw of all such disarmament schemes, however, is that they will not work to eliminate the threat of nuclear war to the West unless the United States is resolved to use nuclear weapons in defense of itself and its allies. If it is not so resolved, as Schell believes it should not be, then there is no reason for the Soviet Union to agree to mutual nuclear disarmament because the United States would already in effect have disarmed itself.

Recently, McGeorge Bundy has given new prominence to an alternative theory of deterrence, called "existential deterrence," further elaborated upon by David Lewis in this volume.[13] Bundy is vague about the requirements for existential deterrence, but for Lewis the mere possession of the capability to inflict unacceptable damage on the Soviet Union will suffice for deterring any size nuclear attack, including limited nuclear attacks (the problem case for U.S. strategists), because Soviet leaders cannot reasonably discount the worst-case scenario for them, which is that the United States would reply in kind to a large-scale Soviet nuclear attack or that a limited nuclear war would escalate (deliberately, inadvertently, or accidentally) to attacks causing unacceptably high levels of damage.[14] The upper limit on unacceptable damage for the Soviets is usually thought to be "assured destruction" – a level of civilian casualties and economic damage that would effectively destroy the Soviet Union as a functioning society – but the actual threshold for Soviet leaders could be far less. Assuming that Soviet leaders are cautious and relatively risk-averse (a not unreasonable assumption), then no realistic security threat or opportunity to effect a favorable shift in the "correlation of forces" would be compelling enough to tempt them to take the risks of "great" destruction by attacking the West with nuclear weapons. As Lewis explains it:

> It is our military capacities that matter, not our intentions or incentives or declarations. If we have the weapons, the worst case is that somehow – and never mind why – we use them

in whatever way [the enemy] likes least. . . . In short: [The enemy] will be deterred by the *existence* of weapons that are *capable* of inflicting great destruction.[15]

Existential deterrence offers an elegant way out of two problems that have plagued philosophers of deterrence for years. The first is the classic paradox of deterrence: How can deterrence work if it requires threats that it would be grossly immoral or suicidal to carry out? The second problem arises if one accepts the intuitive moral principle that it is morally wrong to be resolved or to intend to do that which it would be wrong to do. For then, if nuclear war is morally wrong, it would seem to be wrong to even try to deter nuclear war. With existential deterrence these conundrums are dissolved, because deterrence can be maintained without threats or the resolve to carry them out.[16] The question of the morality or credibility of nuclear threats and intentions is irrelevant for deterrence.

Taken literally, however, as the claim that the mere existence of an assured destruction capability (or less) is sufficient for deterrence, existential deterrence is, I believe, questionable.[17] In the first place, as an empirical hypothesis it seems vulnerable to the following reductio ad absurdum argument. If it were correct, the United States could deter Soviet *aggression of any sort* (not only limited nuclear attacks but also conventional force invasions, insurgencies, even military assistance to Third World countries) *anywhere in the world* by simply declaring potential target areas "off limits." If the mere capability to inflict assured destruction deters limited nuclear attacks against the United States, it should deter all forms of aggression against U.S. interests as well, because the worst-case scenario in all cases is the same: The United States inflicts assured destruction on the Soviet Union. Of course, the Soviets as well could declare regions of the world "off limits" to the United States, thus creating a rigid superpower stalemate worldwide. A world order of this kind has not evolved, however, for the good reason that it is simply not credible that the United States would start a nuclear war to keep Soviet troops out of Afghanistan (at least in the strategic environment of 1979) or to block Soviet military assistance to Ethiopia or Nicaragua. U.S. nuclear weapons can deter only blatant military attacks on regions that are clearly perceived to be of vital interest to the United States, such as Western Europe, because only in these cases is it plausible that the United States would be *willing* to use nuclear weapons in defense. Indeed, a U.S. vital interest can be defined as an interest that the United States is willing or resolved to defend with nuclear weapons.

Admittedly, deterrence may not require that government leaders and the public wholeheartedly embrace the use of nuclear weapons. Given the enormous damage from a U.S. assured destruction attack, substantial ambiguities about U.S. resolve are probably tolerable. But suppose every American were convinced that the only safe and sane function of nuclear weapons is deterrence. Suppose also that this national consensus is apparent to all (opinion polls reflect it, politicians and presidential candidates of all political parties regularly support it in public speeches on national defense) and that "deterrence only" is embodied in official statements of U.S. nuclear doctrine. Under these assumptions, even cautious Soviet leaders might be sorely tempted to attack the West if confronted with a pressing security threat, especially if the Warsaw Pact has significant conventional force advantages over NATO.[18] Even if NATO has conventional force parity with the Warsaw Pact, the Soviets might still be able to prevail using only a small number of low-yield nuclear weapons on key NATO military targets, such as staging areas for reinforcements, major air bases, or the like.[19] Such limited nuclear attacks could give the Soviets a comparatively cheap victory while greatly decreasing the risks of a fatal miscalculation. The Soviet leadership could never be 100 percent sure, of course, that with Soviet nuclear weapons exploding on NATO soil or with NATO's conventional defense collapsing, the U.S. president might not suddenly acquire a newfound appreciation for nuclear weapons and order their use (with or without NATO concurrence). But would the president's launch orders be carried out by those down the chain of command? After all, the president would be acting contrary to an overwhelming national preference. As for bluffing, this may be a feasible option for the president and his close advisors, although even here one cannot dismiss the possibility that Soviet agents would discover the administration's secret "no use" policy. But bluffing is not an option for an entire democratic society that seeks to conceal a "no use" stance from the Soviets.

"Deterrence only" advocates are faced with a pragmatic dilemma similar to that confronting moral subjectivists. Moral subjectivism is not bound to lead to moral dissolution of the individual. But given human psychology as it is, it could have this effect on many individuals, and widespread public adherence could lead to the collapse of the moral order. Moral subjectivists who enjoy the material and psychological benefits of a well-behaved society – and most do – must hope that their own metaethical creed does not become too popular. Similarly, widespread public commitment to a "no use" nuclear policy (which is just another name for "deterrence only") could undermine the very thing McNamara and other critics of U.S. nuclear policy are keen on strengthening. "Deterrence only" advocates cannot press their case too vigorously. At the same time, it would be particularly disingenuous for critics of nuclear-use policies to rely on the resolve of those favoring nuclear retaliation to endow U.S. nuclear threats with sufficient credibility to ensure that deterrence does not fail.

Unfortunately, both critics and defenders of U.S. nuclear strategy have not squarely confronted the risks and challenges of a "no use" policy. In their effort to stop damage-limiting force deployments from going too far, for example, advocates of finite deterrence rely heavily on the argument that it is pointless to try to fight a limited nuclear war because *"any* use of nuclear weapons carries with it an *unacceptable* risk of escalation to all out nuclear war."[20] The policy

Robert E. Foelber

implication of this argument seems to be that the United States should make no nuclear response at all to a limited Soviet nuclear attack. But a "no use" policy threatens finite deterrence just as much as it threatens deterrence through damage limitation.

The architects and defenders of U.S. nuclear doctrine, on the other hand, have failed to adequately answer the "no use" challenge. It is all well and good to insist, as countervailing strategists frequently do, that a damage-limiting strategy is morally superior to an assured destruction strategy. A good argument can probably be made that if the United States ever uses nuclear weapons it should (morally) aim these weapons at Soviet military targets and not at the Soviet population. But the central issue in the nuclear debate is not whether to attack civilians or military targets if deterrence should fail. Very few finite deterrence theorists would actually propose attacking Soviet cities in retaliation for a Soviet nuclear attack on the United States, which almost certainly would be counterforce in nature. While some would not be opposed to some sort of limited counterforce retaliation, many apparently would favor no nuclear response at all in the belief that any U.S. nuclear retaliation would just make things worse for everyone.

The reluctance of U.S. government officials to publicly articulate a strategic rationale for nuclear retaliation is understandable. It is not easy to describe a sensible, moral nuclear strategy that would be convincing to the American people when the outcome of a nuclear war could well be national annihilation or worse. On the other hand, many critics of America's nuclear warfighting strategy are also suspiciously silent about what the United States should do if the Soviet Union ever attacks with nuclear weapons. A no-use policy may be still less acceptable to American citizens. The growing public concern, however, about the implications of using nuclear weapons even in retaliation leaves both sides no choice but to address the question of nuclear weapons use more directly.

124

THE MORAL USE OF NUCLEAR WEAPONS

The distinction was made earlier between the moral and strategic dimensions of nuclear weapons use. Some would draw a sharp line between the two, arguing that strategy has to do with protecting national interests, the most fundamental of which is the independence and survival of the state, whereas morality deals with rules of behavior that take into account the interests of all people and nations. It is in this sense of "morality" that so-called "realists" claim that morality does not apply to international relations – that no binding moral obligations exist to respect the interests of foreign individuals or nations in determining state policy. National interest, it is argued, should be the sole standard for assessing national security policy, including the decision to use nuclear weapons. Some moral philosophers today, however, distinguish another sense of "morality," which encompasses the basic values, whatever they might be, guiding the conduct of an individual or society.[21] In this sense, the concept inescapably applies to all actions of state, and military strategy – including nuclear strategy – is merely a tool of morality that aims at preserving and protecting national values, one of which could be respect for all human life regardless of nationality. If "morality" is understood in this broad sense, the debate over the use of nuclear weapons is at bottom a moral issue.

But if morality is the issue, can it ever be morally right to fight a nuclear war, and under what circumstances, and for what purpose?

The most widely discussed and restrictive moral critique of U.S. nuclear weapons policy proceeds from Just War principles. As formulated by the U.S. Catholic bishops and secular Just War moral philosophers such as Anthony Kenny, the basic argument has three premises:[22]

1. It is absolutely wrong to intentionally kill innocent human beings; hence, "under no circumstances may nuclear weapons or other instruments of mass destruction be used

125

for the purpose of destroying population centers." Classic assured destruction attacks designed to kill Soviet civilians are absolutely forbidden, even in retaliation for Soviet destruction of U.S. cities – a position fully endorsed by many damage-limiting theorists and reflected in U.S. nuclear doctrine, which does not target civilians per se.

2. Even if civilian deaths are not intended, nuclear attacks against military, political, or economic targets that would bring about the deaths of "many" innocent human beings as unintended "collateral damage" would still be immoral, because such attacks would be "indiscriminate" in destruction of innocent human life, and in general would cause "disproportionate" harm compared to the good achieved.

3. Although it may be possible theoretically to execute highly limited strategic or tactical nuclear attacks against enemy military targets that cause few civilian casualties and are, in themselves, morally permissible under Just War principles, there is an "overwhelming probability" that such attacks would escalate to a large-scale nuclear war that would cause "disproportionate" loss of innocent life. Hence it is highly doubtful that *any* use of nuclear weapons would be morally acceptable.

At a general level, Just War reasoning is straightforward and commonsensical. It says simply that the good consequences of using nuclear weapons must outweigh the bad consequences. The conclusion of the U.S. bishops, however, rests on particular factual and value premises that have been questioned by many, including other Just War theorists such as William O'Brien, who believes that the bishops have not given sufficient weight in their moral calculations to the values that are to be defended with nuclear weapons, that they have underestimated the Soviet threat to these values, and that they fail to appreciate what can be done to limit damage from nuclear weapons and thus to broaden the range of a just nuclear defense.[23] Despite their differences, however, all Just War theorists hold that innocent human life is so valuable that, even if a no-use policy led to the destruction of free society worldwide, nuclear retaliatory attacks that would kill tens of millions of the other side's innocent civilians would be immoral.

If the orthodox theory of deterrence is right, a steadfast U.S. national commitment to Just War morality could well be fatal for deterrence, despite the bishops' "centimeter of ambiguity" about some limited uses of nuclear weapons. For even if Just War doctrine sanctions more extensive use of nuclear weapons at the lower end of the spectrum than that endorsed by the U.S. bishops, it rules out everything else. As such, in extreme circumstances the Soviets could be dangerously tempted to launch a large-scale nuclear attack on a United States that, if it genuinely *embraced* Just War principles, would be restrained by its morality from retaliating with a counterforce attack large enough to prevent a Soviet military victory. (It is assumed that the United States acts consistently with its moral views and takes appropriate action known to Soviet intelligence services to ensure that nuclear weapons are not used immorally.) With future improvements in guidance technology (allowing for the use of lower-yield nuclear weapons and perhaps even conventional warheads for strategic missions) as well as the development of "third-generation" nuclear weapons with tailored effects, the United States might be able to substantially reduce collateral damage to innocent civilians from attacks on Soviet military targets.[24] But the Soviet Union in turn might be able to offset these technological developments and keep America strategically hamstrung either through active and passive countermeasures to thwart U.S. weapons improvements[25] or as a last resort by deploying its military forces closer to urban areas to ensure levels of innocent casualties that would be unacceptable to Just War morality. Soviet strategic doctrine has long emphasized protecting the Soviet population from nuclear attack – not exposing it to greater danger. But if the United States genuinely adopted Just War constraints on its strategy, the Soviet leadership could find it advantageous to redeploy its military forces so that a U.S. retaliatory counterforce attack would cause immorally high Soviet civilian casualties.

Although classic Just War doctrine is taken for granted by many Western moral philosophers and religious moralists, there are other moral attitudes about nuclear weapons use that have some appeal in the West and may have as legitimate a claim as Just War doctrine to moral commitment. One of these, which I will call Nuclear Protectionism, says that, if the Soviet Union ever used its nuclear weapons to destroy the United States as a functioning society, the United States would be entirely justified in destroying the Soviet state in turn to protect free societies elsewhere in the world from the threat of Soviet Communism.[26] The basic assumptions of Nuclear Protectionism are, first, that with the United States a "smoking, radiating ruin," Soviet military dominance would seriously jeopardize the survival of other free societies; and, second, that the survival of free society is more important than the lives of tens of millions of Soviet citizens (many unfortunately innocent children) who could be killed by a U.S. retaliatory nuclear attack.

Nuclear Protectionism, it should be emphasized, is not a policy of revenge or moral retribution. It is motivated by a noble and moral purpose: the protection of free society. It is in fact a damage-limiting policy – not with regard to the United States, of course, which is assumed to have been destroyed by a massive Soviet nuclear attack – but in terms of limiting damage to surviving free societies. For Nuclear Protectionists, the purpose of nuclear retaliation is not wanton destruction of the Russian people and its culture, but destruction of the Soviet regime so that it will not be a threat to free society in a post–World War III world. The targets of a U.S. retaliatory nuclear attack, therefore, would be confined to Soviet security forces, the Communist Party leadership, and Soviet armed forces, not the Soviet civilian economy or general population. Indeed, for Nuclear Protectionists everything possible should be done to limit the death and destruction of nonhostile elements of Soviet society. Admittedly, given the characteristics of today's nuclear weapons, a large-scale U.S. counter–military/political retaliatory attack could kill as many Soviet civilians as an assured destruction attack.[27] But (again) with improvements in missile accuracy, deployment of tailored-effects nuclear weapons, and the like, it may be possible to destroy the Soviet state while limiting Soviet civilian casualties to a level below that of assured destruction. In any case, nuclear retaliation would be justified for a Nuclear Protectionist even if Soviet casualties reached or exceeded assured destruction levels.

By sanctioning the destruction of the Soviet regime in retaliation for destruction of the United States, Nuclear Protectionism provides the moral underpinning for deterring nuclear attacks at the high end of the spectrum. But a morality that justifies retaliation only in response to a large-scale nuclear attack could be as fatal for deterrence as Just War doctrine, if not more so. If deterrence is to work, the United States must be resolved to use nuclear weapons in response to at least some kinds of *limited* Soviet nuclear attacks as well.

The decision to respond in kind to a limited Soviet nuclear attack could be more anguishing for U.S. leaders than the decision to retaliate for a massive Soviet attack that had already rendered America a nuclear wasteland. Because of the possibility of escalation leading to national annihilation, the United States has a lot to lose in fighting a limited nuclear war. But not retaliating for limited Soviet nuclear attacks also risks a great disaster – the "Sovietization" of the United States and much of the free world. What it would mean for the United States to be Sovietized has been vividly portrayed in a recent book by the noted historian Robert Conquest, who uses the historical record of Soviet occupation and oppression as a model.[28] The picture is a grim one, but then so, of course, is the aftermath of a nuclear war.

Nevertheless, some Americans value freedom (political, economic, social, religious, and intellectual) so highly that not only would they prefer personally to be dead rather than red, but they believe that the threat to free society posed by a Soviet military victory over the West is so severe that the United States would be morally justified in using whatever force is necessary to prevent such an occurrence – even at the cost of the nuclear destruction of the United States. According to this expanded version of Nuclear Protectionism, NATO should deploy whatever conventional forces are needed to have high confidence in defeating a Warsaw Pact conventional force invasion of Europe (or a Soviet attack on other vital interests) under a prudent range of scenarios. If NATO were to lose the land battle on the Central Front, Nuclear Protectionists would not immediately resort to nuclear weapons, as envisioned in some NATO war scenarios,[29] but would instead continue fighting a conventional war for as many years as it might take for the West to fully mobilize its vast military potential and to regain lost territory. Although a long-war strategy runs the risk that over the years U.S. and European populations would lose hope at the prospect of a prolonged armed struggle whose destructiveness could far exceed that of World War II or even some limited nuclear wars, use of nuclear weapons before all conventional defense has failed would put the survival of free society unnecessarily at risk. Nevertheless, if NATO's conventional forces suffer an irreversible defeat or the Soviets initiate limited nuclear warfare, Nuclear Protectionism holds that the United States should retaliate with limited nuclear attacks against Soviet military targets with the aim of convincing Soviet leaders that they will not be allowed to achieve their military objectives. But if it takes a massive counter–military/political attack to stop the Soviets, or if a limited nuclear war escalates out of control to a massive exchange – so be it. At least the Soviets have not won. For Nuclear Protectionists, the preservation of free society in the world is more important than the survival of the United States.

A nation whose morality sanctions the full range of nuclear responses to prevent the victory of its enemy would have solved the problem of deterrence. Soviet leaders would have to be mad to start a war (nuclear or conventional) with such a country. A potentially fatal defect of this heroic strategy, however, is that the United States is not the only free country that could perish in a nuclear conflict. America's European NATO allies, Japan, and other democratic nations could also become nuclear battle zones. Indeed, some analysts believe that a nuclear war is more likely to begin with tactical nuclear attacks in Central Europe than with an outright U.S.–Soviet strategic exchange. Moreover, if the "nuclear winter" hypothesis is true, the survival of neutral societies (free and potentially free) could also be threatened.

The prospect of nuclear winter, in fact, may be the most serious challenge to Nuclear Protectionism. In the past, scientific study of the worldwide indirect effects of nuclear war focused on global fallout and the possible depletion of the atmosphere's ozone. Scientists are now more concerned with the possibility that a nuclear war would produce large amounts of smoke and dust that would cause a prolonged period of subfreezing temperatures that would destroy agriculture and have other disastrous biological effects. According to early estimates, an attack of as few as 100 megatons on cities would be enough to cause a devasting nuclear winter in the Northern Hemisphere, and a counterforce exchange of several thousand megatons (what strategists call a "limited" nuclear war) would produce a global nuclear winter that could threaten the human species with extinction.[30] This outcome is now considered unlikely, although a 1985 study by the Scientific Committee on Problems of the Environment (SCOPE), part of the International Council of Scientific Unions, estimates that a large-scale countervalue/counterforce exchange of 5,000–6,000 megatons (about half the total combined megatonnage of the U.S. and Soviet nuclear arsenals) could cause a nuclear winter that would kill one to four billion people worldwide, mainly through starvation, in addition to the tens of millions who would die from direct effects of blast, heat, and prompt radiation.[31]

Analysts are just beginning to explore the implications of nuclear winter for U.S. nuclear strategy and deterrence. Some contend that the nuclear winter hypothesis should have no effect on deterrence because the direct effects of nuclear war on the superpowers are by themselves sufficiently destructive to deter nuclear conflict.[32] If the argument of this paper is correct, however, the nuclear winter hypothesis could profoundly impair deterrence, for the prospect that *all* free societies – not just the United States – might be at risk in a nuclear war could undermine any justification for U.S. use of nuclear weapons and, in consequence, could (for Jonathan Schell, "should") lead the West to adopt a "no use" policy. It has been argued that the Soviet Union would be self-deterred as well from using nuclear weapons because of the possibility that it would be destroyed in a nuclear winter of its own making. But if the United States is genuinely unresolved to use nuclear weapons, the Soviets may conclude that they can achieve military victory using only a small number of nuclear weapons well below the nuclear winter threshold.

While nuclear winter stretches Nuclear Protectionist logic close to the breaking point, it may nonetheless be too early to abandon a nuclear-use policy. The original nuclear winter hypothesis is by no means accepted as fact by the entire scientific community. Some scientists have concluded from independent investigations that even a large-scale nuclear war would cause only small temperature drops with no catastrophic consequences for noncombatant nations.[33] As models have been refined and subjected to closer scrutiny, estimates of destruction have steadily declined from the original apocalyptic assessments, although damage levels are still enormous. Some analysts are also skeptical about the realism of base-case nuclear winter scenarios that tend to assume either countercity attacks only or massive counterforce exchanges with little reduction in each side's nuclear arsenal. Moreover, there are a number of measures that can be taken to reduce the potential for a nuclear winter, including deployment of more accurate low-yield weapons, earth-penetrating warheads, and more discriminate targeting. A final verdict on Nuclear Protectionism must await the outcome of further research on the global climatic effects of nuclear war.

In the meantime, U.S. strategic planners must confront the devastating direct effects of a nuclear war on armed combatants. The loss of the United States in a nuclear war would be a crippling blow to the preservation of freedom in an unfriendly world, but (for a Nuclear Protectionist) it would be an acceptable loss if in consequence free society elsewhere were saved from Soviet domination. On the other hand, nuclear destruction of both the United States and Western Europe (which together account for three-fourths of the "free world's" population and about one-half of the world's total GNP) could leave remaining free societies so psychologically demoralized and economically deprived that they would not survive as free, despite the absence of a Soviet Communist threat. Nuclear Protectionists, consequently, favor whatever policies would be effective in limiting the damage that nuclear war would inflict on free society, provided that these policies do not at the same time undermine deterrence. For example, a Nuclear Protectionist is by no means opposed to a European "nuclear-free zone," unilateral nuclear disarmament by Britain, or for that matter decisions by free non-NATO states (such as New Zealand) to stay neutral in a U.S.–Soviet or NATO–Warsaw Pact conflict, if these or similar policies would genuinely spare European and other free countries from destruction in a nuclear war.

American Nuclear Protectionists also are not averse to the United States' bearing the full burden for NATO of the risk of nuclear destruction, if taking this risk is essential for a moral nuclear strategy. At the same time, however, they would demand, as a fair quid pro quo and to ensure domestic political support for America's singular nuclear vulnerability, that NATO Europe bear more of the burden of conventional defense of Europe and other regions of mutual interest, and in particular the burden of closing the conventional force gap with the Warsaw Pact, if such a gap exists. Without a NATO conventional force buildup (if needed) and other actions to demonstrate West European resolve to resist Soviet military and political aggression, European denuclearization and the like could reinforce West European neutralist and appeasement sentiments, leading Soviet leaders to militarily test NATO political cohesion and resolve.

One major drawback, though, with all these schemes to spare Western Europe and other free societies nuclear war damage is that they require Soviet cooperation in targeting, and it is uncertain whether the Soviets would cooperate. For one thing, it is Soviet military doctrine to use whatever weapons are necessary, including nuclear weapons, to achieve war objectives. And Helmut Schmidt's recent warning that "it is unrealistic to believe that West German soldiers would fight after the explosion of *the first couple* of nuclear weapons on West German soil" reminds us that some European allies may be especially vulnerable to nuclear blackmail.[34] The danger is that, if war breaks out, the Soviets might find it in their interests to use nuclear weapons against West European targets either to coerce our European allies into surrender or to achieve specific military objectives. Moreover, if the Soviets credibly threatened to deliberately expand a nuclear war worldwide to all free societies, to deter the United States from nuclear retaliation, a nuclear-use policy would lose all justification.

There are several reasons, however, why the Soviets might *not* use their nuclear weapons in the ways just mentioned. First, although Soviet military doctrine appears to countenance limited nuclear attacks to achieve war objectives, it is also Soviet doctrine to seize enemy territory relatively intact, not to destroy it, and to avoid or limit nuclear damage to the Soviet homeland and armed forces.[35] Assuming (reasonably) that the Soviet leaders do not want to "lose it all" in a nuclear war, clear resolve by the United States to ensure that the Soviet state does not survive to enjoy the fruits of military victory or nuclear coercion should have a powerful deterrent effect on Soviet leaders contemplating the use of nuclear weapons against Western Europe. Moreover, there is nothing in Soviet military writings available to the West for public scrutiny that would suggest a war strategy based on threatening *neutral* states with nuclear destruction in order to deter U.S. nuclear attacks. For the Soviets, military victory and war survival are accomplished through destruction of the enemy's military capability – not destruction of third-party societies, which are viewed as potential converts (voluntary or otherwise) to Soviet Communism.

But is it realistic to suppose that American citizens would

risk not just their own lives but their families and their nation in using nuclear weapons to save Western Europe and other free societies from Soviet domination, especially if the United States' allies are not willing to risk nuclear destruction themselves? According to one 1984 poll, 74 percent of Americans queried believe "the U.S. should *not* use nuclear weapons if the Russians invade Western Europe."[36] Nuclear Protectionists, however, would reply that further public debate might convince more Americans that deterrence cannot be had on the moral cheap. If the United States is determined to deter a Soviet attack on Europe, it must have a moral nuclear strategy that it is willing to implement. Without effective population defenses, such a strategy could require that the United States accept an unequal risk of nuclear destruction to ensure the survival of free society. In the extreme, this could mean that the United States must be willing to sacrifice itself for values higher than its own national survival. Thus, Nuclear Protectionism views both Just War morality and national "self-centered" realism as unworkable foundations for U.S. security policy.

But even if nuclear war directly threatens our European allies and indirectly all free society as well, or if, perchance, the survival of free society would be best served if the United States were not destroyed in a nuclear war, at least some limited uses of nuclear weapons might still be morally justified. Two key factors in such an assessment are, first, the probability that limited U.S. nuclear retaliation would lead to fatal nuclear damage to the United States and NATO Europe and, subsequently, to the economic and social collapse of all free society; and, second, the odds that withholding nuclear weapons would lead to the Sovietization or other tyrannization of NATO and, subsequently, of the rest of the free world. If the "disvalue" of the first set of outcomes is far greater than the disvalue of the second set of outcomes, then the risks of nuclear escalation will have to be quite low and the likelihood of tyrannization quite high to justify limited nuclear weapons use. If the disvalues are more equal, higher risks of escalation are tolerable. The odds of escalation for any given use of nuclear weapons are highly uncertain, but in some cases, such as retaliation in kind for limited Soviet attacks against NATO reinforcement choke points, they may be morally acceptable if one ascribes very high value to free society and believes that the consequences for free society of a no-use policy would be extremely odious. This, anyway, is the kind of reasoning that apparently has led some Just War philosophers, such as William O'Brien, to defend limited use of nuclear weapons as morally justified in certain circumstances.

A modified version of Nuclear Protectionism that sanctions some limited nuclear attacks as well as retaliation in kind for massive Soviet nuclear aggression provides a moral foundation for deterrence of Soviet nuclear attacks at both ends of the spectrum. It leaves a considerable range of attacks in the middle for which a proportional U.S. response would be morally forbidden because of the high risk of escalation to all-out nuclear war. But Soviet strategists face serious obstacles in planning a nuclear attack against the United States if it subscribes to a "high–low" nuclear strategy: If the attack is too small, U.S. command authorities may feel they can retaliate without undue risk of escalation; if the Soviet attack is too large, U.S. leaders may interpret it as a mortal blow (intentional or not) to the United States that justifies a state-busting response. While it does not support as strong a deterrent as heroic Protectionism, a "high–low" strategy nonetheless may sanction a wide enough range of nuclear attacks to provide a solid deterrent against Soviet nuclear aggression. Moreover, improvements in damage-limitation capabilities through more survivable and effective command and control, more discriminating nuclear weapons, and more extensive strategic defense (if truly effective) could lead to a widening of the range of morally acceptable nuclear retaliation.

Nuclear Protectionism makes a number of controversial *factual* assumptions about the consequences of both the use and the non-use of nuclear weapons. Uncertainties abound regarding these issues, but, as with a nuclear use policy, Nuclear Protectionist assumptions about the threat of Soviet nuclear dominance to free society cannot be dismissed out of hand. Western society serves as an example to the entire world of a successful alternative to the political oppression and economic failings of Soviet-style regimes and, as such, is a perpetual threat to the survival of Soviet Communism. Tyranny cannot coexist with freedom in a true state of peace, as the Soviets acknowledged for years in their official definition of "peaceful coexistence."[37] Given the bloody history of the Soviet regime's brutality toward its enemies domestic and foreign, exemplified most recently in the deliberate Soviet campaign of terror against the civilian population of Afghanistan,[38] it may not be farfetched to suppose that if the West adopts a hard-and-fast "no use" nuclear policy the Soviet Union might eventually seek to eliminate by force – using whatever weapons are necessary, including nuclear, chemical, and biological – what its Leninist political ideology has long viewed as a mortal threat. Efforts by the Soviet Union to Sovietize a denuclearized free world would at first face massive opposition, backed in some nations by formidable conventional forces, but the Soviets would not need a successful military invasion and occupation to accomplish their goal. The use of nuclear weapons against Western populations, if it went unanswered in kind, could be sufficient to convince Western leaders that they had no choice but to submit to the imposition of pro-Soviet puppet regimes in their own countries.

Skeptics might demur that, even if the Soviet Union had the capability to Sovietize a denuclearized West, it has "softened" considerably, especially in the last few years under Mikhail Gorbachev's rule. Gorbachev's program of economic "restructuring" (perestroika) and "openness" (glasnost) reflect a fundamental change in attitudes that could lead to significant liberalization of Soviet society. Accompanying this historic process of internal reform are a number of initiatives in the area of national security – including announcements of unilateral arms reductions, reductions in military spending, the adoption of a defensive military strategy, and a rethinking of the guiding Soviet principle that socialism and capitalist "imperialism" are irreconcilable enemies – that portend a dramatic lessening of hostility toward the West and perhaps even an end to the Cold War. In light of these startling developments, Nuclear Protectionist assumptions may be overdrawn and out of date.

Nuclear Protectionists ardently hope this is the case. But at this writing the direction and outcome of Gorbachev's reform effort are much in doubt. The Soviet military, which acquired immense power and influence during the Brezhnev regime, apparently agreed several years ago to a partial shift in resources away from defense and toward economic modernization (although Soviet defense spending has continued to grow) in the belief that a strong, technologically sophisticated economy is essential to meet Soviet military requirements in the future. But Soviet generals reportedly are not happy with Gorbachev's recently proposed unilateral conventional force cuts and in a few years may press hard for new increases in defense spending as the Soviet military prepares for a new phase of weapons modernization.[39] One way Gorbachev could reduce the huge burden of defense on the Soviet economy (about 17 percent of GNP, versus 6 percent for the United States) is by reducing Western military capabilty through arms control agreements, but Gorbachev's arms control initiatives, in addition to buying time for reform, could also constitute another "peace offensive" aimed at the demise of NATO and the achievement of Soviet dominance over Western Europe. If the West does not keep a clear head, it could negotiate itself into a worse military situation than it currently faces. (For example, symmetrical conventional force reductions could worsen NATO's defense posture by lowering force densities, which would make it easier for the Soviets to maneuver and mass its forces for encirclement attacks.) The Soviet military threat to Western Europe would be substantially reduced if the Soviets adopt not only a defensive strategy (in fact Soviet military strategy by definition has always been "defensive," since Soviet ideology decrees that the Soviet Union will never be the aggressor in a war) but also a defensive operational art and force structure. But so far Soviet "defensive" thinking remains a mere slogan backed by offensive weapons procurement, operational planning, training, and deployments.

Politically, the Soviet government has loosened somewhat its iron grip on the population (for example, by allowing freer public discussion of national problems), but free speech and other human rights are still severely limited by Western standards, and it is unclear whether recent constitutional reforms have indeed made the Soviet Union a more democratic nation or have merely centralized power in new hands that are still not responsible to the Soviet people. Finally, on the economic front there has been only marginal improvement, and in some cases (for example, agriculture and the availability of consumer goods) things may be getting worse. The question is whether Gorbachev's economic program will succeed in revitalizing the Soviet economy without greater economic and political liberalization that could undermine the dominant role of the Communist Party and its ideology in Soviet society and unleash uncontrollable popular demands for more freedom. The failure of economic reforms or a glasnost-inspired popular revolt that threatens the Soviet empire, domestic stability, or Communist Party dominance could lead to Gorbachev's removal and a return to more traditionally ideological foreign and domestic policies. Even if economic reform can be accomplished without radical political reform, it is possible that economic modernization could lay the foundation for a period of more confident pursuit of traditional Soviet security objectives.

These musings may be too pessimistic. The Soviet Union in fact may be in the process of abandoning its seventy-year Leninist–Stalinist–Brezhnevian heritage of political oppression, militarism, and hostility toward the West. If so, then Nuclear Protectionism and all the other tortuous schemes concocted by strategists to solve the puzzle of nuclear deterrence can be filed away and forgotten until a new unfriendly nuclear power emerges with the capability to destroy the United States. So far, however, events do not warrant testing Soviet intentions by adopting a "no use" nuclear policy.

The dispute between Just War theorists and Nuclear Protectionists, however, is not just about certain "facts," such as the Soviet regime's willingness to use nuclear weapons against denuclearized populations. It is also a classic example of a moral controversy based on a disagreement over fundamental *values*. Both disputants hold the same core Western values, including innocent human life and basic individual freedoms, in very high esteem. Indeed, it is the strong commitment to these values that distinguishes both positions from Soviet morality and places them in the same broad moral tradition. Nevertheless, Just War theorists and Nuclear Protectionists disagree strongly on how precisely to rank Western values relative to each other. For the former, innocent human life is so valuable that it is impermissible to sacrifice "many" wholly innocent lives even to save Western society from a dark age of totalitarianism. For the latter, the basic freedoms of Western society are so precious that it may be morally permissible for the United States to slaughter millions of innocent Soviets or to run a considerable risk of national annihilation to preserve the political and social order needed to ensure respect for individual rights and liberties.

Who is right, if either? It would not be dogmatic to assert that no moral philosopher so far has been able to establish "by reason alone" or any other putative philosophical method that any one particular ranking of values or set of moral principles is objectively correct. Indeed, most modern moral philosophers long ago abandoned the ambition (if they ever had it) of demonstrating the objective truth of a particular morality. Proponents of many of today's mainstream philosophical moral theories, such as utilitarianism, neo-Kantian deontologicalism, and contractarianism, typically do not claim that the basic principles singled out by these theories are demonstrably true but, rather, that they either are part and parcel of the "logic of ordinary moral discourse" or represent a reflective balance between everyday moral intuitions and theoretical moral principles that appear sensible and reasonable after careful thought. For some moral philosophers, the prin-

ciples of traditional Western morality nonetheless corre-
spond to some objective moral order of the universe. Others
would not deny that morality can be objective in the sense
that particular moral judgments are derivable from the core
principles of a given "moral image," or that there are some
things valued by all (or most) human beings, or that the principles of Western morality define a social order in which many
human beings would be happy – or at least more happy than
in any other kind of society. What is denied, though, is that
morality is objective in the stronger sense that basic moral
rules are categorically imperative or authoritative for all rational agents, or that values exist "out there" in the world
apart from human acts of valuing, or that some human interests are intrinsically higher or more noble than others according to some nonsubjective standard.

The absence of demonstrated fundamental principles in
moral reasoning, however, does not mean that anything goes
in the moral debate over nuclear weapons use. I take it as a
given that, at the minimum, our moral judgments about nuclear weapons should be consistent with the basic set of values and principles that are at the heart of the Western moral
tradition. Within this tradition, though, flow subcurrents that
give different priorities to the core values and principles. It
is not self-evident which of these subcurrents, if any, represents objective moral reality, assuming there is such a thing.
As a result, disputes sometimes erupt within the Western
political community between men and women of good moral
character not only about the facts in a moral controversy but
about how to order commonly accepted values and principles.

Given the philosophical obstacles to resolving moral disputes, there are at least two approaches one can take in dealing with the issue of the morality of nuclear strategy. One
approach is to stick doggedly with one of the established moral
theories constructed by philosophers to "rationalize" or "make
sense of" everyday moral intuitions, and to accept the verdict of the theory, whatever it might be, on the morality of

nuclear weapons use. A more pragmatic alternative approach assumes that trade-offs in moral values and principles are inevitable in response to constantly changing threats, and that the emergence of novel, unforeseen challenges may impel citizens of Western societies to adjust the way they rank their values and principles to ensure that the moral order survives. Nuclear weapons are putting just such a strain on our moral beliefs. Before the emergence of a nuclear-armed communist state capable of threatening the existence of Western civilization, the slaughter of millions of innocent human beings to preserve Western values may have appeared wholly unjustifiable under any possible circumstances. Today, however, it may be that Western democracies, if they are to survive as guardians of individual freedom, can no longer afford to provide innocent life the full protection demanded by Just War morality.

It might be objected that the freedoms of Western society have value only on the assumption that human beings are treated with the full dignity and respect assumed by Just War theory. Innocent human life is not just another value to be balanced side by side with others in moral calculations. It is the raison d'être of Western political, economic, and social institutions. A free society based on individual rights that sanctioned mass slaughter of innocent human beings to save itself from extinction would be "morally corrupt," no better than Soviet society, and not worth defending.[40] The only morally right and respectable policy for such a society would be to accept destruction at the hands of tyranny, if need be.

This objection is partly right in that a society based on individual rights that *casually* sacrifices innocent human lives for the sake of common social goods is a contradiction in terms. On the other hand, even Just War doctrine allows for the unintentional sacrifice of some innocent human life under certain hard-pressing circumstances. It is essentially a consequentialist moral doctrine that ascribes extremely high – but not absolute – value to innocent human life. The problem for any nonabsolute moral theory, of course, is where to draw the line.

142

It is not obvious that Nuclear Protectionism is wrong to draw the line where it does. Charges of "moral corruption" beg the question. Certainly no convincing case has yet been made on consequentialist grounds that the adoption of a moral standpoint sanctioning the use of nuclear weapons, including massive nuclear retaliation, weakens commitment to Western values and institutions. The stakes in a nuclear war with the Soviet Union would be astronomically high. Thus, nuclear retaliation against the Soviet Union must be viewed as an extreme case of killing innocent human beings for a high moral purpose. Indeed, it is possible that, in all other practical cases where innocent human life is at stake, the moral judgments of Nuclear Protectionists would be identical with those of Just War moralists and perhaps condemnatory as well of some past U.S. military actions. For example, a Nuclear Protectionist might conclude that Allied conventional bombing of German and Japanese cities in World War II as well as the atomic attacks on Hiroshima and Nagasaki were immoral because the fate of Western society did not hinge on the carnage wrought by such attacks.

Of course, nothing said above shows that Nuclear Protectionism is the correct moral view regarding nuclear weapons use. The fact that it enhances deterrence does not make it right. As Richard Wasserstrom has pointed out, the use of nuclear weapons cannot be morally justified on grounds that a strategy for use would have the morally beneficial consequence of bolstering deterrence, because if deterrence fails the moral question is opened up anew.[41] Nonetheless, Nuclear Protectionism can be seen as a reasonable extension of one legitimate subcurrent of Western morality. Moreover, if the orthodox theory of deterrence is correct, a nation of Nuclear Protectionists may have a better chance of surviving the nuclear age than one that subscribes to Just War theory or a secular variant. In light of philosophical uncertainties about moral values, this is a most relevant fact in making practical moral decisions about nuclear-use policy.

NUCLEAR PROTECTIONISM AND STABILITY

One of the main criticisms of damage-limiting countervailing force postures, however, is that they can be dangerously destabilizing if too effective or too threatening to the other side. Thus, even if it would be morally right to *implement* a damage-limiting strategy once war breaks out, *deploying* a countervailing type of force posture, it is argued, would dangerously weaken deterrence, and hence would be immoral. All strategists agree that a bilateral strategic environment in which both sides believe that they and the other side have a so-called "splendid" first-strike offensive capability – i.e., the capability to destroy enough of the enemy's strategic forces in a first strike to survive all-out retaliation from an enemy second strike – would be exceedingly unstable. But nothing remotely like this condition exists today, and it is unlikely to emerge in the future if each side maintains its historical determination to prevent the other from acquiring a first-strike capability.

Where the threshold of instability lies (below the level of mutual first-strike capability) depends on a number of factors, including among others the perceived targeting doctrine, force survivability, and counterforce capability of both sides, as well as the resolve of national leaders to use nuclear weapons. Based on these factors, America's countervailing force structure, even when fully modernized with the MX ICBM, the Trident II submarine missile, the B-1B and Stealth bombers, and other programmed offensive strategic systems, could be fairly stable in a crisis, in the sense that neither the United States nor the Soviet Union would have a strong incentive to launch a nuclear attack.

Constructing first-strike scenarios is enormously complicated because of the number and uncertainty of the assumptions involved. But under certain assumptions, after a U.S. "bolt-out-of-the-blue" surprise first strike in the year 2000 (when the current U.S. strategic offensive force modernization program will be complete) the Soviet Union would have about 4,700 surviving strategic nuclear warheads (out of a total of 15,700), and it would have about 7,700 surviving warheads if its forces were on alert. After a Soviet counterforce second strike, both sides could have just about the same number of warheads for assured destruction and a wide range of counterforce missions, assuming no deployment of ballistic missile defenses. (See Table 1 for details and assumptions.) If the Soviets were to strike first,they would have an advantage of between 1.5:1 and 2.0:1 in surviving warheads after a U.S. second strike, but the United States would still have about 4,200 strategic warheads after a Soviet surprise attack and about 7,600 warheads if its forces were on alert.

More refined analysis may show that in the above scenarios one side or the other could achieve an advantage in some category of military capability (e.g. enduring survivability of hard-target kill weapons) that could tempt some military planners to favor a "preemptive" first strike. But a Nuclear Protectionist would have no incentive to launch a nuclear first strike against the Soviet Union, crisis or no crisis. Because the United States lacks a disarming first-strike capability, all a U.S. first strike would accomplish is to precipitate a large-scale nuclear war that most likely would end with the destruction of the United States. Even if U.S. national command authorities knew *for sure* that the Soviets were about to launch a nuclear attack (information that is in practice unattainable), a U.S. first strike would probably not be able to meaningfully limit damage to the U.S. population and economy. On the other hand, the United States has sufficient survivable nuclear capability to ensure that the Soviets cannot escape unacceptable destruction if they strike first. Thus, the prudent and moral policy for a Nuclear Protectionist is to wait and see what the Soviets do first in a crisis. If the Soviets do not attack, the world has been spared a nuclear war. If the Soviets do attack, the United States has sufficient capability to ensure that they are not victorious.

The Soviets also would seem to gain nothing by launching a nuclear first strike in a crisis. Although they may have an advantage in surviving warheads if they attack first versus second in a strategic exchange, retaliation from a Nuclear

Table 1. *First-strike scenarios (year 2000)*

Item	Forces[a]		Surviving warheads							
			U.S. first-strike				Soviet first-strike			
			Surprise[b]		Alert[c]		Surprise[b]		Alert[c]	
	Launchers	Warheads	(1)[d]	(2)[e]	(1)[d]	(2)[e]	(1)[f]	(2)[g]	(1)[f]	(2)[g]
United States forces										
ICBMs										
Minuteman II	450	450	240	(240)	240	(240)	45	(45)	45	(45)
Minuteman III Mk12	200	600	30	(30)	30	(30)	60	(60)	60	(60)
Minuteman III Mk12A	300	900	45	(45)	45	(45)	90	(90)	90	(90)
MX silo-based	50	500	25	(25)	25	(25)	50	(50)	50	(50)
MX rail-garrison	50	500	50	(0)[h]	50	(0)	0	(0)	500	(500)
SICBM (Midgetman)	500	500	500	(500)	500	(500)	500	(500)	500	(500)
SLBMs										
Trident II (D-5)	480	3,840	3,625	(2,319)	3,625	(2,857)	2,534	(2,052)	3,072	(2,590)
Bombers										
B-52H	90	1,800	1,800	(540)	1,800	(1,440)	540	(540)	1,440	(1,440)
B-1B	90	1,440	1,440	(432)	1,440	(1,152)	432	(432)	1,152	(1,152)
B-2 (Stealth)	120	1,440	1,440	(432)	1,440	(1,152)	432	(432)	1,152	(1,152)
Total	2,330	11,970	9,195	(4,563)	9,195	(7,490)	4,683	(4,201)	8,061	(7,579)
Soviet forces										
ICBMs										
Silo-based	798	6,810	288	(288)	288	(288)	3,971	(3,971)	3,971	(3,971)
Mobile	600	1,950	1,950	(1,718)	1,950	(1,718)	1,950	(1,950)	1,950	(1,950)
SLBMs	928	4,908	2,454	(2,312)	3,926	(3,784)	4,908	(2,454)	4,908	(3,926)
Bombers	178	2,056	0[h]	(0)	1,645	(1,645)	2,056	(0)	2,056	(1,645)
Total	2,504	15,724	4,692	(4,318)	7,725	(7,435)	12,885	(8,375)	12,885	(11,492)
Soviet: U.S.	1.1:1	1.3:1	0.9:1		1:1		2:1		1.5:1	

Note: (1) = warheads after first strike; (2) = warheads surviving after second strike.

[a]Launcher and warhead data from U.S. Congressional Budget Office, *Modernizing U.S. Strategic Offensive Forces: Costs, Effects, and Alternatives*, November 1987; and Congressional Research Service, *Strategic Nuclear Forces: Potential U.S./Soviet Trends with and without SALT 1985–2000*, Report No. 86-135F.

[b]Day-to-day alert rates: for *United States*, 0.95 for silo-based, 0.9 for mobile ICBMs, 0.66 for SLBMs, and 0.3 for bombers. Although two-thirds of the Trident force will be at sea at any one time, only 50% will be on station with weapons available for attack. For *Soviets*: 0.95 for new ICBMs, 0.85 for mobile ICBMs, 0.5 for SLBMs, and 0.0 for bombers. Assumes 50% of Soviet SSBNs at sea. Source: U.S. Congress, House Committee on Appropriations, *Hearing on Department of Defense Appropriations for 1986, Part II*, pp. 926–27. Assumes no Soviet bombers on alert. Robert P. Berman and John C. Baker, *Soviet Strategic Forces: Requirements and Responses* (Washington: Brookings Institution, 1982), p. 36.

[c]Generated alert rates: 0.95 for ICBMs, 0.8 for SLBMs, and 0.8 for bombers. Alert rates for submarines and bombers could be higher with additional warning time.

[d]Assumes U.S. attacks 998 "hard" targets and 752 "soft" targets. Source: William W. Kaufmann, *The 1986 Defense Budget* (Washington: Brookings Institution, 1985), p. 10, adjusted for Soviet mobile missiles. Target assignments: 1 MX plus 1 Minuteman III Mk12A against 875 hardened targets, 50 MX against 25 hardened targets, and 190 Trident II Mk5 warheads against 95 hardened targets; 570 Minuteman III Mk12 and 210 Minuteman II against 752 soft targets, with two per bomber and submarine base. Assumes terminal (overall two-shot kill probability (TPK(2)) of 0.86 for MX/MMIIIMk12A, 0.98 for MX (silo), and 0.96 for Trident II against targets hardened to withstand 5,000 pounds per square inch (psi) overpressure. Assumes U.S. bombers are not used in first strike because of slow flight times (approximately six hours or more) to targets in the Soviet Union. See Union of Concerned Scientists, *In Search of Stability: An Assessment of New U.S. Nuclear Forces* (Washington, 1986). pp. 39–45, for arguments that the Stealth bomber might not be used in a surprise first strike and why, in general, the system "does not appear to pose a serious threat to stability."

[e]Assumes Soviets use 374 warheads to attack 116 hardened U.S. strategic targets, including launch control centers, nuclear weapon storage facilities, and national command headquarters with two warheads each with TPK(2) of 0.9. U.S. silos and small ICBMs not targeted, although Soviets attack seven rail-mobile MX bases with two warheads each. To even out the score after a U.S. first strike, the Soviet Union does not need to attack U.S. ICBMs. Eighty-three soft targets are attacked with one warhead each, except two for submarine, bomber, and mobile MX bases. Target data for Soviet weapons from William Daugherty, Barbara Levi, and Frank von Hippel, "The Consequences of 'Limited' Nuclear Attacks on the United States," *International Security* 10, no. 4 (Spring 1986). 30.

[f]Assumes a Soviet attack of 2,839 warheads against U.S. strategic forces. See Daugherty et al. Assumes TPK(2) of 0.9 for new Soviet heavy ICBM against hardened (2,000 psi) U.S. targets, including missile silos. Assumes Soviets attack seven MX rail-garrison bases but not small ICBM force in surprise scenario and no attacks against U.S. mobile missiles in alert scenario because of excessive warhead requirements. Source: U.S. Air Force.

[g]Assumes U.S. second strike of 482 warheads against Soviet missile launch control centers, ABM launcher sites, nuclear navy bases, bomber bases, national and strategic rocket forces HQs, and communication facilities. For target data, see Barbara G. Levi, Frank von Hippel, William H. Daugherty, and David Thickens, "Civilian Casualties from 'Limited' Nuclear Attacks on the USSR," *International Security* 12, no. 3 (Winter 1987–88), 174.

[h]Assumes that attacks against rail-mobile MX, non-alert bombers, and submarines in port are virtually 100% effective.

Protectionist America would be swift and sure. A Soviet military victory would be impossible and annihilation of the Soviet state a distinct possibility. On the other hand, the chances of a U.S. strategic first strike under a Nuclear Protectionist regime are virtually nil. To do any rational war planning at all, the Soviets cannot ignore U.S. disinclination to launch first strikes.[42] Here the adoption by a Nuclear Protectionist America of a no-first-strike strategy, supported by official military–civilian analysis demonstrating the disutility of preemptive uses of nuclear weapons, should be reassuring. For Soviet planners as well, then, a first-strike strategy would gain very little compared to a policy of restraint.

A more serious problem for stability than countermissile attacks may be that the mutual vulnerability of both sides' command and control systems could tempt U.S. or Soviet authorities in a crisis to launch a preemptive attack on the other side's command and control assets to avoid being "decapitated" by an enemy first strike. Offsetting (at least partly) the potential for destabilization in this case, however, are two factors. First, U.S. and Soviet planners may not be confident that they can execute a successful decapitation strike. Soviet command and control is highly centralized, but according to a 1985 CIA assessment,

> Although US attacks could destroy many known fixed command, control, and communications facilities, the Soviets' emphasis in this area has resulted in their having many key hardened facilities and redundant means of communications; thus, *it seems highly likely that the Soviets could maintain overall continuity of command and control,* although it would probably be degraded and they could experience difficulty in maintaining endurance.[43]

Cautious Soviet planners may have a less optimistic view of the survivability of their own command and control systems, but they also "probably credit the U.S. command system with greater resilience" than do many U.S. defense analysts.[44] Second, as with a countermissile attack, if a decapitation strike fails, it fails in a big way; the other side is likely to respond immediately with a massive second strike to frustrate any follow-on attacks. A second-strike strategy also entails enormous risks, of course; if the other side succeeds with decapitation, it wins the war. Nevertheless, given the uncertainty of successful decapitation, reducing command and control vulnerability would seem to be a more prudent course for both Nuclear Protectionists and Soviet planners than adopting a first-strike strategy.

From the point of view of the "logic of deterrence," therefore, it may be possible to have an acceptably stable strategic balance in which both sides have considerable counterforce and other damage-limiting capabilities.[45] What worries some critics of damage limitation and nuclear warfighting, however, is that logic and reason will not prevail in U.S.–Soviet war planning or crisis response. Against the backdrop of "worst-case" threat assessments, irrational fears, suspicions, perceptual biases, institutional interests, and other psychological factors, U.S. adoption of an offensive nuclear warfighting strategy, it is argued, could provoke the Soviet Union into launching a preemptive nuclear attack out of fear that U.S. planners, taking their nuclear warfighting doctrine too seriously, might perceive some narrow military advantage in striking first in a crisis.[46]

The study of the "psychology of deterrence" is in its fetushood. To date, the bulk of research consists either of analyses of historical cases of deterrence failure, which mercifully have not involved nuclear-armed combatants, or theoretical speculation based on limited and incomplete empirical data.[47] Regrettably, today's decision makers and their staffs are not immune to the mental weaknesses of their historical counterparts. It is a matter of considerable debate, however, to what extent worst-case threat assessments and other psychological factors are operative in U.S.–Soviet decision making and what their effect is or could be on deterrence. Moreover, it can be argued that the potential for national annihilation posed by nuclear weapons makes problematic a straightforward application of historical analyses of deterrence failure to U.S. deployment of nuclear damage-limiting capabilities. True, the "concept of disaster is subjective"; during crises that preceded the two world wars, some decision makers expressed the fear that war would mean "the end of civilization."[48] Still, the horrors of nuclear conflict give a new meaning to this phrase and seem to exert an enormous deterring effect on contemporary political and military leaders on both sides.[49] Certainly Nuclear Protectionists have no illusions about the possible consequences of nuclear war for the United States.

A detailed review of the psychological critique of damage-limiting nuclear strategies lies outside the scope of this paper. But I would like to briefly address two specific concerns some may have about the effect of Nuclear Protectionism on stability: (1) that because Nuclear Protectionists are willing to commit national suicide to deny the Soviets victory, they may be too eager to take risks of nuclear war; (2) that to sustain the resolve needed to support a nuclear-use policy, Nuclear Protectionists must perpetuate the decrepit myth of the Soviet Union as an "evil empire", thus dooming U.S.–Soviet relations to a dangerous level of Cold War tension that increases the risk of nuclear war.

To the first objection Nuclear Protectionists would reply that they are not moral crusaders dedicated to destroying communism with nuclear weapons. Because Nuclear Protectionists are first and foremost committed to the survival of free society, only the gravest threat to that survival – namely, Soviet use of nuclear weapons or imminent defeat in a conventional war – would justify U.S. use of nuclear weapons. The fact that Nuclear Protectionists are more willing than "deterrence only" theorists to use nuclear weapons if the West should ever find itself *in* a desperate war for survival does not mean that Nuclear Protectionists are more willing to get *into* a war. Indeed, their determined resolve to use nuclear weapons to prevent a Soviet military victory makes it highly unlikely that a U.S.–Soviet nuclear or conventional war will ever occur in the first place, at least by design. And to reduce the risks that nuclear war would occur by accident or inadvertently through misunderstandings, Nuclear Protectionists favor a variety of so-called confidence-building measures, including risk reduction centers, more extensive observation of military maneuvers, and agreed restrictions on the movement and deployment of military forces, although these measures could have a deleterious effect on Western security if readiness slackens or Soviet noncompliance is ignored by Western governments to avoid aggravating political tensions.

Second, although skeptical about the long-term objectives of Gorbachev's reform program or its prospects for success if benign, Nuclear Protectionists welcome any genuine change in the Soviet Union toward a free, democratic society. The resolve of Nuclear Protectionists to use nuclear weapons is purely conditional on Soviet armed aggression. If it is true, as most Western (and probably most Soviet) strategists believe, that NATO is politically incapable of firing the first shot in a NATO–Warsaw Pact conflict, and thus that the decision to go to war rests primarily in the hands of Soviet leaders, then a full-fledged Soviet attack on the West, especially supported by nuclear weapons, would suggest a hostile intent that would justify the strongest defense measures possible, including the use of nuclear weapons. Indeed, it is difficult to imagine the Soviet Union, or any country, embarking on a war that could result in the nuclear annihilation of itself and its victim unless it perceived its victim as a mortal enemy threatening its own survival and very way of life. Even if the Warsaw Pact invaded Western Europe in confusion with no politically expansionist objectives in mind at the outset, it is quite possible that Soviet leaders, if things were going their way, would come to view the war as an opportunity to eliminate once and for all the Soviet Union's major security threat from the capitalist West. After taking the ultimate gamble of nuclear annihilation, is it likely that a victorious Soviet Union would allow the West to remain free and thereby pose a persistent threat to the continued survival of Soviet Communism?

In sum, it is not obvious that Nuclear Protectionism supported by a damage-limiting countervailing force posture is either logically or psychologically destabilizing. More analysis and research are needed before this issue can be resolved with confidence. But suppose the weight of future evidence is that a countervailing strategy is destabilizing. One alternative might be to base deterrence on a "pure" assured destruction force (i.e., a force of inaccurate low-yield weapons with only sufficient megatonnage for inflicting massive damage on the enemy's population and economy). For some finite deterrence theorists, the fact that Just War morality absolutely forbids attacking Soviet cities should not stop us from adopting such a strategy, at least for deterrence purposes. George Quester, for example, argues that "if the prospect of torturing and killing the innocent works to keep the prospectively guilty from becoming the actually guilty, perhaps we ought . . . to adjust our morality, without obfuscation."[50]

There is something to be said for Quester's moral pragmatism when the survival of free society is at stake, but the chief defect with a genuine assured destruction strategy that deliberately aims at killing Soviet civilians is that it is hard to conceive any situation in which it would be rational to implement the strategy. It is the Soviet regime and not the Soviet people that is generally assumed to be a threat to the United States. If deterrence ever fails, a more sensible strategy would be to use one's assured destruction force to attack soft Soviet military targets, such as troop concentrations, air bases, logistic and transportation centers, and the like. Warfighting strategies are thus morally and strategically inescapable.

NUCLEAR PROTECTIONISM, U.S. STRATEGIC FORCES, AND ARMS CONTROL

I conclude with two brief observations about possible implications of Nuclear Protectionism for U.S. strategic force deployments and arms control.

(1) If it is not obvious that a countervailing strategy is destabilizing, it is also not obvious that deterrence requires all the warfighting capability of a countervailing strategy. A key

implication of the orthodox theory of deterrence often forgotten by countervailing strategists is that resolve can substitute for warfighting capability in deterring an aggressor. The French *force de frappe* is not a logical or political absurdity.[51] A Nuclear Protectionist might settle for less damage-limiting capability than he or she would prefer for military purposes if, for example, nuclear damage-limiting strategies were destabilizing or if there were other pressing demands on national resources, although savings from budget cuts are limited by the fact that total funding for U.S. nuclear forces constitutes at most 20 percent of the military budget and less than 1.5 percent of the U.S. Gross National Product.

Nonetheless, for Nuclear Protectionists there are two reasons for deploying countervailing-type damage-limiting capabilities, if they are not destabilizing. First, nuclear war could occur, despite the best efforts of the West to prevent it, and countervailing-type damage-limiting capabilities, if employed judiciously, could limit damage short of national annihilation. Second, despite the fact that a large proportion of Americans (41 percent according to one poll) apparently "would rather die in a nuclear war than see communism come to their country," public resolve to go "all the way" with the Soviets in a nuclear war is uncertain and could weaken in a crisis with the prospect of nuclear war looming more real.[52] What conclusions the Soviets might draw from our national debate over using nuclear weapons to defend vital national interests is uncertain. For a nation of Nuclear Protectionists, sophisticated warfighting capabilities would not be essential for deterrence. On the other hand, if national resolve to risk nuclear damage in a war is flaccid, the modest damage-limiting capabilities of a countervailing strategy are not going to save deterrence.[53] If national resolve to use nuclear weapons is more ambiguous, however, the damage-limiting capabilities of a countervailing strategy may contribute significantly to deterrence, because Soviet leaders may reason that with such capabilities U.S. leaders might believe they could retaliate without unduly risking national survival.

(2) According to Nuclear Protectionists, the only moral jus-

tification for using nuclear weapons would be to protect free society from a mortal threat. Thus, the sand in the logical gears of Nuclear Protectionism – and deterrence in general – is the possibility that a U.S.–Soviet nuclear war would directly or indirectly threaten the survival of *all* free society. Technology may prove useful in limiting nuclear damage inflicted both on innocent Soviet civilians and on free society, although it is unlikely to eliminate entirely the remote threat of nuclear annihilation hanging over the United States. Arms control, if approached realistically, could also help to limit nuclear war damage on the West. In particular, from the point of view of a moral nuclear strategy, an arms control agreement that would limit U.S.–Soviet strategic forces to a level of megatonnage sufficient only for mutual assured destruction is prima facie highly desirable.[54] On this issue at least, finite deterrence theorists and advocates of damage limitation should concur. Unless the United States is resolved to use nuclear weapons in defense of its interests, however, the Soviets will have little incentive to reduce forces to such a level.

NOTES

1. President Ronald Reagan, First Annual Report to Congress on the National Security Strategy of the United States (January 1987), pp. 21–22.
2. Concerns about the credibility of U.S. threats to use nuclear weapons also contributed to the development of NATO's Flexible Response strategy, adopted in 1967, with its options for graduated nuclear escalation if NATO faces conventional-force defeat.
3. The chief beneficiaries of damage limitation are supposed to be the United States and its allies, but limiting damage to the Soviet population is also a goal, both intrinsically as a moral imperative and as a means to limiting damage to the United States. Through the use of limited, controlled counterforce attacks, and more generally the capability to match Soviet attacks blow for blow, it is argued, a nuclear conflict can be successfully terminated short of attacks on the Soviet popu-

lation that would precipitate Soviet attacks on the U.S. population. The U.S. government no longer publicly emphasizes the importance of civil defense for deterrence because of vocal public opposition, but the rationale for civil defense, given the assumptions of a countervailing strategy, is still valid.

4. As the Reagan Administration saw it, the primary functions of the SDI program are, first, to "enhance deterrence by injecting great uncertainties into Soviet estimates of their ability to achieve their essential military objectives in a first strike" and, second, to "provide incentives for Soviet acceptance of significant arms reduction agreements." National Security Strategy of the United States, p. 22.

5. See, for example, John M. Collins, *The US–Soviet Military Balance: 1980–1985* (New York: Pergamon and Brassey's, 1986), pp. 56–57; and Robert W. Tucker, *The Nuclear Debate: Deterrence and the Lapse of Faith* (New York: Holmes and Meier, 1985), pp. 66–72.

6. Tucker, *The Nuclear Debate*.

7. McNamara, "The Military Role of Nuclear Weapons: Perceptions and Misperceptions," *Foreign Affairs* 62, no. 1 (Fall 1983), 59–80, at 79.

8. U.S. National Conference of Catholic Bishops, "The Challenge of Peace: God's Promise and Our Response," *Origins, N.C. Documentary Service,* May 19, 1983.

9. Brodie, "Development of Nuclear Strategy," *International Security* 2, no. 4 (Spring 1978), 73.

10. Quoted in Jonathan Schell, *The Abolition* (New York: Avon, 1984), p. 45.

11. Even against the current or an expanded Soviet nuclear threat, strategic defenses might still be worth deploying for less demanding missions that do not require the high level of effectiveness associated with protecting the U.S. population against an all-out Soviet nuclear attack. See Leon Sloss, "The Case for Deploying Strategic Defenses," Chapter 8 of this volume.

12. See Schell, *The Abolition*. The Reagan Administration originally insisted that the President had only proposed the elimination of all nuclear *ballistic* missiles at the Reykjavik summit in October, 1986, but later concurred with other reports that a ban on all nuclear weapons had been offered. U.S. Library of Congress, Congressional Research Service, Arms Control:

Overview of the Geneva Talks [by Steven A. Hildreth], CRS Issue Brief 85157 (updated regularly).

13. McGeorge Bundy, "Existential Deterrence and Its Consequences," in Douglas MacLean, ed., *The Security Gamble: Deterrence Dilemmas in the Nuclear Age*, Maryland Studies in Public Philosophy (Totowa, N.J.: Rowman and Allenheld, 1984), pp. 3–13; and David Lewis, "Finite Counterforce," Chapter 2 of this volume.

14. Bundy's point seems to be that for purposes of deterrence the United States can get by with less warfighting capability than required by a countervailing strategy, but he does not specify what the minimum level of capability might be, and some of the examples he cites of successful existential deterrence involve capabilities exceeding a minimum assured destruction capability. Lewis is perhaps truer to the concept of existential deterrence, for logically, if existential deterrence works at all, it should work as long as the United States possesses the capability to inflict unacceptable damage on the Soviet Union.

15. Lewis, Chapter 2 above.

16. This is not to say that either Lewis or Bundy would solve these two problems by appeal to existential deterrence. Lewis, for example, has argued that there is no necessary connection between the morality of an action and the morality of the intention to perform it. See "Devil's Bargains and the Real World," in MacLean, ed., *The Security Gamble*, pp. 141–54.

17. Lewis distinguishes existential deterrence as a conceptual thesis – given that a nation's leaders have certain attributes, the mere capability to inflict unacceptable damage is sufficient to deter them from using nuclear weapons – from existential deterrence as an empirically true description of how deterrence works in the case of the Soviet Union. While Lewis is not wholly convinced that the mere capability to inflict unacceptable damage would work completely in all cases where leaders of a nuclear-armed country are to be deterred, he seems fairly confident that such a capability has been effective in deterring Soviet leaders past and present – assuming (that is) that Soviet leaders need deterring.

18. For example, if faced simultaneously with an economic crisis and internal revolt by nationalist-minded Muslims in the Soviet Asiatic republics or by several Eastern European satellites, Soviet leaders might conclude that the time had now

come to solve the problem of "capitalist encirclement" to ensure that the West would not emerge with an overwhelming
advantage in the "correlation of forces" if the Soviet Union
should suffer catastrophic economic or political setbacks.

19. Reportedly, some high-level U.S. intelligence officials believe
that limited Soviet nuclear attacks against "reinforcement"
targets are much more likely in a NATO–Warsaw Pact war
than large-scale attacks against U.S. strategic forces. See Albert Wohlstetter, "Between an Unfree World and None: Increasing Our Choices," *Foreign Affairs* 63, no. 5 (Spring 1985),
962–94, at 985 n. 32.

20. Union of Concerned Scientists, *In Search of Stability: An Assessment of New U.S. Nuclear Forces* (Washington, 1986), p. 6. Emphasis added.

21. See, for example, J. L. Mackie, *Ethics: Inventing Right and Wrong*
(London: Penguin, 1977), p. 106.

22. U.S. National Conference of Bishops, "The Challenge of Peace,"
and Anthony Kenny, *The Logic of Deterrence* (London: Waterstone, 1985; Chicago: University of Chicago Press, 1985).

23. William O'Brien, "The Bishops' Unfinished Business," *Comparative Strategy* 5, no. 2 (1985), 105–33.

24. See, for example, Carl Builder, *The Prospects and Implications of
Non-nuclear Means for Strategic Conflict*, Adelphi Paper No. 200
(London: International Institute of Strategic Studies, 1985), and
Theodore B. Taylor, "Third-Generation Nuclear Weapons,"
Scientific American 256, no. 4 (April 1987), 30–39. Third-gen-
eration nuclear weapons, also called nuclear directed-energy
weapons (NDEWs), "would suppress certain effects, heighten
others, and perhaps channel them in certain directions as well."

25. Achieving the high accuracies needed to reduce warhead yields
to levels that would limit collateral damage from a counterforce attack to acceptable Just War levels would probably require either sophisticated terminal guidance systems that would
match microwave, infrared, or optical images with a stored
image of the target, or else mid-course guidance information
from satellites and other sources. Terminal guidance systems,
however, are vulnerable to various active and passive countermeasures, such as jamming and changing the shape of the
target. Data senders for mid-course guidance correction may
be vulnerable to destruction. For a discussion of techniques
for improving missile warhead accuracy and possible coun-

termeasures, see Matthew Bunn, *Technology of Ballistic Missile Reentry Vehicles*, Report No. 11, Program in Science and Technology for International Security, Massachusetts Institute of Technology, March 1984.

26. A "free society" is a society in which the chief governmental authorities are elected by "a meaningful process" (e.g., candidates for election are not chosen by the ruling party) and in which citizens are guaranteed a wide range of civil liberties, such as freedom of speech, assembly, religion, education, and travel, and equality before the law. Free societies are by and large Western-style democracies. For further details regarding the notion of "free society", see Raymond D. Gastil, "The Comparative Survey of Freedom," *Freedom At Issue* no. 94 (January–February 1987), 19–33. Gastil has sought to classify the countries of the world as "free," "partly free," and "not free" based on the degree of political rights and civil liberties guaranteed by the state government or other ruling authorities. According to Gastil, 37 percent of the world's population lived in free states (in January 1987), 24 percent lived in partly free states, and 39 percent lived in not-free states.

27. See, for example, Desmond Ball, "U.S. Strategic Forces: How Would They Be Used?" *International Security* 7, no. 3 (Winter 1982–83), 31–60, at 40–41; rpt. in Steven E. Miller, ed., *Strategy and Nuclear Deterrence: An "International Security" Reader* (Princeton: Princeton University Press, 1984), pp. 215–44.

28. Robert Conquest and John Manchip White, *What To Do When the Russians Come: A Survivor's Guide* (New York: Stein and Day, 1984).

29. Under current NATO doctrine, the Supreme Allied Commander Europe (SACEUR) must request use of nuclear weapons before NATO loses the cohesiveness of its conventional defense. Bernard Rogers, "Arms Control and Deterrence," *Global Affairs* 3, no. 1 (Winter 1988), 1–15, at 13. Some NATO–Warsaw Pact war scenarios envision NATO political leaders approving the use of nuclear weapons at this point, which Rogers (a former SACEUR) estimates could come within two weeks of the start of the conflict.

30. Carl Sagan, "Nuclear War and a Climatic Catastrophe: Some Policy Implications," *Foreign Affairs* 62, no. 2 (Winter 1983–84), 257–92. In general, the dust from counterforce attacks is less likely to cause nuclear winter phenomena than fires from

attacks on cities, but larger counterforce attacks, it is alleged, could still produce a global nuclear winter.

31. Mark A. Harwell, Thomas C. Hutchinson, with Wendell P. Cooper, Jr., Christine C. Hartwell, and Herbert D. Grover, *Environmental Consequences of Nuclear War*, vol. II: *Ecological and Agricultural Effects*, SCOPE 28 (Chichester and New York: Wiley, 1985). For a discussion and response to the nuclear winter hypothesis by Defense Department spokesmen and independent analysts, see U.S. Congress, *Nuclear Winter and Its Consequences*, Hearings before the Senate Armed Services Committee, S. Hrg. 99–478 (Washington: U.S. Government Printing Office, 1986).

32. See, for example, statement of Russell Murray II, in U.S. Congress, *The Consequences of Nuclear War*, Hearings before the Joint Economic Committee, S. Hrg. 98–1303 (Washington: U.S. Government Printing Office, 1986), pp. 51–55.

33. See, for example, Starley L. Thompson and Stephen H. Schneider, "Nuclear Winter Reappraised," *Foreign Affairs* 64, no. 5 (Summer 1986), 981–1005.

34. Helmut Schmidt, "Zero-Zero Option: On Equilibrium in Arms Control," *Fort Worth Star Telegram*, May 3, 1987, p. AA3. Emphasis added.

35. See, for example, Wohlstetter, "Between an Unfree World and None," and John G. Hines, Phillip A. Petersen, and Notra Trulock III, "Soviet Military Theory from 1945–2000: Implications for NATO," *Washington Quarterly* 9, no. 4 (Fall 1986), 117–37.

36. It is not clear, however, what the response would be if the issue were clearly stated as responding to Soviet use of nuclear weapons against Western Europe. The Public Agenda Foundation, *Voter Options on Nuclear Arms Policy: A Briefing Book for the 1984 Elections* (New York: Public Agenda Foundation, 1984), p. 22.

37. According to Alvin Rubinstein, implicit in the traditional Soviet view of peaceful coexistence are "continued rivalry, endemic suspicion, and unrelenting effort to weaken the adversary in order to alter the correlation of forces through a combination of political, economic, cultural, and ideological means." *Soviet Foreign Policy Since World War II: Imperial and Global* (Cambridge, Mass.: Winthrop, 1981). For quotations from Soviet sources, see Albert L. Weeks and William C. Bodie,

Robert E. Foelber

ed., *War and Peace: Soviet Russia Speaks* (Washington: National Strategy Information Center, 1983).

38. The Soviet state policy of terror against the Afghan people, including indiscriminate bombing of civilians, massacres, and the use of booby trapped toys to maim children, continued to be implemented even during the Soviet's military withdrawal from Afghanistan, leading one longtime observer of the Afghan war to wonder what Gorbachev's new Communism might really mean. Rob Schulteis, "The Soviets' Ugly Exit: Do Atrocities in Afghanistan Belie Moscow's PR?" *Washington Post*, January 8, 1989, p. C1. For documentation of the Soviets' "human rights abuses" in Afghanistan, see United Nations General Assembly, Report of the Economic and Social Council, *Situation of Human Rights in Afghanistan*, November 5, 1985; see also Helsinki Watch, *"Tears, Blood and Cries": Human Rights in Afghanistan Since the Invasion 1979–1984*, December 1984.

39. Michael Dobbs, "Soviet Officers Vent Unease at Cutbacks," *Washington Post*, December 16, 1988, p. 37. For an analysis of some of the military implications of Gorbachev's economic modernization program, see Central Intelligence Agency and Defense Intelligence Agency, *Gorbachev's Modernization Program: A Status Report*, August 1987.

40. See C. A. J. Coady, "Escaping from the Bomb: Immoral Deterrence and the Problem of Extrication," Chapter 4 of this volume, and Kenny, *The Logic of Deterrence*, pp. 21–22.

41. Wasserstrom, "War, Nuclear War, and Nuclear Deterrence: Some Conceptual and Moral Issues," *Ethics* 95, no. 3 (April 1985), 424–44; rpt. in Russell Hardin et al., ed., *Nuclear Deterrence: Ethics and Strategy* (Chicago: University of Chicago Press, 1985), pp. 15–35.

42. It might be argued that prudent Soviet planners cannot afford to consider U.S. intentions; they must plan on the basis of U.S. military capabilities only. If so, we are back to either existential deterrence, in which case the Soviets will be deterred by U.S. capabilities to inflict assured destruction on the Soviet Union, or to what might be called existential nondeterrence: In a crisis the Soviets will assume the worst, namely an all-out first strike by the United States, and will launch a desperate preemptive nuclear attack. If we assume existential nondeterrence, however, even a finite deterrence posture would be destabilizing.

43. Robert M. Gates and Lawrence K. Gershwin, *Soviet Strategic Force Developments*, Testimony Before a Joint Session of the Subcommittee on Strategic and Theater Nuclear Forces of the Senate Armed Services Committee and the Defense Subcommittee of the Senate Appropriations Committee, June 26, 1985, p. 7. Emphasis added.

44. Bruce Blair, *Strategic Command and Control: Redefining the Nuclear Threat* (Washington: Brookings Institution, 1985), p. 283.

45. An expanded civil defense program, such as that recommended by both the Carter and Reagan Administrations, would not give the United States a reliable war-winning capability either, even in combination with the Reagan Administration's strategic force modernization program, because it could not ensure the survival of the U.S. population against direct nuclear attack, although it could save millions of American lives in a limited counterforce nuclear conflict. U.S. Congress, Office of Technology Assessment, *The Effects of Nuclear War* (Washington; U.S. Government Printing Office, 1979).

46. For a recent statement of one version of this argument, see Stephen Van Evera, "The Cult of the Offensive and the Origins of the First World War," *International Security* 9, no. 1 (Summer 1984), 58–107; rpt. in Steven E. Miller, ed., *Military Strategy and the Origins of the First World War: An "International Security" Reader* (Princeton: Princeton University Press, 1985), pp. 58–107. Using organizational theory, Van Evera argues that military establishments inevitably adopt offensive military doctrines, which are viewed as in general destabilizing. This applies to U.S. and Soviet nuclear warfighting doctrines as well. For a critique of the "cult of the offensive" thesis as it applies to the origins of World War I and the stability of nuclear counterforce postures, see Scott D. Sagan, "1914 Revisited," *International Security* 11, no. 2 (Fall 1986), 151–75.

47. See, for example, Robert Jervis, Richard Ned Lebow, and Janice Gross Stein, ed., *Psychology and Deterrence* (Baltimore: Johns Hopkins University Press, 1985), and Ralph K. White, ed., *Psychology and the Prevention of Nuclear War* (New York: New York University Press, 1986).

48. Richard Ned Lebow, *Between Peace and War: The Nature of International Crisis* (Baltimore: Johns Hopkins University Press, 1981), p. 16.

49. For a critical review of *Psychology and Deterrence* that questions

the relevance of nonnuclear deterrence failure to problems of nuclear deterrence, see James G. Blight, "The New Psychology of War and Peace," *International Security* 11, no. 3 (Winter 1986–87), 175–86.

50. Chapter 5 of this volume.

51. Since the 1960s France has based nuclear deterrence on a strategy of all-out retaliation against Soviet urban–industrial areas. Some analysts speculate that as France expands and modernizes its nuclear forces over the next decade it might modify its strategic doctrine to include options for limited counterforce attacks. See John Prados, Joel S. Wit, and Michael J. Zagurek, Jr., "The Strategic Nuclear Forces of Britain and France," *Scientific American* 255, no. 2 (August 1986), 33–41.

52. Indeed, according to the same poll, 79 percent of those queried believe "there is nothing on earth that could ever justify the all out use of nuclear weapons."Public Agenda Foundation, *Voter Options on Nuclear Arms Policy*, p. 37.

53. This is the valid criticism of offense-dominated damage-limiting strategies made by some finite deterrence theorists, such as Robert Jervis, as well as by some advocates of nuclear war-winning strategies, such as Colin Gray. See Robert Jervis, *The Illogic of American Nuclear Strategy*, Cornell Studies in Security Affairs (Ithaca and London: Cornell University Press, 1984), pp. 35, 74, 83–84; and Colin S. Gray, "Targeting Problems for Central War," *Naval War College Review* 33, no. 1 (January – February 1980), 3–21, at 7.

54. Such a treaty would not be in the United States' interests, however, if it undercut Western resolve to resist Soviet political and military aggression, or if the Soviets could achieve a significant military advantage through clandestine deployment of strategic defenses or strategic counterforce weapons.

Chapter 4

Escaping from the bomb: immoral deterrence and the problem of extrication

C. A. J. Coady

Objections to nuclear deterrence have been around almost as long as the Bomb itself. Broadly, and too crudely, they take two forms. On the one hand the policy (or mix of policies) is criticized in terms of its pragmatic framework – it is too costly, it is too dangerous, it doesn't deter enough (witness Hungary, Czechoslovakia, Vietnam, Afghanistan, etc.), its empirical assumptions (e.g. about the degree of the enemy's malevolence) are false. On the other hand the policy is rejected on the ground that the particular kind of threatening attitude it embodies violates deep moral constraints on how anyone should act or set himself to act. These constraints operate even, indeed especially, when the agent has good ends in view, and this is worth remembering since defenders of deterrence are naturally quick to stress the good they hope to achieve. It should also be noted that both lines of criticism usually involve moral concerns, since those who, for instance, object to the cost or risk of deterrence are not merely concerned for their own pockets or hides. More generally, some concern for avoiding harmful consequences and seeking beneficial ones clearly has a place in morality, though it must be insisted that it is not the whole of it.

I have spoken of constraints, and it is natural to do so since the area of morality I have in mind often comes into play by way of restricting our choice of programs, techniques, or means to achieving what we see as worthwhile objectives. Paul Ramsey's fantasy of the surely immoral, though possibly efficacious, technique of strapping babies on to the front of motor cars to reduce (by a kind of deterrence) the dreadful carnage of our roads is just one illustration of the way such moral constraints operate.[1] Then again there is William James's example of a world in which general happiness and wellbeing were purchased at the cost of subjecting one "lost soul," one innocent individual, "on the far-off edge of things" to a life of "lonely torment." James thought the policy of so acting towards this individual clearly immoral as an act of injustice whatever its beneficial effects.[2] Another example would be the prohibition, in Just War theory, on the taking and killing of hostages even in pursuit of good ends. More positively, the existence of such constraints is at least partly due to an interest in the nature of the acts one does and the kind of person one is in doing them. Morality has, in other words, as much to do with character and deeds as with long-term public outcomes. To mark the distinction I will follow recent usage and call the orientation to outcomes "consequentialist," and with less deference to recent usage I will call the area marked by constraints "internalist."[3]

Much public discussion of nuclear deterrence is, very understandably, dominated by a discussion of possible and probable consequences. My own view is that the consequentialist case for nuclear deterrence is much weaker than its supporters believe. Insofar as the probabilities are calculable (which is not really very far at all) they seem to me to indicate that deterrence makes nuclear war more probable rather than less probable, and this prospect is more hideous by far than that of domination or invasion by some communist power – which is, in any case, nowhere near as probable in the absence of deterrence as is often maintained. In the case of the United States, the fear of such domination or invasion is now almost ludicrous, so that discussions of deterrence or invasion couched in terms of unprovoked Soviet nuclear attacks on the United States have an air of more than usual unreality about them. This does not of course stop them from going on.

The prospect of Soviet conventional forays into Western Europe makes a little more sense, though not in terms of "Soviet expansionism" in the abstract but in terms of local flare-ups in precarious areas like Berlin. Such an eventuality is in any case remote, but it would be folly to propose nuclear solutions for it. The folly arises both from the availability of nonnuclear responses, especially in the early stages of any such crisis, and from the idea that a contingency such as the East German or Soviet occupation of West Berlin would be a sufficient disaster to require nuclear measures. (I do not mean to minimize the misfortune this would be for West Berliners; but their incorporation into East Germany would be roughly comparable to the fate that has in fact been politically negotiated, over their heads, for the people of Hong Kong.) The slogan "Better dead than red" not only distorts the values at stake (since nuclear war involves more than the sacrifice of individual life) but also embodies a misunderstanding of strategic realities, and the same is true of its Eastern bloc equivalent – presumably, "Better blight than white." [4]

Nonetheless I want principally to address not the consequentialist questions but, rather, the internalist ones. I shall raise first of all some questions about the arguments for and against the immorality of the deterrent stance and then move on to what might follow from admitting its immorality. Those who do not agree with the admission may nonetheless be interested in what I have to say about the moral considerations relevant to acting on it.

THE INTERNALIST CRITIQUE OF DETERRENCE

The basic internalist moral objection to nuclear deterrence proceeds from the prior judgments, first, that all-out nuclear war is immoral and, second, that any military use of nuclear weapons plausibly likely to follow on the failure of deterrence is also certain to be immoral even where it goes under

some such heading as "retaliation." I shall begin by sketch-
ing a familiar line of defense of these judgments[5] and then
proceed to rebut certain important objections.

It is simplest to begin by invoking the Just War tradition,
though we need not take a stand on some particular interpretation of that tradition, since on virtually any account of
it there will be moral prohibitions on how a war can be waged.
It is, I think, quite compelling that any morality concerned
with the waging of war must include both some principle of
discrimination and some principle of proportion, the former
dealing with the nature of legitimate targets and the latter
with whether the proposed military response will create
damage and evil disproportionate to the goods it is designed
to achieve. The former principle most significantly prohibits
direct attacks upon noncombatant populations, and the latter seeks, among other things, to keep even "incidental"
damage to noncombatants under moral control. The categories of combatant and noncombatant and those of direct and
indirect action raise many complex philosophical issues into
which we cannot now plunge, but in broad terms the operation of these distinctions is not hard to manage.[6] Moreover,
their moral significance within Just War theory is clear enough
since, if any justification can be given for the resort to massive lethal violence, then the status of those against whom
the violence is directed must be that of *perpetrators* of some
serious evil. This is a minimum necessary condition, and,
though it may be possible to include those who have been
forced to participate in prosecuting the evil, such as conscript soldiers, we have here no license to attack ordinary
civilians who live under the enemy's rule. One must surely
conclude that all-out or large-scale nuclear war cannot satisfy
either principle. No doubt there are some purely military targets that could be destroyed by an accurate nuclear weapon
having virtually no disproportionate side effects – an enemy
war fleet at sea is a plausible candidate. Nonetheless it is
fanciful to suppose that the present war plans of the Eastern
and Western powers can find moral comfort in such a fact,
since if deterrence fails they are embarked upon a course of

prodigious slaughter of the innocents and immense devastation of culture and nature.

It may be replied that such a critique fails to take account of significant changes in Western policy concerning nuclear war and deterrence. Deterrence is no longer based upon assured destruction of enemy populations but upon the more moral though equally fearsome prospect of flexible response and counterforce. This reply is sufficiently fashionable to deserve close attention, though such attention reveals fairly readily that its charms are largely cosmetic.

We should begin by resolving it into two interrelated elements which are not always sufficiently distinguished. On the one hand there is the claim that, even in the event of large-scale nuclear war, the West no longer targets the enemy's civilian population; on the other there is the claim that the West, in any case, now rests its deterrent upon the prospect of "limited" nuclear war in which civilian populations are not the object of attack. Let us examine these successively.

It is certainly true that the targeting policies of the United States have undergone a complex series of developments over the last forty years, but it is far from clear that they have become any less objectionable morally. The current state of the Single Integrated Operational Plan (SIOP) places much less emphasis upon the capacity to destroy Soviet cities. Indeed, partly in response to (or in deflection of) moral criticism, though mostly for strategic reasons, current policy claims to eschew population targeting per se. But this fastidiousness is almost entirely a verbal maneuver, as the following considerations demonstrate.

(1) The change in U.S. policy does not involve abandoning the threat of or the capacity for assured destruction, since the move to counterforce and other "discriminatory" policies is largely a matter of adding to a repertoire rather than abandoning one in favor of another. The basic idea is that the United States should have more flexibility than the sole option of massive destruction in the event of deterrence failure, but if graduated responses fail, the option of city-razing is

clearly retained. The frequently reiterated piety that the United States does not, in the immortal words of Secretary of Defense Elliot Richardson in 1973, "target civilian populations per se" has been deemed by later U.S. officials such as President Carter's Secretary of Defense, Harold Brown, to be perfectly consistent with retaining the capacity to destroy "a minimum of 200 major cities."[7] Nowadays, attacks upon population centers are in the category of "withholds," which seems to mean that such attacks are late resorts but are not wholly excluded. The idea of limited nuclear war requires some such "withholding" if it is to make even minimal sense, but this does not mean that civilian targets are no longer seriously considered for attack.[8]

(2) There is also the fact that the policies of the other Western nuclear powers are explicitly "city-busting." This is one reason why the original unveiling of a shift away from the priority of population targeting, notably in Robert McNamara's famous Ann Arbor speech of June 1962,[9] provoked such a negative reaction among the European NATO governments. Those with nuclear weapons saw their independence eroded, since their smaller arsenals had to have cities as primary targets if they were to retain a shred of autonomy, and those without such weapons were disturbed by the specter of limited nuclear war on European soil. McNamara and others were forced to maintain publicly the primacy of MAD (mutual assured destruction) while actually building up counterforce options in a framework of flexible response. These days U.S. "declaratory" policy includes no targeting of civilian populations "per se," but European leaders are reassured (presumably) by the knowledge that assured destruction policies still play a central role in the defense of Europe.

(3) Civilian populations have, in any case, small reason to be comforted by the thought that they are not targets "per se." In the first place, it is unclear what this means, since even the German civilians attacked in Allied raids during World War II were not bombed just because they were German civilians (though there may have been some admixture

of purely malicious motivation) but primarily because their deaths, sufferings, and homelessness were thought likely to lead to demoralization and an earlier end to the war. Yet the raids clearly violated the discrimination principle. It is interesting that, especially in the early stages of these bombings, the principal British targets were working-class areas.[10] The interest here lies in the fact that during the Vietnam war the United States had an avowed policy of not bombing the enemy population "per se" but exempted workers from this restriction because they were an economic resource, a view which has resurfaced in the nuclear context. U.S. nuclear planning pays a good deal of attention to preventing the enemy's industrial recovery after a nuclear attack, and it is believed that "survival of the work force is by far the most important factor in industrial recovery."[11] This belief bodes ill for the Russian work force and for those who live with them, such as spouses, children, and aged relatives. We should also remember in evaluating political reassurances of this kind that political leaders commonly lie to their people in matters of "national security" when they judge that their policies need a cloak of moral or legal respectability. A classic case was the behavior of the British government over Suez when Prime Minister Anthony Eden and Foreign Minister Selwyn Lloyd lied boldly and convincingly to Parliament and the electorate about the background and objectives of that notorious misadventure.[12] Nor should the grand deceptions of the Vietnam era in U.S. politics need recalling (does the phrase "Tonkin Gulf" ring a bell?), especially since the Reagan Administration did its best to bring the point home once more.

(4) Even if a genuine attempt were made to rule out noncombatants as targets, it is unclear that this would be either possible or desirable within the present framework of American deterrence theory and capabilities. As Richelson puts it, "An SIOP level attack that involved targeting of Soviet military and political assets as well as major manufacturing installations would produce civilian casualties at a level that would make population-avoidance a theoretical footnote."[13] But not only is there abundant evidence that there would be

massive "incidental" civilian death and damage from present strategies that could be regarded only broadly as having military targets; there is also reason to believe that this figures as a welcome feature of military targeting from the point of view of current deterrence theory. The fact that such a high proportion of the enemy population will suffer death or severe injury in the event of a large-scale nuclear attack on military targets is still an essential ingredient in what is supposed to make deterrence work and also in what is supposed to make limited nuclear strikes feasible.

So much for the first element; but what of the possibility of limited nuclear war? It will be urged that technological developments, especially more accurate missiles and better intelligence about the adversary's dispositions, now make limited war and deterrence based upon it a real possibility. The trouble with this is twofold. On the one hand, either the limited nuclear war scenarios are too limited to serve the full purposes of deterrence, or they deter primarily by the scary likelihood of escalation or by their horrendous side effects. The United States wants its nuclear weapons policy to deter its enemies from making an attack, primarily a nuclear attack, upon its own territory, but it also wants the policy to deter attacks upon its allies and to protect supposedly vital interests around the world. This is the sphere of extended deterrence. It may well be that the threat of a war that involved some restricted use of tactical nuclear weapons, but that conformed to Just War criteria and was certain (or was generally thought certain) not to escalate, would provide *some* disincentive to a hostile power's belligerence, but nothing like the disincentive that nuclear deterrence is supposed to give. Such a threat makes nuclear war look more like "ordinary" war, and if extended deterrence works at all then it works because the enemy believes that nuclear war will be nothing like ordinary war and that the U.S. threat is not the restricted threat discussed above. It is hard to deny the validity of this belief.

Take the case of a limited nuclear engagement in Europe. The collateral effects of nuclear attacks directed only against the Warsaw Pact forces invading Europe are likely to be devastating for the civilian populations of East Germany, Poland, and Czechoslovakia even before one considers the effects on Western Europe of similarly surgical retaliation by the Soviet Union against the military targets of NATO – not that the Soviets, if they respond, are likely to make a merely surgical retaliation. But grim enough as this prospect is, we must also consider the dangers of escalation. It is not enough to counter these by reference to the bare possibility that human beings will remain rational enough on both sides to favor negotiation or capitulation ahead of the resort to a higher level of nuclear attack. Sloss makes some play with this possibility,[14] and it is indeed a genuine one, but what we need here, given the enormous stakes, is strong probability or even certainty. This we emphatically do not have, especially when we consider that either contending party might reasonably think that his cause would be decisively furthered by resort to a higher nuclear level without occasioning a similar response from the enemy. In so thinking, each power could make use of the comforting thought that his opponent is surely too sensible to respond with a further escalation, and this thought is seductively and successively available. In addition to this, many of the conditions for rational decision making may well be absent or damaged as a direct result of nuclear weapons having been used. Either panic or impairment of communications could easily lead to misjudgment of the scale of the nuclear attack and a disproportionate reprisal. All things considered, it is not surprising that the impressive team of McGeorge Bundy, George Kennan, Robert McNamara, and Gerard Smith concluded in 1982: "No one has ever succeeded in advancing any persuasive reason to believe that any use of nuclear weapons, even on the smallest scale, could reliably be expected to remain limited."[15]

ATTEMPTS TO NEUTRALIZE JUST WAR PRINCIPLES

There are two other criticisms of the Just War objections to the various forms of nuclear war which I should briefly discuss. One tries to neutralize the principle of discrimination and the other the principle of proportion. The first is due to Gregory S. Kavka, who has sought to show that at least some attacks upon enemy population centers will not violate the requirements of discrimination because the population of the unjust aggressor government is somehow implicated in his unjust aggression (or whatever other injustice justifies our violence). Kavka moves from the fact that we do not insist on full moral responsibility to justify our use of violence against a madman attacking us or a conscript soldier coerced to attack us to the claim that the citizens of an enemy aggressor state are not immune (or are merely "semi-immune") from our violent response.[16] But this argument won't do – for, whatever difficulty the madman or the conscript poses, he is at least *attacking* us, whereas vast numbers of the enemy's noncombatants are not by any stretch of the imagination doing anything like that. In the case of nuclear war between East and West an attempt to implicate Soviet, Polish, Hungarian, and Czech citizens in the guilt of the Soviet leaders is particularly distasteful even if we ignore the slaughter of their children.

Kavka also helps himself to the intuition that "most of us believe" that, assuming equal effectiveness, it is "substantially more objectionable" to deter country Y from attack by threatening retaliation against the cities of uninvolved nation Z than by threatening Y's own cities.[17] I don't myself believe anything of the sort. Except for the fact that the onslaught on Y's cities would presumably kill some aggressors and the attack on Z's would not even do that, the cases seem to me (and, I dare say, to many other critics of nuclear war) quite comparable. What defenders of deterrence believe about such matters can hardly be seen as neutral intuitional data for our moral problem. No doubt in the Palestinian camps or in Libya "most of them" believe that it is "substantially more objectionable" to kidnap and hold hostage for political ends a Swedish than an American civilian. Once again this belief is bolstered by certain genuine facts about differences in behavior and policy toward Middle East affairs by the Swedish and American governments, but individuals do not belong to governments and are not to be seen as agents of their policies merely by virtue of being citizens or inhabitants. Of course the matter is *somewhat* different if they have opted to become agents, even unwilling ones. I do not doubt that there are interesting and difficult issues about the exact nature of a citizen's relation to government policy; what I hope to have made doubtful in this brief discussion is that the relation by itself can be sufficiently intimate for mere citizenship or residence to qualify one as a legitimate target for lethal violence.[18]

David Lewis, in his paper in the present volume, concentrates more upon challenging the position that substantial nuclear attacks by the United States on military targets must violate the principle of proportionality.[19] To do this he invokes both the idea that a very large number of enemy civilian deaths might be morally acceptable as long as their deaths were counterbalanced by the lives saved, and the idea that in doing such calculations one is entitled (at least if one is the commander-in-chief) to discount the enemy's lives at some unspecified (and unspecifiable) rate. The first idea is the more plausible and challenging for the case I am defending, and it is, perhaps fortunately, detachable from the second. Nonetheless I will begin by briefly commenting on the second.

Lewis defends the Chief's right, indeed obligation, to weigh deaths "with a finger on the scale"[20] by recourse to the theory of what might be called "special responsibility." This tells us that if we have undertaken or otherwise incurred a particular responsibility for some individual or group, then we may (or must – it is not always clear which) put the welfare of that person or group ahead of the welfare of others. So parents are entitled or obliged to spend more money, time, and thought on, say, the education of their own children than on that of the child next door or some victim of the Ethiopian famine. In such small-scale illustrative contexts the theory has obvious appeal, but it is far less compelling when exported wholesale to such entities as nation-states and their rulers. The theory is sometimes invoked to provide moral support for inertia, if not complacency, about the present distribution of wealth and wellbeing in the world today. Those who see the persistence of this distribution as signifying callousness and injustice have cause to be suspicious of the theory. From the point of view of the world's victims, the idea that the rulers of the affluent world are obliged to discount their interests to an unspecifiable degree by dint of having gone through certain electoral processes is likely to appear grotesque – a version of "I'm all right Jack" sung in Gregorian chant. Clearly what truth there is in the theory needs closer analysis, but we should note that, even in the small-scale cases where it has most appeal, special responsibilities are constrained by broader, less partial moral considerations. If the success of the child next door is likely to block my child's access to some important educational good (he will probably just beat my child for a crucial scholarship), this may entitle me to hire a special tutor, which his parents can't afford, but it doesn't entitle or oblige me to go out and kill him or give him a beating that will reduce his study potential. Nor can I always treat other children's lives as less significant in the matter of risks. I do not suggest that these points decisively prove that Lewis is wrong to draw so strongly upon the theory of special responsibility, but they certainly cast doubt upon the ease with which he employs the theory to support tampering with the scales.

More centrally, he argues that, although a policy of direct nuclear attacks upon cities is "wicked," a policy of "modest" counterforce which attacks military sites in or near major Soviet cities with devastating collateral effect can be morally justified. This is basically because the American lives saved would outweigh the Soviet lives lost (especially with the Chief's finger on the scale). Lewis expresses a degree of dissatisfaction with Just War theory, or what he calls the "self-regarding" part of it, but, as he notes, his defense of finite counterforce could be put in terms of the Soviet civilian deaths being foreseen but unintended consequences of a military attack. They would then be permissible if they were proportionate,[21] but, forgetting about loaded scales, would they really be proportionate?

Certainly some counterforce strategies would fail this test. A full attack upon the SIOP targets (excluding direct city-busting) in order to deal with a Soviet conventional invasion of West Germany would be not only imprudent but morally disproportionate. Lewis, of course, does not advocate such responses, though it is unclear that the structure of the policy of extended deterrence does not encompass them. What Lewis does claim is that, in the event of a major Soviet nuclear attack upon the United States, a retaliation of a somewhat restrained counterforce nature in a situation of great uncertainty would be morally licit even if it involved the collateral killing of millions of Soviet citizens. He thinks this because he believes that despite the uncertainty (about how many enemy missiles remain unlaunched, how many are invulnerable, how substantial the enemy attack is, what further intentions the enemy has, and so forth) a counterforce retaliation is likely to be sufficiently *damage limiting* for the United States to compensate for the noncombatant deaths. How can such an issue be decided?

Suppose we think it very probable that 14 million Soviet civilians will be killed by our modest counterforce response. Lewis would think it proportional if it saved anything above 14 million American lives (with a finger on the scales it will be far fewer).[22] To this there are several possible lines of response, but in a spirit of modest counterforce I will make only two. The first is that Lewis fudges somewhat on the options. In the event of a nuclear attack on the United States, the counterforce response may not be the best available, for there is the option of not making a military response at all, and there are various more moderate military and indeed nuclear responses than Lewis's. He acknowledges the no-counterattack option and even admits that, on certain plausible assumptions, it is the best response but rejects it basically because the uncertainties and confusions created by a nuclear attack are so great that we couldn't know whether nonretaliation would work to limit damage. In this part of his discussion Lewis rightly stresses both how little we know and how much less we are likely to know in the context of a serious nuclear attack ("all is guesswork").[23] Yet he really does not allow the different options impartial use of this ignorance. Our lack of certainty that not responding would achieve a cease-fire rules it out as an option, though what seems at least as great an uncertainty about the consequences (for us) of resort to counterforce responses does not impair its appeal as an option in the least, even though it requires us pretty certainly to bring about the deaths of millions of Soviet noncombatants. Lewis takes this line because he is convinced that "it is likely that there will be follow-on attacks no matter what we do."[24] Out of the fog of uncertainty and guesswork to which his critics are still confined, Lewis emerges mysteriously with this confident belief, but, on his own showing, he is not entitled to such confidence.

This brings me to the second objection. Even if we set aside the question of specific nonnuclear options for damage limitation, the question whether our near-certain killing of 14 million Soviet civilians is a proportionate response cannot be decided by weighing their deaths against some merely possible saving of life that may thereby be accomplished. Lewis is, of course, aware that the calculations have to make reference to likelihoods, but he does not seem sufficiently impressed by the contrast of the practical certainty of the enemy deaths against the great uncertainty of the damage limitation – i.e. the saving of more than 14 million American lives. I readily concede that traditional Just War talk of "proportion" is not as clear as it should be, but when its representatives speak of the need for the evil foreseen side effect not to be disproportionate to the good sought by the action they clearly have in mind the matter of likelihood as well as degree of evil. This is why the comparison is usually with objectives close at hand and epistemically firm.[25] You can refuse to take a man on board your lifeboat even where this means his death if you are pretty sure that taking him on board will sink the boat and probably kill him and all thirty others on it. But the case is very different if you think merely that his presence on board *might* endanger the lives of others because his is another mouth to feed and water and you don't know how long you will be adrift. Similarly with warfare: All sorts of actions will have proportionately acceptable, though hideous, side effects if the long-range, often speculative, goals they are hoped to promote are allowed the same currency for practical thinking as the immediate and certain evils they cause.

It might be replied that, even if all this were allowed, I would have conceded Lewis an important point of principle in the very act of rejecting his application of it. Pivotal to his thinking is the idea that proportionality is the essential issue and that it is basically to be understood in consequentialist terms. I have rejected his way of doing the sums, but have I not also implicitly abandoned the centrality of the principle of discrimination? This reaction is mistaken in several ways. First, noncombatants have a different moral status from combatants (for reasons given earlier), so that causing their deaths, whether directly or indirectly, is generally of graver moral concern than killing combatants, though there remain important questions about our duties toward the latter. Second, I seriously doubt whether the deaths of the Soviet civilians can be treated as unintentional and hence within the scope of the double-effect principle. The principle of double effect seems to me (though not to Lewis) to have a useful role in moral thinking, but it is easily prone to abuse.

Suppose that someone who is very hostile to flies sees a fly land on a companion's bald head. The fly-hater has a sledgehammer handy but no normal flyswatter, and the fly is elusive. Fully realizing the costs, he smites the fly and smashes his companion's skull. In explanation he points out that he didn't intend both deaths but only the fly's. The companion's demise was a foreseen but unintended side effect. Such an explanation would plainly not excuse, but – more important – it does not add up as an explanation. The connection between killing the fly and killing the man is too intimate for the killer to be able to disavow the intention to kill the man. Similar considerations apply to Lewis's suggested description of a possible direct nuclear countervalue attack upon a city: The attacker intends only the creation of the visible flight of the warhead and the visible fireball, since these are all the enemy needs to detect to respond as we want him to.[26] The carnage subsequent upon flight and fireball is merely an unintended side effect. But in the real world this carnage is so intimately related to the flight and fireball, and so central to our planning of these, that it would be incomprehensible to claim that the attacker did not intend the death and destruction. True, the attacker's desires are achieved through the enemy's beliefs, and these arise from seeing the fireball; but the attacker aims at the death and destruction in order to create those beliefs, since he cannot realistically think of the fireball and the carnage as separable effects related in quite different ways to his will.

In the case of Lewis's modest counterforce it is not so obvious that those who attack the missile sites intend the closely associated civilian slaughter. This is one reason why I chose to dispute the example partly on Lewis's own grounds. Nonetheless a case can be made for this conclusion, although to make it effectively would require a close analysis of intention, action, and double-effect doctrine. Such a case would have to attend not only to the question how inevitable the civilian deaths are but also to the degree of responsibility we bear for the situation in which their lives are in jeopardy and are made to seem a fair price to pay for the protection of our citizens. This is a point of more general significance for the moral status of modest counterforce as strategic doctrine. It can seem plausible to treat a policy as morally tolerable when it is justified in terms of some worst-case scenario for saving millions of our innocents by sacrificing fewer millions of theirs, but we do not know that our use policy is designed for only such extremities, nor should we assume that if such extremities eventuate they will have come about because of the enemy's evil and folly rather than our own – including our continued reliance upon nuclear war policies for "normal" political goals such as "containing" communism.[27]

178

I conclude that the first stage of the internalist critique of deterrence is successful. We must now look to the second stage.

Given that the foreseeable uses of nuclear weapons on which deterrence rests are immoral, does it follow that the policy of deterrence is itself immoral? The policy threatens to do what is immoral; but let us suppose (with its defenders) that it does so solely or principally to prevent the enemy's using nuclear weapons against us and our responding in kind. Let us also suppose that it is at least reasonable to believe that the policy has been successful in this aim in the past and has some chance of continuing to be successful in at least the near future. It is clear that not all threats to do what is immoral are themselves immoral. Insincere threats, i.e. bluffs, need not be immoral though they threaten what it would be immoral to do. True, they usually involve an element of deceit, but I am prepared to concede that lying can in certain situations be justified, and some bluffs do not even involve outright lying. A sincere threat to do what is morally wrong, however, is much more problematic since it involves the intention to act immorally, and it seems to be a secure moral intuition that if it is morally wrong to do x it is morally wrong to intend to do x. This enshrines what Kavka has called the Wrongful Intentions Principle (WIP). As Kavka points out, the WIP is supported by three common features of our moral thinking: First, someone who fully intends to do some morally wrong act but is prevented by external circumstances is nonetheless blameworthy for having had the intention; second, we view the man who intends to do what is wrong and then changes his mind as having corrected a moral fault; third, there seems to be a way in which intentions are parts of the acts that fulfill them, so that someone who forms an intention to do some act x is thereby embarked on the act.[28]

Does it make a difference that the intention involved in nuclear deterrence is a conditional intention, i.e. an intention to slaughter millions of people only if the enemy does something first? Surely not. Suppose I form the intention to shoot you dead if a coin I tossed comes down heads. Its coming down tails does not show me to be blameless, even though it deprives me of the chance of executing that intention. This is true, incidentally, even if the coin is biased so that the chance of its coming down heads is only one in a hundred.

SOME REPLIES TO THE CRITIQUE DISCUSSED

We seem, then, to have a powerful objection to the morality of nuclear deterrence, but several lines of reply to it have recently been developed in the philosophical literature. The replies vary in detail but basically either deny the presence of the conditional intention or deny its moral significance.

1. The deterrent does not embody the conditional intention, because

(*a*) It is on *our* part, at any rate, a bluff. That is, we declare or signify that, if *c*, then we will do something terrible, *x*, but we intend not to do *x*. We naturally describe bluffing as threatening to do something which we don't intend to do. But the phrase "don't intend to do" is ambiguous between "intend not to do" and "not intend to do," and characteristically the former is a better rendering since the bluffer has typically excluded the execution of his threat.

(*b*) It is unclear that it embodies any definite intentions other than to frighten the enemy with the prospects of what we might do. That is, we declare or signify that, if *c*, we will or might do *x*, but right now we have neither the intention to do *x* nor the intention not to do *x*. Even if the enemy realizes that this is the situation he, like us, will not know how to predict our behavior if *c*, and so will act on the assumption that we will do *x*.

2. The deterrent does embody the conditional intention, but this does not have the moral significance attributed to it by the WIP, because

(*a*) The WIP implies that where doing *x* is seriously immoral, intending to do *x* is just as seriously immoral, and this is counterintuitive, especially in such situations as the nuclear deterrent, where the intention functions precisely to prevent anyone's having to do *x*.

(*b*) The WIP requires the judgment of immorality of the intention to flow entirely by derivation from the judgment of immorality of the contemplated action, but this ignores the fact that forming the intention is one act and performing the intended action another, so that the forming of the intention can be judged morally good on the basis of its "autonomous" consequences even where it would be wrong to do the action.

(*c*) The grain of truth in the WIP is that intentions are open to moral assessment just because they usually make the actions they are directed upon more likely to occur. They have no independent moral interest, however, and when the probability link is severed or greatly weakened then the WIP fails. (This is related to (*b*) but is not quite the same.)

I have gathered this scheme of objections from the writings of Gregory Kavka, David Lewis, Bernard Williams, and Jeff McMahan, and a proper treatment would have to consider their careful presentations in specific detail.[29] I have no space to do that here, but I shall simply comment on the objections as abstractly posed above.

1(*a*). We can be brief with this, for we have no reason at all to believe that the actual deterrent is a bluff and every reason to believe that it is not. The record of both superpowers is not such as to suggest an aversion to violating noncombatant immunity, so we have historical evidence aplenty that their threats are sincere. There is also abundant empirical evidence about the attitudes, dispositions, and instructions which lie behind the U.S. deterrent. Of course all this empirical evidence might remain just as it is were the deterrent to be a perfect bluff, but that is no consolation for the bluff hypothesis. The perfect bluff could be known to be so only to the very few who are utterly discreet, perhaps only to the Ultimate Decider. He (be he one person or a small group) may have it in mind not to make a nuclear response to a failure in deterrence, but the institutional pressures and powerful government forces that inevitably surround such a figure will probably make his ideas irrelevant. In the light of his past belligerent attitudes, he will be seen as having cracked under pressure and will be replaced. We have every reason to believe our leaders sincere in their nuclear threats, and we have good reason to believe that, were they not, their insincerity would be of no avail.

1(b). As stressed by McGeorge Bundy and David Lewis, a great deal of what force deterrence has in international affairs resides in its uncertainties rather than in its declared intentions.[30] A nuclear strike by one side or the other, even of the most "surgical" kind, would bring with it an extraordinary degree of confusion and uncertainty, which in turn would make a response to it highly unpredictable and uncertain. Deterrence is in this sense "existential" because it is sustained on both sides not by a fear of what the enemy is known definitely to intend to do but by his existing capacities and by uncertainty about how he will use them in an emergency. There is certainly a degree of truth in this, but it is surely inadequate as a rebuttal of the moral argument against the deterrent, and this for two reasons.

In the first place, we must not discount altogether the frequently reiterated declarations of intention to use nuclear weapons, at some stage, in reprisal against Soviet population centers or against "military" targets that would, as I argued earlier, have disproportionate civilian casualties associated with the military destruction. These intentions may be adjusted or abandoned in the chilling face of an actual attack, but we cannot ignore the fact that they give structure and shape to the attitudes decision makers will bring to the crisis. The uncertainties created by deterrence, both for the enemy and for us, are mostly ones about how monstrously we will behave, and not (predominantly) about whether we will respond at all. There are serious government plans for slaughtering the enemy's civilians in certain eventualities, and the fact that it may be hard to tell on the spot if those eventualities have occurred, or the possibility that the Ultimate Decider may abandon the immoral intention, can provide at best marginal comfort.

In the second place, the internalist argument about intention rests upon certain psychological orientations toward action, of which intention to act is the strongest and most central but not the only one. Even if it were true that the nuclear deterrent did not embody the specific intention to do x (where x is, say, the immoral breach of noncombatant immunity) it would still embody states of mind that are immoral – for instance, the readiness to do x or to let others do x, the intention to set up (or connive at the setting up of) a political situation in which the doing of x is one of the possible options ("plans") to be realized, and so on. What, for instance, are we to think of the moral standing of a man who arranges to defend himself by setting up a device which when triggered by an intruder will either kill the intruder, do nothing, play a Mozart concerto, kill the intruder's innocent relatives, or kill a whole lot of innocent people in the neighborhood where the intruder happens to live? His attitude is at least one of moral irresponsibility, and this is true even if his device serves for a time to deter his enemy. Nor would the matter be improved by leaving the operation of the device not to chance but to the choice of an Ultimate Decider, who might have the moral outlook of, let's say, Richard Nixon or, if you prefer, Spiro Agnew.

CONDITIONAL INTENDING AND CORRUPTION

This really brings us to 2(*a*), (*b*), and (*c*). Let us concede that the conditional intention or some related mental set is involved in the deterrent. Let us also concede that its presence has the "autonomous effect" (as Kavka calls it) of making an enemy attack less likely and to that extent making it unlikely that the intention will have to be put into effect. Reply 2(*a*) argues that it is absurd to claim, as the WIP would have it, that such a conditional intention is just as immoral as actually firing the missiles or as malevolently intending to do so for the sheer pleasure of it. Bernard Williams and Jeff McMahan, in different ways, have forcefully urged this difficulty,[31] but whatever force it might have against some proponents of the WIP objection, it seems clear that the objection itself makes no such claim or assumption. The argument concludes that deterrence is immoral because it incorporates a seriously immoral intention, but it does not insist that this conditional intention is as bad as various other conditional intentions or other categorical intentions. Nor does it imply that the agent is as great a scoundrel as certain other agents who have less attachment to the good than the operator of a deterrent policy may have. It seems that something can be very seriously wrong without being as wrong as certain other serious wrongs. Destroying someone's reputation is not as wrong as torturing him slowly to death, but nonetheless it is immoral. An internalist may perfectly consistently hold that two acts or two intentions are both seriously immoral, both above the threshold of the seriously immoral, and yet that one is, *in the nature of the act or state*, worse than the other. It is impermissible to kill one's spouse even if he or she has been quite provoking, but this admission is compatible with regarding Hitler's genocide as a greater crime in terms of what is done.[32]

With regard to 2(*b*), we may separate the deeds of forming the intention and acting upon it or the phenomena of intending and acting, but the two are profoundly linked conceptually and dynamically. Given that the proposed action is morally monstrous, we cannot treat the agent who sets himself to do it as a simple benefactor just because he also hopes for the autonomous effects that supposedly flow from such an orientation. In pursuing these effects the nuclear deterrer becomes, as Anthony Kenny has put it, a person with "murder in his heart."[33] We should be wary of trading off character and all that its destruction involves against the hoped-for benefits of the nuclear cold war. Lewis and Kavka have sought to deal with the so-called paradoxes of deterrence by arguing that it may be rational to form an intention that it would be irrational to execute and, by parity, morally right to form an intention that it would be morally wrong to fulfill.[34] I will not discuss the rationality debate (though I have views on it) but will focus instead on the parallel puzzle for morality. This involves, as Kavka and Lewis both see, judgments not only about actions and outcomes but also about agents and their character.

The agent who sets himself to do an act which he knows to be seriously immoral is contaminated by his orientation to evil, by his plans and thoughts and schemes as they are directed onto the malevolent act. He becomes someone who will do such acts if needs be. Both objections 2(*b*) and 2(*c*) miss the mark partly because they ignore or make light of the question of contamination or corruption and partly because they tend to exaggerate the degree to which the probability link between intention and outcome is weakened in the case of deterrence. On the latter point, the deterrent intention clearly does not make its own implementation impossible. If that were so and known to be so, then the intention could not be formed – you cannot intend to do what you know cannot be done. In fact the forming of the conditional deterrent intention, though it is indeed supposed to make our recourse to nuclear war a remote eventuality, does make it more likely than certain other options such as unilateral nuclear disarmament. Certainly this is true of *our* recourse, though supporters of deterrence will argue that the crucial outcome is not what we do but the occurrence of nuclear war whoever wages it. That is of course an important consideration, though it does not make the doing of murder insignificant. Nor is it easy to show that our willingness to use nuclear weapons makes nuclear war less likely than our renouncing such readiness. If "we" are the United States, then our withdrawal from the nuclear race may have several political drawbacks, but the increase in the likelihood of nuclear war in the foreseeable future is not, I think, one of them.

Were the United States and the Soviet Union the only contestants, then this would scarcely need arguing; but the arms race now has many runners, and it is hard to be sure of their reactions to such a turn of events. Supporters of deterrence try to turn this uncertainty to their advantage by arguing that various situations would arise to make the world even more dangerous from the point of view of nuclear war. One is an

Asian nuclear alliance between Japan and China, another an Anglo-French nuclear umbrella over Europe or a Franco-German nuclear force, and so on. I cannot deny that these speculations evoke possibilities, but they are nonetheless basically speculative and face massive obstacles on the road to more pertinent probability. As things stand, the prospect that Japan and China will forge such an alliance, given their historical enmities and ideological differences, is little short of fantastic. In the case of Franco-German or Franco-British or Anglo-German cooperation there is not only historical mistrust and enmity to overcome but present firm strategic policy. The French, in particular, have adamantly refused, in the name of "autonomy," to engage in any form of nuclear cooperation with their European neighbors or with the United States; and the British are hardly likely to welcome an expanded nuclear role, especially in partnership with the Germans. In short, we have no real reason to believe that U.S. nuclear renunciation would increase the likelihood of other powers resorting to such warfare, though of course they might. In addition we know that such a renunciation would have extensive effects upon the world political climate, and it is at least plausible to suppose that most of these would be beneficial. This plausibility is bolstered by the fact that throughout much of the world the United States is now viewed as a belligerent and interventionist power whose possession of nuclear weapons is a cause for anxiety rather than reassurance. One should no doubt be wary of facile optimism about these beneficial effects, but the facile pessimism of the strategic "realists" is, I think, even more dangerous. I shall return to this issue in the last section of this chapter; I discuss it here because objections 2(c) and, to some extent, 2(b) make such strong play with the supposed failure of any probability link between deterrent intention and nuclear war.

Nonetheless the immorality of such mental states as intentions is not only a matter of their increasing the probability of the occurrence of the projected outcome; it is also a matter of the contamination or corruption of the agent. This issue of corruption is not one that has received a great deal of attention from modern philosophers, but it should in debates about internalism and consequentialism. Stanley Benn has raised it in connection with the deterrent, arguing that the deterrent intention does violence to the moral natures of those who harbor it, and by extension corrupts the society that supports them.[35] To evaluate this claim we must resist the temptation to think of intentions, or related psychological phenomena, as ghostly, insubstantial "Cartesian" entities. If we think that way it will indeed seem strange that they could have moral significance. We must think of them, first, as orienting the person toward ultimate action; second, as connected with other intentions, beliefs, and desires in an overall stance toward the world, a stance that contains a more or less coherent frame of reasoning about conduct; and, third, as involving intermediate acts of planning, adjustment, and preparation for the ultimate action where it is not itself immediately to hand. Those involved in maintaining and supporting the nuclear deterrent must think it permissible (if regrettable) to hold noncombatants hostage to the good of national security, placing them under threat of death, disease, or devastation on a great scale in order to further political purposes. Moreover, they must stand ready actually to inflict such harm and damage and must presently engage in acts of preparation for such slaughter and in conditioning their own populations to accept it and its consequences.

Two recent comments on corruption, relevant to my discussion of 2(*b*) and 2(*c*), deserve some attention. The first is McMahan's argument that even if the leaders and decision makers are corrupted the corruption does not extend beyond them. He claims that only a relatively small number of people need to have the conditional intention, and for "the rest of society, it is sufficient if people simply give no thought to the policy, which is in fact what most people do."[36] The factual claim here is pretty certainly false. Very few people have the policy constantly in their thoughts, no doubt partly because it does not bear too much concentrated attention, but this is far from "giving no thought" to it. The most common reaction is to think it a good thing, to dwell on the protection it affords and on the awfulness of those whom we threaten with annihilation, and to scorn those who oppose it. It is also, very significantly, to be prepared to accept a deterioration in the conditions of healthy political existence. The nuclear cold war has seen a tremendous extension of the powers of the state in democratic societies and a surrender of rights and checks that citizens previously had against sovereign power. In the United States, for instance, no one knows exactly how the decision to launch nuclear weapons will be made, but it will have no reference to representative bodies or public opinion. Nor is it accidental that so many governmental activities in the nuclear age are shrouded in secrecy and illegality, both of which are explained and even defended in terms of the sacred cow of national security. It is true that governments have always had a predilection for the furtive and underhand, but this tendency has been given new impetus and license by the huge stakes supposedly involved in everything to do with the nuclear confrontation and any of the hostilities associated with it. In this connection one could cite countless examples, but two must suffice. There are the covert idiocies of the Reagan Administration's attempts to subvert U.S. law by funding its proxy war against the Soviets in Nicaragua with money from Iranian arms deals, and there is the Thatcher Government's fiasco over the Zircon spy satellite involving a secret police ("Special Branch") campaign against the media, especially the BBC.

Let us suppose, however, that McMahan is right to say that most people give little or no thought to whether their government is prepared for and is threatening a (conditional) massacre of the innocents. Would this not itself be a corruption of public life? We are sometimes told that most Germans in the 1930s and early 1940s gave no thought to their rulers' intentions and plans for their Jewish fellow citizens. If true, this may absolve them of direct complicity in the Nazi crimes, but, given the notorious facts of Nazi anti-Semitism and what was increasingly publicly available about their plans, it surely exhibits grave moral defects in their outlook. Government policy about nuclear weapons is overtly proclaimed in broad terms and is a matter of frequent media debate in the West. In this respect, an attitude of unconcern on our part is even more reprehensible.

The second comment is Lewis's statement that we have no use for "a simple, unified, summary judgment" on those who have corrupted themselves in this good cause. They can be (to quote Lewis) both "great patriots" and "fiends in human shape"; it is basically a question of separate judgments on separate aspects of the person at one time or even on the whole person at different times (first he is good, then he is evil).[37] It is of course true that we can judge thus, but there are reasons why we need something like a unified verdict. Lewis thinks such a judgment can be required only by a Last Judge in a Last Judgment if there is such a thing, but it is not only the Last Judge but the First Judge who needs such a perspective. The agent cannot view himself as so many aspects but needs, as a moral being, to decide on courses of action in the light of what he will be or become in so acting. He needs a sense of his own integrity, and he aims ideally at moral integration. The conscientious Nazi mentioned by Lewis[38] cannot rest content in the judgment that he is admirably conscientious in his attention to duty if he becomes aware that his conception of duty is leading him into gross immorality. One of our problems with such a character is how he could honestly fail to see the nature of what he is doing, but if he does he must surely act on the unified judgment that to behave thus is to abandon virtue. Indeed, the conscientiousness merely makes the overall character of the acts worse, as it makes the evil policy more efficient and lends to genocide a spurious air of virtue. I am inclined to think the same of the patriotic fiend, except that I rank patriotism even lower on the scale of virtue than conscientiousness. I am conscious, however, that there are those who think it can be morally right to corrupt oneself in a good cause. Such a thought is available to the defenders of deterrence. Putting it this way, however, shows how little we defuse the moral paradox of deterrence by separating the judgments we make on the formation of the intention and on its fulfilling act, since in corrupting himself the agent makes himself (and perhaps others) the sort of being who will do such fulfilling acts even though he now judges them monstrous.

Before leaving the issue of corruption, we should confront two other objections that are rather more dismissive. The first originated with McMahan and appears again in Robert E. Foelber's contribution to this book. Their argument is that the charge of corruption is question-begging.[39] To summarize McMahan: If intending to do what it is wrong to do is corrupting that is because it is wrong; it is not wrong because it is corrupting. This pithy objection seems at first blush very powerful, but on closer examination it emerges as confused. To begin with, it appears to prove far too much, since if it were valid then there would never be any specific point to a criticism of corruption, and that is surely implausible (and probably uncongenial to the objectors). What is true is that the wrongness of an intention derives from the wrongness of the act upon which it is directed. Nevertheless, the orientation to evil so involved is itself something that has effects on the agent's personality and character even if he doesn't get to do the specific act intended. Those effects are themselves action-orienting states of the person, and the actions they tend to produce are evil. This is not the place for a full analysis of the concept of corruption, but one important aspect of corruption is that the agent comes to view, as perfectly moral and acceptable, behavior which he would once have recognized, or in other contexts can still recognize, to be morally unacceptable.

An example may prove helpful. Suppose you are a parent wondering how best to educate your young child. A behavioral scientist suggests enclosing the child for a time in a controlled room where his actions and reactions can be dominated and monitored by machinery. Among other inputs the child will be prompted to do many evil actions, but these actions will never actually eventuate from his intentions and designs. (He had better not know this, or he would be unable to form the relevant intention.) The child will be prompted (the scientist says "educated") to such things as planning the torturing of its brothers and sisters, the killing of its parents, the brutal dismembering of live animals, and, of course, lying strategies for pinning the blame on others. A great deal of ingenuity will be needed to work out the implementation of these purposes, and the scientist assures you that this would be good intellectual training for your child (perhaps even better than learning Latin). No actual harm is done to others by the child's intentions, plans, and strategies or even by what he says, since we hearers can see through his lies.

The scientist is surprised when (as I hope) you reject his scheme with indignation. You point out that the child would be corrupted by such an experience, but the scientist replies by asking for some independent account of what is *wrong* with the child's intentions and state of mind given that they produce no harm in "the world." The scientist, like Mc-Mahan and Foelber, is a kind of reductionist about states like corruption or depravity; in his tough, pragmatic way, he does not want to be bothered with such phantom evils. But corruption is real enough, and of course we can say quite a lot about the kind of wrong it is. What is wrong with corruption is that it orients the person toward what are known, independently, to be bad actions, and in various complex ways it affects for the worse his understanding of and orientation to the world of good and bad actions. To talk about corruption is to draw attention to the multiform ways in which an agent's moral outlook and his further actions and attempts at actions are liable to dangerous distortion by some particular orientation. The concept of corruption belongs with such concepts as character and virtue, and they are part of how we cope and have coped for ages with the understanding of good and evil. The effects and connections of corruption are subtle and complex but nonetheless perfectly factual and very much related to the evil and harm that occur in the public world. The parent who objects to the scientist's proposal does not need empirical research to know that the child's state will be disastrous, and any suggestion that the experiment go ahead in order to see afterwards whether the child will behave badly outside the room would be contemptible.

The point in the nuclear context is that the orientation to what is agreed to be evil (i.e. the killing of millions of noncombatants) can itself plausibly be regarded as evil via the concept of corruption even where it is claimed to be unlikely ·– and the agent himself believes and hopes that it is unlikely – that he will have to act on the specific intention. Nor does it matter that the deterrers believe they are preserving the peace. It is, after all, characteristic of certain sorts of corruption that agents are given to justifying their behavior by appeal to the good they believe it will achieve. The KGB see themselves as defending the Revolution, just as American "dirty tricksters" are out to protect national security and South African government torturers to defeat communist subversion.

Of course, the analogy with the child in the room is not exact in all respects. In particular, the child thinks that its plans and intentions are all given immediate effect, whereas the deterrer thinks that his probably won't be. I do not deny that this is an important difference, but it does not affect the value of the illustration as a reply to the dismissive objection, particularly since the difference is, by hypothesis, one of mental outlook. Lest the example of the child be thought entirely fantastic, I would refer the reader not only to the writings of psychologists in the tradition of B. F. Skinner but more particularly to the famous experiments of Stanley Milgram. Milgram, it will be recalled, arranged for his subjects to inflict, as they thought, increasing levels of pain upon victims in another room. The "victims" were not in fact connected to the machinery that was supposedly inflicting the suffering, and Milgram was no sadist – he was interested in exploring the degree to which people are disposed to obey authority. In view of the good he was hoping to achieve by the experiments Milgram seems to have largely discounted (at the time) what he might be doing to the inner lives of the subjects.[40]

This brings us to the second dismissive objection. Admitting the effects on the child, our scientict might still claim that the possible scientific benefits to the world of going ahead outweigh what is done to the child's "heart and soul." Somewhat similarly, David Lewis, in this volume, is dismissive of the corruption argument (or something close to it) because he thinks of it as part of the merely "self-regarding" element in Just War theory and thinks we may wonder "whether some murderous hearts may not be preferable to the heart of one who cares more for the state of his own heart than he does for the lives of his countrymen." He concludes that, in any case, "other things at stake in warfare are just much more important than the state of the warrior's heart and soul."[41] This way of putting the point loads the case unfairly against the corruption point by making it sound as if "hearts and souls" had no connection with social ills and harms, whereas the point – as Lewis saw more clearly, I suspect, in his earlier paper "Devil's Bargains and the Real World" – is that the corrupted agent is likely to be a menace to others as well as a disgrace to himself. Perhaps there are things in warfare that are more important than the corruption of a single agent, but, in the first place, more than the single agent is involved since the corruption is also socially ramified and, secondly, the corruption is clear and relatively certain whereas the benefits to be achieved are mostly speculative and ambiguous. These facts underpin the traditional moral concern with character and support the view that caring about one's character just is a central way of caring about one's fellows (and not only one's countrymen).

RESPONDING TO IMMORALITY

We are now in a position to confront the interesting question of what follows from the admission that the deterrent is immoral. Even granting the success of the arguments presented against the deterrent, a critic might still urge that we cannot simply ignore the consequentialist case for the deterrent. As I noted earlier, there are frequently beneficial consequences to acting immorally and they are usually rightly ignored, but the critic wants to insist that when the stakes are high enough the consequences can make the immorality the right thing to do. This is part of what moves those who, like Lewis, think it is right for the deterrers to corrupt themselves. This way of speaking may (and, I think, should) sound strange, but it points to a genuine perplexity that is one of the things behind the recent fashion for antimorality writings by British and American philosophers. Michael Slote has spoken in this connection of "admirable immorality" and insisted that morality should not always be the supreme, overriding consideration concerning conduct.[42] Among other examples he gives that of Churchill's policy of bombing civilian targets in World War II. Michael Walzer uses (part of) the same example to argue that in circumstances of "supreme emergency" it may be necessary to override the moral prohibition on attacking noncombatants. Walzer thinks that the bombing, in its early stages, was necessary but immoral. After 1942, it was just immoral.[43] What Walzer and certain other philosophers seem to be saying is that weighty internalist considerations normally override consequentialist ones but that in certain extreme situations the consequentialist argument should prevail. We are then in the region of what some have called "moral immorality."[44] Other theorists, such as Thomas Nagel, seem to hold that in such extremities there is a kind of breakdown of the moral system so that neither type of consideration can be decisive.[45]

This family of responses needs a fuller treatment than I can here produce. I will only say that I am deeply uneasy with it both at the level of argument and at the level of moral judgment. At the level of argument its principal difficulties seem to me to reside in too vague and elastic an appeal to such categories as "supreme emergency," "disaster," and so on, too little attention to the ramifications of immorality, and too abstract and static a view of the situations in which an agent confronts such choices. This is very sketchy, but some of what I have in mind should emerge later. At the level of moral judgment, I find many of the examples given unpersuasive, partly because of a certain sentimentality in their selection. Nonetheless, I shall not carry the argument any further, but I shall assume that the judgment of grave immorality is not normally to be overridden by the prospect of good consequences and that the call to self- (and societal) corruption needs a most powerful consequentialist justification in terms of both weight and certainty of achievement if it is even to gain a hearing. Against this background, I want to turn to a response to our question that seems to me to have better credentials and draws upon a type of consideration not hitherto invoked.

This response admits in full the immorality of the conditional intention to use nuclear weapons but argues that the matter of retreating from the policy of threat has pragmatic and moral aspects itself such that temporary persistence in the policy may be the price to pay for successful withdrawal from it. There is thus room for a gap to arise between the judgment that x is seriously immoral and the decision what to do about avoiding or abandoning the doing of x. The fact that there is sometimes room for such a gap makes a point of contact with Bernard Williams's complaint that the conditional intention argument "makes it sound as though the issue might as well be whether we should bring nuclear weapons into existence. But it is absolutely central to the discussion that this is actually a world of nuclear weapons."[46] Unfortunately, he takes this to mean that the question is "how to live with them" rather than "how to get rid of them," so our positions do no more than touch briefly. Nonetheless, I suspect that his complaint gains what force it has from the existence of the gap I am interested in.

The possibility of such a gap seems to be ignored, or denied by implication, in the writings of many who have been most eloquent in arguing for the immorality of the deterrent. Commonly such critics have assumed that their position commits them to advocacy of a policy of unilateral nuclear disarmament: The deterrent is gravely immoral, so we should give it up at once whatever the costs and whatever the adversary does. Even more strongly, and at a more personal level, Michael Dummett has argued that there is an absolute obligation upon citizens not to join the armed forces of their country if it is "potentially involved in conducting nuclear warfare." His argument seems to imply also that there is an obligation on present members of such armed forces to resign.[47] Now, it may be that such powerful prescriptions can be derived from the internalist critique but not, I think, in one move since the gap to which I am drawing attention must first be crossed. This is a complex and difficult issue, and I am certain that I do not see my way as clearly as I would like here; but let us begin by noting certain pragmatic questions that arise concerning the *implementation* of the judgment that some action or policy is immoral. These are to do with various degrees of unlikelihood that the most natural and direct route to implementing the judgment of immorality will succeed. Consider, for instance, the case where the judgment is that someone else's behavior is immoral, but outright denunciation of it may be unlikely to stop it. I do not want to deny that answers to the pragmatic questions involve moral thinking; my point is merely that they involve somewhat different, and less disturbing, issues than objections to acting on a moral judgment directly which are concerned more explicitly with its morality rather than its feasibility.

I want to explore a range of such possibilities in what follows; to explore, in other words, the different types of gap between the judgment of immorality and its natural implementation. I will distinguish some categories and then deal with them in turn. In each category both pragmatic and more purely moral arguments against immediate implementation can be made, and the border between these styles of argument is not at all sharp. My concern is primarily with ongoing immorality: policies being enacted, complex activities in train, recurring patterns of behavior, and so on. This focus results naturally from the problematic embodied in discussions of deterrence, but it is also of interest just because it is so seldom adopted by moral philosophers, whose perspective on morality tends to be relatively static, atomistic, and ahistorical. As theorists, we tend to consider agents faced with highly specific choices and ask questions about whether their obligations are absolute or prima facie, or whether what would normally be wrong is here right. Should Jones lie to the murderer seeking his victim who is hiding in Jones's house? Should Smith break her promise to meet Jones in order to save a child from a burning house? (The answer "Yes" is particularly felicitous in Smith's case, since she will thereby also avoid a possibly clumsy intervention in the conversation between Jones and the murderer.) When we raise our eyes to the institutional level we tend to consider questions like what the principles of justice should be for a well-ordered society in which full compliance is commonplace. Or we ask, in our "dirty hands" tone of voice, whether a ruler should authorize a single act of torture in the hope of saving many innocent lives. I do not mean to belittle the interest of any of these questions, but concentration upon them can blind us to the ways in which moral choice must often operate in situations already enmeshed in evil so that a primary moral concern is how best to reshape the situation and change its dynamics in conformity to a moral imperative rather than how to fulfill the moral imperative *simpliciter*. Let us turn to the categories. I distinguish four in terms of different sorts of relation that might exist between agents: distance, intimacy, representation, and identity.

1. *Distance*. The matter is clearest when the judgment of serious immorality is made by one agent A upon policies, acts, or states of mind of another agent or group of agents B. It is plausible to suppose that A's negative judgment commits him to some hostile attitude to B's policies etc., but many factors may reasonably prevent his opposition even from gaining public expression, still less from becoming a campaign of confrontation. B's immorality may be none of A's business; A may have other priorities that make it reasonable for him to ignore the matter; the expression of his opposition may be futile or, worse, counterproductive. The first two considerations are predominantly moral, the third is pragmatic, though it is important and is guided by a moral perspective. It seems clear that someone's immorality, even when it is serious, may be none of your business either in the weak sense that intervention is not morally obligatory or even in the strong sense that it is morally forbidden. There is such a

thing as a moral busybody, and we object to him not only because his obsessive interest in other people's misdeeds leads him to ignore his own and to intervene in situations that he mistakenly judges to be immoral, but also because, hypocrisy and misjudgment aside, there seems to be a moral case for nonintervention in the affairs of others even where they involve immorality. The exact lineaments of this case are beyond our concern here, but it surely rests in part upon the value of zones of freedom for the conduct of one's life – a value that puts limits not only on legal but, to some extent, on moral interference. The liberty to conduct my own life puts restrictions upon how much correcting of others I can be morally obliged to do, and this reinforces the fact that the autonomy of others deserves some respect.

Take the case of the people down the road who regularly beat their children in the spirit of "spare the rod." One may regard this with strong moral disapproval but find that morally consistent with nonintervention even of a verbal kind. The matter is different where the children are in danger of, or are now sustaining, severe physical damage, since there intervention may well be necessary. Where such danger is not at issue we may nonetheless judge that the less tangible effects are morally alarming but still think it wrong to intervene even with (unsolicited) advice. Part of our reluctance may be pragmatic; where the behavior is culturally entrenched, moral remonstration is unlikely to be effective and may be counterproductive. Some will argue that this is all there is to our reluctance, but I think there is a good case for the stronger conclusion. It would be interesting to consider our reactions to an adult version of the case where the husband physically chastised his wife, in line with cultural traditions, or in which she was so subservient to his wishes as to make us fear for her moral autonomy, growth, and wellbeing. But even if the apparently moral arguments for nonintervention turned out upon examination to be pragmatic in complex ways, this would provide a strong indirectly moral constraint upon implementing our original moral judgment by direct action. The general point is that action designed to prevent another's persistence in immorality may lead to its persistence and even the perpetration of other and greater immoralities. This is clear in the present category of cases – it is one of the issues raised in debates about the best way for outsiders to deal with the immorality of apartheid – but it seems to apply in the other categories as well.

2. *Intimacy.* Suppose A's judgment of B's policies etc. is made in a context where there is a relation of intimacy between them – friendship, close familial ties, love. Here the idea that B's behavior is none of A's business or that A's other priorities allow him to ignore it gets much less purchase, if any, but the problem of *effective* action remains. It may be no easy thing to decide on the best way to act to help in B's reformation and to protect others from him, but it is at least possible that the best policy involves making no immediate protest at his actions and even allowing them to continue for a time by avoiding interventions that could stop them but have other disadvantages, such as making it likely that they will shortly be resumed. Many complex psychological factors that enter into relations of intimacy may indeed militate against B's receiving moral criticism from A in an appropriate way. We sometimes react better to such criticism or advice when it comes from a total stranger.

3. *Representation.* An important class of cases for our present concerns is that in which B is somehow representing A and his immoral actions are done, in some sense, on A's behalf. My rather vague qualifications are necessary here if the category is to include both the strong cases of representation, such as A's explicitly authorizing B to act on his behalf in some matter, and the weaker cases where B is the government of A's country or where B is acting for some institution or group to which A owes loyalty. Here A may well feel a kind of implication in B's wrongdoing even though he is not himself doing wrong. It is hard for him to claim, *simpliciter*, that it is none of his business or to ignore the matter altogether. It is a rather puzzling matter why this should be so in cases where one has had no direct responsibility for what the institution or government has done. Yet such implication

can have quite a long reach, as for instance when one feels a twinge of shame or annoyance at something one's old school has done or at a revelation about one's ancestors' behavior. What is involved here are issues of identification, and these are brought into play by the weaker notions of representation. Yet once again the question of how best to deal with the situation is a real one not settled by the judgment of immorality alone.

Let us concentrate on the government–citizen relation. Denunciation of one's government's immoral behavior will naturally flow from the judgment that it is immoral and will normally be the way to dissociate oneself from implication in it, but, on some given occasion it may be politically and morally less effective than some other response that may seem to involve a less full-blooded rejection of the policy as immoral. The policy of nuclear deterrence is very much to the point here. The natural political response of the citizen who judges such a policy to be seriously immoral is advocacy of unilateral disarmament. Of course he also judges the enemy's policy to be immoral and advocates their abandonment of the weapons too, so, like all sane unilateralists, he favors what we might call general unilateralism. This is not quite the same as advocating multilateralism, however, since this, as usually understood, involves the idea that you will give up your nuclear arsenal only if the other side(s) will reciprocate, and those who advocate this view seem not to recognize the intrinsic immorality of deterrence. But if unilateralism is the natural response it is not inevitably dictated by a recognition of the immorality of deterrence.

The citizen who believes that there is no possibility of his government's adopting unilateral nuclear disarmament in the near future may advocate instead policies that still embody the threatening attitude he objects to but at least offer more hope that the intention will not be put into effect, and can be seen as steps on the way to eventual abandonment of the deterrent. McMahan objects to both the U.S. Catholic bishops' and Barrie Paskins' advocacy of measures short of unilateralism on the grounds that such advocacy shows that they can't really believe that the conditional intention is seriously immoral, but his objection misses the point being made here.[48] The bishops' statement is not entirely clear on this matter, but the "strictly conditioned moral acceptance of nuclear deterrence"[49] that they give is at least based upon the proviso that steps be taken to move away from deterrence to nuclear disarmament and so may fit the pattern of reasoning I have been trying to explore. Paskins is quite explicitly operating in this way when he argues for "deep unilateral cuts in the West's deterrent" as a step on the road to eventual abandonment of it.[50]

I have discussed this issue as if the only problem for the citizen were the *unfeasibility* of a unilateralist proposal, but similar considerations apply if we suppose immediate unilateral disarmament to be possible but probably much more *harmful* than a policy that temporarily tolerates the deterrent while moving steadily toward its abolition. Here, what the citizen should urge upon his government may parallel what a friend should advise a man in the grip of some dangerous and immoral habit. Perhaps the best advice is to make a sharp and complete break, but perhaps, in certain cases, a policy of gradual withdrawal is the better recommendation – think of certain cases of drug addiction, for example. For a non-nuclear political example we might think of the choice between advocating an immediate end to a well-entrenched social immorality such as slavery and seeking more gradual disentanglement on both practical and moral grounds – one of these latter being that the government's policy has brought about a situation in which slaves could not cope with immediate freedom.[51]

In the nuclear case, it is often said that for one nation to disarm nuclearly is to invite total devastation from its enemy, which retains such weapons. If this were true it would be exactly the sort of consequence that calls for extrication strategies. It must be insisted that maintenance of the deterrent involves persistence in corrupt and dangerous practices. Nonetheless, its immediate abandonment by a government that is responsible both for the safety of its people and for the immoral practices by which that safety has (let us suppose) so far been secured would involve such moral costs as to make it imperative to seek less costly ways to abandon the practices. This is especially so since many of the costs are likely to be borne by innocent people. Of course, the hypothesis of total nakedness before probable nuclear attack is hardly a compelling account of our predicament in the real world; it is, I suspect, a sign of the corruption of political sensibilities that it surfaces so often in popular debates about deterrence. There would nevertheless be moral costs to immediate one-sided abandonment of the deterrent and calculations of how to retreat in good order from the policy of immoral threat must look to the minimizing of such costs. I shall return to these questions in discussing the next category of cases.

THE MOST DIFFICULT CATEGORY

4. *Identity.* Finally there is the most difficult category of all, that in which B is identical with A. Is there really room here for the prudent disentanglement from evil that we analyzed in the other three categories? It is important to face this question since we can raise it directly, in the nuclear case, as an issue for the rulers and their subordinates. No doubt category 3 is the most pertinent to the decision making of ordinary citizens, but category 4 is applicable to those who are actually operating the policy of deterrence. And, as suggested above, the advice one gives an agent must take account of moral costs as well as political possibilities. Even here I would argue that prudent disentanglement gets some grip.

McMahan, who fails to distinguish categories 3 and 4 (or any of the others) in his criticisms of the bishops and Paskins, claims that there are some immoral policies from which it would be absurd to talk of gradually extricating ourselves, and he instances "the nuclear incineration of cities" and "nuclear genocide."[52] This may, of course, be true, but its truth arises partly from the fact that there seems to be no room for a category 4 question like "What is the best way to

202

disentangle ourselves from this policy?" If the question makes any sense, then the obvious answer to it is "Stop the bombing now." That is, don't disentangle, just stop. We are forced to this conclusion because the two policies are such that if either is being put into effect by people who realize the moral enormity of what they are doing, then there can be no better moral scenario than ceasing at once. Of course, as a category 3 question the matter may not be so straightforward. Imagine that you were in a position to offer what was likely to be effective advice to President Truman in the final weeks of World War II. You know, let us suppose, that nothing you say can prevent the president from using an atomic bomb on a population center, but you can affect the decision on how many cities are bombed and which ones. If you urged the bombing only of Hiroshima, you would be recommending a gross immorality, but arguably you would be doing the best you could and effecting a partial disentanglement of American policy from evil. But if this is true, it is so because you do not have it in your power to persuade the president to do what he ought.

The principal interest of category 4 cases lies in the fact that this constraint normally does not obtain. Truman may have suffered certain disadvantages from a decision not to use atomic weapons, but the decision was within his power. Nonetheless, gradual disentanglement from seriously immoral policies does seem morally licit for at least some types of category 4 cases. Part of the reason for this is that even where A is identical with B there can be, in the public arena at least, problems of feasibility. The ruler may know that his decision to discontinue x at once will certainly be blocked by a hostile house of review, whereas gradual moves away from the policy will be accepted. I want, however, to concentrate on moral objections to immediate cessation of immoral conduct.

Paskins gives the example of a man engaged in an immoral, adulterous affair with a woman who is "suicidally dependent on the relationship"[53] and argues that it would be wrong to end it abruptly. It may be even more pertinent to

C. A. J. Coady

the nuclear issue to consider cases in which the agent B (here identical with A) inherits an immoral situation that is already replete with institutional ramifications that themselves have moral significance. Suppose B inherits his father's business and is carrying it on to the best of his ability when he discovers that part of the business is involved with the promotion of serious immorality – prostitution, heroin dealing, or protection rackets. The business is a closely interlocking whole, so simply calling an immediate halt to the criminal operations would wreck the business, thus putting thousands of innocent people out of work and creating economic and social disruption of a grave kind. This must be done if there is no other way to end the immoral involvement, but if there is a possible course of more gradual disengagement, which nonetheless offers real hope for a speedy but less traumatic end to the evil, then it is, I think, arguable that B should take it.

It is important that these two examples are both cases in which the agent is implicated in an evil brought about either by himself or by persons for whom he somehow must take responsibility. This is what makes them cases of extrication or disentanglement. In the first and simpler case, he cannot just decide to stop without thereby taking responsibility for some continuing consequences of the policies he had immorally set in train, including certain consequences of immediate withdrawal from the evil course of action. The consequences in question are plausibly viewed as at least partly *his* immoral acts, and so his previous behavior has put him in a position whereby, whatever he does, he will be acting immorally – at any rate, for a time. Here he should choose the course that will have him acting less badly, but this choice situation is clearly different from the characteristic dilemma posed for internalists by utilitarian and other critics, where the choice is between acting immorally or allowing great evils to flow from someone else's action for which one has no responsibility but that contrived by the choice situation itself. Bernard Williams's well-known example of the tourist Jim faced with killing one Indian at the behest of the corrupt police chief who will otherwise kill ten Indians is such a case. Internalists are, I think, rightly suspicious of "lesser evil" resolutions of such examples, but disentanglement cases are quite different in kind. As for the second type of case, matters are similar though more complex just because the conditions for inheriting moral responsibility or otherwise having it devolve upon one are none too clear. This is not the place to investigate such conditions, but it is apparent that such situations exist.

A different type of case again is that of restitution.[54] It is commonly held that someone who has wronged another has some duty to remedy the wrong. It may be no simple matter to determine what a just remedy or restitution amounts to, especially when, as is frequently the case, the wrong does not translate readily into monetary terms. Where the wrong is a case of theft, matters are a bit simpler. To take such a case: Millicent stole money from Clair years ago and has now seen the error of her ways. She stole the money by altering certain documents, so that Clair never realized it was hers. Millicent put the money into a business that flourished but has now taken a somewhat precarious turn. Clair is hard up but not destitute. Millicent reckons she should give Clair $50,000 to make full financial reparation, but that is just the sum she needs to put the business back on its feet, and there are a number of innocent workers dependent on Millicent's business who had nothing to do with the original crime. Add, if you like, that Millicent's business is serving noble ends which no other local entrepreneur is liable to be interested in promoting – she is providing much-needed physiotherapy equipment for handicapped veterans. Millicent is surely right to try to rescue the business and postpone full restitution even though she thereby persists in the immoral use of Clair's money. She is making the best of the bad lot she has created, but her course of action is still to be governed by the judgment that restitution is a matter of some urgency. This may lead her, for instance, to send $5,000 anonymously at once to Clair even at some risk to her efforts to keep the business afloat, but in any case it will not allow her to keep the money indefinitely even if there is always some good use to which it can be put and some harms it can prevent.

I allow such a possibility as category 4 envisages with some misgivings. One source of these misgivings is the fact that a spurious appeal to considerations or prudent disengagement can always arise as a temptation to continue in immorality, and it is a temptation to which those in power are particularly prone. Another is that it may appear to blur the distinction between my position and that "family of responses" mentioned earlier. For myself and for them there will be cases in which an agent has good reason to persist in serious immorality. Nonetheless an important difference remains, since it is essential to my view, though not to theirs, that such persistence can be allowed only as a temporary measure designed to extricate the agent from the immoral situation, and then only when alternative ways of disengaging are either unavailable or morally disastrous. For them no such stringent provisos are required. To cite a favorite example, owed originally to Bernard Williams, Gauguin (or a romanticized version of him) exhibits "admirable immorality" (or whatever) in treating his family and friends cruelly and irresponsibly in order to follow the promptings of his artistic vision. There is no suggestion, however, by Slote, Stocker, or Walzer that such figures (Churchill *qua* terror bomber is another) must be working their way out of the immoral stance they have temporarily adopted. Extrication, by contrast, may involve some persistence in evil, but not only is this temporary, it is governed by the understanding of immorality and the orientation *away* from it. The agent's orientation to the evil he does is thus different from that of someone who chooses evil (reluctantly, perhaps) as an enduring means toward some good.

My position is then very different, but it clearly needs more elaboration and refinement than I can give it here. One urgent question is what I say to someone who concedes the existence of an area for extrication morality but insists nonetheless that some immoral situations are inextricable: not in the sense that the agent lacks the power to disengage (as he might be unable to make restitution because the victim and all his relatives are dead), but in the sense that it would be wrong to do so. All too briefly, let me say three things. First, the existence of such situations would not mean that others amenable to prudent disengagement were lacking in interest or importance, especially in view of their previous theoretical neglect. Second, it may be that even if inextricability situations are possible the moral agent should not think of his own predicaments in terms of them. The moral life is part of the practical life and so has essential reference to action, challenge, and problem solving. Having it in mind that there may be no way out of one's moral predicament is liable to blunt imagination and resource. There are parallels here with the sportsman who can win only if he doesn't entertain the truth that he is likely to lose. Third, a full answer would require the solution of problems about the degree of coherence to which a moral outlook can or should aspire and the role, if any, of absolute constraints in it. This suggests that if there is room for the inextricably immoral situation it will be at the tragic limit of moral consciousness rather than at its center. Consequently the envisaged possibility should provide no prop for complacency, even grim complacency, about our nuclear predicament.

From a different direction it might be objected that my view of extrication concedes too much to consequentialism. The harmful consequences of the agent's abandoning immoral behavior should not count in her decision no matter how sorry she may feel about them: The choice to act on the judgment of serious immorality simply is the choice to stop at once, and an internalist stance should have no truck with consequences. But it must be said against this that an internalist cannot so simply dismiss a concern for consequences in the case where they are consequences of the agent's evil acts or intentions. The internalist stance itself seems to dictate that there is an asymmetry between moral responsibility for the harmful consequences of bad and of good actions. You may plausibly disavow moral responsibility for the harms consequent upon refusal to do some disgraceful act where another is threatening to do something dreadful if you don't comply. By contrast, an agent's original commitment to some evil will often carry responsibility for many of the harmful consequences of the evil and of perseverance in it. My claim is that such responsibility extends even to some of the harmful consequences of ceasing the bad actions. After all, it is the agent's evil will, not just the vagaries of life and history, that has brought about the situation in which acting to abandon evil will harm innocent people. (More generally, the fact that internalism and consequentialism stand opposed as theories doesn't mean that an internalist stance requires no attention to consequences of any sort. How could it? A concern for the nature of actions must involve an interest in tracts of behavior exhibiting certain characteristic causal relations.)

Can anything else be said at this level of generality about the morality of extrication? Not, I suspect, very much. Extrication lies within the domain of that most concrete of virtues, prudence, and generalized comments on its features are difficult to give and are liable to mislead. Nonetheless I will try for a little more clarification. Since the governing idea is prudent disengagement from immorality, the option of just ceasing the wrongdoing must remain an option, and this applies in both categories 2 and 3 for the question of advocacy and advice, as well as in category 4 for that of implementation. This implies that where one advocates a policy of extrication one must remain sensitive to the other party's (say, the government's) failure to respond or to respond with sufficient seriousness. If you are getting nowhere with such advocacy this will suggest that you may actually be better off, even from the point of view of feasibility, in advocating more immediate and drastic solutions. Where one implements the first step in a policy of extrication, one must monitor the effects of that step with a view to doing more or moving in another direction or, if progress is blocked, simply abandoning the wrongdoing. Impatience must be avoided, but so must complacency.

Another point is that prudent disengagement may apply more to some sorts of immorality than to others. I suggested earlier that we cannot make much sense of a policy of extrication in connection, say, with an action such as the nuclear bombardment of cities – not, at any rate, if it is treated as a category 4 question. There has to be something in the situation that gives plausibility to talk of disengaging from wrongdoing with a minimum of harm and opens up several possible routes for discussion. It may be that projects aimed at the production of some evil that is itself still at a distance are more amenable to this than actual ongoing performances of great wrongs.[55] The Millicent case is not, however, of this kind, nor is the example of an inherited business (nor are many of the category 3 cases, but I am here principally considering category 4 problems where mere lack of feasibility is not usually the problem). Nonetheless, they may present something similar in reverse. The principal damage or the major wrong has (we may suppose) already been done, and the restitution or reform process concerns an attempt now to remedy and restore from a context where other wrongs could result depending upon the methods we choose.

We might also wonder whether extrication tactics could ever require that we do a greater wrong on the way to most effectively getting out of our present mess.[56] This would, I think, be merely self-defeating. The driving force behind extrication is precisely the recognition of the grave immorality of what we are engaged in; it can hardly be a dictate of morality that we engage in an even greater wrong in order to avoid continuing with the first. Something might turn on how the wrongs and their gravity were characterized: An extrication course might *appear* to involve a greater wrong, but I do not think it can actually do so. I suspect that the worry raised here is best seen as another way of posing the inextricability issue discussed earlier.

One final clarification. I do not mean to suggest with this talk of extrication that we must be continually on the lookout for an opportunity to temporize with evil. Clean breaks are often the best thing to advise and the best thing to make. It cannot be denied that people are often seduced into an enduring and deadening complicity with evil by hopes of extri-

C. A. J. Coady

cation or amelioration. Sometimes fundamentally good men continue to serve evil political regimes – as judges in corrupted legal systems, for instance – when they would do better to oppose the regime in exile, or even just resign and return to private life. The public renunciation of evil has a value that must not be neglected. Nonetheless, sometimes the course of gradual extrication is to be preferred, and it is not possible to decide in the abstract on the circumstances or conditions required for this preference to operate. This is because so much depends on the concrete situation, on the real possibilities for change, on the resources of the individual.

In any case, my position allows that someone might judge that nuclear deterrence is seriously immoral but argue for a political policy short of full-scale unilateralism as long as this could be realistically viewed, in the light of plausible answers to certain empirical questions,[57] as a genuine step toward abandoning nuclear deterrence. Such a step involves acknowledging that the idea of immediate unilateral nuclear disarmament has severe conceptual and pragmatic defects. It has often been remarked that the knowledge and technology that lie behind the nuclear arsenals cannot be abolished, so that the possibility of relatively rapid nuclear rearmament will survive the demise of present weapons. This is a problem for multilateral disarmament as well. There are also the moral and political costs that a self-disarmed nation must face. I have claimed that some of the starker fears here are wildly unrealistic, but even at lower levels of apprehensiveness it is hard to be confident about the plausibility of various scenarios. If only one of the nuclear powers disarms (my use of "disarm" here always refers merely to nuclear disarming), then there must remain some problems about how the remaining powers will behave. If all the present nuclear powers disarm, then what is to prevent the emergence of new nuclear powers who will look to our past malicious practice rather than our present good example? What is to prevent terrorist groups from holding nations hostage to nuclear blackmail?

It can rightly be replied that some of these prospects already exist in some form or another, even without any moves to nuclear disarmament. The superpowers' possession of nuclear weapons gives them no immunity against the terrorist danger, since there is no sane nuclear targeting policy they could deploy to deter such an attack. The Middle Eastern hostage crises show the impotence of massive firepower in dealing with terrorist tactics, and nuclear weapons would be equally ineffective in dealing with the possibility of terrorists smuggling small nuclear weapons into a superpower's territory. Similarly, there are already nonnuclear powers that confront the rest of the nuclear world in something like the way a newly disarmed power would have to, and with the cry of "nonproliferation" the rest of us are urging them to stay that way. Switzerland, Sweden, Austria, Finland, Yugoslavia, and Egypt are just some of the nonnuclear powers without nuclear alliances or bases, and to these we could add nonnuclear powers that are loosely allied with nuclear powers and for whom those connections are dubiously advantageous, such as Australia, New Zealand, Indonesia, Norway, and Cuba. Their present plight is hardly catastrophic. Similarly again, there are already problems posed for peace by the prospect of newly emergent nuclear powers such as Pakistan, Israel, South Africa, and possibly India. The surprising, and perhaps hopeful, fact is that these powers have not yet fully "emerged" in spite of predictions stretching back a decade or so. This line of reply suggests that nonnuclear status need not be the horror often imagined, especially when we add that the disarmed power will still have great military, political, and economic strength.

Nonetheless qualms remain, and understandably so. For the fact is that there are few grounds for certainty or even probability about what the move to nonnuclear status would involve. This uncertainty is part of the reason why the governments and electorates of Western nuclear powers are so unlikely to countenance unilateral nuclear disarmament in the near future and are not even particularly enthusiastic about general nuclear disarmament. But it is not only politically impractical to think in terms of a swift transition to a nonnuclear United States or a nuclear-free world; there is also a sense in which the picture of such a transition is epistemically beyond us. So much would have to be changed, so much again would be altered by those changes, that it is almost idle to speculate about the dangers, risks, and potentialities of the disarmed condition on the basis of how things *now* are. What is urgent is that we take steps in that direction which minimize genuinely foreseeable risks and which testify to our awareness of both the immorality and the danger of deterrence. If necessary, these steps should be unilateral, though the present regime in the Kremlin – if Gorbachev's initiatives can survive internal reactionaries – may make talk of unilateralism out of date.

What first steps are most appropriate for extrication? A totally effective "Star Wars" (SDI) shield, equally available to all Cold War adversaries, might eliminate all our problems by simply eliminating nuclear deterrence, but no one, with the possible exception of Ronald Reagan, believes that either element – total effectiveness or equal availability – is anything but a fantasy for the foreseeable future. Moreover, even were the fantasy to be taken seriously there would still be strong temptations to maintain some form of nuclear deterrence in case the defenses didn't work or new technology rendered them obsolete. But fantasies aside, the best that can be said for SDI is that it offers certain prospects of damage limitation but thereby encourages nuclear warfighting and prevailing strategies. Its moral claims are best considered, therefore, in the framework of moralized versions of flexible response and counterforce. If anything, it adds to the difficulties they face by increasing the likelihood of deterrence failure, but I shall not be able to argue this here.

From among the other possibilities for extrication steps I shall briefly discuss two that are represented by contributors to this volume. One is to abandon assured destruction as a retaliatory policy and adopt "modest" counterforce objectives, and the other is to abandon all idea of counterforce and rest deterrence on a minimal assured destruction capacity. These are of course rough, polarized schemes for detailed proposals – David Lewis's ingenious discussion may stand for the first approach, and Harold Feiveson's for the second.[58] (Matters are a little more complicated than the schemes suggest since Lewis, for instance, wants the United States to "buy like a MADman and use like a NUT," which means having an assured destruction capacity and planning options but a policy of modest counterforce for use. Nor does Lewis himself advance his proposals as "first steps" in my sense.)

The first approach seems more to respect Just War criteria and the second far less, if at all, but, partly for reasons already given, I think this moral advantage is largely an illusion. I have argued that "modest" counterforce as proposed by Lewis (and *a fortiori* the ambitious counterforce of present policy) fails to respect Just War criteria because of the unacceptable levels of likely collateral damage to noncombatants. It is hard to give a decisive demonstration of this just because it is difficult to know how "modest" Lewis's mix of assured destruction capacity and finite counterforce weaponry turns out to be. He is trying to walk an honest but very delicate tightrope between counterforce weapons aimed at targets modest enough to avoid the problem of unacceptable collateral damage and an assured destruction capacity strong enough to guarantee robust deterrence. His view that present deterrence policy is not far from the ideal and his apparent readiness to accept the damage-limiting scenarios discussed earlier convince me that this sort of modesty should not beguile us. It is true that the retaliatory policy of modest counterforce is more respectful of Just War restraints than the retaliatory policy of modest assured destruction, but its moral and political dynamic is all wrong. In spite of the undoubted benefits of "existentialism," modest counterforce is liable to be destabilizing in promoting the idea of feasible nuclear warfighting, and it is therefore likely not only to generate crises but to keep some momentum going in the arms race. It is, I suppose, possible that there could be some really *very* modest counterforce policy which fully respected Just War criteria, but by itself it must at least appear a less likely deterrent, and this appearance would make it much less appealing to our leaders as a first step. The best first step for the West's extrication from the deterrent therefore lies in the direction of Feiveson's "finite deterrence," even though it still preserves the immoral threat against cities.

There is undeniably an air of paradox about this endorsement. My critique of deterrence concentrated upon the immoral intention involved, and yet my recommended extrication move still embodies that intention. Nonetheless, finite deterrence does represent a genuine moral improvement in the direction of abandoning the deterrent intention. For one thing, I have already allowed that some grave wrongs may nonetheless be worse than others and that the known degree of likelihood of an evil intention's being implemented makes a difference to its moral evaluation. The step to a massively reduced finite deterrent, such as Feiveson describes, would be a much more hopeful political sign to our adversaries (and to many of our friends), and for that reason the chances of severe crisis and hence of deterrence failure would be reduced. It has been estimated that every forty-eight hours the equivalent of the entire firepower used in the Second World War is added to the world's arsenals, which already contain over three thousand times that quantity. To a very large extent the deterrence race is a cause of superpower enmities, suspicions, and bitternesses rather than a protection against them. This is where the importance of the INF Treaty lies. In itself it is of no great moment – it is more a slight stumble in the direction of extrication than a firm step – but it opens up new possibilities, one of these being the move to finite deterrence, which has good prospects of improving further the political climate and of reducing the risk that the weapons will be used. It is regrettable that the immoral intention is still embodied in finite deterrence, but it is an improvement in the moral situation that there is much less risk of its being implemented.

In the second place, we are talking of first steps, and the move to such deep cuts as are envisaged in finite deterrence would naturally be accompanied by such associated initiatives as a ban on all nuclear testing. The Soviet Union offered this and unilaterally practiced it for over eighteen months, to a shameful lack of response by the West. This lack of response exhibits the political folly and danger behind so many Western policies, especially in the United States, where an absurdly Manichaean picture of world politics has gained the ascendancy. (That its mirror image dominates much Soviet political thinking merely adds to our problem.) A sign of the dominance of this picture is the immense popularity of such mindless pieces of political pornography as *Rambo* and *The Hunt For Red October*.[59]

In the third place, the force reductions envisaged by Feiveson's project could very naturally be accompanied by efforts to persuade the British to abandon their nuclear role altogether, efforts that could build upon the strong antinuclear sentiment within the British Labour Party and much of the electorate. It should also be joined to a determined exploration of the feasibility of limited conventional defenses of Europe as presented by Lutz Unterseher (Chapter 7 of this volume). Some defenders of nuclear deterrence rightly stress the very considerable horrors of large-scale conventional warfare, and opponents of the deterrent should not fall into the trap of glorifying anything nonnuclear. Many strategies for conventional war (not to mention chemical and biological strategies) would violate Just War criteria, particularly when they may soon be able to deploy conventional weapons that are virtually as destructive as some nuclear weapons.[60] Unterseher's proposals, and some other conventional defensive methods, do not, however, violate Just War constraints and have genuine possibilities for deterrence in the European context. They also need to be considered in the light of the recent revival of interest in conventional arms reductions in both Western and Eastern Europe, and the widespread European unease about the presence of U.S. nuclear weapons on their soil.[61]

These, then, seem to me the most hopeful paths for an extrication strategy. We have no guarantees of success, but the Reykjavik conference, although it failed at the time to produce agreements, did produce a significant shift in the possibilities available to us. The leaders of the United States and the Soviet Union came close to agreeing on drastic nuclear arms reductions previously regarded by the hardheads as the merest fantasies of "greens" and peaceniks. Much now turns upon how sympathetically Western leaders continue to respond to the new spirit abroad in Soviet politics, but the INF Treaty is at least a hopeful sign. The destruction of any nuclear weapons gives a glimmer of what transformations are possible, and when our first real steps toward nuclear disengagement have been taken it will be time enough to examine the next extrication steps. Such examination must be guided by the judgment that finite deterrence is still gravely immoral inasmuch as it embodies an immoral intention or some related commitment to evil. Nonetheless, we will have a better picture of what needs to be done and of what really are the moral risks and possibilities attending our next moves. Anthony Kenny has argued for an extreme version of existential deterrence in which, somewhat in the spirit of finite deterrence, the West keeps only its SLBMs but declares that the weapons will never be used, come what may, and moreover trains its military personnel never to respond to orders to launch.[62] Kenny seems to see the retention of an SLBM force as basically a bargaining counter on the way to total nuclear disarmament, but he thinks that the residual force would remain an effective deterrent despite the renunciation of use because the Soviets would be too cautious to put our renunciatory policy to the test. Viewed from our present situation this may well seem fantastic, but in a relatively denuclearized world it may point the way toward further extrication. From our vantage point now, we really don't know and can't say. What we do know is that an extricative move to finite deterrence is certainly no worse morally than sticking to present policies, which also embody the immoral intention and have many more disadvantages.[63]

NOTES

1. Paul Ramsey, *The Just War: Force and Political Responsibility* (New York: Scribner, 1968), p. 171. Ramsey's comparison has been criticized by Michael Walzer in *Just and Unjust Wars: A Moral Argument with Historical Illustrations*, (New York: Basic, 1977), pp. 270–71, and by Bernard Williams in "Morality, Scepticism and the Nuclear Arms Race," in Nigel Blake and Kay Pole, ed., *Objections to Nuclear Defence: Philosophers on Deterrence*, (London: Routledge & Kegan Paul, 1984), pp. 105–6. Williams endorses Walzer's argument that the analogy breaks down because the babies' lives are considerably disrupted by the basket arrangement, whereas the enemy citizens are not affected at all in their day-to-day existence by the nuclear threat hanging over them. Although I make no direct use of Ramsey's analogy, I think that this line of criticism leaves it largely unscathed. It would still be a gross mistreatment of the babies if they were strapped in cozy baskets and enjoyed being where they were. In any case, it is simply false that the role of nuclear hostage "makes no difference to the citizens at all" (Williams, p. 106). Many people (no doubt less complacent than those Walzer and Williams have in mind) are made very anxious by the position they find themselves in, as is evident in the antinuclear protest movement and in the resistance that such countries as New Zealand show to being made targets.

2. The example has been turned by the science fiction writer Ursula LeGuin into a short story entitled "The Ones Who Walk Away from Omelas," in vol. II of *The Wind's Twelve Quarters* (New York: Harper and Row, 1975). The example comes from James's essay "The Moral Philosopher and the Moral Life," in William James, *The Will to Believe* (New York: Longmans, Green, 1897), p. 188.

3. It is more common to talk here of "deontologist"; but not only is this ugly, it tends to have theoretical implications that I want to avoid. I choose the expression "internalist" to indicate both that we are narrowing focus to deal with the kind of act performed, rather than with its possibly remote outcomes, and that this interest is inseparable from a concern with the moral life of the agent.

My references to these issues in the text are unpardonably sketchy, or at least would be if my principal concern here were with foundational issues in the theory of morality. Fortunately, perhaps, it is not. I am primarily interested in providing a background and framework for what follows in the hope that they will have at least some prima facie plausibility for the reader. Hence I feel at liberty to set aside important questions such as just how deep the distinction between consequentialist and internalist elements in morality really goes. Act utilitarians see the distinction as relatively superficial and tend to be dismissive of internalist thinking. Rule and other indirect utilitarians are best seen as trying to show that at the very deepest level of moral thinking the internalist considerations are vindicated by an appeal to consequentialist argument. Some consequentialists argue that the best outcomes will be promoted if the common herd, at any rate, do not seek to maximize good outcomes but rigorously observe the common moral rules and constraints. Exceptions are usually made for the theorist himself and a few gifted colleagues, but one can imagine a quite general argument of this kind without such disfiguring elitism. A theorist who views the internal aspects as irreducible will probably remain unimpressed by the advocates either of dismissal or of deep reduction, and tensions of varying kinds remain between him and them. To acknowledge this I sometimes contrast internalists and consequentialists in what follows, but it is often enough for my purpose that the practice of morality forces some such distinction upon us whatever its final philosophical import be.

4. The consequentialist pros and cons are discussed in Anthony Kenny, "Better Dead than Red", in Blake and Pole, *Objections to Nuclear Defence,* pp. 12–27, and also in Douglas Lackey, "Missiles and Morals: A Utilitarian Look at Nuclear Deterrence," *Philosophy and Public Affairs* 11 (1982), 189–231, plus comments by Russell Hardin, "Unilateral versus Mutual Disarmament," and Gregory Kavka, "Doubts About Unilateral Nuclear Disarmament," and a reply by Lackey, "Disarmament Revisited," all in *Philosophy and Public Affairs* 12 (1983).

5. See also Walzer, *Just and Unjust Wars;* Richard Wasserstrom, "War, Nuclear War and Nuclear Deterrence: Some Conceptual and Moral Issues," *Ethics* 95, no. 3 (April 1985), 424–44; rpt. in Russell Hardin et al., *Nuclear Deterrence: Ethics and Strategy* (Chicago: University of Chicago Press, 1985), pp. 15–

35; Kenny, "Better Dead than Red," and *The Logic of Deterrence* (London: Waterstone, 1985; Chicago: University of Chicago Press, 1985); also Michael Dummett, "Nuclear Warfare," in Blake and Pole, *Objections to Nuclear Defence,* pp. 28–40.

6. Whether they have appropriate theoretical underpinnings is a matter of debate, but some such distinctions seem required by any model of the Just War that seeks to put moral constraints upon the waging of war. Difficulties arise not only for determining worrying borderline cases but for giving principled accounts that display the moral significance of the distinctions. For some discussion of the combatant/noncombatant distinction, see G. E. M. Anscombe, "War and Murder," in Richard Wasserstrom, ed., *War and Morality* (Belmont, Calif.: Wadsworth, 1970), pp. 42–53; Thomas Nagel, "War and Massacre," *Philosophy and Public Affairs* 1, no. 2 (1972), 123–44; Walzer, *Just and Unjust Wars;* Jeffrie G. Murphy, "The Killing of the Innocent," *The Monist* 57 (1973), 527–50; and Jenny Teichman, *Pacifism and the Just War: A Study in Applied Philosophy* (New York: Basil Blackwell, 1986). For the direct/indirect distinction, see Jonathan Bennett, "Morality and Consequences," particularly section III, in *The Tanner Lectures on Human Values,* vol. II, ed. Sterling M. McMurrin (Cambridge: Cambridge University Press, and Salt Lake City: University of Utah Press, 1981), pp 47–116; Thomas Nagel, *The View From Nowhere* (Oxford: Oxford University Press, 1986), pp. 180–85; and Gerald Dworkin, "Intention, Foreseeability and Responsibility," in Ferdinand Schoeman, ed., *Responsibility, Character, and the Emotions: New Essays in Moral Psychology* (Cambridge and New York: Cambridge University Press, 1987), pp. 338–54. These discussions are only a small sample of the wide literature on these topics.

7. Both quotations are cited by Desmond Ball, "Towards a Critique of Nuclear Targeting," in Desmond Ball and Jeffrey Richelson, ed., *Strategic Nuclear Targeting* (Ithaca and London: Cornell University Press, 1986), p. 27.

8. As Jeffrey Richelson has put it, what we now have is "an increased emphasis on the military and political targeting and the requirement of a capability for conducting a prolonged nuclear exchange," but "urban–industrial targeting remains a possibility – at least as a 'final' option when war has escalated to spasm level." Jeffrey Richelson, "Population Target-

219

ing and US Strategic Doctrine," in Ball and Richelson, *Strategic Nuclear Targeting*, p. 234.

9. This was actually not McNamara's first statement of the shift, but it was the one that had the most impact. Its effect on European governments is described by Ball in "The Development of the SIOP, 1960–1983," in Ball and Richelson, *Strategic Nuclear Targeting*, pp. 67–68. As Ball also points out in his introduction to that volume, it is likely that, in the event of an outbreak of nuclear hostilities in Europe, "British and French nuclear forces would be employed against Soviet urban–industrial centers (including Moscow) before U.S. capabilities for escalation control could be exercised" (p. 20). This point is pertinent to my discussion below of the likelihood of escalation for limited nuclear war scenarios.

10. For an excellent account of the "area bombing" policies of World War II, see Barrie Paskins and Michael Dockrill, *The Ethics of War* (Minneapolis: University of Minnesota Press, 1979), ch. 1.

11. These issues are discussed by Richelson, "Population Targeting and US Strategic Doctrine," and he gives (pp. 241–42) the quotation from an official Joint Committee on Defense Production report.

12. Fuller information about this episode has recently become available in the U.K.: see *The Observer*, January 4, 1987.

13. Richelson, "Population Targeting and US Strategic Doctrine, p. 245. Richelson goes on to argue that even much less ambitious targeting projects that ostensibly avoided populations "per se" would still result in massive civilian casualties.

14. Leon Sloss, "The Case for Deploying Strategic Defenses," Chapter 8 of this volume.

15. Bundy et al., "Nuclear Weapons and the Atlantic Alliance," *Foreign Affairs* 60, no. 4 (Spring 1982), 753–68, at 757.

16. Gregory S. Kavka, "Nuclear Deterrence: Some Moral Perplexities," in Douglas MacLean, ed., *The Security Gamble: Deterrence Dilemmas in the Nuclear Age*, Maryland Studies in Public Philosophy (Totowa, N.J.: Rowman and Allanheld, 1984), pp. 131–32.

17. Ibid.

18. Kavka talks primarily, in the nuclear case, of immunity from and liability to threat of violence, but presumably the differ-

ence in status would carry over to the implementation of threats were that called for.

19. Lewis, "Finite Counterforce", Chapter 2 of this volume; see especially pp. 90–3.
20. Ibid., pp. 92–3.
21. Ibid. I think that Lewis misunderstands several aspects of Just War theory, though in some presentations they are eminently open to misunderstanding. Combatants and noncombatants are to be defined not in terms of their guilty or innocent souls but in terms of role in prosecuting an evil, even unwillingly. Nor can proportion be treated quite as Lewis treats it; but I deal more fully with this later in the text, as I do with the "self-regarding" aspects of the theory.
22. I use the figure of 14 million because that is a figure Lewis thinks within the bounds of probability. I find it hard to believe that it could be fewer, but we are heavily into guesswork here.
23. Lewis, Chapter 2 of this volume, p. 79.
24. Ibid., p. 80.
25. In a note, Lewis wonders about my earlier reference to "disproportionate side effects" and claims that it "makes no sense to ask whether some particular effect is proportionate" since "the relevant proportionality is between total harm done and total good accomplished" (Chapter 2, note 43). But in Just War theory considerations of proportionality operate at two levels. The first is concerned with very broad issues to do with whether, say, the resort to a war of national self-defense will be worthwhile, given reasonable estimates of overall likely harms and benefits. The second is concerned more explicitly with the operation of the double-effect principle or any related principle to do with the permissibility of evil side effects. Here it is natural to narrow focus and ask whether the (usually certain) evil of the particular side effects may not be too great for us legitimately to proceed with our direct purpose of achieving some military good. In either case our perspective is that of an agent facing a choice, so the proportionality is not between harm done and good accomplished but between reasonable expectations of harm and good. I do not see that it "makes no sense" to restrict our focus in the second type of case, where we are dealing with some proximate certain good directly sought and some more or less equally cer-

C. A. J. Coady

tain evil side effect. Our overall goals and hopes will have some bearing here, but, for reasons given in the text, we have to be cautious about intruding them illegitimately.

26. Lewis, Chapter 2 of this volume, note 45.
27. Of course it is a point in favor of Lewis's proposal that it involves *some* restriction of targets according to moral criteria, but (as I urge later) this has negative implications as well.
28. See Gregory Kavka, "Some Paradoxes of Deterrence," *Journal of Philosophy* 75 (June 1978), 289.
29. Kavka, "Nuclear Deterrence: Some Moral Perplexities"; David Lewis, "Devil's Bargains and the Real World," in MacLean, *The Security Gamble*, pp. 141–54; McMahan, "Deterrence and Deontology," *Ethics* 95, no. 3 (April 1985), 517–36; Bernard Williams, "Morality, Scepticism and the Nuclear Arms Race." I have discussed the views of McMahan and Williams in overlapping but somewhat different terms in "Deterrent Intentions Revisited," *Ethics* 99, no. 1 (October 1988), 98–108.
30. Lewis, "Devil's Bargains"; and McGeorge Bundy, "Existential Deterrence and Its Consequences," in MacLean, *The Security Gamble*, pp. 3–13.
31. McMahan, "Deterrence and Deontology," especially pp. 526–29; Williams, "Morality, Scepticism and the Nuclear Arms Race," p. 107, and in an earlier version, "How to Think Sceptically about the Bomb," *New Society* 62, no. 1044 (Nov. 18, 1982).
32. When we say that it is a serious wrong not only to do x but even to intend to do x, we mean that it is equally the case that both are seriously wrong but not (necessarily) that both are equal in their degree of wrongness. It seems to be a failure to notice this which confuses McMahan in "Deterrence and Deontology."
33. Kenny, *The Logic of Deterrence*, p. 56.
34. Lewis, "Devil's Bargains," pp. 142–43; Kavka, "Nuclear Deterrence; Some Moral Perplexities," especially pp. 156–57.
35. S. I. Benn, "Deterrence or Appeasement? or On Trying to be Rational About Nuclear War," *Journal of Applied Philosophy* 1 (1984), 15.
36. McMahan, "Deterrence and Deontology," p. 522.
37. Lewis, "Devil's Bargains," pp. 144–45.
38. Ibid., pp. 145–46.
39. McMahan, "Deterrence and Deontology," p. 523, and Foel-

ber, "Deterrence and the Moral Use of Nuclear Weapons, Chapter 3 of this volume.

40. Cf. Stanley Milgram, *Obedience To Authority* (London: Tavistock, 1974).
41. Lewis, Chapter 2 of this volume.
42. Michael Slote, *Goods and Virtues* (Oxford: Oxford University Press, 1983), ch. 4.
43. Walzer, *Just and Unjust Wars*, pp. 260–62 and 323–62.
44. Michael Stocker, "Plural Values, Imperfect Beings and Moral Immorality," unpublished.
45. Nagel, "War and Massacre," in *Mortal Questions* (New York: Cambridge University Press, 1979), pp. 73–74.
46. Williams, "Morality, Scepticism and the Nuclear Arms Race," p. 108.
47. Dummett, "Nuclear Warfare," p. 38.
48. McMahan, "Deterrence and Deontology," p. 530.
49. "The Challenge of Peace", the Pastoral Letter of the U.S. Catholic Bishops, *Origins, N.C. Documentary Service*, May 19, 1983, p. 18.
50. Barrie Paskins, "Deep Cuts are Morally Imperative," in Geoffrey Goodwin, ed., *Ethics and Nuclear Deterrence* (London: Croom Helm, 1982), p. 100.
51. I owe this example to Gerald Dworkin.
52. McMahan, "Deterrence and Deontology," p. 531. McMahan keeps pressing the objection as if his opponents must hold nuclear deterrence and nuclear slaughter to be "equally wrong," but we have seen that this is ambiguous: It is true but no longer damaging if it means "equally the case that both are seriously wrong" and false if it means "both are equal in their degree of wrongness."
53. Paskins, "Deep Cuts are Morally Imperative," p. 99–100.
54. I am grateful to John Langan for suggesting this sort of example.
55. I am indebted to Robert Fullinwider for a suggestion along these lines.
56. David Lewis suggested this worry in discussion.
57. The fact that some proponents of the conditional intention argument ask such questions is seen by Williams as a reason for doubting the value of their argument. Their argument, he says, "either settles the question very quickly, or it does not settle it at all." ("Morality, Scepticism and the Nuclear Arms

C. A. J. Coady

Race," p. 107). My argument is that there are two questions; it settles one decisively but does not settle the other though it gives rise to it.

58. See Chapters 2 and 6 of this volume.

59. I have given more substance to this claim about *The Hunt for Red October* in a broadcast review of the book for the Australian Broadcasting Commission's radio program *Books and Writing* in June 1986.

60. For a good discussion of some of these issues relating to conventional wars, see John Keegan, "Nuclear Shadows on Conventional Conflicts," in William V. O'Brien and John Langan, ed., *The Nuclear Dilemma and the Just War Tradition* (Lexington, Mass.: Lexington Books, 1986), pp. 199–207. Some of the other contributions in this book bear upon my topic but came to my attention too late for me to include any comments about them.

61. The fears, reactions, and apprehensions of "our European allies" are frequently cited by U.S. "hawks" and "neo-hawks" (as well as by "doves" when it suits them – as with SDI), but there is seldom much attention paid to opinion poll evidence which suggests that, for instance, surprisingly large percentages of the populations of the NATO countries do not want U.S. nuclear forces on their soil. A recent poll in *The Guardian* (February 16, 1987) showed that 66 percent of Germans, 56 percent of Britons, and 78 percent of Italians disapproved of the presence of American nuclear bases in Europe. The poll also showed that 57 percent of Germans and 79 percent of Italians wanted European nuclear weapons dismantled. Interestingly, 54 percent of Germans and 41 percent of Britons (as compared to only 19 percent of Italians and 26 percent of Frenchmen) wanted to keep military links with the United States. The same poll showed a high level of support for the U.S. alliance. These two attitudes are perfectly compatible, though such is the strength of the nuclear disease that many American politicians find their combination incomprehensible. This is clearly illustrated by the difficulty so many Americans have in understanding New Zealand's position, which is antinuclear but pro-ANZUS.

62. Kenny, *The Logic of Deterrence*, especially section III.

63. I have benefited from many criticisms and comments made upon earlier versions of this paper when they were presented to philosophy groups in Brisbane and Melbourne, and to the

Working Group on Nuclear Policy and Morality in Washington, D.C., from whose discussions the present volume arose. Here and there I have mentioned some of these debts, but there are many critics not cited who made helpful suggestions. Three other specific acknowledgments should, however, be made. Benjamin Gibbs made useful comments on an early draft. Steven Lee's impressive chapter in this volume, "Morality, the SDI, and Limited Nuclear War," persuaded me that I did not have to consider SDI at any length as a candidate for extrication. The tireless editor of this volume, Henry Shue, provided a great number of structural and material suggestions and criticisms, which always proved helpful, even where I was not fully persuaded by his argument, and which saved me from many mistakes and infelicities. Unfortunately for the reader, his encouragement to expand and elaborate has helped produce a much longer paper than I had originally planned.

Chapter 5

The necessary moral hypocrisy of the slide into mutual assured destruction

George H. Quester

The central moral paradox of nuclear deterrence theory is that peace (a morally very desirable good) is preserved by each superpower's immorally threatening the lives of millions of innocent people on the other side. The victims are people who would probably not have approved of the conventional aggression or nuclear surprise attack that began a war, but who must bear the brunt of the retaliation that turns the war into our worst nightmares of World War III. The prospective suffering of such innocents, the prospective destruction of the cities in which they live, presumably deters their leaders from ever beginning such wars in the first place, i.e. deters the prospectively guilty from becoming the guilty.

Various proposals for alternatives to deterrence can be supported by practical arguments that they might actually improve the situation of Americans or others, as we balance all the contingencies against each other. Yet such proposals for disarmament, or for antimissile systems as in Reagan's Strategic Defense Initiative, or for a reliance on conventional defenses so as to limit nuclear weapons to deterring each other and nothing more (perhaps this is where the 1987 Reagan–Gorbachev INF Treaty is to take us?) all also stem in part from the moral problems of continuing to accept Mutual Assured Destruction.

Preventing crime by punishing the loved ones of those who

would have become criminals is certainly an alien and distasteful idea for anyone accustomed to the cultural traditions of the Western world. We cannot think of anything else for which we use such a bizarre mechanism, except the preservation of peace in the years after 1945. Merely reflecting on how this nuclear deterrence system is presumed to work thus becomes distasteful and disturbing, producing a great search for alternatives among those who reject deterrence,[1] and producing a great deal of obfuscation and redefinition among those who defend deterrence as the best of available options. If these hypocritical attempts to escape facing up to the nature of deterrence were nothing more than a balm for troubled consciences they would not create such serious problems. But the attempt to conceal something so morally strange and alien from oneself could have serious consequences for policy, since a move to a more moral approach might indeed very much endanger peace.

The intent of this essay is to describe some of the ways in which Americans and others have repressed the essential nature of deterrence here, specifically how we have over and over again refused to admit that we were engaged in the countervalue punishment of civilians, rather than a more traditional counterforce disabling of an adversary's armed forces.

The history of such repression of unpleasant facts is also the history of our slide into such facts. It was not always the case that war plans were designed around the torturing of an enemy's populace. The bulk of such a shift away from the simple disablement of the enemy's military, away from "deterrence by denial" to today's "deterrence by punishment," has emerged only in the twentieth century.[2] If deterrence is bothersome, it may be because it is immoral, or it may be more because deterrence is new in its central structure, so new that morality has not had the time to adjust and accommodate to it. We shall return, toward the end of this chapter, to the ultimate moral excuse for the deterrence approach, the excuse for planning for the punishment of the innocent, as a means of keeping the potentially guilty from becoming the actually guilty – namely, that "it works."

A reasonable person with philosophical inclinations will have to address the historical frequency of warfare, and the historical patterns by which weapons that are produced soon come into use.[3] Weapons since 1945 have come into use a little less frequently, and a little less rapidly after being produced, and a fair slice of the weapons produced have not come into use at all.

It is sometimes instead argued that mutual assured destruction policies may be workable for basic deterrence, i.e. for the prevention of attacks on the United States itself, but that they are much less credible and usable for extended deterrence, i.e. for protecting such valuable allies as the NATO countries or South Korea. Would a president of the United States be willing to escalate to the use of nuclear weapons when no damage had as yet been inflicted in the cities of the United States itself? Is MAD "the right solution to the wrong problem"?

Yet the philosophical distinctions are hardly so clear here. Would it be moral, or in any way sensible, for the leaders of the United States to retaliate against Soviet population areas even after North American cities had been destroyed? We would, in such a case, clearly be murdering the innocent in order to punish the guilty; in terms of our future material national interests, moreover, we would merely be cutting off one source of possible relief supplies for American survivors of the original attack.

If such problems, and issues of credibility, get raised more often for the situation where only Western Europe or South Korea has been attacked by Soviet nuclear forces, or has been occupied in the purely conventional attack of communist forces, it is not because of the immorality of mutual assured destruction. Revenge would not make any practical sense or moral sense in any of these cases, but revenge might very well occur, in each case, for reasons that are as much instinctive as rational.

There are indeed good reasons to worry more about extended deterrence than about basic deterrence, but the difference here is much more practical, a function of our judgment of superpower national interests. Critics of the morality of mutual assured destruction will thus reject nuclear deterrence whether it is applied to shield simply the United States or also its allies; they will in fact criticize either even if "it works." Critics of attempts at extended deterrence in particular instead focus most on the risk that the necessary American responses would be viewed in Moscow as an incredible bluff, i.e. that this deterrence might not "work." If the Soviets then call a bluff that in fact was not a bluff, a needless round of warfare will have occurred.

But the alternatives for the shielding of Europe can only be a reliance on conventional defense or a reliance on Soviet good intentions, each of which is highly problematical. The idea that nuclear targeting could also somehow be configured differently for such scenarios, perhaps aiming more honestly at true counterforce targets, rather than sliding into countervalue targeting by any kind of euphemism or moral evasion, is plagued by all the risks of collateral damage that nuclear warheads are almost inevitably going to pose.

Everyone's favorite approach to defending any kind of target on this earth is simply to be able to blunt an attack on that target, i.e. to keep physical damage from being inflicted on cities, and also to keep our cities from being occupied by any force that intends to impose a very alien political, economic, and social regime on them.

If we could accomplish this without threatening the other side, without making Moscow sense that its own cities are threatened with destruction, then we could have the kind of peace that moral analysts would also approve of. Yet it is highly probable that we will be physically unable to make our cities safe against nuclear attack; and it is almost as probable that we will be unable to make Western Europe secure against physical occupation of its cities by any regime convinced that Brussels should be given the same communist system that has been installed in Warsaw.

If we care enough about sparing Brussels what has been installed in Warsaw, then the best of a bad bargain may yet be to threaten all the cities of the world with nuclear destruction, if the armored forces commanded from Moscow ever move toward Brussels.

SOME ELEMENTARY LOGICAL QUESTIONS

Analysts sometimes confuse what exactly has brought about this change in war planning. With the mobilization of the masses behind regimes after the French Revolution, mobilization on the basis of ideology or of nationalism, it might be thought that "total war" simply came to include the targeting of populations and cities as part of the totality. While this has proven a useful rationalization for the expansion of target lists, it is neither a necessary nor a sufficient condition for what has occurred. Even if the Soviet people are no more behind their rulers than the Prussians were behind Frederick the Great (a comparison I regard as apt enough), they are now exposed to mass homicide by the targeting plans of the U.S. Strategic Air Command.

What is rather necessary (and then becomes sufficient, in that each side exploits whatever serves its national interests here) is that each side shall have acquired an ability to strike at the other's rear areas, at civilian residences and the civilian economy, without having first won victories on the battlefield. One could not have punished the Prussian subjects of Frederick without first defeating the Prussian Army, without halting that army's advance. If Maria Theresa had possessed an air force equipped with nuclear weapons, however, she might have tried to deter Frederick's seizure of Silesia by the simple prospect of the destruction of the cities Frederick had begun with.

Wherever such a possibility of worsening the lives of the adversary's civilians emerges, it brings with it some prospect of influencing the behavior of the adversary government. Whether those civilians control that government, or are responsible for its policies, or even identify with its policies, will make less difference, for the important variable is the reverse: whether the government identifies with, or cares about, the suffering of its people. Redefining those civilians as soldiers, accusing them of having an active and crucial role in the enemy war effort and in the decisions for war, is useful only as a way of redefining those civilians as "military targets," thus making it morally easier to blaze away at them. But the important point is not how much they contribute to the war effort, but how much an otherwise successful war effort can be made unprofitable in the calculus of the relevant government.

For all the reasons and burdens of moral tradition we have cited, it is easy and tempting to confuse and blur counterforce and countervalue impact. The two impacts are indeed never utterly separate. To be made to suffer intense pain *may* weaken one's ability to fight; and to be disarmed *may* also cause substantial psychological pain. Yet the two impacts are surely distinct and not synonymous. To destroy an enemy missile silo is mainly to disarm him, and only incidentally to cause him pain. And to destroy one of his cultural treasures would be mainly to cause suffering, and only incidentally to weaken his ability to fight as a result of the anguish.

To make clear how separable these impacts are, it is certainly possible that what causes pain will not reduce an enemy's *ability* to fight, but might even increase it. Albert Speer discovered that he had more people available to work in munitions plants a few weeks after a heavy British air raid on a German city than a few weeks before, as delicatessens, etc., not essential to the German economy, had been destroyed, and their former owners had to find other means of employment.[4] (This is not to suggest that Speer or Hitler or other German leaders welcomed the bombings, for they did not, identifying with the German people's suffering in such raids.) Conversely, one could imagine a situation where being disarmed was actually not so painful, relieving a country of the burdens of world power, getting the contest of war over with once and for all.

Counterforce and countervalue approaches to warfare are thus indeed distinct. If we confuse them, it is only because we have not thought about the problem carefully enough; or, more probably, it is because we have been reluctant, on moral grounds, to admit that we are actually conducting a countervalue operation. We will be reluctant to admit it to neutrals, because such neutrals might lean against the side that has violated moral traditions here. We will be reluctant to admit it to ourselves, because of the disquiet and sleepless nights this may produce.

THE "NEWNESS" OF THE ISSUES

One should not exaggerate the novelty of the separable countervalue possibility by painting it as so entirely new. There has always been some global trade, so that there was always something one side could do to degrade the living standard of the other, even if no prior military victory had been imposed. Whether the raids from the sea were by Vikings or by the British fleet approaching Cadiz or Baltimore, the sea has offered some such options for bypassing the enemy force. There has also always been the possibility of some penetration by secret agents, or assassins, or bomb throwers, or guerrilla bands, so that pain could be inflicted without first conquering the enemy and overpowering his fortifications. For as long as there has been warfare, men have applied strategic reasoning to whatever avenues of leverage they possessed, so that a weighing of the alternatives of the counterforce and countervalue approaches is an old story.

One might wonder whether this pattern of the imposition of suffering on the adversary's home front did not then begin much earlier than World War I. If the blockades producing hunger in that war were the moral equivalent of aerial bombing producing other miseries (dissuading an adversary even while his armed forces remained intact), would this not have been the pattern with naval blockades over all of history? What of the British Orders in Council, and Napoleon's Continental System, at the beginning of the nineteenth century? And what of the interaction of maritime forces over the preceding centuries?

World War I was interestingly different from the Napoleonic era, however, in that countries were now much more dependent on international trade for the maintenance of their living standards. The British policies adopted in "economic warfare" after 1914 thus had a much greater prospect of success than those adopted by Napoleon in 1806. The Napoleonic approach was also interestingly different (apart from its lack of prospects for success) in that it sought to force Britain to make peace (i.e. sought to deter London from continuing with the war) not by keeping goods from reaching Britain, but by cutting Britain ("a nation of shopkeepers") off from markets in Europe.[5] Revolutionary France had gone through an interesting evolution of thinking on international trade, rejecting the liberal ideas of Adam Smith and reverting to the mercantilist assumptions that had guided national economic policy in peace and war for the prior century: specifically, the assumption that the total of trade was some sort of zero-sum game in which one state could increase its own reserves and prosperity only by reducing those of another.

If Britain was just beginning to understand the ideas of Adam Smith on the eve of the French Revolution, France and the bulk of the world would see such ideas prove themselves only after the final defeat of Napoleon. The ensuing growth in the total of world trade and prosperity mocked considerations of gold reserves or protectionism but also gave all the world's economies a powerful vested interest in the maintenance of trade, with a very painful withdrawal then to be suffered if such trade were interfered with. Napoleon, with the Continental System, was striking only most indirectly (and ineffectively) at the innocent civilians of Britain, and was much hoping to confront the British government with a threat to its base of material power, since a positive balance of payments was still viewed as a fundamental ingredient of the power of a state regime. When the British blockade kept food from reaching Germany after 1914, this was instead striking (whether it was to be admitted or obfuscated) heavily at the civilians on the German side.

The important measure thus is obviously the fraction of the adversary's value items that can be struck at and damaged by countervalue attacks. Trade may have been important for Holland, and the flow of silver and gold from America was once crucial to Spain, but trade became crucial to the quality of life for the larger portion of the world only as we approached the twentieth century. However great a lever of influence the British Navy may have had in options for countervalue retaliation after Trafalgar, it came to have even more as World War I drew nearer.

And the additions of aerial means of delivery and, penultimately, the atomic bomb and the hydrogen bomb have now placed the entirety of what we hold dear under the control of someone whom we might have beaten on the battlefield. To have been beaten by the Mongols in battle was to lose everything one held dear. To have instead beaten the Mongols would have been to leave very little at risk. Today one might not dare to defeat nuclear-missile-equipped Mongols too resoundingly.

WORLD WAR I

Some of the most interesting development of theory for our purposes emerges here in 1917 and 1918 in the British Imperial War Cabinet, contemplating the impact of German Zeppelin and airplane raids on London, contemplating also the possibilities offered by Allied air attacks against German cities, especially as the war along the Western Front threatened to remain stalemated into 1919 and 1920. While the number of bombs that fell on London seems trivial by the standards of World War II and by the possibilities of a nuclear war, the impact in terms of sensed damage had been great, as large numbers of Londoners had panicked and rushed into the Underground stations at even the first hint of a German air raid. German raids did damage to British production of war materials, and British raids against Germany might have a similar impact in reverse – clearly a counterforce kind of argument. Yet the German raids also made Britishers, outside the government or within it, reevaluate their desire to continue the war, regardless of whether the capability for fighting was at all diminished, and here we are of course already across the line into a countervalue argument. Perhaps the Germans might react even more adversely to being bombed; perhaps this was a way to get the Germans into the mood to surrender, if the blockade or the unpromising prospects along the front did not suffice for this.

Air Marshal Trenchard (known as "Boom" Trenchard to his friends) dismissed the possibility of any effective British counterforce air raids against the airfields from which the Germans had been launching their attacks. Rather, the best target would be German industry *and* population, in a line of argument that still contained enough traditional "military target" explanation to extract some moral cover but that surely also now presupposed that a war stalemated at the front could be won by the pain delivered over and past that front.

> The policy intended to be followed is to attack the important German towns systematically, having regard to weather conditions and the defensive arrangements of the enemy. It is intended to concentrate on one town for successive days and then to pass to several other towns, returning to the first town until the target is thoroughly destroyed, or at any rate until the morale of workmen is so shaken that output is seriously interfered with.
>
> British experience goes to show that a great deal of time may inevitably be occupied in creating a large striking force, but that once a nucleus is created with its necessary aerodromes, depots, stores, &c., the work can be carried on and the force regularly increased. In order that the bombing of Germany may have its maximum effect it is of the first importance to carry through systematically, in spite of losses and other adverse conditions, the plan which has been made.
>
> Long-distance bombing will produce its maximum moral effect only if the visits are constantly repeated at short intervals, so as to produce in each area bombed a sustained anxiety. It is this recurrent bombing, as opposed to isolated and spasmodic attacks, which interrupts industrial production and undermines public confidence.
>
> On the other hand, if the enemy were to succeed in interrupting the continuity of the British bombing operations, their achievements (as the Allies' success against Zeppelins show)

would be an immense encouragement to them which would operate like a military victory.

The Allies must therefore adopt a programme of bombing operations which, whenever the weather permits, must be constantly kept up and under which it can be assured that the heavy losses, which are bound to occur, can be instantly made good.[6]

What was being considered and debated in London as World War I continued is illustrated in a memorandum prepared by Winston Churchill as Minister of Munitions in October of 1917.

It is not reasonable to speak of an air offensive as if it were going to finish the war by itself. It is improbable that any terrorization of the civil population which could be achieved by air attack would compel the Government of a great nation to surrender. Familiarity with bombardment, a good system of dug-outs or shelters, a strong control by police and military authorities, should be sufficient to preserve the national fighting power unimpaired. In our own case we have seen the combative spirit of the people roused, and not quelled, by the German air raids. Nothing that we have learned of the capacity of the German population to endure suffering justifies us in assuming that they could be cowed into submission by such methods, or, indeed, that they would not be rendered more desperately resolved by them. Therefore our air offensive should consistently be directed at striking at the bases and communications upon whose structure the fighting power of his armies and his fleets of the sea and of the air depends. Any injury which comes to the civil population from the process of attack must be regarded as incidental and inevitable.[7]

The last sentence here amounts to the loophole, of course, through which a great deal of civilian suffering was to be inflicted in the later history of air warfare. Churchill's quite sincere deprecation of a more deliberate assault on civilian targets shows, moreover, that such an assault already had advocates in London in 1917, advocates of getting a German

237

government to surrender when it had not yet been defeated on the battlefield.

The same dichotomy has applied to applications of naval blockade. Were we cutting off food to Germany in World War I, or to Japan in World War II, to keep German and Japanese soldiers from eating to renew their fighting abilities, or were we doing this to inflict hunger pangs on the civilians of these countries so that their governments would have to sue for peace even if their soldiers remained reasonably well fed? For a relatively frank admission that the painful countervalue impact may be as important as the disabling counterforce impact, we can turn to the very prescient writings of Sir Julian Corbett, who offered this analysis in 1911, after the counterforce analysis of Mahan had won such wide acclaim, but before the outbreak of World War I:

> The destruction of your enemy's forces will not avail for certain unless you have in reserve sufficient force to complete the occupation of his inland communications and principal points of distribution. This power is the real fruit of victory, the power to strangle the whole national life. It is not until this is done that a high-spirited nation, whose whole heart is in the war, will consent to make peace and do your will. It is precisely in the same way that the command of the sea works towards peace, though of course in a far less coercive manner, against a continental State. By occupying her maritime communications and closing the points of distribution in which they terminate we destroy the national life afloat, and thereby check the vitality of that life ashore so far as the one is dependent on the other.[8]

It is important to remember that not only the German U-boat campaign against British shipping (itself publicly justified on counterforce military grounds, of course, rather than on its real countervalue impact), but also the first German Zeppelin raids on Britain (justified the same way), came as explicit retaliation for the British naval blockade.

Germany and Britain might in any event have gotten into an exchange of air attacks in World War I, serving as a logical rehearsal for the air attacks of World War II (and World War III?), even if there had been no naval countervalue operations. But the analogy between the two hardly went unnoticed at the time.

As in almost every discussion of the targeting of civilians, a blanket is wrapped around the argument at the end by which the civilians being bombed (or starved) are somehow employed in war production. If they had not been so employed, would that have made them a less legitimate target? Or would their "morale" then have been identified as another key element in the German war effort?

References to "morale" are thus often also a part of the obfuscation here. If your morale is lowered, you may be distracted and rendered less functionally effective, so our air strikes can be viewed as a legitimate military ploy. Yet the lowering of morale may reflect no loss of effectiveness at all, but rather merely a change in the stakes and payoffs for any continuation of the combat, as every day of the war, whether you win or lose, will be that one more painful day for you.

LESSONS OF WORLD WAR I

Reminiscences of World War I tend to stress the horror of the trenches while normally treating the air war instead rather lightheartedly, as a succession of dogfights with Red Barons flying canvas aircraft. Yet the prospect of delivering high explosives or poison gas into the enemy's rear area, inflicting death and destruction on his cities and population, was taken rather more seriously at the time, setting the stage for a great deal of planning between the wars, and indeed activating such thinking even as World War I's end was nowhere yet in sight.

Giulio Douhet's writings on air war, often remembered as imaginative prophecy, were thus in actuality based on what had already happened to London and German cities in 1917 and 1918, and what was almost certainly in store for 1919, for Douhet, passing through London during the war as a liaison officer, had noted some of the ideas and proposals of people like Trenchard, Sykes, Smuts, and Churchill.

Douhet's forecast of future air warfare makes the people of the opposite side a target. Still burdened by the Western philosophical tradition condemning any unnecessary targeting of civilians, Douhet adopts the same device that every advocate of countervalue bomber and missile targeting tends to adopt (a device used also by advocates of naval blockades), a redefinition of the people as a counterforce target:

> The prevailing forms of social organization have given war a character of national totality – that is, the entire population and all the resources of a nation are sucked into the maw of war. And, since society is now definitely evolving along this line, it is within the power of human foresight to see now that future wars will be total in character and scope.[9]

Douhet thus justifies his war plans by borrowing ideas from Clausewitz. Clausewitz is widely accused of having *advocated* such a total commitment of society to warfare, whereby every part of society is committed to war and inferentially is therefore to be targeted by the other side. Clausewitz might more fairly be credited not so much with advocating this as with *describing* it, in comparing European political and military style after the French Revolution with the style before. Before 1789, the bulk of the civilian population of the countries of Europe had been left out of the wars fought between their rulers in minor scrambles over provinces. As the French Revolution brought in governments meant to be responsible and responsive to the people, it also made possible mass conscription and total war.

The introduction of the vertical dimension of war pulls in all of society in a second and more important way, since it can be struck at. Yet such total war, in carrying bombs back to cities behind the lines, was then often justified morally with the prior argument that the war had *already* become legitimately total because of the ideological and nationalistic involvements that make all of the people being bombed the functional equivalent of soldiers. "They're all Nazis" would thus be the World War II Bomber Command's interpretation of the German population of a city like Hamburg; if they contribute to the war effort by working in factories, or even by cheering on the soldiers at the front, they can be attacked as part of an effort to disarm those soldiers at the front. Civilian workers who have been demoralized contribute less to the war effort; those who have been killed contribute still less.

The honest truth of such a campaign might instead have been that the punishment of civilians would not greatly diminish the enemy's ability to fight, but might remove that enemy's willingness to fight. Destroying civilian residences would no longer be defense, or "deterrence by denial," but instead "deterrence by punishment," an approach that could work, but one for which very little moral groundwork had been laid.

Hence the tendency toward confusion and hypocrisy, the tendency in all such approaches to warfare toward exaggerating the counterforce impact (the reduction of the enemy's capabilities for fighting) and understating and concealing the countervalue impact of attack, an impact that is mainly painful.

Do the people thus become a target because they are politically involved in a war? Or are they a target more directly because they can be reached, and because their safety is of importance to their government? The latter is indeed more significant than the former, with the former being more excuse than reason. That Douhet was not the only one to suggest such an excuse can be shown in the arguments summarized in the British official history of aerial warfare in World War I, commenting on how London and German cities came to be the target of air attacks:

> On the question of morality little need be said here. Opinion during the war was divided, certainly in Germany, where some pleaded for air attacks on Great Britain directed solely towards the breaking of the spirit of the civil population, while others wanted the raids confined to objects of military importance.

Long before the aircraft bomb was invented it was a military teaching that a nation resorted to war to impose its will on another nation, a statement of no great profundity, but one which has some advantage over another, at one time in common currency, that war is the sport of kings. Democracies, perhaps, get the sort of war they deserve. So long as war was confined to strictly professional armies so long might a code of manners survive, but as soon as it became an affair of nations it was inevitable that popular clamor should often override purely military considerations.[10]

The British planners contemplating future air warfare between 1919 and 1939 thus often contemplated an attack on civilian populations and on the entire fabric of the enemy's society, sometimes labeled a "knockout blow." As in the writings of Douhet and J. F. C. Fuller, they lumped the entire target system together as one gigantic warmaking complex, thus avoiding any admission that the enterprise would be to hurt rather than to handicap. Perhaps a capital city that had been blasted into rubble, and doused in poison gas, would lose the war because it was incapable of coordinating its side of the fighting anymore. Perhaps one would thus never have to evaluate morally the situation where an adversary remained able to fight but had been dissuaded (deterred) from continuing to fight by fear of a continuation of such punishment.

If World War I had continued into 1919, rather than being terminated by the German surrender in 1918, there is evidence that British and French air attacks would have been conducted against German cities with the use of poison gas. Perhaps that would similarly have been labeled counterforce; yet, just like the blockades that had so much lowered German home-front morale in 1918, it would more truly have been countervalue.

Perhaps as much aware as anyone of the slippery slopes and hypocrisies of such "military" bombings of civilian urban areas, the United States Army Air Corps, in its declarations of air warfare theory after 1919, stuck a little more to the moral high road, repeating numerous times that it was

not American policy to wage air warfare against cities, whatever tie one might make between such cities and the enemy's
war effort. The laws of war had for decades called for an
avoidance of unnecessary civilian destruction, and for a careful aiming of fire at military targets:

> Against industrial centers. Industrial centers, especially those
> devoted to the manufacture of war material, are important
> strategic targets, while under favorable conditions day bom-
> bardment may be used in their attack, it is in raids on such
> objectives as these that night bombardment comes into its own.
> Whichever is used, particular subtargets should be selected
> and each plane or formation should be assigned a certain
> building or group of buildings to destroy. It is wrong to send
> out planes simply to drop their bombs when over a large tar-
> get. . . .
> Against political centers. The bombing of political centers is
> prohibited by the laws of warfare. However, since they are the
> nerve centers of the nation, they are apt to be important tar-
> gets for bombardment in reprisal for attacks made by the en-
> emy on such centers in our own country, especially since they
> are apt to contain important factories or stores of war material.
> Nevertheless, such employment is purely strategical. In the
> World War the Germans bombed London and Paris, while the
> dream of all the Allies was to bomb Berlin. Whether such
> bombing actually accomplishes its avowed purpose – to weaken
> the morale of the hostile nation and thus hasten the end of
> hostilities – is doubtful in some cases. The reactions may be in
> exactly the opposite direction. The G.H.Q. commander will
> know whether or not bombardment should be used in this
> manner in any given case.[11]

Suggesting that American policy here was a matter of more
than mere words, the bombers that the Air Corps was allowed to procure were to be significantly different from those
procured in the same years by the British Royal Air Force.
The RAF bombers developed in the 1930s were designed to
attack their targets by night, and thus required less machine-
gun protection and protective armament, counting on dark-
ness to help them escape the enemy's interceptor aircraft.

Having devoted less weight to warding off the defenders, these bombers could carry a larger bomb load; flying by night, they were expected to be less accurate in attempting to hit any particularly precise target, and thus set the stage for the RAF's "area bombing" in World War II.

The U.S. Army Air Corps, by contrast, purchased the B-17 and B-24, designed to drop their bombs by daylight and thus necessarily equipped with protective armament. The protective armament reduced the weight of bombs that could be carried, which then put all the greater premium on the precise accuracy of bomb aiming that American planners were hoping for. Touting the wondrous Norden bombsight as capable of directing bombs "into a pickle barrel," all Americans – Air Corps planners, Congressmen, and men-on-the-street – thus came into World War II with a stronger moral commitment to the sparing of civilians.

While the debate about the morality of nuclear deterrence is today being carried on, openly or subliminally, in many corners of the world, its most important round may be the one that occurs in the United States, the one superpower that can have a public soul-searching on such subjects. We should not exaggerate the uniqueness of American moral feelings. It is still the norm almost everywhere to condemn Guernica and Rotterdam and Coventry; it is still the norm everywhere to claim that any destruction of urban areas was more an inadvertent byproduct than a deliberate goal. Yet Americans may still have taken these moral issues a little bit more seriously over the decades. And this may cause problems rather than solving them.

WORLD WAR II

The pattern of American and British bombing campaigns in World War II is complicated in some interesting ways. The RAF air attacks on Germany for most of the war were conducted by night, in area attacks that leveled the residential areas of Hamburg and other cities. The commander of this offensive, Air Marshal Arthur ("Bomber") Harris, sometimes argued that he was reducing German war production, but at other times conceded that he was trying to destroy German willingness to continue the war. In the final victory over Germany, the disquiet that British political leaders felt about the area bombing approach was illustrated by the fact that Harris was the only one of the major commanders not immediately knighted at the end of the war.

Harris's outlook in "area bombing," and on the general approach to winning the war, is illustrated in a progress report he prepared in 1943:

> This achievement is expressed in terms of acreage destroyed per tons of bombs dropped and of acreage destroyed in comparison with acreage attacked. The acreage dealt with refers throughout only to areas which are 40% or more built up where results can be accurately measured, and a true indication given of what has already been accomplished. The figures to the end of October show that 167,230 tons of bombs dropped on the 38 principal towns which had been attacked have destroyed 20,991 acres or about 25% of the 84,160 acres attacked. Of this total 18,641 acres or nearly 22% (out of the total of 25%) have been destroyed by the 102,000 tons dropped during the first 10 months of this year, a clear indication of the great advance in efficiency due to the use of navigational aids combined with the policy of heavy concentration raids. The acreage destroyed is judged from vertical photographs which, as is obvious, cannot and do not show the full extent of the actual damage.
>
> It is not possible to dogmatise on the degree of destruction necessary to cause the enemy to capitulate but there can be little doubt that the necessary conditions would be brought about by the destruction of between 40% and 50% of the principal German towns.[12]

How far the direction of targeting strategy had come here is illustrated in an Air Staff directive sent to Bomber Command in 1942, completely inverting the logic of whether countervalue impact was a spinoff from counterforce efforts:

> Whilst the primary aim of your operations must remain the lowering of the morale of the enemy civil population and in

particular that of the workers in industrial areas vital to the enemy's war effort, every effort consistent with this aim should be made to reduce the output of aircraft factories, and particularly those producing fighter aircraft.[13]

This message from the Air Staff was in effect urging that in the normal leveling of urban areas and residential areas some greater consideration be given to whether the particular city being bombed played any role in the production of airplanes for the Luftwaffe. Having made the people of Germany an alleged counterforce target, the proposed amendment was that some attention be paid to more indisputably counterforce targets.

The U.S. Eighth Air Force joined with the British in bombing German targets after 1942, but it elected to carry through its raids by daylight, aiming at such "precision" targets as the ball-bearing industry, and then railroads and the oil industry. While there was no open disagreement between the two air forces, some American officers were privately inclined to comment that they saw the British approach as immoral, not sufficiently attuned to avoiding civilian residences and hitting military targets.

Whatever moral superiority Americans might have felt here was vitiated by the frequency with which American bombardiers, even with their Norden bombsights, missed their intended targets, thus imposing a substantial collateral damage although no "area bombing" philosophy had been adopted. Any criticism of the British was further rendered empty when the two air forces sometimes coordinated on joint night and day attacks on the same German city, as with Dresden in February of 1945, making it impossible for German firefighting and damage-control teams to do anything to prevent the total destruction of the city. If the RAF was aiming bluntly at night and the USAAF hitting the same rubble more "precisely" by daylight, the moral distinction had become very thin indeed.

The final erosion of the American commitment to precise targeting then came in the air assault against Japan. General

Curtis LeMay, commander of the B-29s of the Twentieth Air Force, concluded from the early reports of the United States Strategic Bombing Survey studying the air attacks on Germany that the precise attacks had too often failed to hit their intended target, and thus had not generated enough impact. LeMay decided to shift to a night area offensive in attacks on Japan, stripping his B-29s of the defensive armament they would not need so much at night, so that they could carry a larger bomb load. In a first major use of this tactic, some three hundred B-29s attacked Tokyo with incendiary bombs to start a firestorm which took more than 100,000 lives – more people killed than at Hiroshima or Nagasaki.

To save the cover that this was a counterforce attack aimed at Japanese military capability, various American news reporters were now informed by Army Air Force intelligence that the Japanese had been using an extensive array of machine shops scattered across the garages and backyards of residential areas, so that these entire residential districts had to be burned out in order to prevent the production of Japanese fighter planes, etc. Once again, some kind of military impact was to be the official goal, with the collateral consequence – that life in Japan might become so horrible for its civilians that the government would be deterred from continuing the war – being only an unintended byproduct.

The naval blockade imposed on Japan, as noted, was covered by the same kinds of convoluted logic. And thus was Hiroshima described as having been chosen as the first target for a nuclear weapon because it was the home base for several Japanese army units.

The Japanese surrendered after the bombings of Hiroshima and Nagasaki not because these bombings had crippled the effectiveness of Japanese military units, but because such bombings would be a fate too painful to bear, far more painful than surrender.

Critics of the Hiroshima and Nagasaki bombings base much of their argument on the likelihood that the Japanese government would soon have surrendered in any event. Such a prediction is surely somewhat debatable. Even if correct, moreover, it hardly settles the moral issue, for one must ask what would so surely have made Tokyo surrender and withdraw its troops from China, except for the conventional bombings and the naval blockade, and in particular the countervalue aspects of such bombings and blockades, i.e. the suffering already being imposed on Japanese civilians.

SINCE WORLD WAR II

The same kind of reluctance to face up to the new nature of targeting shows up in U.S. plans after 1945 for the possibility of war with the Soviet Union. The Strategic Air Command, in planning for the delivery of nuclear weapons to Soviet targets, always chose "military" targets, but always found five or six such targets within Moscow, and within Leningrad, etc., so that the "collateral damage" in such a war would include the killing of millions of Russians. For SAC to regard this as collateral damage was to avoid the moral opprobrium of having aimed at civilians directly, still basically a war crime. Since such civilians would be killed simply as the unavoidable and presumably unintended consequence of a strike at legitimate military targets, consciences could be set at ease.

The paradox, of course, was that the civilian analysts projecting the future of mutual deterrence as an underpinning for peace between the Soviet Union and the United States were at the same moment counting on such destruction of civilians. Such "collateral damage" at times also came to be labeled "bonus destruction," a little more frank as an admission of what was the most important here.

Historians who use the Freedom of Information Act to uncover the war plans of the 1950s sometimes gasp at the counterforce tone of many such plans and then direct ridicule at the civilian analysts of the time who wrote as if countervalue targeting was predominant, setting the stage for mutual deterrence and Mutual Assured Destruction. Yet such documents may not amount to such solid grounds for gasping at or questioning the relevance of MAD, for the documents are only in part serious war plans, and in another part euphemisms intended to avoid moral guilt and thoughts of future war-crime indictments.

The same kinds of doublethink were applied to all the applications of conventional air power in the limited wars fought after World War II. In the Korean War, U.S. Air Force bombings of North Korea were always officially directed at military targets. Yet, less openly stated, the intention, besides weakening the enemy's capabilities, was also (or perhaps even more) to punish his economy and society, to make life less pleasant. The moral obfuscation here is delightfully illustrated in a directive from General Smart:

> Whenever possible, attacks will be scheduled against targets of military significance so situated that their destruction will have a deleterious effect upon the morale of the civilian population actively engaged in the logistic support of the enemy force.[14]

The final phrase, by which all the North Koreans who would suffer a loss of electricity or other services in such bombings were already part of the North Korean war effort anyhow, completes the normal looping we have seen before. The bombs are to be aimed at value targets, but all the human beings connected to such value targets have become redefined as force targets, restoring another layer of targeting legitimacy in case too many moral doubts had been aroused.

In all of these cases one could hardly argue that American planners saw no counterforce possibilities in air attacks. Rather, the important point is that such planners have also always seen countervalue possibilities, and have then been inclined to pretend systematically that these were simply counterforce, and hence less immoral. If we can win a counterforce victory in a conventional war or a nuclear war, or if we can pose the mere threat to our adversaries that we would win in such a force exchange, all well and good. But if this is not attainable, one may still be able to deter or coerce an enemy by the "collateral" damage that will be inflicted on things he values.

In the Vietnam War, U.S. air raids were similarly always described as intended to achieve an "interdiction" of the flow of war supplies from North Vietnam to the South, but in actuality they were intended at least as much to have a countervalue impact, to set back North Vietnamese industrial development and the quality of life under the Communist regime, to impose a price for the continuation of the war. For example, note Defense Secretary McNamara's testimony in 1967:

> Our primary objective was to reduce the flow and/or to increase the cost of the continued infiltration of men and supplies from North to South Vietnam.
> It was also anticipated that these air operations would raise the morale of the South Vietnamese people who, at the time the bombing started, were under severe military pressure.
> Finally, we hoped to make clear to the North Vietnamese leadership that so long as they continued their aggression against the South they would have to pay a price in the North.[15]

Critics had a field day with the official "primary" explanations offered for the bombings, pointing out that the bombings were not effective in slowing the movement of war material (any more than the bombings of Germany had any early impact in reducing German war production). Such criticisms missed the mark in a way that the Johnson Administration could not so easily discuss, for the more important focus would have been a "deterrence by punishment" rather than a "deterrence by denial," an approach as immoral and difficult to discuss in public as always, but one that certainly was not so devoid of prospects for success. (Lest anyone somehow remember that bombing clearly "failed" in Vietnam, he should ask himself what the situation would have been if Nixon had not been handicapped by the Watergate scandal, and if the Congressional bans on further bombing campaigns, by sparing North Vietnam from the threat of B-52 attacks, had not freed Hanoi to dispatch tanks to finalize the conquest of the South.)

Israeli air attacks on Arab targets are similarly always advertised as counterforce in intention, with any countervalue impact simply being a regrettable but unavoidable collateral impact. After any terrorist attack within Israel, the normal response is an air strike at a Palestinian target, which the Israelis will (with some justification) describe as a PLO training base, and which the Arabs (also with some justification) will describe as a Palestinian refugee camp. Since Israeli fighter-bombers can never discern exactly which house they are hitting or are meant to hit, some women and children are always wounded and killed in the process. Officially, this is something that the Israelis did not intend to have happen; privately, of course, Israelis relish the sense of "getting even," here hoping that the prospect of such retaliatory inflictions of pain will reduce and deter such Arab attacks in the future.

In the 1970 "war of attrition" along the Suez Canal, as Egyptian artillery persisted in shelling the Israeli forces on the east side of the canal and Israeli artillery and air forces responded by shelling the Egyptian forces on the west side, each of the combatants could similarly face the world with a claim that a clean war was being fought, in that only explicitly military targets on the other side were being brought under fire.

Yet the nature of the contest – the explanation of why the Egyptians in the end had to concede and end it – nonetheless included an important countervalue element, namely the fact that a great many young men in uniform were being killed. Neither side expected to impose a defeat by incapacitating its enemy on this front in 1970, or to follow up with a breakthrough and an advance. The Egyptians rather intended to impose a daily toll of casualties on the Israelis, so as to make them wish to quit the advanced positions; and the Israelis struck back in a similar manner, calculated to force Nasser to send condolences to the grieving parents of a great number of dead Egyptian soldiers.

The example of such a war of attrition, analogous to what the Germans were hoping to inflict on the French in 1916 in the Battle of Verdun, illustrates again that this less moral policy of warfare by the infliction of pain has a longer history.

More people were killed at Verdun than at Hiroshima. Such people were in each case killed as part of an attempt to make the other side's government less willing to fight, rather than less able to fight. In the Battle of Verdun, the German commander Falkenhayn has been accused of having deliberately slowed the initial German advance so as to draw more French reinforcements into the battle, reinforcements that could then be subjected to German artillery fire. If enough letters had to be sent home to the parents of dead French soldiers, Paris might have to sue for peace.

Countervalue attacks were thus being inflicted here rather than counterforce attacks, even if the "value items" were human beings wrapped in French army uniforms. As had been made clear earlier by Sir Julian Corbett, an element of countervalue may indeed have been crucial to victory in any war.

These reflections on the targeting of uniformed soldiers, rather than "innocent civilians," might seem to question some of the traditional moral judgments we bring to bear in this area. The traditions are surely important, as a means of imposing at least some restraints on warfare; but we should not credit their internal logic with being so very whole and complete.

Confining the contest of attrition to men in uniform at least sets limits to it. And no one is going to propose that men in uniform be exempted from enemy fire as part of some grand effort to humanize war. Our major point, indeed, is the great extent to which people out of uniform have now been added to the target list – and how they came to be added.

It should be noted that the 1970 "war of attrition" is not typical of Middle East warfare. Most rounds of fighting in the region have instead been characterized by a seemingly genuine emphasis on counterforce targeting in the strictest sense, without any seeking for "collateral damage." Cities have by and large not been attacked; thus, the Israeli Air Force in 1967 struck Cairo airport's military facilities without hitting the city itself, and the Arab air forces have largely spared Israeli population centers.

In part this can be explained by a mutual-restraint logic of limited war. But a larger portion is due to the extreme urgency of the preemptive counterforce motives in any war like that of 1967, with the Israeli Air Force sparing the city of Cairo because it had no forces to direct against it, being so intent on destroying the Egyptian Air Force.

All in all, this amounts to a nice miniature illustration of our moral paradoxes here. The confrontation of the two sides' air forces in 1967 so much favored the first strike that it may have caused that war to break out, even while it also drove the two sides to spare cities. An ability to hit targets precisely allows one to spare civilians, but it tempts one to strike first, to preempt, in an attempt to wipe out those of the other side's forces that might be capable of striking with comparable precision.

EPISODES OF CANDOR

The natural temptation is thus to deny any deliberate infliction of pain in warfare, to claim that this is always inevitable and collateral, to hide any deliberate intention of inflicting such suffering, hide it from others and from ourselves. Where in the history of aerial warfare are we to find more honest and open statements of intention?

Air Marshal Harris comes close, in his description of the Bomber Command offensive against German cities during World War II. Secretary of Defense Robert McNamara also comes very close, in the briefings on "assured destruction" he delivered in the Department of Defense Posture Statements in the middle 1960s.

American strategic writers outside the government have stressed such targeting policies candidly enough and often enough, of course, in outlining their interpretations of how peace has been maintained in the world since Hiroshima and Nagasaki. Such theorists, in a way that could rarely if ever be echoed in public statements by responsible government officials, have indeed often endorsed such targeting as desirable in both directions. That is, it has been portrayed as advantageous to the United States that millions of Russians would be killed in an American retaliatory strike, and also as advantageous *to the United States* that millions of Americans would be killed in a Soviet retaliatory strike. The prospect of our retaliation will keep them from deliberately beginning a war; the prospect of their retaliation will assure the Soviets that *we* are deterred and so will lessen their fear of being attacked by our forces in some kind of first strike.[16]

This is the logic that condemns anti-ballistic-missile weapons (which normally cannot kill anyone, but could only – in the event of war – keep hundreds of thousands of people alive). To be precise, it condemns ABM when such defenses hold the prospect of shielding people, but not when such ABM protection would only shield weapons systems. What protects weapons is good, what protects people is bad: Such is the inverted moral wisdom of nuclear deterrence, and our traditional morality is a major obstacle to any full and deep acceptance of this.

At the outset of the Kennedy Administration, Secretary of Defense Robert McNamara is reported to have developed a soon-aborted interest in shifting away from countervalue targeting toward something more legitimately counterforce.[17] Such an approach might reduce the number of Russians killed if war ever came and, by offering Moscow an incentive to withhold and limit its own nuclear attacks, would also reduce the number of Americans killed. By targeting the fledgling Soviet intercontinental missile force, such a carefully orchestrated "no cities" approach might additionally reduce American casualties by a "damage limitation" approach of expeditiously removing the Soviet capability for imposing such casualties. Finally, in brandishing such a U.S. strategic superiority, the new American targeting approach enhanced the deterrence of Soviet conventional aggression around West Berlin or in Western Europe generally.

McNamara quickly despaired of any success in this direction, however, retreating within a few years to a focus on assured destruction rather than such damage limitation.

First of all, McNamara discovered that a counterforce targeting list would again become a justification for programming a very large number of warheads against targets inside the Soviet Union, with a great deal of collateral damage still imposed. If the countervalue damage inflicted in an attack designed to be mainly counterforce was greater than that of the originally less counterforce approach, the moral or practical preferability of such an attack was very much in doubt. More important, the Soviet investment in strategic missiles based on submarines or in hardened underground silos might soon make any serious shielding of American cities by counterforce "damage limitation" attacks relatively ineffective. Finally, if one wished the Soviets to rest secure against the possibility of a U.S. first strike, one would wish them to have such secure second-strike forces.

It is often pointed out that McNamara, in giving up on strategies intended to reduce damage to Soviet or American civilians in a nuclear war and instead settling for Assured Destruction (a term to which critics later appended "Mutual" to show that it was "mad"), did not thereby succeed in reducing the momentum of the U.S. Air Force and Navy toward adding more nuclear warheads, delivery systems, and targeting points.

McNamara's more open admission that the intention of strategic forces was to inflict countervalue punishment may thus have been refreshingly honest, but the rest of the U.S. defense decision-making system was simply not prepared to be this honest.

Yet it would be a mistake then to conclude that McNamara's "assured destruction" view of what U.S. targeting choices were all about was factually incorrect, or that this view was not shared in the Air Force. Rather, a gap opened between them because the Air Force, for all the reasons cited, would see it as inadvisable to call a spade a spade, to be so honest about the balance of terror. But if anyone had been concerned that talk of counterforce targeting might have left

Soviet cities insufficiently threatened in the 1960s, the plans formulated by SAC in Omaha would always have been enough to eliminate this concern.

OTHER SOURCES OF CONFUSION BESIDES MORALITY

Apart from traditional morality, we can list a few other intellectually less respectable factors that reinforce our delay in facing the new reality of deterrence. First, there is always some wishful thinking to be indulged in here, as people are genuinely appalled by the possibilities of civilian suffering in a nuclear war and seek to convince themselves that such suffering can be avoided or moderated.

Elementary civil defense preparations, accurate aiming of weapons, and a stress on counterforce targeting are thus somehow combined in imagination to make most of us want to survive a World War III, rather than hoping for an early death in such a war.

Since the destruction caused by air attacks in World War II never measured up to the horrible levels predicted before 1939, we are now somewhat inclined to tell ourselves that the most dire forecasts of destruction in World War III may be crying "Wolf," and that civil defense might thus be effective. Moreover, the sheer momentum of older patterns of thinking on a subject will often enough stand in the way of change. Military officers still read Mahan and Clausewitz, as well as Douhet, and still regard the disarming of an enemy military force as their natural calling in its highest form. If the mutually deterring impact of two assured destruction second-strike retaliation forces is to change all this, one cannot expect this new reasoning suddenly to replace that of the last several centuries.

What military officers see here as their calling is itself very much the result of the moral traditions of their society, intertwined with their professional estimates of what is possible. To protect one's own people has never been condemned in the courts of victors or of public opinion. To have served in the anti-aircraft units of Nazi Germany, shooting at the Allied bombers on their way to Dresden or Hamburg, is the best war record a German could have to avoid later criticism. To attack the civilians of the other side has, by contrast, been to render one vulnerable at war-crimes tribunals.

A third source for a continued stress on the military uses of nuclear weapons, rather than on their deterrent threat against population centers, has been an American tendency to overrate the possibilities of accurate bomb aiming. If we as Americans have been unusually moral, in avoiding until very late the commitment made by the British to deliberate bombing of civilian target areas, we have also been unusually inclined to regard technology as the solution to problems, expecting that an application of engineering would allow us to destroy what we wanted to on the other side, without destroying too much of what we did not want to destroy.

Such a fixation on the technological implementation of moral approaches is illustrated in our earlier expectations for pinpoint daylight bombing and the Norden bombsight. More currently, it may be illustrated in optimistic expectations of the accuracy to be achieved with cruise missiles, or with new guidance systems for ballistic missiles. Perhaps engineers have been corrupted by the same sales practices that more generally afflict the military–industrial complex, as the performance characteristics of weapons are typically oversold as a way of "buying in" to a contract, while the overall costs to the taxpayer are understated until it is too late to cancel the procurement. But American engineers have probably more genuinely exaggerated what could be accomplished with their gadgets, convinced that the "fog of war" could be cleared by American ingenuity and confident that in the end we will surely be able to hit what we are aiming at.

Reinforcing such wishful thinking is a certain kind of bureaucratic political game: The commanders of air forces will stress the opposing air force as a much more important target than the adversary's cities, not just to look moral, but subtly to remind taxpayers of the importance of our own air force by stressing the significance of air forces in general. This translates soon enough into more mundane considerations of budgeting and manning. To aim at military targets is to add to the total target list, thus leading to larger appropriations and larger force levels. Military commanders always reject the charge that they are guided by such considerations in their development of strategy and war plans, but civilian skeptics about these commanders, as about any government bureaucracy, often find such charges plausible.

A "MODEST COUNTERFORCE" APPROACH?

A few advocates of a U.S. stress on counterforce targeting contend that this strategy will never stampede Moscow into launching "on warning" or induce in the Soviets an attitude of "use them or lose them" with regard to their missiles. Because (this argument runs) the Soviets saw us restrain ourselves during our monopoly possession of nuclear weapons between 1945 and 1949, or because they know that as a liberal democracy we would never initiate a war – i.e. because they see fundamental asymmetries in the political confrontation of the superpowers – they would tolerate new hard-target accuracies in our arsenal, just as they would tolerate a breakthrough in the Strategic Defense Initiative.

A very different response, from advocates of a counterforce targeting approach, would instead be to acknowledge that we must indeed be worried about possible Soviet worries, and therefore to advocate preparations for only a "modest counterforce" capability, adequate to weaken Soviet military forces in the event of a war, but never really able to strip the other side of its ability to destroy American cities.[18] This would allegedly comply with morality without threatening peace.

But there are many practical problems with this approach. Would not the collateral damage associated with such a "modest counterforce" scheme again be vastly greater than anticipated, such that tremendous numbers of civilians would be killed in any event? The ideal of a modest counterforce weaponry would be a system that imposed no damage at all on civilians, but that substantially weakened the military capability of any forces Moscow sent forward on the attack. If this was realizable at all, it could most probably be so only with conventional warheads. But there are substantial doubts about whether any reliable and stabilizing defense will ever be so attainable.

Whether one is using conventional forces or nuclear forces, any scrupulously observed policy of aiming only at military targets would run great risks of being insufficient as a deterrent, as soon as the military calculations of Soviet planners indicated that the new NATO defenses would not be effective. If there is no concomitant collateral damage to civilian targets to go along with the application of weapons to battlefield pursuit of victory, then aggression would make sense whenever the victory seemed likely to go to the attacker.

With regard to the deployment of "tactical" battlefield nuclear weapons since the 1950s, we have been relying, in effect, upon such collateral damage as the sure means of keeping aggression from looking attractive. If we were serious now about avoiding such collateral damage, perhaps relying on the new accuracies that may be attainable, we would be betting everything, for the status quo we seek to protect, on the military reinforcement for the defense that such new accuracies may promise. But what if these emerging technologies cannot deliver all of such a promised reinforcement for "conventional deterrence" – i.e. what if new conventional weapons trends strengthen the offensive as much as the defensive?

Would not the counterforce possibilities of such a force also still be plausibly effective against Soviet missile and bomber forces, causing undiminished anxiety in Soviet command centers? As we improve accuracies to avoid collateral countervalue damage, we confront a greater problem in avoiding panicking the other side, i.e. in assuring them that our counterforce capability is truly as modest as we claim.

But there is a broader moral paradox in such proposals for "modest" counterforce, for they suggest that we should be

betting on Soviet countervalue capabilities even if we are for-
swearing our own. Why are we restricting our own counterforce capabilities, except that we are seeking to assure the
other side of their ability to destroy some civilians, namely
our civilians?

For my own part, I am indeed firmly convinced that it is
desirable for the United States, for the Soviet Union, and for
the world that American cities remain vulnerable to Soviet
nuclear warheads: Proponents of a "modest counterforce"
capability are endorsing exactly the same moral heresy. But,
being very symmetrical in how I see the world, I am equally
firmly convinced that the world, including the Soviet Union
and the United States, is better off if Soviet cities remain as-
suredly vulnerable to destruction by U.S. strategic nuclear
forces. This portion of the new strategic wisdom is not being
accepted by the advocates of modest counterforce approaches and in effect is being treated as morally repugnant.

The advocates of modest counterforce might thus be accused of being very selective about which portions of the
new moral heresies they are prepared to tolerate and which
they are not. If they do not get the majority of American
decision makers and of the American public to go along with
this division of the issues (the typical American will find the
prospect of the unilateral assured destruction of the United
States even less appealing than the idea of mutual assured
destruction), we run the risk that something much less modest in counterforce options will emerge.

It has all along been regarded as more moral to aim at the
other side's military forces than at his civilians; but it has
been even more highly approved to seek to shield one's own
civilians. The idea of deliberately tolerating the vulnerability
of one's population to the deadly weapons of the other side
is far less easily reconciled with the moral and philosophical
traditions we are discussing here.

Finally, is it possible that some "modest counterforce" advocates are, in actuality, nothing more than disguised proponents of "finite deterrence," in effect counting (like everyone else in the evolution of these choices) on the collateral

damage that may be unavoidable, and thereby escaping any admission that such civilian destruction is being sought for its own sake? The more straightforward advocate of finite deterrence is quite open about espousing a countervalue targeting strategy, on the same premises as an advocate of MAD; but he wishes to avoid the expense of redundant nuclear retaliatory weapons systems, and he presumably also wants to hold down the total of destruction inflicted on the two sides, and on the rest of the world, in case deterrence should fail.

An advocacy of limited counterforce options might thus be based only partly on the premise that this would better deter Soviet military initiatives by the prospect of a defeat of Soviet armed forces, and might be based much more on the inevitable (but finite) damage that would be inflicted on Soviet cities, people, and economy if such counterforce options were ever exercised.

But the moral issues remain in place as before. Some of us might feel that our consciences were clean, in that every opportunity had been undertaken to reduce the suffering of civilians in any future exchange of nuclear attacks, and would then allow ourselves to welcome the residual of unavoidable collateral damage for its contribution to overall deterrence. Yet the side effects of even such a welcoming of unavoidable countervalue impact might still be insidious. What if technology next year offers us ways of reducing the number of Soviets killed in a nuclear exchange to one-tenth of those now exposed? Would we regret these developments because they made deterrence less reliable? Would not such a regret about any "changes in the inevitable" drive us again to seek "assured destruction"?

As noted throughout this chapter, the "acceptance of inevitable damage to civilians" has very often become a cover for *welcoming* such damage, and all the problems of troublesome moral analogy might thus be ready to be activated. If we welcome some suffering by the innocent here, because it deters those who otherwise would become guilty, are we not thereafter inevitably drawn into similar reasoning on other social issues?

SOME CONCLUSIONS

The reader might object that we have been lumping together too many different degrees of countercivilian pressure here, as we flounder on the slippery slope of countervalue targeting. Dropping H-bombs on cities is surely far more immoral than cutting off those ships that merely sustain a higher standard of living in peacetime. Harassing the overseas spice trade of a rival power in the eighteenth century might already have been as much countervalue as counterforce. Imprisoning a lawbreaker in domestic society could be counterforce (if he is a threat to society when left at large), but it is often also mainly countervalue, intended to deter crimes by the example of punishment (for instance, an embezzler who would never be put in a position of financial trust again, and hence would be no threat if left at large). Is all of this history so relevant to Mutual Assured Destruction?

Yet millions of people died as a result of the influenza epidemic of 1918, which was tied not very indirectly to the malnutrition caused by the Allied blockade of Central Europe. The blockade worked to make Germany ready to quit the war; countervalue here was no mere harassment of a distant spice trade, and it does have relevance to MAD.

We deal in our century with the prevention of wars that have not yet begun and/or with the termination of wars that are already under way, in either case working to achieve peace by trying to influence the incentives of our adversary's government. In short, we are dealing with very high stakes, and the incentives have thus had to involve higher costs. To dissuade an enemy from something as big as war, to accomplish instead something so morally significant as the attainment of peace, it has become necessary to threaten something morally as damaging as the suffering and death of millions of people, people whose involvement in state decisions is exaggerated as an excuse.

The philosophically honest response to countervalue target planning might thus be to cease the hypocrisy and obfuscation, to call a spade a spade and stop pretending that we are trying to disarm our adversary when we are rather trying to torture him. If the prospect of torturing and killing the innocent works to keep the prospectively guilty from becoming the actually guilty, perhaps we ought simply to adjust our morality, without obfuscation, and this is what most elementary textbooks on nuclear deterrence have done, relatively forthrightly and honestly.

Such philosophical candor emphatically would not require us to adopt a morality by which people see nothing wrong in destroying cities and killing millions of people. What it would require, rather, is a new contingent morality by which we see nothing so wrong in posing the *threat* of such destruction, on the no-longer-strange logic that this threat keeps itself from having to be exercised. The "rationality of irrationality" is a concept that has lost its paradoxical tone since first being enunciated by Thomas Schelling and others at the end of the 1950s. What we would need is the parallel concept of "the morality of immorality."

It is indeed possible that some ordinary people and others have already begun to develop such a new morality of contingent situations, what many might label as consequentialist morality, by which "deterrence is acceptable because it works." Threats that we would hate to have to execute *ex post*, threats that would indeed serve no practical selfish interest of our own country if executed, might still be very desirable *ex ante* if they kept us from having to respond to any aggressions, if they kept Soviet nuclear attacks and Soviet conventional attacks from occurring in the first place.

But what would be the results of an attempt at philosophical honesty here? What of those many Americans, including elected officials and military officers, who cannot so easily adjust their moral thinking to the new logic of mutual assured destruction? If their morality persists, will they not still feel driven to "clean up their act," in pursuit of new options that are not simply defined as counterforce by the logic of evasion, but are more truly counterforce? The Strategic Defense Initiative, at least in some of the forms in which it has been presented, amounts to an example of this kind of effort.

So does the accuracy of the warheads on the MX missile system, capable of hitting Soviet missile silos very accurately while avoiding cities that we do not wish to hit.

Our greatest worry, of course, is that such a traditional moral approach, of not bombing civilian targets but aiming carefully at military targets, might make war much more likely by threatening to push Soviet strategic force commanders into a position of "use them or lose them." The technologies that allow us to be careful to avoid hitting Soviet civilians will perennially be the technologies that plausibly allow us to strike precisely at Soviet military targets, in particular at the Soviet missiles that are aimed at or close to our civilians; this could one day make the two sides sit in nervous expectation of each other's attack.

Unless one can ensure the strategic nuclear forces of each side against the other's temptation to preempt, perhaps by concealing the missiles' location on board submarines or on mobile land-based vehicles, enhancements of accuracy will always have this dual impact. It has always been moral to avoid hitting the other side's civilians, and it has always been just as moral to try to shield one's own civilians; but now we face the new *consequentialist* argument that this may actually make a war much more likely.

Does this then have to be a chapter in defense of hypocrisy? The argument here is very simplemindedly practical. The old morality is inappropriate for holding the risks of nuclear war, or even the risks of a repetition of World War II, to their minimum. But the old morality has a strength and life of its own; though I treat it with no great reverence, I regard it simply as an important political and social fact.

If the new morality of Mutual Assured Destruction could indeed be implanted in place of the old standards of war, our task would be much more straightforward and would call for no duplicity and hypocrisy. But there is no early date in sight when this is to be expected, with the U.S. Roman Catholic bishops' letter[19] and President Reagan's Strategic Defense Initiative being very fine illustrations of how far we still have to go. The cultural product of several millennia cannot be revised and amended in four decades, or perhaps not even in ten decades. Thus we have found it necessary to lie to others, and to ourselves, on how the prevention of wars is related to the cultural standards to which we are all in thrall.

This is admittedly an approach that does not take philosophy very seriously in its own right; but philosophers should be assured that it takes the sociological facts of philosophical traditions very seriously. If these traditions were not as powerful as this analysis takes them to be, then there would be no *need* for hypocrisy; and, in fact, much of the muddle and confusion about bombing strategy in this century would never have occurred (indeed, would be quite impossible to explain).

Aside from the difficulty of overcoming centuries of moral tradition, there is yet another argument to be offered for hypocrisy: that it avoids the exploration of logical but damaging analogies. The position of some of the other authors in this volume is that current policies of mutual deterrence plunge us into a deontological absolute immorality, and that such policies will also soon enough contaminate our morality on other subjects.[20] I must confess to being utterly uninterested in the first consideration but to being very taken with the latter argument, itself a "consequence" of deterrence. What if we, after having come to understand and accept the logic of deterrence, begin applying it to discourage murder (by punishing the innocent relatives of murderers where we cannot apprehend the criminal himself)? Would we then also sanction torturing teenagers as a way to discourage them from becoming addicted to narcotics, and so on?

Yet the closing of logical gaps here is hardly such a sure thing. The important point is not whether such connections and analogies *can* be developed logically, but whether they actually then get accepted so widely as to produce such contamination on other fronts. People see analogies, or they choose not to see them. Sometimes the best way to avoid an analogy is simply to avoid thinking very much about a subject.

The professional philosopher may contend that a moral stance based on such evasions, on such a failure to contemplate the analogies, is faulty. But the more practical social scientist would welcome such arbitrary drawing of distinctions, concluding that much of what we do in ordinary life depends on this. "Hard cases make bad law" is an aphorism among modern analysts of the legal scene, contending that we should avoid pressing laws to their logical limits, for fear we will then never be able to legislate anything that is useful and practical most of the time.

One could thus argue that the issue of deterrence is very much like the issue of abortion. Does a tolerance of abortion lead logically to a tolerance for euthanasia, and then for murder? Anyone having seen sonic photographs of a one-month-old fetus, sucking its thumb and moving about in its mother's womb, can be forgiven for concluding that this is already a human being. If it were judged socially desirable that this fetus be aborted, it might then be easy enough for an individual who thinks logically about the issues, after watching such visual displays of the earliest weeks of life inside the mother, to become more callous about the termination of other lives later along. Yet the majority of us, who tolerate abortion and oppose murder, can avoid such moral contamination by simply refusing to dwell upon this analogy, by ceasing to watch such video displays, i.e. by taking steps to lead ourselves to believe that there is a difference.

Similarly, it is also possible that anyone who dwells upon the logic of deterrence will become ready to depart from the moral traditions of Western culture on other subjects; but it is just as possible that the majority of us, who favor deterrence and oppose mass murder, will find ways to avoid the analogy here too, i.e. again by drawing comforting if arbitrary distinctions. If most Americans and most West Europeans have been engaged in this kind of escape on deterrence (and on abortion), the practical "consequentialist" conclusion might thus be that contamination can be contained, that the bad side effects of these policies are much less than might have been feared. We are dealing here less with logical relationships than with a task of measuring psychological impact.

Perhaps we are thus better off living with a combination of hypocrisy and the old morality, amid all the analytical confusions of target planners pretending to do one thing while doing another; for in this way we do not in other areas of life get into any game of aiming at the innocent to dissuade the potentially guilty (other areas of life where this would be much less necessary, and much more costly).

All of this reads like social engineering of the most extreme sort. Yet anyone questioning current policies or moralities, anyone opposing hypocrisy as well as anyone quixotically favoring it, has already joined in a debate about an engineering of public attitudes. There is only a certain amount of leverage to be applied, and the argument is really about the direction in which to apply it.

We are thus in the paradoxical position of welcoming incompetence or subterfuge among some of our colleagues. When missile engineers or Strategic Air Command target planners voice a strong moral commitment to counterforce instead of countervalue warfare, we could try to talk them out of it, and try to change also the moral and philosophical attitudes of the constituencies to which they have to respond. But if that should be impossible, we would not find any reassurance about the impact of all this on crisis stability until we discovered that engineers and target planners were less competent than they pretended, or less truly committed to striking the sword from the enemy's hand. In the end, most of them are likely to welcome the collateral damage from whatever missile strikes they have to orchestrate, because (to our relief) they have found no way to dispense with a retaliatory capability directed at Soviet value items.

One can illustrate this well in the dialogue on Ronald Reagan's Strategic Defense Initiative. The president himself offered a clear and logically consistent version of SDI, proposing to do away with MAD and to have, in the end, no cities in the United States or anywhere else menaced with nuclear destruction. Some of his advisers and spokesmen (and many of the project managers in the SDI program) have offered a far more subtle form of SDI, in which a space-based anti-missile system will be important for shielding U.S. missile silos against a Soviet ICBM attack, i.e. for reinforcing MAD rather than abolishing it. The latter version of SDI is the more devious, and thus the more reassuring for any of us concerned about crisis stability, concerned that any move actually toward Reagan's vision of a nuclear-free future would very much endanger world peace. Living in a world where no city was threatened by nuclear destruction (whether we got to that world by general and complete disarmament or by SDI) might be very good. But getting there might impose the most horrendous strains on each side's apprehensions about the other.

A SUMMARY

The proposition that wars have been prevented by the mere threat of nuclear bombardment is unprovable, but it is nonetheless believed by this author and by most students of contemporary strategy. Similarly, wars have been terminated by the actual imposition of countervalue pain: World Wars I and II both fit this model, in a manner that is considerably more provable.

Some philosophical writers might approve of the threat and never of the actual imposition. The important point, however, is that the bulk of traditional morality condemns both, and that exactly the same euphemisms and confusions have thus had to be wrapped around both. We lie to ourselves when we say that we are only planning for a counterforce response to Soviet aggression, and that the countervalue damage we would thereby impose would be only inadvertent and collateral. We similarly lied to ourselves when the Germans were starved into surrender in 1918, and when the Japanese were starved and bombed into surrender in 1945. If such lies and hypocrisy continue to be needed, we have a real-life experience here from which we have been learning.

Obfuscations have let us live with deterrence. But we might

one day die in "a war nobody wanted" if those obfuscations are too much exposed to the light of day, are too much shown to be as hypocritical as this essay has noted. Clarifying documents such as the Roman Catholic bishops' statement might thus drive a reader to work harder to develop real counterforce weaponry, the very kind of weaponry that (despite its conformance to traditional morality) would upset deterrence.

A different respondent to the bishops might become a more fervent supporter of disarmament, of course, but here the burden of argument and proof remains enormous on whether disarmament can succeed, on whether it can be carried through with sufficient mutual confidence and verification to avoid yet another form of war nobody wants.

The world has slid into a hypocritical application of countervalue techniques because our culture has made it hard to accept such techniques openly. My own favorite outcome might be a frank and honest acceptance of the contingent moral logic of mutual assured destruction, by which threats to civilians are justified when they prevent or end wars. Short of that, I would prefer more hypocritical sliding into such an acceptance, amid all the kinds of euphemisms noted here, rather than accept any philosophically honest pursuit of alternatives that made war more likely.

NOTES

1. For some valuable sortings-out of the moral difficulties of nuclear deterrence see "Ethics and Nuclear Deterrence," special issue of *Ethics* 95, no. 3 (April 1985).
2. Glenn Snyder, *Deterrence and Defense: Toward a Theory of National Security* (Princeton: Princeton University Press, 1961), pp. 14–16.
3. A well-articulated expansion of such an argument can be found in Robert Jervis, *The Illogic of American Nuclear Strategy*, Cornell Studies in Security Affairs (Ithaca and London: Cornell University Press, 1984).
4. See United States Strategic Bombing Survey, *Overall Report (European War)* (Washington: 1945).

5. For a discussion of the logic behind Napoleon's economic attack on Britain, see E. F. Hecksher, *The Continental System: An Economic Interpretation* (Oxford: Oxford University Press, 1922).

6. Quoted in H. A. Jones, *The War in the Air*, Appendixes (Oxford: Oxford University Press, 1937), pp. 26–27.

7. Ibid., p. 19.

8. Sir Julian Corbett, *Some Principles of Maritime Strategy* (London: Conway Maritime Press, 1911), pp. 90–91.

9. Giulio Douhet, *The Command of the Air* (New York: Coward-McCann, 1941), p. 6.

10. Jones, *The War in the Air*, vol. 5 (Oxford: Oxford University Press, 1935), pp. 152–53.

11. United States Army, Air Service Tactical School, *Bombardment* (Washington: U.S. Government Printing Office, 1926), pp. 63–64.

12. Quoted in Sir Charles Webster and Noble Frankland, *The Strategic Air Offensive Against Germany*, vol. 2 (London: Her Majesty's Stationery Office, 1961), p. 53.

13. Quoted in Webster and Frankland, *The Strategic Air Offensive Against Germany*, vol. 4, p. 148.

14. Quoted in R. F. Futrell, *The United States Air Force in Korea: 1950–1953* (New York: Duell, Sloan and Pierce, 1961), p. 481.

15. Cited in *The Pentagon Papers*, vol. 4, ed. M. Gravel (Boston: Beacon, 1972), p. 200.

16. See Oskar Morgenstern, *The Question of National Defense* (New York: Random House, 1959).

17. For a detailed discussion of the evolution of McNamara's policies on nuclear war planning, see Desmond Ball, *Politics and Force Levels* (Berkeley: University of California Press, 1980).

18. See David Lewis, "Finite Counterforce," Chapter 2 of this volume.

19. *The Challenge of Peace: God's Promise and Our Response* (Washington: National Conference of Catholic Bishops, 1983).

20. See C. A. J. Coady, "Escaping from the Bomb: Immoral Deterrence and the Problem of Extrication," Chapter 4 of this volume.

Chapter 6

Finite deterrence

Harold A. Feiveson

OVERKILL BEYOND ASSURED DESTRUCTION[1]

The numbers of nuclear weapons in the arsenals of the United States and the Soviet Union are well beyond what is needed for "assured destruction" – the capability to absorb a first strike by the adversary and to inflict "unacceptable" damage in retaliation. This is the mission that defines the balance of terror in which the United States and the Soviet Union have become each other's "mutual hostages." By virtue of the great destructiveness of nuclear weapons, the assured destruction mission has become the bedrock of nuclear deterrence.

Very few weapons are required for this mission even after allowance is made for the survivability of the retaliatory forces. In 1968, the U.S. Department of Defense estimated that a U.S. nuclear attack with a destructive power of 200 equivalent megatons (EMT) – i.e. the equivalent of 200 one-megaton warheads – could kill 50 million people and destroy over 70 percent of Soviet industry.[2] Figure 1 shows more recent estimates of Soviet – and of U.S. – casualties that could be expected from attacks on urban areas. The figure shows two alternative estimates: The lower estimates are based on assumptions traditionally used by the U.S. government and are similar to those published by the Department of Defense in 1968; the higher casualty estimates assume the possibility

271

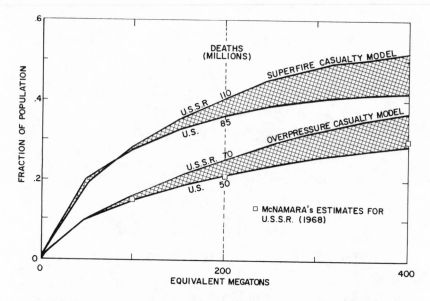

Figure 1. Estimates of the numbers of persons who could be killed in either the United States or the Soviet Union by the direct effects of one-megaton nuclear explosions shown as a function of the number of explosions. The curves labeled "overpressure casualty model" use methods similar to those that were used to make the calculations for Secretary of Defense McNamara in 1968. The curves labeled "superfire casualty model" take into account the lethal effects of the "superfires" that might be ignited by large nuclear bursts over urban areas. (Von Hippel et al., *Scientific American* [see text, note 3], p. 38)

that high-yield weapons exploded over urban areas might cause large and highly lethal "superfires." In the latter case, fifty 1-MT weapons exploded over the urban areas of either the United States or the Soviet Union would immediately kill 25 to 50 million people. In either case, a 50-to-100-megaton attack on urban areas would virtually obliterate the social and economic infrastructure of the major U.S. and Soviet cities.[3] By comparison, as of the middle of 1988 the United States had deployed over 13,000 nuclear warheads on long-range strategic delivery vehicles with a total destructive power of approximately 4,600 EMT, or the equivalent of about 75,000 Hiroshima bombs; the Soviet Union had deployed about

11,000 strategic nuclear warheads with a total destructive power of over 6,000 EMT.

Historically, however, the United States and the Soviet Union have sought more than secure retaliatory forces. Each has acted as if protection of its vital interests depended upon a capability to attack the full range of enemy targets, including economic, political, and military targets and including especially the enemy's nuclear forces and their associated command and control facilities. The most critical and numerous of these targets, those associated with the enemy's nuclear forces, are often referred to as "counterforce targets." In U.S. strategy, this has led to "target coverage requirements" of at least several thousand nuclear weapons, of which a high fraction are designated for counterforce missions.

The adoption of "finite deterrence" by the United States and the Soviet Union would require them to reject this reliance on counterforce weapons and to recognize the futility of seeking goals for nuclear weapons beyond the maintenance of the mutual hostage relationship. In large measure, U.S. and Soviet counterforce weapons have become each other's principal targets. For this reason, it should be possible to drastically reduce both sides' nuclear arsenals without affecting very much the number of retaliatory (second-strike) weapons in the arsenals. Disarmament is a far surer and less catastrophic way to reduce the counterforce capabilities of the nuclear arsenals than counterforce attacks.

Therefore, under finite deterrence each side would drastically reduce its nuclear arsenal and move toward a small highly secure nuclear force capable of inflicting great destruction in retaliation but not suited to counterforce missions.

AN ILLUSTRATIVE ARSENAL:
TENFOLD REDUCTIONS

If the number of nuclear warheads in the arsenals of the United States and the Soviet Union were reduced substantially, it would make sense to do so in ways that put as few warheads as possible at each potential target. By putting few eggs in each basket, such a reduction strategy would maximize the number of targets that a country contemplating a first strike would have to attack. For this reason, any measure of deep reductions of nuclear forces should largely do away with multiple-warhead (MIRVed) ballistic missiles, especially land-based ballistic missiles, which are the most destabilizing elements of today's strategic arsenals. On the other hand, to go very far in this direction could be very expensive if new systems (such as single-warhead ballistic missiles or small submarines) were deployed.

Under any practical reduction scheme to achieve finite deterrence, the residual forces of the United States and the Soviet Union would reflect some trade-off of these factors of stability and cost. The trade-off would depend also on what sorts of verification were possible. If, for example, countries could monitor confidently either the total number of warheads deployed by a country or the degree of MIRVing of specific missile types, it might be possible to "deMIRV" directly, simply by removing warheads from missiles rather than by developing an altogether new missile. The size and composition of a finite deterrent force would also depend on political considerations, such as the probable unwillingness of the United States and the Soviet Union to reduce their strategic forces to levels comparable to those of France, Great Britain, and China.

Based on these various considerations, illustrative finite deterrence arsenals for the United States and the Soviet Union might look as follows (see Table 1, which compares finite deterrent forces with strategic forces in 1988 and as they might be under an agreement along the lines then being negotiated in the Strategic Arms Reduction Talks [START]):

- Strategic warheads for each side would be reduced to 2,000 warheads, in large part by replacing multiple-warhead with single-warhead missiles. A reduction to 2,000 warheads would represent roughly an 80 percent cut in the current strategic arsenals. It would leave each of the arsenals about an order of magnitude greater than the *current* strategic forces of France and Great Britain.

- If it were decided to preserve the current triad of strategic forces, the 2,000-warhead arsenal could be divided among warheads on mobile single-warhead land-based ballistic missiles; warheads on submarine-launched ballistic missiles; and warheads on air-launched cruise missiles or other air-delivered weapons.
- Intermediate-range and tactical nuclear weapons would be largely eliminated.
- The destructive capacity of the force could be fixed by constraining the explosive yield of warheads in the arsenal to less than 100 kilotons. That yield is at the low end of the range of warhead yields in the current strategic arsenals of the superpowers, but it is approximately eight times larger than the yield of the bomb that destroyed Hiroshima.
- Such a regime could be adequately verified through a combination of national technical means, notably satellite observations, and of cooperative measures, including on-site inspections of production facilities, test ranges, and certain other military activities. Verification of some aspects of the regime would be daunting, such as of limitations on numbers of sea-launched cruise missiles; but with minimal prudence in designing a finite deterrence regime, no degree of unobserved cheating could undermine either side's ability to continue to hold the other hostage.

Under this force structure, the total number of warheads in each country's arsenal would be about one-tenth the current number. Each arsenal's total destructive power would be 400 equivalent megatons – less than one-tenth that in each of the superpower arsenals today. The force structure does not eliminate ballistic missiles altogether. Although the speed of ballistic missiles makes them ideal first-strike weapons against the enemy's nuclear forces and command and control network, ballistic missiles cannot be defended against as readily as air-breathing weapons systems and thus provide increased assurance of penetration of the enemy's strategic defenses.

Harold A. Feiveson

THE ADVANTAGES OF DEEP REDUCTIONS

At present, the United States and the Soviet Union must constantly measure their strategic forces against an expanding list of enemy counterforce targets, both to secure their own forces against an enemy first strike and to be able to "cover" the enemy's nuclear forces in a damage-limiting attack. In these circumstances, there is little likelihood that both sides simultaneously will find their forces "sufficient" or adequately balanced with the enemy's. The result in the past has been a steady expansion in the number of warheads in the strategic arsenals of the superpowers. If unconstrained by arms control agreements, this expansion would be expected to continue for at least another decade.[4]

If, by contrast with the current insistence on counterforce weapons, each side were willing to rely for deterrence on small, invulnerable retaliatory forces, the pressures for expansion of strategic forces would be greatly diminished. Without a counterforce threat to contend with, each side's retaliatory force would be relatively easy to secure and would

Table 1. *Illustrative U.S. and Soviet strategic nuclear arsenals under finite deterrence compared to 1988 and to possible START agreement*

	Delivery vehicles			Warheads/totals		
	1988	START	Finite deterrence	1988	START	Finite deterrence
United States						
ICBMs						
Minuteman II	450	0	0	450	0	0
Minuteman III	500	0	0	1,500	0	0
MX (silo-based)	50	50	0	500	500	0
MX (rail-based)	0	50	0	0	500	0
Midgetman	0	300	500	0	300	500
ICBM totals	1,000	400	500	2,450	1,300	500
SLBMs						
Poseidon	240	0	0	2,400	0	0
Trident I/II	384	408	126	3,072	3,264	1,000
Missile totals	1,624	808	626	7,922	4,564	1,500

Table 1. *(cont.)*

	Delivery vehicles			Warheads/totals		
	1988	START	Finite deterrence	1988	START	Finite deterrence
Bombers						
B-52 (ALCM)	160	100	0	2,808	2,000	0
B-52/FB-111	164	0	0	1,190	0	0
B-1/2[a]	97	231	100	1,552	3,698	500 (ALCM)
Strategic totals	2,045	1,139	726	13,472	10,262	2,000
Soviet Union						
ICBMs						
SS-11/13	480	0	0	480	0	0
SS-17	138	0	0	552	0	0
SS-18	308	154	0	3,080	1,540	0
SS-19	350	0	0	2,100	0	0
SS-24	10	80	0	100	800	0
SS-25[b]	100	300	1,020	100	300	1,020
ICBM totals	1,386	534	1,020	6,412	2,640	1,020
SLBMs						
SS-N-6/8/12	548	0	0	548	0	0
SS-N-18	224	0	0	1,568	0	0
SS-N-20	100	140	0	1,000	1,400	0
SS-N-23	64	208	120	256	832	480
Missile totals	2,322	985	1,140	9,784	4,872	1,500
Bombers						
Bear-H(ALCM)	60	130	0	480	910	0
Bear	100	0	0	400	0	0
Blackjack[a]	0	200	100	0	3,200	500
Strategic totals	2,482	1,315	1,240	10,664	8,982	2,000
SLCMs (SS-N-21)	Tens	?	0	Tens	?	0

[a] A modern non-ALCM bomber is assumed to carry an average of sixteen nuclear bombs and short-range attack missiles.

[b] Under finite deterrence, it is assumed that the SS-25 or a follow-on single-warhead missile will be put into a hardened-launcher configuration similar to the proposed U.S. Single Warhead ICBM.

Sources: Numbers of warheads on multiple-warhead missiles based on counting rules agreed to in the *Joint U.S.–Soviet Summit Statement* (10 December 1987). Data for 1988 from *Strategic Forces of the United States and the Soviet Union*, Fact Sheet, The Arms Control Association, Washington, July 1988. Although as of July 1988 the United States had not completed its program to deploy 50 MX missiles, it is assumed that the deployment was complete (the Fact Sheet lists 38 MX).

Adapted from H. Feiveson and F. von Hippel, "The Feasibility of Deep Reductions in U.S. and Soviet Strategic Nuclear Arsenals" (see text, note 1).

be compatible with the other side's requirements for a secure retaliatory capability. In addition, target coverage requirements for damage limitation for both sides would be much reduced. The adoption of finite deterrence by the United States and the Soviet Union would therefore remove much of the incentive for these countries to modernize and expand their strategic forces.

The deep reductions in counterforce weapons imposed by finite deterrence could also help to improve stability by drastically reducing the possibility for preemptive attacks to limit damage. They would, in particular, eliminate the possibility of "barrage attacks" against the escape routes for bombers and against mobile land-based missiles. In barrage, the strategic equivalent of indirect fire by conventional artillery, the attacker would position nuclear explosions uniformly over an area where the mobile weapons were expected to be in the hopes of destroying these weapons, which it could not otherwise target directly. However implausible barrage might seem, it is considered by the military under worst-case assumptions, and its removal as an attacking option would increase confidence in the survivability of both sides' retaliatory forces.

Deep reductions could also significantly reduce the capability of a country to attack its adversary's command and control system, in many observers' view the most vulnerable element of the strategic forces. Since there are probably fewer than 150 to 200 critical command and control targets in each country, attacks by the United States and the Soviet Union on each other's command and control networks could be accomplished by a small fraction of the current arsenals (on the order of 500 weapons, or about 4 to 5 percent of today's arsenals). Modest reductions would not make such attacks any less feasible. But the very deep reductions called for by finite deterrence would force a country to expend a substantial fraction of its forces in a command and control attack; and the reductions would not allow a country simultaneously to attack command and control systems and the nuclear forces remaining after the reductions.

A deemphasis of counterforce and accompanying deep reductions should also make it easier to achieve other stability goals. For example, by emphasizing highly survivable systems, finite deterrence forces could sharply lessen the difference between the survivability of strategic forces on day-to-day (peacetime) alert and their survivability on crisis-generated alert. This is important because there would be less urgency in a crisis to move forces to a higher state of alert, a movement that could be provocative, leading the adversary to believe that the side generating its forces was contemplating the possibility of a nuclear exchange.

The greater crisis stability brought by finite deterrence would not end U.S.–Soviet antagonism, but it would lessen the grip which the mutual fear of nuclear war places on the relationship. So too would the dramatic show of actually dismantling and destroying nine-tenths or so of the nuclear weapons in the superpower arsenals.

WILL FINITE DETERRENCE DETER?

Although any realizable finite deterrent would inevitably possess some counterforce capability, some analysts fear that significantly lessening counterforce capabilities would undermine the effectiveness of deterrence by removing the ability to use nuclear forces in what might appear to be selective and militarily useful ways.

Deterrence of direct attacks on homelands

With respect to deterrence of direct attacks on the United States or the Soviet Union, deep reductions in counterforce weapons would hardly appear to matter. Even if one side had counterforce weapons and the other did not, as long as each maintained a secure retaliatory force, what could the country maintaining counterforce capability hope to gain? Mounting a small-scale counterforce attack would mean futilely exchanging a few of one's own warheads for a few of the other side's warheads. A large-scale attack, even against the reduced forces of a finite deterrent, would cause millions of casualties in the attacked country while leaving its retaliatory capability intact – a most uninviting prospect.

Extended deterrence

A source of deeper concern is that an arsenal incapable of a wide range of counterforce attacks could not adequately deter conventional or even nuclear attacks on allies or pose a frightening enough threat to keep the enemy cautious in the Third World. This has been a particular worry of the United States and NATO.

Throughout its history the NATO alliance has relied upon the threat posed by U.S. nuclear weapons to balance the conventional forces deployed by the Warsaw Pact. Indeed, most of the U.S. nuclear arsenal is justified by this goal, not by the need to protect the United States itself against nuclear attack. The desire to make plausible U.S. willingness to risk American cities for the sake of the European allies has been a powerful motive for the constant search for additional credible "nuclear options" and more "usable" nuclear forces.

For those holding this view, the implicit threat posed by maintaining a finite deterrence force capable of destroying population centers but without significant counterforce capability appears suicidal and, therefore, incredible and empty. They see such a force as irrelevant to the deterrence of less-than-all-out attacks by the enemy. These critics of finite deterrence claim that, by contrast, a substantial damage-limiting capability, even if it could not completely disarm the opponent, would pose a far more credible threat to a potential aggressor, for it would give a country an apparent reason actually to retaliate with nuclear weapons.

This presumption that extended deterrence must rely on a damage-limiting counterforce capability is a view forwarded very strongly in this book by Leon Sloss[5] and Robert Foelber.[6] According to Sloss, for example, the United States should seek "a range of targeting options, with enemy military forces and command and control centers as the principal targets."

In Sloss's view, this is largely because the Europeans "want a strategy that makes the Soviets believe that any threat to Europe brings a strong chance of prompt U.S. nuclear retaliation *against the Soviet Union.*"[7]

One trouble with such arguments is that they imagine unrealistic capabilities for strategic forces. A small and relatively ineffective damage-limiting capability would add little to the credibility of deterrence, since the gains from an attack with such a force would be minuscule compared to the terrors it would unleash. An effective damage-limiting capability might under some circumstances constitute a more credible threat but would, by the same token, be dangerously destabilizing; for any damage-limiting capability which looks effective in retaliation would look far more effective as a first strike. A truly effective damage-limiting capability, however, is simply not possible under any realistic circumstances. There are too many ways to conceal and deliver nuclear weapons for either superpower to hope that it could destroy most of the enemy's arsenal and take itself out of hostage.

Furthermore, a large-scale counterforce attack to limit damage would be almost certain to kill tens of millions of civilians. Such attacks would be as unacceptable on moral and strategic grounds as direct counterpopulation attacks. For example, at present force levels, a comprehensive damage-limiting attack by the Soviets on U.S. missile silos and launch control centers, bomber and tanker bases, international airports, nuclear navy bases, nuclear weapons storage facilities, and command and control targets would immediately kill and seriously injure 20 to 35 million Americans.[8] These numbers do not include long-term radiation-induced cancers, famine, and other secondary effects. A U.S. damage-limiting attack on a similar set of Soviet targets would cause even more Soviet casualties – over 50 million killed and seriously wounded – because Soviet nuclear forces are generally sited closer to population centers than is true of U.S. forces. (See Figure 2.)

These casualty estimates are for counterforce attacks not compromised to reduce collateral damage to civilians. But given the proximity of many critical counterforce targets to

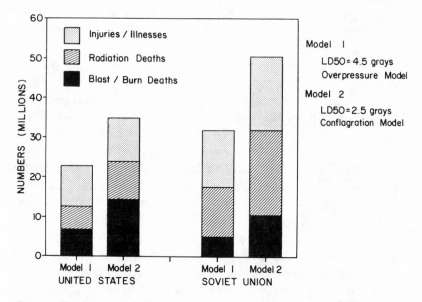

Figure 2. Short-term casualties from counterforce attacks, with typical May winds. Deaths and injuries from attacks on either U.S. or Soviet strategic nuclear facilities would number in the tens of millions. The results shown here were calculated assuming typical May winds (an intermediate case). Model 1 uses the U.S. Department of Defense assumptions that probability of death or injuries from blast and burns is a function of peak blast overpressure and that the median lethal radiation dose (LD 50) for ionizing radiation is 4.5 grays (450 rads). Model 2 takes into account the fact that "superfires" might greatly increase the number of fire deaths and that the median lethal radiation dose, as suggested by the recent reanalysis of Hiroshima casualty data, is only 2.5 grays. (Barbara Levi, Frank von Hippel, William Daugherty, and David Thickens, Research Report 211, Center for Energy and Environmental Studies, Princeton University, June 1987, pp. 20–21)

population, it is difficult to see, in the best of circumstances, how civilian destruction could be much reduced without drastically curtailing the effectiveness of the counterforce attacks themselves.

A nuclear war limited to Europe would also cause unthinkable damage to civilians. Over 400 million people are packed into the relatively small area from the Atlantic to the western border of the Soviet Union. Within this area, there are now thought to be nearly 10,000 nuclear weapons, even excluding the weapons covered by the Intermediate Range

Nuclear Forces Treaty. Clearly, any substantial use of such an arsenal would cause catastrophic damage. Even if a nuclear war in Europe were confined strictly to the Germanies and to a very small set of counterforce targets, there would be very great destruction. For example, attacks limited to the 170 prime counterforce targets in West and East Germany would cause 7 to 25 million immediate deaths and severe injuries, disregarding long-term casualties and disruptions.[9]

The incredibility of any nuclear use does not mean, however, that nuclear deterrence must be ineffective. On the contrary, despite possessing little real damage-limiting potential, the U.S. and Soviet nuclear arsenals today clearly instill great caution in both superpowers, in Europe and elsewhere – as, indeed, do the far smaller arsenals of France, Great Britain, and China. Given the potential for catastrophe inherent in the mutual hostage relationship once nuclear weapons are actually used, deterrence would not seem to depend very much on the details of the arsenals or the plans for targeting them. This is the situation that McGeorge Bundy has termed "existential deterrence"[10] and that David Lewis characterizes as one in which risk-averse states are guided by the admonition, "Don't tangle with tigers."[11]

No matter how unsuited nuclear forces may be to any rational response, their use could never be altogether discounted by a country if the provocation being contemplated, such as an invasion of Europe by the Soviets, was extreme. Even forces scaled to achieve finite deterrence would inevitably have some capability to attack military targets – such as staging bases and airfields – on a limited basis. A large-scale counterforce attack would not be possible with finite deterrence forces, but neither is it truly realizable today.

WHAT IF DETERRENCE FAILS?

Let deterrence look after itself

It is important to distinguish between the capability of the United States and the Soviet Union to destroy each other's society and the actual execution of such an attack if deterrence fails. Given their mutual capability to destroy each other, the two superpowers must act cautiously. They need not continue to search, in ever more refined and esoteric formulations of nuclear strategy, for ways to make their nuclear deterrents more credible. As long as they have secure retaliatory forces, they can decide what to do if deterrence fails without worrying very much about how their decisions in this regard will affect deterrence. How they choose to use their retaliatory forces if deterrence fails can then be determined on pragmatic and moral grounds, not on how the choice affects the credibility of the deterrent.

The capability to inflict unacceptable damage on the enemy need not, and should not, imply the intention to do so if deterrence fails. This is also the point of view taken by David Lewis in this volume: Determine what you want to do if deterrence fails, "and deterrence can look after itself."

Finite deterrence implies the determination of the superpowers to maintain a mutual hostage relationship. However, nothing in the configuration of finite deterrent forces containing several hundred nuclear weapons of great variety would force countries to attack population centers rather than, for example, military installations such as staging bases for conventional war, airfields, etc. Countries would not be forced to undertake massive retaliatory attacks rather than small "demonstrations." They would not be forbidden to attack selected targets of value, such as power plants, transportation centers, oilfields, or electric grids that were remote from population centers. And they would not be forbidden to do nothing if that seemed the best path to take to end a nuclear war as quickly as possible.

Nuclear war would be so novel that no country could be sure beforehand what it would do once nuclear weapons were actually used, and still less could it be confident what its enemies would do. It is, therefore, not unreasonable for countries to rely on capabilities and uncertainties to effect deterrence rather than on statements of intentions and refinements of doctrine. It is not unreasonable for a country to say both that it will maintain the mutual hostage relationship and that it intends not to attack populations if deterrence fails.

It is true that, by insisting on maintaining the mutual hostage relationship, a country adopting finite deterrence is relying ultimately for deterrence on the threat of retaliation, even against cities. But this is true for counterforce doctrines as well, certainly including our present nuclear doctrines.

For the past decade or so, U.S. spokesmen have repeatedly insisted that the United States does not target cities as such. By 1976, the Chairman of the Joint Chiefs of Staff was explaining that "we do not target population *per se* any longer. We used to. What we are doing is targeting a war recovery capability." A recent Assistant Secretary of Defense for International Security Policy has testified that "as a conscious matter of policy, we have not planned for the deliberate destruction of the population."[12]

The United States does, however, target industrial sites which are collocated with population centers. According to Desmond Ball, "simply by virtue of associated industrial and military targets, all of the 200 largest Soviet cities and 80% of the 886 Soviet cities with populations above 25,000 are included in U.S. war plans." A study by the U.S. Arms Control and Disarmament Agency noted that in 1978, on average, nineteen warheads per million population were targeted on the 200 largest cities in the Soviet Union (excluding Moscow). Approximately sixty-four warheads were targeted within 10 nautical miles of the Moscow city center. Ball estimated that a large-scale U.S. attack on Soviet strategic, other military, and economic recovery targets would kill 50 to 100 million people, and that "if population was deliberately targeted, rather than casualties being only side effects of attacks on military and economic targets, then somewhere between 20 and 30 million additional people would be killed."[13]

The situation would be similar for Soviet attacks on the United States. For example, a 100-megaton attack aimed to hit the U.S. urban population directly would kill and injure immediately 40 to 60 million people; a 100-megaton attack on the U.S. military–industrial base would kill and injure 25 to 40 million.[14]

Even some radical schemes of disarmament depend ultimately on deterrent threats. For example, Jonathan Schell's proposal to abolish all nuclear arms depends for stability on the prospect that a threatened country would be able in a relatively short period to reacquire nuclear weapons. The principle underlying the "abolitionist" position – the stability afforded by the mutual hostage relationship – is not dissimilar to that underlying the illustrative finite deterrent.[15] The abolitionist position is, in effect, one of finite deterrence with the level of nuclear warheads set at zero.

Comparison to finite counterforce

In several critical respects, David Lewis's arguments in support of "finite counterforce" also support finite deterrence. Under both concepts, the United States and the Soviet Union would "buy like a MADman" – that is, would deploy forces capable of mutual assured destruction. And under both concepts the forces "impl[y] nothing about what we ought to do in case of war, or what we ought to intend beforehand."

The principal difference between finite counterforce and finite deterrence lies in the second part of Lewis's maxim, "buy like a MADman, use like a NUT." To "use like a NUT" means to undertake counterforce attacks to limit damage. Lewis does not want forces capable of doing so "ambitiously," for this might look like a first-strike capability. But he advocates that some counterforce potential be included in his otherwise MAD forces and that these forces be used to limit damage in case deterrence fails.

One problem with this view is that even a modest counterforce damage-limiting capability is likely to be more effective in a first strike than in retaliation. The situation would be much worse, as Lewis points out, if the counterforce were ambitious. But even if it is not, so that there can be no prospect of a disarming strike, there could be incentives for a country to strike first if by doing so it could reduce damage to itself, at least a little.

More important, if damage limitation made sense for one country in a second strike, it could make sense as well for the other side in a third strike, so that both sides would have incentives for counterforce attacks even after a nuclear war had begun. This is no recipe for war termination, which would be the main hope for damage limitation once deterrence had failed. In any case, a determination of one country to act like a NUT would, in all probability, simply lead the other to withhold fewer missiles in its initial strike with a corresponding increase in damage to the first.

Therefore, "use like a NUT" is not a very helpful prescription for what a country ought to do in case of war. In this case, there is little reason deliberately to include counterforce systems as part of a finite strategic force, although any realizable finite deterrence force is likely to have some counterforce potential, including high-accuracy components.

What to target?

If one should not target cities and not target the enemy's nuclear forces in the event deterrence fails, what then should be targeted? One answer is to target nothing or, rather, to the extent possible, to design the retaliatory force to allow time after a nuclear attack for the political authorities to decide what to do in the real context of a nuclear war rather than having them rely on some prepackaged contingency plans designed during peacetime. In any case, there are many targets other than nuclear forces and cities. These include many power plants, some oil refineries, dams, possibly certain key transportation nodes, and various military installations.

The principal guideline for what to do if deterrence fails must be to keep the war as limited as possible and to end a nuclear exchange as quickly as possible. And finite deterrence forces and command and control networks should be designed accordingly, no matter how skeptical one may be of the possibilities for limiting nuclear war once nuclear weapons were used.

Defense

Without dramatic restraints on offensive systems, the achievement of a strategic defense that could effectively protect population is surely a futile dream. But what about the compatibility of strategic defense with drastic reductions in strategic offensive arsenals?

In practice, strategic defense, no matter how ambitious, would be unlikely to unravel the mutual hostage relationship between the United States and the Soviet Union, even if offensive forces were reduced to finite deterrence levels. If each side saw matters in this light, then strategic defense could be compatible with very deep reductions in strategic forces.

If, however, the defense promised to limit damage very effectively, and eventually to take the nation out of hostage altogether, its compatibility with drastic disarmament looks more dubious. In such circumstances, countries could conceivably accept the erosion of the mutual hostage relationship; but in that case it is difficult to see why defense should provide a better course to save lives than still more drastic disarmament.

If, as is more likely, the United States and the Soviet Union remain unwilling to give up the assurance of the mutual hostage relationship, then defense of population by one side is likely to provoke offensive responses by the enemy, which could well result in still greater damage in the event the arsenals were actually used. And if, despite the offensive reactions, the strategic defenses remained effective in protecting population, in a crisis this would merely lead to the temptation to attack the defensive systems preemptively.

At present, in fact, the superpowers show no intention of allowing each other out of hostage. If so, successful strategic defense looks incompatible with significant disarmament. Whatever strategic defense is pursued by the United States and the Soviet Union should follow the achievement of disarmament to finite deterrence levels, rather than being trumpeted as a precondition.

CONCLUSION

Eventually, we should want to move away from the balance of terror. In the meantime, however, as long as the United States and the Soviet Union remain determined to hold each other hostage, finite deterrence is the best concept for nuclear forces that can be obtained. It rejects as a delusion arguments that countries must be able, with a large and diverse array of counterforce weapons, to "cover" the full spectrum of enemy targets, including thousands of ballistic missile silos, other nuclear weapons facilities, and related command and control sites.

It is incredible that the United States or the Soviet Union would ever undertake a first strike on the other. Even if they expected that none of the enemy's nuclear weapons would survive such an attack, there would be overwhelming reasons for restraint: Such an attack would kill tens of millions of people, would raise risks of severe and ill-understood global environmental consequences, and would shatter the four-decade taboo against the use of nuclear weapons.

But, of course, many weapons would survive such an attack at virtually any practically achievable level of disarmament – certainly at the levels considered in this paper. A few tens of warheads exploded in the populated regions of the United States or the Soviet Union would cause unthinkable damage. Even under finite deterrence, hundreds of weapons would be available for retaliation after any first strike. This is all widely understood, but it suits the pretensions of academic experts, the institutional interests of the militaries and of the industries that the militaries support, and the caution and prudence of political leaders to pretend otherwise.

The massive arsenals that exist today have no rational purpose. The weapons cannot be used, and we may as well get rid of them in an orderly and reciprocated way. Doing so in a sensible manner could reduce the possibility of accident and could also sharply reduce pressures for an endless arms race. Despite the real stability of the present situation, both the United States and the Soviet Union constantly act as if they have to modernize and expand their arsenals in the face of the enemy's counterforce threat. Reductions in counterforce weapons would, therefore, significantly undercut arguments for new weapons. They will make it harder for worstcase analysts in the United States and the Soviet Union to invoke concerns over crisis stability and images of a remorseless enemy as reasons for new armaments.

NOTES

1. This paper is based partly on work reported elsewhere. See especially H. Feiveson, R. Ullman, and F. von Hippel, "Reducing U.S. and Soviet Nuclear Arsenals," *Bulletin of the Atomic Scientists* 41 (August 1985), 144–50; and H. Feiveson and F. von Hippel, "The Feasibility of Deep Reductions in U.S. and Soviet Strategic Nuclear Arsenals," in *Verification of Nuclear Warhead Reductions and Space-Reactor Limitations,* a collection of articles prepared under the cooperative verification project of the Federation of American Scientists and the Committee of Soviet Scientists (New York: Gordon and Breach, forthcoming).

2. Department of Defense, *Annual Report Fiscal Year 1969* (Washington: U.S. Government Printing Office, 1968).

3. Frank N. von Hippel, Barbara G. Levi, Theodore Postol, and William H. Daugherty, "Implications of Counterforce for Nuclear Arms Reductions," *Scientific American* 259, no. 3 (September 1988), 36–42. See also W. H. Daugherty, B. G. Levi, and F. N. von Hippel, "The Consequences of 'Limited' Nuclear Attacks on the United States," *International Security* 10, no. 4 (Spring 1986), 3–45. B. G. Levi, F. N. von Hippel, W. H. Daugherty, and D. Thickens, "Civilian Casualties from 'Limited' Nuclear Attacks on the USSR," *International Security* 12, no. 3 (Winter 1987–88), 168–89.

4. E. L. Warner III and David Ochmanek, "1986: The Year in Arms Control," RAND Corporation, Washington, November 1986 (manuscript).

5. Leon Sloss, "The Case for Deploying Strategic Defenses," Chapter 8 of this volume.
6. Robert E. Foelber, "Deterrence and the Moral Use of Nuclear Weapons," Chapter 3 of this volume.
7. Sloss, Chapter 8 of this volume (emphasis in original).
8. Daugherty et al., "The Consequences of 'Limited' Nuclear Attacks on the United States" (cited note 3 above).
9. William M. Arkin, Frank von Hippel, and Barbara G. Levi, "The Consequences of a 'Limited' Nuclear War in East and West Germany," *Ambio* 11, no. 2–3 (June 1982), 163–73, at 163. The attack scenarios assume two 200-KT weapons delivered to each target. The lower part of the range of casualties assumes two airbursts; the higher part assumes one airburst and one groundburst. The combined population of the two Germanies is 76 million.
10. McGeorge Bundy, "Existential Deterrence and Its Consequences," in Douglas MacLean, ed., *The Security Gamble: Deterrence Dilemmas in the Nuclear Age*, Maryland Studies in Public Philosophy (Totowa, N.J.: Rowman and Allanheld, 1984), pp. 3–13.
11. David Lewis, "Finite Counterforce," Chapter 2 of this volume.
12. Desmond Ball, *Targeting for Strategic Deterrence*, Adelphi Paper No. 185 (London: International Institute for Strategic Studies, 1983), p. 32.
13. Ibid., pp. 15, 34.
14. Von Hippel et al., "Implications of Counterforce for Nuclear Arms Reductions" (cited note 3 above).
15. Jonathan Schell, *The Abolition* (New York: Knopf [also Avon]), 1984.

Chapter 7

Defending Europe: toward a stable conventional deterrent

Lutz Unterseher

INTRODUCTION

This contribution does not discuss details of nuclear policy. It accepts arguments advocating the conversion of the West's current nuclear forces into a minimum deterrent: The idea of controllable nuclear warfighting options has to be regarded as illusory because of the simple fact that the adversary's reactions are in principle incalculable.[1] The call for a radically restricted role for nuclear forces appears to be very plausible, and consequently a "No First Use" policy should be adopted as a first step toward the broader goal of substantially reducing nuclear firepower.[2]

According to this line of argument, the resulting minimum deterrent should enhance crisis stability by not provoking the adversary (through threats to decapitate him) and by not providing him with lucrative targets (which, given today's state of the art, would suggest sea-basing). Within this context the concept of "finite deterrence" can be seen as a convincingly pragmatic step in the right direction.[3] The INF Treaty and the commitment of the United States and the Soviet Union to START give rise to the hope that the two dominating military powers are already on the right track.

As the role of nuclear deterrence is played down, the question arises what a complementary conventional defense would

293

look like. This conventional posture, of course, should in itself be a strong deterrent and should minimize damage (e.g. the risk of escalation) if deterrence fails. The long-term sustainability of such a defense is a third and equally important requirement. So most of this paper's attention is concentrated on exploring several approaches to "conventionalization," confronting different lines of thought within NATO's establishment with security policy alternatives from outside. But before this exploration is carried out, it may be helpful to take a look at the potential attack options of the Warsaw Pact.

SOME NOTES ON THREAT SCENARIOS

In studying the other side's conventional military options vis-à-vis Central Europe, it is of vital importance to avoid NATO's two typical fallacies of perception:

1. Exaggerating the Warsaw Pact's combat strength in order to support political campaigns for higher defense budgets. This is done by basing the assessment of the adversary's forces almost exclusively on numbers of weapons and military formations – virtually neglecting variables such as organizational complexity, quality of equipment, leadership and initiative, troop morale, and the relative loyalty of each superpower's allies.
2. Tailoring conflict scenarios to NATO's political convenience. The implication is that the Warsaw Pact respects NATO's often slow-moving institutional process of consensus building and the weaknesses of its military machine: no aggression before large parts of NATO's active forces are in place; no early preemptive strikes even though West Germany, for instance, is stuffed with vulnerable targets (armored vehicles in their home bases and in storage facilities for transatlantic reinforcements, fighter-bombers on a rather limited number of airfields, launchers of nuclear missiles, etc.).

These fallacies show themselves strikingly to the independent long-term observer, who has seen NATO posit an increasing Soviet threat potential yet at the same time rule out any imminent danger. Admittedly, the following attempt to give a brief overview of the current debate about military conflict scenarios for Central Europe is biased by this observer's impression.

The 1985 White Paper of the German Federal Minister of Defense on "The Situation and the Development of the Federal Armed Forces" considers three different military options of the Warsaw Pact:[4] full-strength attack, attack combining surprise and strength, and attack seeking strategic surprise. "In case of a full-strength attack, the Warsaw Pact would seek to achieve far-flung strategic objectives from the start. The attack would not commence until extensive preparations of both the armed forces and the population would have been made. Such preparations would be identifiable for NATO and would afford the Alliance a comparatively long warning time. This would leave the Alliance time to make political decisions and to prepare its defence psychologically and militarily. . . . Under the present circumstances, NATO considers this kind of aggression unlikely."

This official statement contrasts sharply with a recent analysis conducted by Kaufmann – based on advanced model simulations – claiming that the Warsaw Pact, and the Soviet Union in particular, could "out-mobilize" the West during a long-lasting crisis: the longer its duration, the more favorable the Pact's odds.[5] Our sympathy is with the official statement, which shows a rare degree of self-confidence against the opponent and refrains from exaggerating Eastern capabilities to mobilize. This sentiment is supported by the impression that Kaufmann's assessment has some shortcomings: For instance, it omits from the force balance almost half of the well-equipped and trained German territorial formations for frontline deployment, and numerous units for rear area protection.[6] However, Western – in particular, German – force planning for the 1990s should not overestimate NATO's ability to "countermobilize." The oncoming demographic crisis, resulting from the sharp fall in the birth rate during the late 1960s, calls for new military structures that can make better use of the reservists.

What the Federal Minister of Defense says he fears most is an attack combining strength and (operational) surprise. That is the eventuality – most obviously – for which he would like to prepare his forces. Certainly, this mode of aggression would put NATO decision making to a tough test. But, given that related expert estimates of the time available after the first warning vary between six and nine days, making up one's mind and getting the troops where they ought to be seem to be manageable problems.

Furthermore, the American political scientist Mearsheimer has convincingly demonstrated that even a (rather unlikely) Soviet lead in quick mobilization, resulting in a force ratio of 2:1 in armored divisional equivalents, would not inevitably present a deadly challenge to the West.[7] (The term "armored divisional equivalent" [ADE] refers to a measure developed by the U.S. Army, not adopted by NATO, in order to base its assessment of comparative combat value not only on the quantitative but also on the qualitative aspects of firepower.)

Based on the assumption that NATO's standing forces would be in place at the time of an attack by the Warsaw Pact, Mearsheimer has argued that – thanks to a sufficient force-to-space ratio and the effects of the "crossing-the-T phenomenon" (meaning that the attacker cannot make full use of his firepower while concentrating) – NATO could hold even in the face of massive thrusts and at least deny the enemy any chance of gaining a quick success. This is essential, Mearsheimer says, because only the availability of attractive blitzkrieg options would be adequate to tip the Soviet cost–benefit balance in favor of war. As we shall see later when discussing the doctrine of "Active Defense," there are legitimate doubts about the structural reliability of NATO's current conventional posture. Despite these concerns it can be said, however, that the defender would have enough forces, after proper frontline deployment, to give him a fair chance of bringing a massive conventional attack to a halt.

Mearsheimer's analyses seriously consider only the prospects for an assault after several days of warning. How about a "true" Soviet blitz: namely, an "attack seeking strategic surprise"? The German Federal Minister of Defense concedes initial advantages to such an attack, but then rejects it because of the Soviets' alleged inability to exploit their success in the face of incoming Western reserves. The underlying message, however, is different from the argumentation on the surface: Such a Soviet attack does not fit in with either NATO's political process or its military posture.

In recent years several British authors, among them Dick, Donnelly, and Vigor of the Royal Military Academy at Sandhurst, have developed their idea of Soviet blitzkrieg thinking against the background of an intensive study of the military debate carried on in the Eastern bloc.[8] These British analysts find it quite conceivable that the Soviet leaders, feeling themselves driven up against the wall by worldwide American pressure and an ailing economy, might decide to go to war. After long-term clandestine planning involving deception and camouflage, and possibly using a crisis somewhere along the periphery to divert the West's attention, they would go for a surprise attack (preferably during a "time window" of vulnerability such as Christmas Eve), giving NATO considerably less than two days of actual preparation time.

With only parts of the Soviet standing forces in the German Democratic Republic (GDR) and Czechoslovakia committed, and no satellite troops involved for security reasons, the defender would be superior – but only on paper. NATO's peacetime posture is full of holes: Numerous units are unwisely deployed, and particularly during holiday weekends the manning of vital weapons systems is incomplete. So the aggressor might succeed in bypassing NATO's formations, overrunning and dodging those nuclear weapons of the defender not neutralized by the initial air strike. The general aim would be to prevent NATO from using nuclear weapons, seize the West's bases of mobilization, and block or destroy those airfields and ports that would have to receive American, British, and Canadian reserves, while at the same time commencing full-scale mobilization within the Pact.

These British analysts are well aware of the enormous risks inherent in the concept of strategic surprise attack from a

Soviet perspective (things might go wrong because of the flagging initiative and resulting slow progress of Eastern forces). This is why the Sandhurst scholars give it a rather low probability, albeit higher than the likelihood of an attack on NATO after its forces have managed to "line up" – then NATO's posture would indeed enjoy the Pact leaders' respect. It should be mentioned here that if Gorbachev's plan for unilateral troop reductions in the GDR, Czechoslovakia, and Hungary, made public at the United Nations in December 1988, is actually carried out, and if there are no strings attached in the sense of streamlining the remaining forces for the offensive, the probability of a surprise attack appears to be further reduced.

So far the discussion has focused on scenarios of well-prepared intentional aggression from the East. But this is only half the story. An equally important cause for a hot conflict may lie in either party's shooting first in a crisis situation with faulty inter-bloc communications and rising mutual fears. The side that strikes early – before the opponent disperses his risky peacetime force concentrations and prepares his defenses – may want to create "strategic holes" in the other side's posture that promise rapid exploitation.

The possibility that a political crisis might get out of hand, owing to the inherent advantages of a – nuclear or conventional – early strike, is usually not discussed in official circles. This scenario is the special nightmare of the majority of Europe's peace researchers. They believe that mechanisms of preemption could contribute substantially to the transition from crisis to war. While both alliances appear to be politically defensive, their opposing military postures are seen as incorporating offensive elements and vulnerable structures that undermine mutual understanding and invite military action.

Recently, the European NATO establishment has been supporting this notion, although indirectly and unintentionally. The evolving support for a European Defense Initiative, as the offspring of SDI, implicitly admits that targets on NATO's territory – e.g. bases for dual-capable means of Deep

Strike – may require costly protection from an enemy's (early) blow. So far, however, little analytical work has been devoted by the "authorities" to the abolition of those dangerous targets as a potentially better and cheaper solution to our security problems.

LOOKING AT NATO'S APPROACHES TO CONVENTIONALIZATION

To get an idea of what current "official" concepts to strengthen NATO's conventional capabilities are building upon, it may be useful to look back at the doctrinal development of the 1970s.

"Active Defense": Key doctrine of the 1970s

In 1976 the U.S. Army Training and Doctrine Command (TRADOC) issued a new version of the Field Manual 100-5 (Operations). This can be seen as a highlight of doctrinal development, as the most uncompromising formulation of a fire-oriented defense that had evolved within NATO so far.[9]

Initiated and inspired by General Depuy, TRADOC's first commander, the development of the "Active Defense" concept – as the FM 100-5 of 1976 was soon called – conceived operations and tactics for a positional yet highly flexible defense. Having absorbed the lessons of the Arab–Israeli War of 1973, the authors of FM 100-5 made it their main objective to optimize the use of modern firepower (typically a mix of high-precision tank guns and second-generation antitank guided missiles). This implied fully exploiting the advantages of prepared positions in a friendly environment, careful planning of one's own fire in order to benefit from synergistic effects stemming from different kinds of weapons "working" together, and deployment of forces in high density blocking the prospective axes of the enemy's advance. The latter was to be achieved by doing away with the traditional concept of keeping mobile reserves in the rear: Most of a divisional commander's assets of fire were to be com-

299

mitted frontally. Swift lateral movements "up or down the line" would get sufficient counterconcentrations at the right spot, at the right time. To accomplish this, the role of intelligence and covering forces, which would detect and delay the aggressor's thrusts, was much accentuated.

Active Defense must be understood in its historical context. During the period of its development the Soviet Union was rapidly drawing even at practically all levels of nuclear armament. In the West this process was perceived as a gradual neutralization of its own nuclear options. One consequence was the call for the creation of an improved conventional deterrent, stable in its own right. This was not easy for the U.S. Army to achieve, given budgetary constraints following the Vietnam War and the enormous organizational burden of the transition from conscription to an all-volunteer force. Under these circumstances it seemed plausible to make better use of scarce resources by building upon the advantages of one's own terrain plus modern firepower, while sticking to the well-established pattern of armored and mechanized formations in order to avoid further "institutional" unrest caused by structural experimentation. Compared with the previous operational concept, if there had been any, the deterrent value of this kind of defense was seen in denying the aggressor deep penetrations into NATO territory. Massive firepower (maneuver playing only a subsidiary role) would inflict high attrition rates upon the intruder, thus enabling NATO's forces to win the first battle and thereby prevent the aggressor from gaining territory that might be used as a bargaining chip.

Soon after its appearance the new doctrine met with unexpectedly vivid criticism. Critics, reflecting the recuperation of American pride after the Vietnam disaster, followed a political line of argument and charged that Active Defense was too defensive, confining the offense to the tactical context. According to their perspective, a superpower like the United States should maintain initiative options on all military levels when facing a conflict with the other side. The idea was to have parity of options, whether defensive or offensive. Only this, it was said, could adequately support the role of the United States as the guardian of global peace. Other skeptics, discussing Active Defense within a strictly military frame of reference, have argued that Western force allocation "along the line" may get in trouble for three basic reasons:

1. Aggression by the Warsaw Pact could come as a multipronged rapid advance and not, as hitherto assumed, in the form of easily detectable main thrusts. (This particular concern has developed into the assumption that the Soviets might use "operational maneuver groups" [OMGs] to rapidly bypass Western positions.)
2. Intelligence may not be sufficiently reliable, and NATO's covering screen could turn out to be weak, inconsistent, and full of holes. Thus the prospects might be dim for early detection and checking of the enemy's advance.
3. Lateral movements of armored and mechanized formations – the basic force elements of Active Defense – would almost certainly result in a "logistical nightmare" (S. P. Huntington), because "up-or-down"-moving units would run across the supporting "tails" of their neighbors.

This criticism has led to a reassessment of NATO's conventional capabilities and, consequently, to new lines of thought. While the first of the most relevant approaches to reducing NATO's dependence upon an early use of nuclear weapons, which are discussed below, seems to accept the doctrinal development of the seventies, the second calls for rather radical change.

Attrition, Deep Strike, and FOFA

The most prominent proponents of this school are General Bernard Rogers, the former Supreme Allied Commander Europe, and the ESECS panel.[10] They seem to take a modified concept of Active Defense as given. Their modifications can be seen as a reaction to the critique just described. For instance, there is – again – more stress on mobile reserves, which are of vital importance in case the lateral allocation of forces fails. Nevertheless, the overall posture that both Rogers and ESECS seem to have in mind accentuates fire and attrition: a somewhat linear defense that denies (optimistically all of) Western territory to the potential aggressor.

To make this posture more resistant, Rogers and ESECS follow an "add-on" strategy; structural problems of NATO's current posture are neither tackled nor even explored. So they suggest two sets of measures:

1. To upgrade Active Defense by providing it with high-performance C^3I (command, control, communications, and intelligence) systems, more modern ammunition for direct and short-range indirect fire, and scatterable "smart" mines supporting positional defense.
2. To complement the frontal scheme with assets of medium- and long-range fire. These conventionally armed rockets, cruise missiles, and combat drones, whether of the ground-launched or the airborne stand-off type, are claimed to be functional equivalents of nuclear weapons. This claim has been based mainly on two developments: dramatic increases in both warhead (or submunition) effectiveness and precision (the latter through improved inertial, as well as terminal, target-related, guidance). Usually three kinds of missions are mentioned in this context: offensive counter-air missions, destroying the enemy's airfields before he has managed to send the bulk of his planes westward; hitting small stationary targets like C^3I installations or depots; and attacking the adversary's follow-on forces (FOFA) while they are on the move or after they have been stopped at choke points.

This second component of the Rogers plan has been widely criticized. The criticism may be summed up as follows:

1. The concept of Deep Strike is destabilizing because it nourishes preemptive thinking. If the steadfastness of NATO's forward defense depends on an early destruction of assets stationed in the enemy's rear, it appears to be imperative for us to shoot first although we legitimately see ourselves in the role of defender.
2. If one uses weapons that could carry chemical or nuclear warheads as well (which happens to be the case with some of the proposed means of delivery), the opponent has no way of

knowing what is going to hit him next: Escalation could become a plausible reaction.

3. Employing conventionally armed smart weapons against second-echelon forces could prove unexpectedly problematic. Hitting targets on the move demands real-time intelligence that requires redundant observation platforms and an integrated communication system of the utmost complexity. Yet the frictions of war put a premium on ruggedness and simplicity. Even hitting stationary objects in the enemy's rear is impossible without first-class reconnaissance plus a high IQ built into each weapon. Making our target acquisition foolproof against relatively cheap countermeasures, like dummies, flares, and jamming, could trigger a cost explosion.[11]

Thus the Rogers plan confronts the Western public with a serious dilemma: Either the proposed array of conventional lightning-strike missiles functions well, giving rise to fears of early use and subsequent escalation, or there are going to be grave technological problems. In the latter case we could either give up and accept the resulting credibility deficit of our conventional deterrent (we would have nothing left but good old Active Defense with its built-in inconsistencies), or else spend a vast amount of money to make these exotic weapons work (for consequences, see above!).

Maneuver and punishment

Many Western military experts maintain that defending the Central European front with a phalanx-type deployment of mechanized and heavily armored units is a contradiction in itself. As a way out of this dilemma they suggest that our armored forces utilize space for maneuver. In order to develop their true talents they should be allowed to move freely across wide areas, both backward and forward, penetrating deep into Warsaw Pact territory. Going east is regarded as a better use of one's scarce resources and easier to accomplish organizationally (avoiding "logistical nightmares").

Going east, thus staying in line with the logistic flow, has also been given a political rationale. As Huntington believes, the present nuclear balance at all levels has led to a neutralization of retaliatory options, thus weakening nuclear deterrence. This in turn calls for a renaissance of conventional deterrence, which he suggests can be achieved only by using our armored formations as the means to punish a potential aggressor.[12] Only retaliatory options, which put an opponent's territory at risk, would make him abstain from aggression. Denial by attrition, as in the case of Active Defense, says Huntington, could render our military posture calculable and a weak deterrent.

The "AirLand Battle" doctrine, as contained in the 1982 version of U.S. Army Field Manual 100-5, is well within this conceptual framework. Downplaying the implicit departure from Active Defense by stating that (counter) offensives have been confined to the operational level, which still comprises maneuvers of about a 100-km range, is not very helpful. Given the very fragility of the Eastern bloc, even tactical (!) intrusions, about 50 km deep, could be perceived as a strategic challenge. In East Germany and Czechoslovakia, within a belt along the western borders of about this depth, lie important population and industrial centers. A potential NATO invasion, causing a political upheaval in this vital zone, may be among the worst nightmares of the Pact leadership.

The most recent version of FM 100-5, which appeared in 1986, seems to confirm the concept of far-reaching maneuver warfare – although sounding much less provocative. It cannot appease those who show grave concern over the consequences of this doctrinal development. They have put forward the following arguments:

First, offensive operations aimed at penetrating enemy territory may require very high troop concentrations, higher even than those for Active Defense, thus inviting massive – early – strikes from Warsaw Pact tactical air and missile forces.

Second, as most Western armor and mechanized units suitable for offensive action become "really dangerous" only after they have been filled up with reservists, the Soviets may find that there is a premium on *very* early preemption (with

304

the additional advantage of hitting Western forces still as-
sembled in their bases).

Third, concentrating on the operational or strategic offense creates open flanks which can be exploited quickly by
the opponent. Even if one protects the areas aside from the
main effort with terrain-oriented light formations, the rule is:
The more investment in offensive maneuver, the higher the
vulnerability of flanks and basis. It is in this context that a
historical study of conventional armed conflicts comes to the
following – cautious – conclusion. War is more likely to break
out when both adversaries are concentrating on the offensive or counteroffensive, whereas an area-covering defense
adopted by one side *frustrating the other's intentions for a rapid
invasion* has a good chance of preventing an open clash.[13]

Moreover, one can view conventional maneuver warfare
as a risky strategy that may well provoke an *early* nuclear, or
chemical, escalation. How is the commander of the Warsaw
Pact forces likely to respond if he cannot halt a conventional
thrust with similar means? And how will NATO respond
when sizeable elements of allied forces are trapped by defensive formations of the Warsaw Pact, say, east of Magdeburg?
Most people who irresponsibly speak about going east tend
to forget that the Soviet Army does not consist solely of offensive elements. About half of the Soviet forces in Europe,
and more than 40 percent of those belonging to the Group of
Troops in Germany, are motorized rifle divisions. These force
elements must be regarded as well suited to a terrain-oriented
defense with infantry deployed in depth and reinforced by
armored elements for tactical counterattack. Following the
tradition of Kursk (where in 1943 Red Army infantry, employing mines and antitank guns, brought a massive attack
by the Wehrmacht's armor to a halt), modern Soviet forces
may well be able to render the enhanced-maneuver concept
suicidal.

Finally, military experts affiliated with the Pentagon, who
are proud to have rediscovered the "art of war" (World War
II German-style), seem to share the belief that fire-oriented

attrition is calculable (you know how much you need to out-gun your foe) but resource-consuming. On the other hand, maneuver warfare is said to be risky but less expensive. Critics concur with the evaluation of risk but disagree over cost. They argue that the days of Bill Sherman's raiders have gone, and also the days of elite tank corps sent against unprotected terrain and unprepared infantry. Moving in a modern hostile environment demands winning the battle for dominance in the field of electronic intelligence. It also requires the protection of flanks and the delaying of oncoming enemy forces by mobile precision-guided fire, as well as an anti-aircraft umbrella provided by numerous organic AA batteries, able to neutralize simultaneous assaults by enemy aviation in a quick-reaction manner. Furthermore, we should not forget combat engineers, who would need more high-performance bridging and advanced mine-clearing equipment (i.e. robotics). All would not work without a sophisticated logistics organization capable of responding quickly to the needs of highly mobile formations over extended distances.

So far only the key – maneuver-oriented – element of the AirLand Battle doctrine has been discussed. Since maneuver alone does not kill, there also is an element of fire. Interestingly, the assets of fire supporting the AirLand Battle are conceived to comprise means of delivery with ranges between 50 and 100 km. The rationale is that it may be wise to disrupt the enemy's rear echelons before or while friendly forces are heading east.

Affordability

Today the Rogers plan in its original version seems to have lost its viability. Being reluctant or unable to increase their defense budgets annually by 4 to 7 percent above inflation, as suggested by the former Supreme Allied Commander Europe, the majority of the NATO partners did not get beyond a formal acceptance of FOFA and conventional Deep Strike. Instead interest has focused on the concept of a more shallow strike which has been accentuated by ESECS II. "Shallow" means 50 to 100 km deep. Here we see a similarity to the fire element of the AirLand Battle. Although that seems more realistic than ranges of up to 500 km, which Rogers originally had in mind, some skepticism remains concerning this concept's technological feasibility.

At first glance it looks as if this more moderate plan could be implemented with rather limited resources. Nevertheless, it poses financial problems for a number of NATO countries. If we take the Federal Republic of Germany as an example, we may find that a mere modernization of the Bundeswehr, not a buildup, could increase the defense budget's share of overall federal spending from about 20 to more than 28 percent within the next twelve years.[14] Fundamentally, two factors lie behind this phenomenon:

1. The introduction of a new generation of main weapons systems and modern ammunition throughout the 1990s will almost certainly be accompanied by an unprecedented rise in unit costs, because of a gradual "Europeanization" of arms markets, as well as developmental risks inherent in high-tech sophistication. (Europeanization is just another word for locking out American or other competitors.) The Europeanization of the market for tactical aircraft, for instance, has already resulted in a price level higher than in the United States (the TORNADO program is an especially frightening example).
2. The concept of mechanized, mobile warfare requires a relatively high level of active troop strength which, given adverse demographic conditions, can be maintained only if additional volunteers are attracted through costly pay increases. (There are political limitations to dramatically extending the conscripts' term of service.) Present West German long-term defense planning is sticking to target figures of personnel strength close to the current level of 500,000 active soldiers, despite the fact that a "natural" course of development, following the demographic situation, would lead to a Bundeswehr of only 290,000 by 1995.

In West Germany at least, the conflict between defense expenditures and social policy (in the widest sense of the word) will become acute if current defense planning is continued and executed.

Model simulations based on official data concerning economic growth estimates and budgetary planning indicate that the projected development of defense spending plus the financial demands of social policy will reduce the government's resources for other purposes from today's 50 percent of the federal budget to 36 percent (or less) in twelve years.[15] This would be caused not only by the growth of defense spending but also by the increasing needs of the social sector. To give just one example: As the elderly population grows in both relative and absolute terms, more government money will be needed to support the public pension system.

Such a development, narrowing the government's scope for maneuver, is simply intolerable for an advanced industrial society. It could not accept devoting an ever-smaller share of public resources to high technology, the development of new energy bases, structural reform of the economy, and environmental protection. The dim prospect of reduced "investment in the future" could put either the social sector or defense under pressure. The inherent dilemma is obvious: Substantial reductions in social expenditures would almost certainly lead to public unrest and a gradual political destabilization. As indicated by numerous public opinion polls, West Germany's young and still frail democracy relies heavily on public care for the poor, the weak, and the elderly as a guarantee of internal peace. Drastic cuts in defense spending instead would – in the eyes of the ruling elite – weaken our conventional deterrent and lead to a renuclearization with all its problems of credibility. The implication is that external and internal stability are conflicting values.

ALTERNATIVE DEFENSE: PHILOSOPHY AND HISTORY

Fundamentals

The basic orientation of the "Alternative Defense" school of thought becomes clear when presented against the background of a pointed critique of NATO's mainstream thinking. The following arguments against NATO – as it is and as it is feared to develop – represent views shared by most of the European experts who work on Alternative Defense.

NATO's particular concept of strengthening the conventional forces while keeping theater nuclear weapons tightly interwoven with them is seen as undermining the stability of both the nuclear and the conventional deterrent. The current "unhappy mix" of theater nuclear weapons and traditional formations is said to render Western conventional forces lame and to result in "self-deterrence." "Lame" because the necessarily rigid command and control system of the nuclear forces reduces the flexibility of conventional elements. "Self-deterrence" because the defense, if actually carried out, would immediately destroy the land being defended or that of fellow Germans in the GDR and of other good neighbors. So there are doubts as to what a Western – probably German – field commander can really rely on in case of a military conflict ("de facto No First Use").

Even the recognition that the Warsaw Pact has a higher respect for NATO's atomic artillery than do Western experts themselves would give no grounds for contentment. No matter how weak the Western will to resist, NATO's theater nuclear weapons are seen by the Soviets as potentially dangerous; and these weapons, because they are deployed or stored on land, present targets that must be destroyed or overrun in the opening phase of a war. The Western posture in conjunction with this Soviet view, which can claim a certain military rationality, fuels fears that an inter-bloc crisis might slide into open war due to a "mechanism of preemption."

Apart from its direct hobbling effect on conventional forces, NATO's nuclear posture in Europe has three essential qualities: It consists of dangerously provocative force elements; it presents lucrative targets to the potential aggressor; and it is incapable of damage limitation once deterrence has failed. Interestingly the "alternative" critics claim that the same negative qualities appear in NATO's conventional forces and related planning. It is said that NATO's nonnuclear posture is developing into a mirror image of its nuclear warfighting forces. Indeed, as we have seen when discussing the Alliance's approaches to conventionalization, there are elements assigned to deep penetration for punishment, there are dense concentrations of planes, ships, and tanks (targets), and there is a tendency toward maneuver doctrine, making a restriction of the battle zone illusory (and thus undermining the will to fight).

These built-in inconsistencies lead our critics to rate NATO's current – and planned – conventional posture low on long-term war avoidance and cause concern that this posture may be unable to prevent uncontrolled nuclear escalation because of its many dual-capable elements and its tendencies toward "risk strategy." Furthermore, they argue that NATO's "forward fence" – owing to the partial misdeployment of forces and the slow mobilization process typical of armored units – is full of holes, additionally inviting a Soviet surprise attack through a bypassing maneuver. Another objection is that the current structure of Western ground forces, with its dominance of heavy mobile formations, along with the growing trend toward far-flung maneuver, plays into the hands of the Soviet military leaders. This is the kind of structure they are most used to.

Here we arrive at the critics' core argument: NATO's establishment is hooked on the idea of "answering in kind." The notion is that stability depends on "balance," and balance rests on possessing all of the suspected military (attack and defense) options of the opponent including the related structures. If these structures in themselves lack stability, there can be no reliable equilibrium. Any single move toward force modernization by one side calls for "equivalent" action by the other to get more of the same in ever-increasing quality. These are the dynamics of the arms race, which in the not-too-distant future may weaken the internal stability of modern societies (see the projection of Germany's resource problems).

If indeed a structural change in NATO's posture is needed, even a dramatic reversal of current doctrinal development back to – let us say – a sound philosophy of Active Defense ("denial by attrition") would be utterly insufficient. We should remember that this doctrine was given up mainly because it did not fit the existing structural substratum (heavy armor), and that in turn the inherent qualities of this substratum called for a "suitable" ideology (maneuver warfare and conventional punishment).

Against the background of criticism of official NATO thinking, the resulting plea for substantial structural and doctrinal changes can take on the form of a brief catalogue. In conjunction with the reestablishment of "denial" – as opposed to "punishment" – as the basic defense philosophy, the following measures are considered necessary:

1. Removal of nuclear assets from NATO's European territory, separation of nuclear and conventional forces, adoption of "No First Use" (only if the demands on the American nuclear umbrella are greatly reduced is there a chance for some form of extended deterrence to survive).
2. Creation of an inherently stable conventional deterrent, by
   - tactically and organizationally emancipating it from nuclear weapons (which would no longer be counted upon as "trouble-shooters");
   - giving it the capability to restrict the battle zone, making it virtually safe from being overrun, bypassed, or "out-maneuvered" technically and tactically, and keeping it from presenting valuable targets to enemy fire, thus abolishing opportunities for the opponent;
   - making it structurally incapable of (and doctrinally not charged with) invading or bombarding the other side's territory, thereby removing the reason for preemption.
3. "Decoupling" from the arms race and consequently maintaining and improving the internal stability of our societies by doing away with the traditional concept of balance ("answering in kind") and by specializing in defense in a cost-effective manner.

Back to the origins: The early 1950s

How did alternative thinking about defense evolve? Let us see how it all started in postwar Germany.

In 1952 a certain Bogislaw von Bonin was appointed head of the sub-department of military planning in the Amt Blank – the nucleus of the later Federal Ministry of Defense – in Bonn. This ex-colonel had been a general staff officer in the Wehrmacht but was sent to a concentration camp for refusing to obey an order of the Führer. Bonin naively believed in key foreign-policy declarations of the federal government (which was then a coalition led by the Christian Democrat Konrad Adenauer), according to which there was imminent danger of Soviet aggression, West Germany's allies were highly trustworthy, and the reunification of Germany was the overriding objective.

To fit in with this frame of reference, von Bonin proposed a barrier zone all along the demarcation line, 50 to 70 km deep, intended to wear down, and possibly stop, the armored thrusts of an invader. For this scheme he claimed both "defensivity" and the possibility of quick implementation at relatively low cost.[16] The concept called for numerous small, well-camouflaged field fortifications distributed in depth. The equipment would consist of relatively simple state-of-the-art weapons. Bonin mentioned between 8,000 and 9,000 antitank guns with a limited degree of tactical mobility, complemented by recoilless rifles and plenty of mines. Only relatively small armored reserves were an integral component of the proposed scheme. The highly experienced ex-colonel was particularly skeptical about sophistication. Seeking quick, cheap, and reliable solutions, he proposed procuring ordnance that would be not far above the standard of Soviet equipment in the battle of the Kursk Salient. This decisive encounter of World War II had very much inspired von Bonin's thinking.

According to von Bonin's plan, "defensivity" was to be translated into adequate tactics and force structures, both designed for exploiting the advantages of friendly terrain. Independent, mechanized all-purpose forces were thought of only in the context of Western reserves, which were relatively weak at that time, coming to chop off any enemy

312

spearheads that might eventually pierce through the proposed "shield."

The point of this unambiguously defensive and purely German front layer was to avoid doing anything that might stimulate a buildup of potential Soviet invasion forces in East Germany. The idea was to deny access to one's own territory ("denial"), but not to appear threatening ("nonprovocation"). It was von Bonin's nightmare that foreign mobile forces with offensive capabilities, armed with nuclear weapons, would assemble in ever-increasing strength on both sides of the Iron Curtain, creating a climate of confrontation and instability and minimizing the chances for German reunification.

Contrary to his opponents' claim, the Bonin Plan was never given a fair and thorough military evaluation. Soon after the ex-colonel developed his proposal, he was ostracized as a dissident. Overtly, the main argument against his plan was that it would have the effect of creating another Maginot Line, making the division of Germany intolerably visible. In fact, the plan implied nothing of the sort; on the contrary, it suggested the virtual disappearance of military targets through camouflage and dispersed deployment.

Behind closed doors, Adenauer and the majority of the rapidly evolving politico-military establishment were not as concerned about German unity as they claimed to be in public. In the eyes of this new elite, the Bonin Plan would impede the buildup of heavy armored forces; these forces were seen as the path to respectable status and bargaining power in NATO, which West Germany was on the verge of joining. Contrary to their own declarations, they saw no acute danger of an invasion from the east and distrusted their new allies.

New inputs in the 1970s

The press gave extensive coverage to the Bonin debate, but after 1956 the controversy died away. A new discussion about "defensive defense" began in West Germany during the second half of the 1970s, on a smaller scale.

Somewhat similar thinking received professional publicity earlier in the Anglo-American world.[17] Most of the contributing experts tried to exploit the full potential of second-generation antitank guided weapons (ATGWs), which at that time promised to bring about a revolution on the battlefield. Light infantry forces, either in a deep chessboard deployment or in a techno-guerrilla manner, were thought to be congenial to the new weapons' characteristics. It seemed possible to neutralize the alleged Soviet superiority in numbers of tanks at moderate cost. All these proposals were meant for a Central European environment, but the authors were not much concerned about their allies' chances to survive. None shrank from making urban sprawl or villages military targets by using them as cover. As the Anglo-American debate continued, a more sober view of the role of ATGWs developed, partly caused by an assessment of data obtained in the October War of 1973.[18] As a result, quite a few American concepts specializing in defense, later proposed, rely upon mixed structures and weaponry.[19]

There are no indications, however, that these Anglo-American contributions had much direct influence on the German discussion. Here the first proposal came from the peace researcher Horst Afheldt,[20] who was inspired by the work of Guy Brossollet, a French army officer.[21] Making extensive, yet highly selective, use of what advanced technology seemed to offer, Afheldt developed the concept of "Raumverteidigung" (area defense). This defensive system, to cover most of West Germany, would consist of thousands of platoon-size infantry commandos, homogeneously armed with second-generation ATGWs, in numerous reinforced positions. To protect this highly dispersed and static, terrain-oriented system from massed blows, Afheldt proposed "counterconcentrations" created by indirect precision-guided rocket fire from rear areas of the defense. These artillery rockets, although they represented a leap forward in sophistication, would make a simpler and cheaper defense system,

Afheldt claimed, than those currently under development for Deep Strike purposes. As these weapons would be launched only in support of the stationary infantry commando units, missile design and fire control could benefit from the friendly conditions for reconnaissance and target acquisition in one's own terrain.

Afheldt's approach has been very impressive, mainly because at first glance it seems to be an almost pure translation of the no-target philosophy and the nonprovocation principle into military structure. In his model nothing moves, neither the infantry nor the launchers of artillery rockets. Mobility of fire substitutes for mobility of troops. There would be no invasion capability that the other side might legitimately fear. Concerning the implementation of the no-target philosophy the picture is less clear. On the one hand, it has been argued that the proposed dispersal and protection of infantry teams and rocket launchers would render an aggressor's firepower superfluous. On the other hand, it has been said that infantry platoons cannot be supported by rocket artillery by giving each platoon full authority to call in fire support. In order not to be fooled by probing attacks, the system has to be "hierarchized": In other words, fire control centers would be needed. This runs counter to one of Afheldt's basic ideas, namely "robust decentralization." There would be targets worth attacking, after all. Grave problems of tactical rigidity may also arise if so much depends on the coordination of the infantry commandos and the rocket artillery. This rigidity may invite rapid mop-up operations by the aggressor's first-class mobile infantry. It has to be noted, however, that such elite infantry is a particularly rare asset in the other side's potential.

Besides such military considerations, there are explicitly political ones: Afheldt's original model, covering most of West Germany with a defensive structure, without an eastward-looking front line, and giving no particular role to the NATO allies, has also been criticized for its inherent tendency toward neutralism. Other advocates of an Alternative Defense – most of them retired military men whose contributions appeared during the late 1970s and early 1980s – have stuck to the more traditional concept of exclusive orientation toward aggression from the east, realizing that the minority of West Germans who support neutrality is not likely to expand. One of these experts is Löser, with his concept of tactically mobile commandos on very light vehicles.[22] Another is Hannig, who proposes a fire barrier along the demarcation line, created mainly by precision-guided missiles of various overlapping ranges, launched from mobile carriers.[23] Füreder's proposal[24] is basically a variation on Löser's, Gerber's[25] a very intelligent variation on Hannig's.

Hannig focuses on nonprovocation; none of his (locally) mobile units have the organizational complexity to fight east of the demarcation line. Much depends on the coordination of widely dispersed fire units. This is why the control centers in Hannig's concept present valuable objectives to enemy measures, thus weakening the no-target approach.

Löser seems to put more stress on the no-target philosophy than on nonprovocation. His small-sized mobile teams are capable of far-reaching infiltration, which the opponent might perceive as a substantial challenge. But even the no-target quality of these (mostly nonarmored) motorized units has been questioned. It seems that on the fire-swept modern battlefield, besides dug-in dispersed infantry, only two kinds of mobile formations enjoy a certain chance of survival: armor, if in small formations, and unprotected guerrilla fighters of extremely amorphous fluidity, which, by the way, would pose very serious problems of command and control.

Most of these authors claim that their proposals, once implemented, could stop an invader east of the Weser–Lech line inside friendly territory at much lower cost and with much lower risk of a breakthrough than the present West German–NATO posture. Afheldt, though sure about preventing a breakthrough (there is no "rear" in his model), is less certain about a truly forward defense: Reliably stopping an invader very close to the demarcation line may, he argues, require friendly force concentrations that could offer targets to nuclear fire.

All these experts are aware of the increasing scarcity of fiscal resources (though few have yet made any detailed calculations). And they also recognize that demographic developments, which will drastically reduce available conscripts in Germany, at least partially require force structures with reduced complexity, adequate for the integration of reservists.

All aim at avoiding fighting in inhabited areas: large villages, towns, or urban sprawl. They forgo the use of population centers as bases for friendly fire units, agreeing that to turn such areas into targets would neither make military sense nor protect civilians.

Most of these authors exploit modern technology rather extensively in the interests of cost-effectiveness. They seem to welcome every technical innovation, however sophisticated, that promises to hamper enemy movement. At least to some of these alternative designers technology appears to be more important than tactics or structure. In recent years this notion has been challenged by a team of systems analysts with the Bundeswehr University in Munich, as well as the Study Group on Alternative Security Policy (SAS). Both groups argue that the monoculture of weaponry that figures in Afheldt's or Hannig's concept, and to a lesser extent in Löser's, is likely to make us vulnerable. The enemy could resort to rather simple countermeasures. We would be better off, these groups reason, if we concentrated on the development of tactics and structures of a defensive and terrain-oriented nature rather than on a technological fix.[26] There are no defensive weapons as such! Creating an unambiguously defensive posture is a matter of shaping the overall structure.

SPIDER IN THE WEB: AN INTEGRATIVE PROPOSAL

This section is devoted to a rather detailed description of the interactive forward defense concept developed by the Study Group on Alternative Security Policy (SAS).[27] This approach utilizes elements of the existing force structure, while at the same time sticking to a basic strategy of defense. So far this concept is the only one in Western Europe that has received considerable backing by public institutions or their representatives, as we shall see later.

SAS is an independent group of organization specialists, economists, technologists, military tacticians (active officers), public servants, and younger-generation politicians in the Federal Republic of Germany, the Netherlands, and Britain. The group bases its proposal on a systematic evaluation of a rich collection of contributions emphasizing defense. This includes a broad spectrum of structural formations that were – in theory or in practice – generated in Germany, as well as in the United States, the United Kingdom, Israel, Austria, Finland, and elsewhere.[28]

The design philosophy of SAS suggests that a potential aggressor should be confronted with the utmost complexity on the part of the defender, in both force organization and tactics. There must be no premium for the aggressor in adapting his tactics and operations to the defender's particular way of fighting. This sort of highly resistant complexity can be created by close interaction of a set of functionally different force elements, each based on rather simple organizational schemes and employing easy-to-grasp robust tactics. Thus, the "insider" will enjoy all the advantages of simplicity, which is of key importance in times of war.

Land forces: Design, structure, operations, manning

Structural differentiation of the land forces envisages the following pattern, consisting of three basic elements:

1. A static area defense which uses reactive "wait and see" tactics. This subsystem is in essence a decentralized infantry network, called the *containment force.*
2. Mechanized troops with a certain degree of operational mobility, who are capable of reactive and active missions. This element is called the *rapid commitment force.*
3. A *rear protection force* including light infantry for object defense

and motorized/light armor units to deal with airborne assaults and large-scale diversion.

Up to 90 percent of the wartime rear protection force would consist of reservists who could be mobilized quickly thanks to a regional pattern of organization. More details are not given here because the forward combination of the static area defense and mobile commitment forces is – tactically and technically – more interesting and of greater relevance to the overall SAS model.

As a safeguard against surprise attack, the forward zone of the decentralized infantry network is to be manned by active personnel. This would mean platoons of thirty soldiers for each sector of approximately 16 square kilometers, in a strip of land about 30 km deep stretching out all along the demarcation line. Behind this active part of the containment force there should be a zone, about 50 km deep, which would see one platoon per 6 to 9 square kilometers, following the traditional rule of increasing density with depth. Taking into account Germany's approaching demographic crisis, manning this part of the infantry network would be impossible without relying heavily on regionally integrated reservists, whose quick and flexible mobilization for purely defensive missions would not increase tension in times of crisis but would rather underline NATO's will to resist. Intensive training and repeated on-the-spot exercises would allow these reserves to make good use of "their" terrain – as good as the soldiers in the active forward belt. By the way, the teeth-to-tail ratio of such a defense – that is, the proportion of forces assigned to combat versus support tasks – is excellent.

The survivability of this kind of light infantry appears to be reasonable if troops are deployed in depth and randomly distributed, to maximize the enemy's uncertainty as to their whereabouts. The installations should be small, with two or three men per position. Other inexpensive measures to enhance their survivability further are: hard cover (prefabricated steel or concrete elements); three or four alternative foxholes per team; camouflage, with plenty of decoys and dummy positions. For good protection of the crews, the weaponry of the containment force should be handled by remote control or by adopting a "sensor-triggering" mode.

It has been argued that – in the age of broad-spectrum satellite photography and, particularly, with the advent of advanced sensors, such as forward-looking infrared (FLIR) and millimeter-wave radar, for use by ground forces and tactical air – the proposed scheme of fixed positions would be open to quick and fatal detection. The twofold answer is that mobile objects (e.g. tanks) are much more difficult to conceal than static force elements, and that the competition between multidimensional sensors and, consequently, multidimensional camouflage can be won by the latter at remarkably low cost. (The Swiss Army "employs" cattle in order to blur the infrared image of its static infantry.) The combination of dispersal and deception would result in a degree of "information overload" that might be too much for the enemy artillery commander to cope with. In other words, the job of managing the incoming abundance of dubious messages would drive him crazy.

Basic assets of static warfare to achieve area control and attrition are: multisensor mines (including scatterable minelets); directional mines, which can be seen as automated recoilless rifles simulating density of troops in a highly dispersed setting; other cheap engineer-made obstacles; remote-controlled batteries of large-caliber bazookas; shoulder-launched surface-to-air missiles; mortars and relatively simple RPVs (remotely piloted vehicles) like the U.S. Army's FOG-M, with fiber-optical guidance for short-range indirect fire support. These latter weapons should be at the disposition of battalion commanders, giving them a flexible capability to support subordinate companies and platoons in covering their barriers and obstacles with fire. Modern equipment enabling the network's strong element of combat engineers to create numerous small strongholds speedily, as well as effectively, would be of great importance. Communications would be supported by a robust EMP-proof fiber-optical network.

The static scheme would cooperate with the mobile rapid commitment force, which has been conceived as a standing alert element. This element has not been designed as a homogeneous bloc. It should undergo internal functional differentiation. Besides a well-protected armored force of 40-to-44-ton tracked vehicles armed with state-of-the-art kinetic-energy guns, it would include antitank cavalry with high firepower and operationally mobile infantry, both mounted on the same family of 18-to-20-ton light-armored wheeled vehicles. After all, given the advantages inherent in making full use of "friendly" terrain with an excellent road network, tracked medium tanks are not the only currency to pay with. Incidentally, these mobile infantry forces are to be structured and equipped to deal with light infantry infiltrations in case the opponent changes from tank-heavy thrusts to a new kind of fluid attack.

Fundamentally, one should *not* view containment and commitment forces in a fore-and-aft configuration: The concept proposes tight *overlapping* and close *interaction* between the two elements. The heavier units of the mechanized force are to be based within the 50-km zone, most of the light units within the first 30 km of that zone. (The heavy elements could be moved closer to the demarcation line when actually committed.) A close interaction between static and mobile elements might prove advantageous in many aspects: The distributed area defense would wear down the aggressor's strength, would channel his movements, and could serve as a source of intelligence and means of orientation, as well as cover for counteroffensives aimed at regaining lost terrain. The area defense, along with the rear protection system, would also provide the mobile "trouble-shooting" element with logistic support from numerous decentralized depots (as suggested by the American military analyst Ed Corcoran and successfully tested by the Austrian Army), thereby freeing the commitment forces from most of their clumsy tails. The result would be to optimize force allocation, including operational movements up and down the line.

For these reasons the static element of the SAS model has been called both a space and a force multiplier. The mobile component would, in turn, protect the integrity of the network and serve as a morale booster and potential evacuation facility for frontline infantry positions. (This is an idea SAS has adopted from the work of Steven Canby, another American military analyst.) When members of SAS presented this concept to the young commander of an Austrian mechanized brigade, he said: "I understand you are NATO traditionalists. Your proposal pretty much resembles good old Active Defense, except that it works." The physicist Egbert Boeker, the most prominent supporter of Alternative Defense in the Netherlands, has called this a spider-in-the-web approach, suggesting that a spider remains deadly only as long as it operates within the web.

Because of the force-multiplying effect of the infantry network, overall quantity and unit size of the rapid commitment forces can be reduced, which may be understood as an approximation to both the no-target philosophy and the inability to "cross the line" required by the nonprovocation principle. Consequently the SAS concept contains only about 200,000 mobile troops: 90,000 West German and roughly 110,000 allied forces. In times of crisis or war, the bulk of NATO's ground defense would consist of infantry with up to 500,000 German soldiers (not including replacements). This infantry force would comprise more than 350,000 reservists, integrated into the second layer of the static area defense and into the rear protection force. Because of a regional mode of mobilization, most of these men could be with their units in twelve hours or less. The mobilization procedure can be reliably protected by the combination of the forward mobile forces and the standing element of the area defense (plus some of the active cadres of the skeletonized second layer). The whole process would be much quicker than NATO "filling up" its mechanized formations and "getting them in line," which takes several days.

The NATO allies and the other services

The SAS concept differs from all the other proposals in giving a rather detailed picture of how a – somewhat reduced – component of NATO allied land forces should be integrated into the mobile element of a forward defense. And, whereas most of the "alternative" debate deals with land warfare, the SAS concept is unique in also tackling problems related to a restructuring of the other services.

Some remarks on a future air force: If our ground troops were restructured to minimize the risk of presenting valuable targets – namely, by creating a multitude of unimportant ones – the commander-in-chief of the Warsaw Pact's tactical air would see the raison d'être of his fighter bombers fade away. It is simply not cost-effective to reconnoiter and bombard a loose pattern of very small, well-camouflaged infantry positions from the sky. Neither would the mechanized commitment formations of the Alternative Defense fall an easy prey to the potential aggressor's air forces. Given their relatively compact unit size, they could take cover in the area defense system with its abundance of engineered obstacles and its constantly changing radar and infrared signature. Of course, relatively short periods of potential exposure to the enemy's tactical air cannot be ruled out. To have a good chance of surviving these phases, the rapid commitment force would need organic air defenses of high performance.

If an essential rationale of the other side's offensive air forces were no longer valid, this would raise questions about our own fighter-bombers. As it is now, their main task is to attack the opponent's airfields in order to neutralize his option to break up our present target-rich structure by an early air strike. During a crisis there would be good military reason for our side to be even quicker on the draw (as we have seen already when discussing the Rogers plan). But there is more than just "destabilization" to worry about. A recent NATO study on tactical air, whose findings have leaked out to *The Economist*,[29] is said to have concluded that one enemy plane destroyed on the ground would have to be paid for by the loss of up to one of our own machines, whereas the kill ratio in defensive air combat over friendly territory would be between 4:1 and 5:1 in favor of NATO. And as the other border-crossing task of Western offensive air – namely, to attack mobile and stationary elements of the Warsaw Pact's ground forces – also faces an unfavorable cost–benefit balance (unsolved problems of target acquisition and attrition), SAS arrives at the following scheme.

In the long run NATO should get rid of its fighter-bombers for deep penetration. Instead, the accent should be strongly on air defense – to be optimized against terror attacks, with high priority on the protection of the civilian infrastructure. This could be accomplished by a deep belt comprising a mix of surface-to-air missiles (partly with mobile batteries) plus an element of light interceptors for flexible counterconcentration. Numerous (makeshift) miniature "air bases" and short takeoff and landing procedures should minimize the danger of presenting targets.

SAS has also devoted some conceptual work to naval problems.[30] The general idea is that the German and Danish navies should – much more than today – concentrate on the protection of the Baltic approaches and adjacent coasts, employing mines and light missile carriers like helicopters or fast attack craft, whereas the traditional blue-water navies of the Dutch and British would take care of the North Sea. The underlying notion is that of complementary burden sharing: Relative specialization between services and partners promises an optimization of overall military performance at reduced investment.

Supporting arguments and reply to critics

Let us sum up the arguments that SAS has generated a workable concept which promises a comparably good cost–benefit ratio. High outcome at relatively modest investment may be expected because of

1. greater task-related specialization among the allies;
2. a considerably clearer and much more restricted definition of the three services' roles;
3. a gradual shift of emphasis from highly complex main weapons systems to less sophisticated systems that can be affordably built in greater numbers;
4. a ground force posture that
   - makes optimal use of the defender's terrain (e.g. through dispersal and camouflage),
   - benefits from low-level robust automation (e.g. through the use of smart mines),
   - utilizes the synergistic effects stemming from the interaction between static and mobile force elements,
   - draws profit from a functional differentiation and specialization of mechanized forces,
   - is able to employ regionally mobilized alert reserves as a substitute for a considerable part of today's active strength, which – given the unfavorable demographic prospects – could be maintained only at intolerably high cost, and
   - can, in times of actual conflict, count on more combat soldiers (in relative as well as absolute terms) because the proposed structure promises to improve the teeth-to-tail ratio dramatically.

However interesting these supporting arguments, they might not convince the skeptic. The proponent of the SAS concept (or any similar approach) is confronted with three more fundamental questions:

1. Isn't the proposed scheme just another variant of area defense, which has been shown to be highly calculable in the adversary's planning?
2. Even if deterrence by threatening to punish the potential aggressor in his own backyard invites preemption, doesn't "deterrence by denial," which is content with being able to crush and repel invading forces, encourage probing attacks, since in case of failure the aggressor could go back to the status quo ante?
3. Why are only NATO's approaches to strengthen its conventional capabilities (e.g. Deep Strike, maneuver warfare) criticized for their inherent risks of nuclear escalation? Couldn't the

SAS concept, by proving successful in case of war, also provoke the aggressor to go nuclear?

To these the following replies may be given.

1. Thanks to the work of Sandhurst's experts on Soviet military affairs,[31] we know that more than 50 percent of the Soviet ground combat forces' training time is devoted to the conduct of meeting engagements ("encounter battles") with NATO's armor. Apparently, their standard repertoire of related tactics is becoming more complex. As already indicated, moving armor versus armor on the move is a Soviet favorite. But how about the aggressor's ability to adjust to an area defense system to make his success more calculable? Here there are contradictory opinions. Computer-based combat simulations suggest that a mechanized invasion force could indeed, to a limited degree, adapt its tactics to an area defense if this is defined as a relatively homogeneous system of numerous small fire positions distributed in depth.[32] The renowned infantry expert Eckart Afheldt (former chief of the Bundeswehr's infantry school and an important contributor to the works of his cousin Horst) strongly objects, claiming that a random pattern of obstacles and fire positions would pose a humiliating challenge to a Soviet combined arms commander's initiative.

Be this as it may, SAS is not proposing such a homogeneous defense system. The group's concept is built upon the interaction of structurally different elements, which is supposed to create a "new quality" of defense, a high degree of "unfriendly complexity" that the aggressor cannot cope with. Malcolm Allen has provided us with an imaginative study of how Soviet attack planning would be outsmarted by a close integration of area defense and armored reserves.[33] He points to the cumulative effects of terrain advantage, good concealment, excellent intelligence through area control, uncertainty about what is waiting around the corner (tanks or infantry), and the possibility of flexible, outflanking counterconcentration. Taken together, these would make a Soviet success incalculable.

2. If the risk to the Soviets consisted "only" in a good chance of being defeated in the course of a conventional assault on Western Europe, that would be sufficient. The West needs no further conventional punishment options for stable deterrence. The Soviet leadership cannot take a high risk of defeat, because the option of returning to the political status quo ante (or even preparing for another assault) would not be available. Eastern leaders would have quite a few worries if their armed forces, the main stabilizer of the Warsaw Pact, lost face and grip. In assessing Soviet military options vis-à-vis Western Europe, one should not lose sight of the political context but should remain aware of the deeply rooted latent crisis of loyalty in the satellites' belt.

3. It makes a significant difference if nuclear escalation develops during a conventional military conflict, with risk strategies and vulnerable structures on both sides leading to the slippery slope of preemption, or if an aggressor considers going nuclear after his conventional assault has been repelled by a stable defense. In this latter case (we assume that "stable defense" implies a scheme strongly influenced by the no-target philosophy), there would be no hope of having "surgical" atomic options. Even the formations of the rapid commitment force, the only elements in the SAS ground posture that are by definition not dispersed, would be extremely difficult to target for tactical nuclear weapons (which are – for obvious reasons – incapable of quick-reaction missions). Given both their high mobility and the protective quality of the static net forces, elements for rapid commitment are not easy to track down; and even if they are located in one place they won't be there for long ("hit-and-run"). Consequently, the aggressor could only attack the system as a whole, which necessarily would result in an all-out countervalue strike against the country that hosts such an effective conventional defense. Are there any plausible political scenarios for such a move? Wouldn't a sea-based minimum deterrent with limited countervalue options be adequate to rule out such a dreadful possibility?

Lutz Unterseher

PUBLIC SUPPORT FOR ALTERNATIVE DEFENSE?

Positions of the German political parties

Ever since the Bonin controversy, the Christian Democrats (CDU/CSU) have stuck to the dominant NATO line of answering in kind: tank divisions against tank divisions, fighter-bomber squadrons against fighter-bomber squadrons. If this mode of conventional deterrence fails, a first use of nuclear weapons, even on German territory, is considered. Nowadays, the national leaders of the Christian Democrats, persistently ruling out the possibility of defensively oriented structural change, are attempting to put together five elements of policy:

1. modernizing the heavy armored forces;
2. investing in a moderate form of conventional Deep Strike;
3. but nevertheless insisting upon a First Use doctrine of nuclear deterrence based on assets designed for warfighting;
4. while at the same time trying to get in on the U.S. administration's SDI development expenditure (recently, however, there has been considerable disappointment here);
5. as well as making provision for the evolving European Defense Initiative (EDI) that is perceived to offer complementary protection as well as a substantial stimulus for Europe's high-tech industries.

This combination is inconsistent, totally beyond West Germany's resources, and dangerous. Only one prominent Christian Democrat, Kurt Biedenkopf, who is a widely respected conceptual thinker, has publicly acknowledged that, while the NATO alliance is still supported by a majority of citizens, the established concept of nuclear deterrence is not. Privately, Biedenkopf has shown a keen interest in schemes emphasizing defense. There also is at least some grass-roots protest against the official party line. A small but growing group of CDU members, "Christliche Demokraten für Schritte zur Abrüstung" (Christian Democrats for Steps toward Dis-

328

armament), has publicly criticized SDI, as well as the current development of NATO doctrine. According to the group's policy platform, presented in 1985, the concepts of Afheldt, Hannig, and SAS could provide a point of departure for further considerations.

During the 1950s the Social Democrats (SPD), torn between antimilitarist fundamentalism and an almost blind acceptance of the so-called objective requirements of defense, were unable to seize the opportunity of turning the Bonin Plan into an attractive party platform. In the 1970s, when Helmut Schmidt was Secretary of Defense and then Chancellor, the representatives of the official defense policy prided themselves on their NATO conformism. Schmidt's overriding concern was to protect West German moves toward detente from allied criticism by proving that Social Democrats are no weaklings.

At their national convention of 1984 the Social Democrats, once again out of power, adopted a resolution on defense that contains a number of inconsistencies behind a "progressive" outlook. At first glance the triple formula of gradual denuclearization, "common security/security partnership" with the East, and "structural inability to attack" is impressive. It is somewhat disappointing, however, to be told that only one main road can take us closer to this much desired goal: the process of arms control and disarmament talks. The resolution does not acknowledge that "fair" negotiations, necessarily based on the concept of "balance," are all too often bound for disaster if this balance itself rests on inconsistent structures along with mutual fears and misperceptions. The higher degree of trust that disarmament talks are supposed to produce would generally be a precondition, not a consequence, of success.

The logical sequence would be to create trust first, by reshaping the defense structures, and to negotiate later. This reshaping can be done unilaterally. If NATO closes its windows of vulnerability, removes provocative assets, and adopts a new force mix to render the Warsaw Pact's armored attack formations obsolete, our security would not be undermined:

To the contrary, it could be greatly enhanced by these "independent" measures. But however autonomous these measures are, they should be explained to the other side. Structural change does not always speak for itself. Confidence building needs uninterrupted communication. This is something entirely different from bargaining with and outwitting opponents.

Unfortunately it is very hard to get this message through: A large portion of the SPD's functionaries have been, and possibly still are, addicted to the illusion of negotiating "balance" and "mutually balanced force reductions." Apparently they believe that any unilateral measure would lead to one-sided disarmament, creating additional risks. And they also think that, following the INF Treaty, negotiated conventional disarmament will be a matter of a few years – not decades. They fail to understand that problems of conventional disarmament are more complex – by at least an order of magnitude – than those related to nuclear weapons. Despite the "answering in kind" syndrome, the two sides' military postures are (still) very different, and the question of verification remains open: How, for instance, does one verify the existence of tanks if their exact number – at the beginning of negotiations – is unknown (estimates may err by 20 percent), and if they are hidden in barns (without any signature detectable by "national means")? There is still a long way to go before a majority of Social Democrat representatives can understand that only a shift of political strategy in favor of emphasizing defense – unilaterally, if necessary – promises to open a way out of the arms race.

But there are also hopeful indications. After the 1984 SPD convention the security policy commission of the party Presidium was given the task of developing a more concrete position. Horst Afheldt, Löser, and I got the chance to address the commission. Following this hearing, this body's chairman at the time, von Bülow, presented an outline of a future defense policy that incorporates at least some ideas taken from the alternative school of thought. However, this proposal has been widely criticized for its inherent contradictions and latent anti-Americanism. A real turning point for an emphasis on defense came in June 1985, when Hermann Scheer, the Social Democrats' parliamentary spokesman on arms control and disarmament, strongly supported the SAS concept in the Bundestag.[34] In the meantime, the SAS proposal has developed into an "alternative platform" endorsed by a number of high-ranking politicians, members of the party Presidium, and ministers of state governments.[35] Widely regarded as consistent and NATO-oriented, it could eventually turn out to be the party's compromise for a long-term security policy guideline. The accent is on "long-term," however, as it looks as if the advocates of "balance" and "negotiations" will once again win the day. The party platform on security policy adopted at the 1986 convention is a clear indication of this intermediate development.

During the 1970s, as junior partners of the Social Democrats, the Free Democrats (FDP), liberals in the European sense of the word, came to support Schmidt's NATO conformity in order to protect the Ostpolitik. Now that the Free Democrats have changed sides and become partners of Kohl's Christian Conservatives, they are trying to portray themselves as watchdogs of NATO continuity, willing to protect Germany from adventures like SDI.

Unlike all other parties, the Greens, together with a considerable section of the remnants of the peace movement, tend to favor a withdrawal from NATO followed by complete unilateral disarmament and the introduction of civil resistance schemes in West Germany.

Positions of the churches and the trade unions

Leaving aside the Catholic Church, still one of the solid pillars of conservatism in Germany, we shall focus on the Protestants. In 1981, when the peace movement had gained momentum as a reaction to the U.S. dual-track decision, the Protestant Church published an official memorandum (EKD Denkschrift) addressing questions of peace and international security. The memorandum mentions three groups through which an active Christian might work to prevent war:

1. the committedly pacifist movement "Ohne Rüstung Leben" (To Live without Armament);
2. an initiative started by experts with an ecumenical orientation, called "Schritte zur Abrüstung" (Steps toward Disarmament), whose specific proposals are
   - no nuclear arms in Europe,
   - no arms exports outside of Europe,
   - disarmament by "trans-armament" (which can be understood as a demand for unilaterally emphasizing defense);
3. another initiative, "Sicherung des Friedens" (Securing Peace), supporting the official policy of detente combined with the established military posture.

For a while it seemed that church officials were cautiously developing a preference for the middle position, namely, for nonprovocative restructuring as a formula to appease both the traditionalists, who insist on defending home and family, and those young Protestants who dream of doing away with all weapons at once. Hoping to get such a formula sanctioned, church leaders delegated the task of drawing up a Protestant peace platform to a committee of scholars with nationwide reputations. However, these gentlemen found themselves unable to compromise, and the business of mediation is once again left to the local level.

A short comment on the West German trade unions' position: For a long time their Sunday rhetoric concerning security policy contained nothing but demands for mutually balanced force reductions through arms control talks. Like many Social Democrats, union officials have found it difficult to accept that this approach has already been shown to be a failure. The inherent opportunities that unilateral "trans-armament" measures offer to save the welfare state have only recently begun to be recognized. In 1985 the DGB (German All-Union Congress) published and widely distributed an official brochure recommending discussion of the SAS concept as an alternative leading out of the present dilemma.[36]

Raising public support for Alternative Defense: A dilemma?

NATO's posture for the defense of Central Europe has been sold to the German public with the help of rhetoric that might be called the "pure war-prevention ideology." The standard litany until now has suggested that firm belief in a potential first use of nuclear weapons by the West could guarantee war prevention: Thus it would make little sense to worry about the inconsistencies of NATO's posture, about the consequences to be faced in case deterrence fails. Undoubtedly, this ideology has had a lulling effect on many Germans, lifting a great burden from their hearts.

Any plea for an Alternative Defense based on a comparative analysis of potential consequences of war will almost certainly confront the problem of having to convince people who would prefer not to be concerned. Yet recently the situation has changed somewhat in favor of a true public debate:

1. The peace movement has generated at least some degree of mass awareness concerning security policy (although activism is currently at a relatively low level).
2. Official NATO policy plays into the hands of the proponents of Alternative Defense, as the feasibility of military options – particularly conventional ones – has been given much greater emphasis.

MOVING NATO

It is widely held that the NATO alliance as such has had a high deterrence value. The very fact that the Warsaw Pact has been confronted with a partnership of nations, jointly commanding far superior resources, has strongly helped to prevent war. This contribution, it must be feared, could be undermined by those destabilizing trends inherent in the present development of NATO's strategy.

The proponents of an Alternative Defense within NATO advocate reversing these trends while at the same time en-

333

hancing the solidarity among NATO partners. This is usually seen in the context of a "Europeanization" of NATO that, in substance, implies a two-pillar concept of transatlantic burden sharing. This concept basically means that the United States should take care of nuclear deterrence, preferably reinvesting its assets in minimum-deterrent form, in order to prevent a first use of nuclear weapons by the Warsaw Pact. In return the Europeans would increasingly take conventional defense into their own hands, developing a posture of enhanced stability. This whole scheme would be much to the benefit of the United States' security, greatly reducing the risk that a minor conflict will develop into all-out nuclear war.

Gradual Europeanization focusing on Alternative Defense is not beyond political reach, if three key problems can be solved in the years to come:

1. It has to be made plausible to a majority in the defense communities on both sides of the Atlantic, and to a wider public as well, that a structural change in our conventional posture could enable us to achieve both increased stability and greater affordability.
2. It has to be made clear to the political leaders of the United States that, in their own interest, they should not view Europe as a potential theater for a showdown with the Soviets. They might be induced to realize that a gradual retreat of Europe from the front line of superpower confrontation would lower the risk of open conflict and of escalation as well. Such a process would not call for a total disengagement of American conventional troops from Central Europe. A somewhat reduced force, with a stronger accent on flexible air defense assets than on ground formations, would be welcome as a substantial symbol of continued NATO solidarity – as long as defense treaties are needed in Europe.
3. The United States should be assured of the Europeans' willingness to establish a pattern of mutually profitable cooperation in the field of arms procurement. Europeanization should not become synonymous with locking the Americans out of their traditional markets.

The present trends within the SPD of West Germany and similar developments in the Netherlands and in Italy – both countries whose Christian Democratic parties do show an interest in Alternative Defense – give rise to cautious hope that at least the European pillar has some chance of being built in the long run.

IMPLEMENTATION AND RESPONSE

As we have already seen, initiating a defensively oriented structural change is not dependent upon "equivalent" Soviet (re)action. But, given the prospect of continuing fixation on the idea of "balance," it may be very helpful if the other side responds by reducing offensive elements that have been rendered obsolete by our defensive posture, or even takes the initiative. Such an initiative is easy to understand if one looks at the constant, and even worsening, crisis of the socialist economies, which is obviously caused by the diversion of resources for nonproductive purposes.[37] The other side's willingness to pursue such a course of action, however, would depend on how changes in our posture are perceived. A truly defensive defense, with its relatively high degree of decentralization, could be made transparent to everyone without running security risks. As the structure of such a defense is in itself a confidence-building measure, a policy of full explanation, of open doors and open maneuvers (on a random basis), would be imperative.

Confidence is not enhanced, however, if modules taken from defensive defense are integrated into quite another military concept. For example, under its current structure ("Heeresstruktur 4") the Bundeswehr had begun to put in place a skeleton organization for calling up reservists for relatively strong light infantry elements attached to eleven of its twelve divisions. This measure was taken in the context of a professional debate that basically follows the arguments of General Uhle-Wettler.[38] This respected officer has been a strong advocate of infantry forces designed to make better use of the hilly and covered terrain that characterizes wide areas along the demarcation line, by relying more on reserve manpower plus smart weapons of the light variety than on complex fighting vehicles.

Meanwhile, long-term defense planning has come up with the concept for a new structure ("Heeresstruktur 2000") that envisages a much greater degree of functional and structural differentiation than hitherto observed in the Federal German Army's force design.[39] What can be seen now is the evolution of a three-tier system made up of

- assets of extended-range indirect fire (such instruments – for instance, combat drones reaching up to 100 km deep – are new to the Bundeswehr's *ground* forces);
- "barrier" and mobile light infantry brigades, much stronger and with a far higher proportion of active personnel than the infantry elements of "Heeresstruktur 4," which are designed to fight and hold in a terrain-oriented mode; and
- powerful operational reserves for (counter)attack, consisting of armored forces somewhat reduced in size but considerably upgraded in fighting value, plus strong air-mechanized brigades to be newly created.

One must fear that in the end the Bundeswehr might turn into a "shield and sword" army, the shield protecting the base and the flanks while the sword's strike forces are ready for retaliatory tasks.[40] Such a configuration, if properly functioning and appropriately funded, would confront the other side with a worst case: namely, to be increasingly vulnerable but at the same time deprived of the option to seize Western territory. Given the state of global tensions, the Soviet inferiority complex vis-à-vis the West, and the current trends in Eastern military thinking, it is not likely that a "shield and sword" approach on NATO's side would encourage the Soviets to turn to a thoroughly defensive posture themselves (even though such a posture would undoubtedly have its advantages for them). There is a much greater chance that they would try to neutralize the additional Western capabilities by answering in kind. What a wonderful new impetus to the arms race!

So we have to insist that a confidence-building transition of NATO's forces to a truly nonprovocative posture necessarily has to envisage a gradual reduction of multipurpose (offensive) elements synchronized with the systematic growth of unambiguously defensive formations.

NOTES

1. Already in the 1960s D. Senghaas had provided us with deep insights into the "pathology" of the nuclear system with particular reference to the irrational dynamics built into the concept of the escalatory ladder: "Zur Pathologie organisierter Friedlosigkeit," in E. Krippendorff, ed., *Friedensforschung* (Cologne and Berlin: Kiepenheuer und Witsch, 1968), pp. 217–59.

2. Union of Concerned Scientists (UCS), "No First Use," UCS-Report (Cambridge, Mass., 1983).

3. H. Feiveson, R. Ullman, and F. von Hippel, "Reducing U.S. and Soviet Nuclear Arsenals," *Bulletin of the Atomic Scientists* 41 (August 1985), 144–50.

4. Federal Minister of Defense, *White Paper 1985: The Situation and the Development of the Federal Armed Forces* (Bonn: Ministry of Defense, 1985), pp. 61–64.

5. W. W. Kaufmann, *A Reasonable Defense* (Washington: Brookings Institution, 1986), pp. 65–67.

6. Ibid.; and Federal Minister of Defense, *Weissbuch 1979: Zur Sicherheit der Bundesrepublik Deutschland und zur Entwicklung der Bundeswehr* (Bonn: Ministry of Defense, 1979), pp. 152–54. Kaufmann does not seem to know that after full mobilization the Bundeswehr (German federal armed forces) would be in command of not seven but twelve mechanized territorial brigades. There would also be forty-five motorized battalions for rear area protection. These are relevant to any force assessment that considers Pact forces heading west.

7. J. J. Mearsheimer, *Conventional Deterrence* (Ithaca and London: Cornell University Press, 1983), pp. 167–83. The ratio of *standing* forces along the Central European demarcation line is – according to U.S. Army sources – only about 1.2:1 in favor of the Warsaw Pact.

8. C. J. Dick, "Soviet Operational Art. Part 1: The Fruits of Experience," *International Defense Review* 21, no. 7 (July 1988), 755–61, and "Part 2: The Keys to Victory," *International Defense Review* 21, no. 8 (August 1988), 901–5; "Sowjetische Gefechtsausbildung – Verwundbarkeit oder Stärke," *Internationale Wehrrevue* 18, no 5 (May 1985), 663–65; C. N. Donnelly, "The Soviet Operational Maneuver Group," *International Defense Review* 15, no. 9 (September 1982), 219–27; "Echeloning," Soviet Studies Research Centre, Working Paper A64 (Sandhurst: 1984), pp. 1–23, and "The Warsaw Pact Views of the Future Battlefield," Soviet Studies Research Centre, Working Paper A68 (Sandhurst: 1985), pp. 11–14; P. H. Vigor, *Soviet Blitzkrieg Theory* (London: Macmillan, 1983). A concise summary of Western analyses focusing on Soviet blitzkrieg thinking can be found in D. Farwick, "Eine nationale Option Moskaus? Überraschender Angriff mit begrenztem Ziel," *Europäische Wehrkunde/Wehrwissenschaftliche Rundschau* 34, no. 12 (December 1985), 642–46.

9. J. L. Romjue, *From Active Defense to AirLand Battle: The Development of Army Doctrine, 1973–1982* (Fort Monroe, Va.: TRADOC Historical Monograph Series, 1984), pp. 3–21.

10. European Security Study (ESECS) I, ed., *Strengthening Conventional Deterrence in Europe* (London: Macmillan, 1983); ESECS II, ed., *Strengthening Conventional Deterrence in Europe. A Program for the 1980s. Report of the Special Panel* (Boulder, Colo.: Westview, 1985).

11. S. L. Canby, "The Conventional Defense of Europe: The Operational Limits of Emerging Technology," *International Defense Review* 18, no. 6 (June 1985), 875–80. See also G. Herolf, "Emerging Technology," *World Armaments and Disarmament: SIPRI Yearbook 1986* (London: Taylor and Francis, 1986), pp. 193–208.

12. Samuel P. Huntington, "Conventional Deterrence and Conventional Retaliation in Europe," *International Security* 8, no. 3 (Winter 1983–84), 37–46; rpt. in Steven E. Miller, ed., *Conventional Forces and American Defense Policy: An "International Security" Reader* (Princeton: Princeton University Press, 1986), pp. 251–75.

13. Mearsheimer, *Conventional Deterrence*, pp. 203–12.

14. H. Bebermeyer and B. Grass, "Unsere Streitkrafte in der Ressourcenkrise," in H. G. Brauch, ed., *Sicherheitspolitik am Ende?*

Eine Bestandsaufnahme, Perspektiven und neue Ansätze (Gerlingen: Bleicher, 1984), pp. 176–89.

15. Social Research Group SALSS, "Die Zukunft der Bundeswehr: Eine Durchleuchtung der amtlichen Planung – Gutachten," report for the SPD Presidium (Bonn, October 1985), pp. 1–69. The German Federal Armed Forces Plan 1989, which was presented to the public in early 1988, gives the first indications that official long-term planning is attempting to take the approaching resource crisis more seriously. In the introduction to this plan, which is intended to cover the period until the year 2001, the following statement can be found: "Our armed forces have to meet the challenge, in spite of difficult resource problems, to reach for a balanced comprehensive structure which remains adequate to the threat and exploits the potential of new technology as well as tactical and operational innovation." Federal Minister of Defense, ed., "Bundeswehrplan 1989," *Material für die Presse XXV/3* (Bonn: February 24, 1988), p. 1 (my translation).

This "Bundeswehrplan 1989" envisages a new Army structure – the other services do not have to change substantially – that will be characterized by a much greater degree of functional differentiation than in the current posture. This functional differentiation of force elements, which will be touched upon later in this study, has been conceived as a basis for a more cost-effective weapons mix involving emerging technology. It remains to be seen whether emerging technology can really satisfy the expectations concerning better cost-effectiveness. Another criticism, however, is of more immediate relevance: Since the Bundeswehrplan 1989 adheres to almost the old high level of peacetime strength, even supporters of the federal government (a coalition of Christian Conservatives and Liberals) say that there still may be a long way to go until an appropriate measure of realism is reached. See W. Flume, "Heeresstruktur 2000," *Wehrtechnik* 20, no. 11 (1988), 49–55.

16. H. Brill, "Das Problem einer wehrpolitischen Alternative für Deutschland. Die Auseinandersetzungen um die wehrpolitischen Alternativvorschläge des Obersten Bogislaw von Bonin (1952–1955)," Dissertation, University of Göttingen (Göttingen, 1977).

17. R. Carmichael, "Force-Oriented Defense," *Infantry* 62, no. 3 (May–June 1972), 25–34; J. Keyes, "Tactics for the Force-

Oriented Defense," *Infantry* 62, no. 4 (July–August 1972), 23–27; J. Digby, *Precision-Guided Weapons*, Adelphi Paper No. 118 (London: International Institute for Strategic Studies, 1975); S. L. Canby, "The Wasteful Ways of NATO," *Survival* 15, no. 1 (January–February 1973), 21–26.

18. R. Kennedy, "Precision ATGMs and NATO Defense," *Orbis* 22, no. 4 (Winter 1979), 897–927.

19. See, for a typical example, S. L. Canby, "Territorial Defense in Central Europe," *Armed Forces and Society* 7, no. 1 (Fall 1980), 51–67.

20. H. Afheldt, *Verteidigung und Frieden – Politik mit militärischen Mitteln* (Munich and Vienna: Hanser, 1976); *Defensive Verteidigung* (Reinbek bei Hamburg: Rowohlt, 1983).

21. G. Brossollet and E. Spannocchi, *Verteidigung ohne Schlacht* (Munich and Vienna: Hanser, 1976).

22. J. Löser, *Weder rot noch tot. Überleben ohne Atomkrieg – eine sicherheitspolitische Alternative* (Munich: Olzog, 1981).

23. N. Hannig, *Abschreckung durch konventionelle Waffen. Das David-Goliath-Prinzip* (Berlin: Berlin Verlag Arno Spitz, 1984).

24. G. Füreder, "Non-Nuclear Defense of Europe: Example Germany," Parts I and II, Working Papers (Munich, May 1983).

25. J. Gerber, "Fordert die Wirtschaftlichkeit eine neue Struktur des Heeres?" *Heere International* 3 (1984), 39–51.

26. "Landstreitkräfte zur Verteidigung der Bundesrepublik Deutschland," in Studiengruppe Alternative Sicherheitspolitik (SAS), ed., *Strukturwandel der Verteidigung* (Opladen: Westdeutscher Verlag, 1984), pp. 156–75. During a series of computer simulations conducted by an Operations Research team of the Bundeswehr University at Munich without support from the Ministry of Defense, a model battalion, which was developed there, and a component of the SAS concept proved to be more cost-effective than other German alternatives (and several types of Bundeswehr battalions) in stopping an invader within 25 km. According to this analysis large-caliber recoilless rifles and rather ordinary machine cannons appear to be of higher value in close combat situations, which are typical under bad weather and dirty battlefield conditions, than state-of-the-art sophistication. See H. W. Hofmann, R. K. Huber, and K. Steiger, *On Reactive Defense Options*, Bericht Nr. S-8403 (Munich: Hochschule der Bundeswehr, 1984).

27. SAS, ed., *Strukturwandel der Verteidigung*, Appendix; E. Boeker,

Europese veiligheid: alternatieven voor de huidige veiligheidspolitiek (Amsterdam: VU Uitgeverij, 1986); E. Boeker and L. Unterseher, "Emphasizing Defence," in F. Barnaby and M. ter Borg, eds., *Emerging Technologies and Military Doctrine – A Political Assessment* (London and Basingstoke: Macmillan, 1986), pp. 89–109.

28. SALSS, "Spezialisierung auf die Defensive," survey produced for Hessische Stiftung für Friedens- und Konfliktforschung (Bonn/Frankfurt, August 1984).

29. "NATO's Central Front," *The Economist* 300, no. 7461 (August 30, 1986), 49.

30. H. Bebermeyer and L. Unterseher, "Eine künftige Bundesmarine im Rahmen einer defensiven Verteidigungskonzeption," SAS Working Paper (Bonn, May 1986), pp. 1–48.

31. See note 8 above, C. J. Dick's contribution in particular.

32. See note 26 above.

33. M. Allen, "Combating NATO's Integrated Area Anti-Tank Defense," *Jane's Defence Weekly* 4, no. 3 (July 20, 1985), 139–42.

34. H. Scheer, Bundestagsprotokoll, 10. Wahlperiode – 143. Sitzung (June 13, 1985), pp. 10605–7; see also *Die Befreiung von der Bombe – Weltfrieden, europäischer Weg und die Zukunft der Deutschen* (Cologne: Bund, 1986), pp. 269–79.

35. F. Haeberlin et al., "Konservative Verteidigungsplanung erhöht die Kriegsgefahr in Europa. Für eine realistische und verantwortliche Verteidigungspolitik," *Vorwärts Dokumentation* no. 39 (September 21, 1985).

36. L. Unterseher, "Plädoyer für ein selbständiges Abkoppeln vom Rüstungswettlauf," in DGB, ed., *Nie wieder Krieg! Beiträge zur friedens- und sicherheitspolitischen Diskussion 1985* (Düsseldorf: DGB, 1985), pp. 47–53.

37. Under Gorbachev, the Soviet debate on security policy has indeed moved in the direction of a more defensive defense. Although doctrinal changes so far have only been claimed (witness the creation of the foggy formula "reasonable sufficiency of defense"), and actual structural adjustments have not been observed yet, there is a surprising openness in the exchanges between various military and political factions. This discourse even includes quite radical positions advocating some form of Alternative Defense. See A. A. Kokoshin and Major General V. V. Larionov, "Counterpositioning Conventional

Lutz Unterseher

Forces in the Context of Ensuring Strategic Stability," *Miro-
vaia Ekonomika i Mezhdunarodnye Otnosheniia (World Economics
and International Relations)*, June 1988, pp. 23–31.

38. F. Uhle-Wettler, *Gefechtsfeld Mitteleuropa, Gefahr der Übertech-
nisierung von Streitkraften* (Gütersloh: Bernard & Graefe, 1980).

39. See note 15 above.

40. In one of A. v. Bülow's more recent papers ("Vorschlag für
eine Bundeswehrstruktur der 90er Jahre. Einstieg in die
strukturelle Nichtangriffsfähigkeit," *Europäische Wehrkunde* 35
[November 1986] 636–46) it becomes quite clear that the shield-
and-sword idea also has won proponents outside the armed
forces. The politician's dream (300,000 forward light infantry
and very substantial beefing-up of the armor, plus the current
strong element of strike aircraft) is clearly incompatible with
West Germany's resources and has also been criticized for its
destabilizing potential. See C. Krause, *Strukturelle Nichtangriffsfähigkeit im Rahmen europäischer Entspannungspolitik* (Bonn:
Friedrich-Ebert-Stiftung, 1987), p. 23. The Bülow proposal
contrasts quite sharply with the balanced and comprehensive
approach to "conventional stability" developed by Karsten
Voigt, a member of the SPD Presidium. See "Konventionelle
Stabilisierung und strukturelle Nichtangriffsfähigkeit – Ein
systematischer Vergleich verschiedener Konzepte," *Aus Politik und Zeitgeschichte* (Beilage zur Wochenzeitung *Das Parla-
ment*), B18/88 (29 April 1988), pp. 21–34.

Chapter 8

The case for deploying strategic defenses

Leon Sloss

INTRODUCTION

In a landmark speech on March 23, 1983, President Reagan called for a major national effort aimed at exploring the feasibility and effectiveness of active defenses against ballistic missiles. The speech has been hailed by some and condemned by others as signaling a revolutionary change in U.S. strategy. This characterization is greatly exaggerated. However, the speech did reopen a major debate over the role of defense in the U.S. strategic posture – a subject that had been neglected for more than a decade.

The first concrete outcome of Reagan's address was the launching of the Strategic Defense Initiative as a well-funded, comprehensive research program. SDI has become highly controversial, for it appears to challenge conventional wisdom about nuclear strategy while at the same time introducing new complications in NATO relations and arms control negotiations. It also promises to be extremely expensive.

The purpose of this chapter is to provide a strategic – not a moral or ethical – rationale for strategic defenses. It makes the case for a U.S. strategy that includes such defenses, but not for replacing offense with defense. Nor does it suggest that a deterrent that seeks to deny an aggressor confidence in achieving his military objectives can wholly supplant the

343

threat of retaliation. Thus, the approach advocated here differs in emphasis from the long-range goals that were advanced by President Reagan.

To provide some context for the discussion, I first review current U.S. national security policy and strategy. Next, the role of nuclear weapons is examined, focusing on current strategy and possible alternatives, including one option – finite deterrence – that is the subject of another chapter in this volume. The following section analyzes strategic defenses: the role they could play and the benefits they may provide, as well as potential costs. I conclude by detailing the case for deploying strategic defenses.

U.S. NATIONAL SECURITY POLICY AND STRATEGY

Goals of policy

Throughout its history, the United States has sought to achieve the traditional national security goals of protecting its territory, its citizens, and its way of life. The fundamental national interests we have sought to defend and to promote have been "peace, freedom, and prosperity for ourselves and for others around the world . . . [and] an international order that encourages self-determination, democratic institutions, economic development, and human rights."[1]

Since the end of World War II, the principal challenge to U.S. security has come from the Soviet Union. To meet this challenge the United States has attempted to balance Soviet power in Eurasia by maintaining a globally deployed peacetime defense establishment. Alliances with nations located near the borders of the Soviet bloc have become an integral part of this effort. Such alliances, notably NATO, are needed because neither the United States nor its allies wants to shoulder the burdens of defense individually, and because a common effort is more effective than individual national efforts in discouraging aggression. At the same time, the United States and its allies have sought to settle disputes with the

Soviet Union peaceably and to control and reduce arms through negotiation.

Challenges and threats to U.S. security

While a hostile Soviet Union presents the principal threat to U.S. security, there are two closely related challenges: the existence and potential use of nuclear weapons, and local conflicts that could draw the United States into war. Both of these sources of danger to U.S. security have existed since World War II and are likely to persist in the future – although they may eventually take different forms and present new challenges.

The United States and the Soviet Union have been hostile rivals since the founding of the Soviet state, save for the brief interlude of World War II. This rivalry is due primarily to a fundamental opposition between their respective national objectives and value systems, which in turn creates competing global interests. This competition does not appear reconcilable in the foreseeable future. However, the two superpowers do share at least one common security interest. Both recognize the destructiveness of modern warfare and therefore have a shared interest in avoiding conflict, particularly nuclear conflict. They also have acted in consort to curb the spread of nuclear weapons.[2] Yet even cooperative actions are conducted in a manner reflective of the enduring competitive nature of the relationship.

The existence of nuclear weapons is a byproduct of political hostilities. These armaments do not cause wars, but they can make war enormously destructive. Pressure for their use could come from two sources: the potential for escalation inherent in any superpower conflict, and the instabilities created by local conflicts made potentially more dangerous by the nuclear capabilities of certain regional actors.

There are several developments – above and beyond U.S.–Soviet political competition – that threaten to destabilize the strategic nuclear balance. Most important are improvements in the range, accuracy, targeting flexibility, and payload of nuclear weapons systems, which have brought small fixed targets, such as missile silos, within intercontinental attacking range. In addition to these offensive capabilities, the deployment of active and passive defenses could be a means of limiting the damage to forces and leadership. These developments are creating conditions that many perceive as unstable because they could lead to increasing pressure to strike first in a crisis, in the hope of gaining an advantage or out of fear that the opponent will be the first to do so.

It is important, however, not to exaggerate the risks, for nuclear war remains unlikely. The potential consequences for a large nuclear war and the uncertainties of controlling any war create strong disincentives for initiating one. Even if nuclear weapons are used, escalation is by no means automatic. Most experts agree that a full-scale preemptive strike with no warning is most unlikely. If nuclear weapons were ever used on a more limited scale the parties might well recoil in fear after only a few weapons were employed, for neither the United States nor the Soviet Union has a strong impulse toward suicide.

The other danger of nuclear weapons use comes from regional powers. New nuclear states may simply not be careful or technically sophisticated in controlling their weapons. Inadequate security precautions could allow the weapons of new nuclear states to fall into the hands of terrorists. In addition, these states may not have safety devices sophisticated enough to prevent unauthorized use. Proliferation, moveover, raises uncertainties for U.S. decision makers because new nuclear states represent additional decision centers that if involved in a conflict may not be susceptible to superpower control.

A direct superpower conflict is not likely to become a reality unless activated by some type of political dispute arising from a local crisis or conflict. The United States and the Soviet Union have a variety of competing interests in many areas of the world where tensions already exist. Great-power commitments range from security treaties to military assistance relationships to general political interests. Both major powers could find themselves using their respective military forces in the same local conflict. While it is impossible to predict the consequences, it is questionable whether such a situation could remain "limited" for any extended period of time, particularly if one side achieved significant advantages on the local battlefield.

Strategy and its instrumentalities

A national defense strategy marshals and applies the resources and instruments of power to promote and protect national interests. We will examine below several strategies, each of which has different strengths and weaknesses. We will conclude that there is no "ideal" strategy. However, in the real world there must be a choice; the particular strategy adopted by a government should support the objectives of policy and be supported in turn by the body politic.

Today, in order to pursue its goals and meet the challenges and threats to its interests, the United States employs a strategy based on deterrence and defense. Deterrence combines military strength with the political resolve to convince any adversary that aggression can be countered by retaliation that would deny the attacker any gains.[3] In the event that deterrence fails, the defensive component of strategy would be brought into play in an attempt to limit damage and bring the conflict to an acceptable conclusion.

Several instruments are used to implement U.S. strategy:[4]

1. *Military strength*. This is the most visible and direct component of U.S. strategy. The military instrument is composed of nuclear and nonnuclear weaponry and strategic as well as theater forces. Military strength gives substance and credibility to the strategy of deterrence and defense.

2. *Alliances*. The United States has developed a network of alliances with strategically located nations for two basic reasons: to help defend states with common objectives and values, and to share with such states common security burdens. The U.S. commitment to extend nuclear deterrence to its al-

347

lies (e.g. in Europe and Japan) is the principal military consequence of U.S. security treaties with these countries.

In addition, the presence of forward-deployed U.S. forces in allied countries works to convince an adversary that our capabilities are real and that we would be involved from the outset in a conflict in that area, thus reinforcing deterrence and providing the means for defense. U.S. forces on the scene also reassure our allies of our commitment and assist them in resisting foreign intimidation.

3. *Diplomacy*. Diplomacy establishes channels for consultation and joint planning with our allies. A major role of diplomacy is the coordination of our own and our allies' political and military strategies.

In dealing with adversaries, diplomacy seeks to defuse political disputes through negotiation before such disputes reach the stage of military conflict. Arms control negotiations are one example. The two superpowers use such talks as one method for maintaining a dialogue, managing competition, contributing to the lowering of tensions, and regulating (to a certain extent) military deployments. These negotiations, however, also are often used for propaganda purposes, to put political and public pressure on the opponent or to influence third parties. For instance, disarmament proposals by the Soviet Union often have sought to slow down Western defense efforts.

THE ROLE OF NUCLEAR WEAPONS

Current strategy

U.S. strategy, as reflected in official statements and documents, assumes that nuclear weapons must and do contribute to deterrence across a wide spectrum of threats.[5] These include, as Secretary Weinberger pointed out in his FY 1986 report to Congress, deterring nuclear attack on the United States, deterring nuclear attack on U.S. allies ("extended deterrence"), contributing to the deterrence of nonnuclear attack against the United States and its allies, and contributing to deterrence of the threat of political coercion with military force.[6]

To implement this strategy, the United States has developed plans and capabilities for the use of nuclear weapons in a controlled fashion. The necessity for a variety of nuclear options flows from the belief that we need other choices besides inaction or automatic escalation to general war. Flexible strategic capabilities, including plans for a proportionate response to an enemy attack, are viewed as a means to reinforce deterrence and limit escalation if deterrence fails.

However, we cannot be sure that once nuclear weapons are used (especially in large numbers) escalation will be controlled and the fighting limited. U.S. officials recognize this. President Reagan remarked on many occasions that "a nuclear war cannot be won." Secretary of Defense Harold Brown, who played a major role in crafting an important refinement of U.S. nuclear policy (PD-59), aimed at enhancing the flexibility of U.S. nuclear strategy, remained skeptical of escalation control, stating that he had "very serious doubts" that a nuclear exchange could remain limited. Nonetheless, the need for flexible plans and capabilities remains, because having flexibility seems preferable to having none, and it is held by many strategists to strengthen the credibility of deterrence. In Secretary Brown's words, these measures are intended to "prevent the Soviets from being able to win [a limited nuclear] war and to convince them that they could not win such a war."[7]

Among the components seen as necessary to achieve the objectives of this strategy are: a range of targeting options, with enemy military forces and command and control centers as the principal targets;[8] a durable command, control, communications, and intelligence (C^3I) apparatus that could provide the means to control escalation and lessen the temptation for a "decapitating attack" designed to eliminate command and control; survivable counterforce capabilities sufficiently accurate to destroy enemy military forces and reduce unwanted collateral damage; and a diverse and secure reserve force that would endure beyond the initial attack. The reserve force is designed primarily to protect the United States and its allies from post-attack nuclear blackmail and enable the United States to be in a position to protect its interests and facilitate the termination of hostilities on "favorable" terms.

"Favorable," according to the 1986 formulation of U.S. strategy,

> means that if war is forced upon us, we must win – we cannot allow aggression to benefit the aggressor. It does not mean more territory or other elements of power for the United States. . . . In seeking the earliest termination of conflict, the United States not only would act to defeat the aggression but also try to convince the attacker to halt his advance because his continued aggression would entail grave risks to his own interests.[9]

The plans and capabilities for the use of nuclear forces in a discriminate and flexible manner are intended to facilitate escalation control and also provide a potential means for limiting damage. Damage could also be limited by the use of active defenses. However, except for certain early warning systems and a limited air defense capability, the United States, which once had extensive air defenses and the start of an anti-ballistic-missile (ABM) system, has in the last fifteen years eschewed active defenses (even those permitted by the ABM Treaty of 1972).

This strategy of "flexible response" has many ambiguities and shortcomings. As Soviet nuclear capabilities have grown, the efficacy of escalation control has been widely questioned. Many efforts have been made to reduce reliance on nuclear weapons. Nevertheless, flexible response has persisted as U.S. strategy over two decades and through four administrations – Republican and Democratic – for two primary reasons. First, this strategy has been fashioned to assure or reassure our allies of the United States' commitment to protect them through extended deterrence. Second, flexible response, with all its limitations, is seen by many as the best means to deter Soviet aggression.

A strategy that emphasizes strategic nuclear deterrence (rather than deterrence focused primarily on conventional forces) has been the preferred strategy of our allies. Any strategy that suggests, for example, that a war might be confined to Europe is anathema to Europeans. It means to them that Europe might become the battleground of a future conflict while the United States and the Soviet Union remain sanctuaries. In the absence of the "nuclear umbrella," strengthened conventional forces, as desirable as they might be, may increase the prospect for a war limited to Europe, because there would likely be less hesitation to use them than nuclear weapons. Most Europeans, therefore, want a strategy that makes the Soviets believe that any threat to Europe brings a strong chance of prompt U.S. nuclear retaliation *against the Soviet Union.*

With respect to the role of theater-based nuclear weapons, there has long been a dichotomy between this European perspective and the predominant American strategic outlook.[10] In general, European governments tend to believe that planning and acquiring the forces to fight a "controlled" nuclear war actually undermines deterrence by implying that a nuclear war could possibly be fought and thus be acceptable. They contend that if the employment of nuclear weapons appears manageable war may become more likely. U.S. strategy, in contrast, while aware of these concerns, maintains that planning for operational use of nuclear weapons is necessary to make deterrence credible. A strategy based on the all-or-nothing massive retaliatory strike is, in the view of the past four U.S. administrations, patently incredible and potentially self-deterring – if not suicidal – particularly if the Soviets choose to strike in a limited fashion.

Since the mid 1960s the Soviets have made significant increases and improvements in their strategic forces and capabilities.[11] As a result of these improvements, their ability to inflict damage on the U.S. and its allies equals or exceeds our own ability to damage them. Consequently, confidence in our strategy has declined both at home and abroad. Under these new conditions, relying solely on massive retaliation is seen by many as not being a credible strategy, especially for extending deterrence to others. Even if the survival of the nation is at stake, the threat of massive retaliation (with the likely result of mutual annihilation) without any alternatives is a questionable policy. Nevertheless, such a strategy, which has several permutations and goes under various labels including "Assured Destruction," "Finite Deterrence," or "Deterrence Only," still retains support among many in the U.S. defense community. In this view our ability to retaliate against the high-value targets of the enemy (his cities) is considered absolute, and enough to deter any attack.[12]

Official U.S. strategy has had to come to terms with improved Soviet capabilities and with our perception of Soviet intentions. An examination of Soviet nuclear doctrine suggests that, while the Soviets fully comprehend the dangers of nuclear war, they make very thorough plans for fighting such a war; and while they recognize the difficulty of achieving outright victory, they do not assume that a nuclear war is necessarily unwinnable. Moreover – while this is more controversial – there is some evidence that Soviet doctrine considers limited nuclear exchanges to be a realistic possibility in a nuclear war with the West. This interpretation of Soviet strategy is reinforced by evidence suggesting that the Soviet leadership places a high value on the preservation of the regime throughout a nuclear conflict, and on the survival and continued effectiveness of the instruments of Soviet state power after hostilities have ceased.[13]

A third reason why the United States has relied so heavily on nuclear weapons in the past is that nuclear deterrence – so long as it works – is comparatively inexpensive.[14] A strategy centered on nuclear weapons reassures our allies of our commitment to their security, while allowing both them and us to spend less on comparatively more expensive conventional forces.

The inability of negotiations to reduce forces and manage threats has also been a factor in shaping strategy. Until the 1987 INF Treaty arms control had relatively little impact on either side's defense programs; instead, negotiations have often tended to protect planned programs. It is also evident that from the mid 1960s until the late 1970s the United States unilaterally restrained its arms programs to a considerable degree while the Soviet Union engaged in a massive military buildup. Still, the prospect of arms control agreements has often been a rationale, if not an underlying cause, for restraining Western defense programs. The ABM Treaty, for example, provided an impetus for the United States to cut back research and development on defensive systems and eventually to dismantle its existing ABM system. The Soviets, by contrast, have deployed the systems allowed by the treaty, while continuing a substantial research and development program.

Finally, Soviet compliance with existing arms control pacts has been questioned, suggesting that the United States will be extremely cautious about the verifiability and enforceability of future agreements. This will likely complicate agreements and further lengthen the negotiating period.

All of this is not to say that the pursuit of arms control is fruitless. To the contrary, the arms control process serves the important function of maintaining a dialogue between the two superpowers. Furthermore, negotiated limits add somewhat to the predictability of future defense programs on both sides. Most important, arms control is a political necessity since important segments of political leadership and public opinion in the West demand negotiations. Indeed, as President Reagan's efforts to negotiate with the Soviets demonstrated, even the most skeptical of political leaders feels compelled to try to do something about the nuclear menace.

Some problems and shortcomings

Both policy makers and outside observers recognize the existence of a worrisome gap between the objectives of our nuclear strategy and our current and projected capabilities. This applies to both forces and command and control.[15] Of particular concern are deficiencies in the flexibility, survivability, and endurance of U.S. strategic systems. If these qualities are not improved, the ability of the United States to implement its plans fully, bargain effectively, or resist coercion in a crisis is open to question.

As to flexibility, there is a growing requirement for strategic systems to acquire and attack moving targets (e.g. mobile ICBMs). The Soviet Union is making this task difficult through measures to disperse, conceal, move, and duplicate critical targets.[16] To gain the flexibility to locate targets rapidly and allow decision makers time to weigh options and issue commands requires: near-real-time intelligence with global reach; rapid and reliable communication of that intelligence to processing centers that can survive attack and can rapidly process and evaluate a large volume of information and transmit it to potential users; a rapid retargeting capability that can utilize processed intelligence; and survivable command centers with a capacity to analyze data, make decisions, and transmit orders. Present capabilities fall short of these requirements; projected capabilities will only begin to close the gap.[17] As a result, U.S. policy makers may not have full confidence in their ability to carry out war plans in a crisis. This could put the United States in a disadvantageous position during crisis bargaining.

There is also a requirement for the survivability of national command facilities, strategic forces, and supporting C³I, particularly the survival of attack-assessment systems, national command connectivity to forces, and post-attack damage assessment centers. Improvements in Soviet capabilities (e.g. their large number of hard-target warheads) place increasing demands on U.S. resources and skills to ensure survivability to these assets, which are essential to the effective management of residual forces. Without such capability, U.S. bargaining or warfighting potential diminishes considerably.

Endurance, as compared to survivability, involves the capability to sustain C³I and force effectiveness *over a period of time* should that prove necessary. Endurance is more costly than survivability – not to mention more controversial. Its requirements are less clear, for it is nearly impossible to establish precisely how much endurance can be obtained and at what cost. A truly enduring force would probably require a massive resource expenditure for one contingency – a prolonged nuclear war – whose outcome would at best be problematic.

Continuing Soviet force improvements perpetuate the gap between U.S. capabilities and objectives. The Soviets have improved the survivability of their forces as a result of numerical growth, hardening, dispersal, mobility, redundancy, concealment, and deception. In addition, the Soviets have also expanded air defenses and passive defense programs, and they continue major research and development efforts on ABM and antisatellite capabilities.

Possible alternatives

These shortcomings highlight a dilemma for U.S. strategy. First, U.S. policy is fundamentally based on the maintenance of alliances and of security guarantees to other nations. U.S. strategy, for better or worse, depends heavily on nuclear weapons to meet these commitments. But, as has been previously noted, the United States lacks the military capability to make these commitments fully credible. A major shift to nonnuclear forces is not currently feasible, for the United States and its allies are either unwilling or unable to commit the necessary resources. Equally important, the allies find the prospect of conventional-based deterrence undesirable for the reasons already cited.

Though some arms limitation may be possible, nuclear weapons are not going to go away in the foreseeable future. We must continue to devise ways of utilizing their existence to increase our security. I suggest that the most promising avenue of approach would be a strategy that carefully mixes offensive and defensive forces. Such a strategy could be realized by a planned natural evolution from current U.S. strategy.

To be sure, this is not the only alternative. A number of alternatives to current U.S. strategy – many of them interrelated – can be envisioned. I propose to identify and examine six representative approaches. The following discussion is not intended to create "straw man" options that can be easily dispensed with. Rather, it seeks to demonstrate that some of the most popular alternatives also have their limitations. No panaceas or perfect strategies exist. My own preferred alternative is discussed in further detail in a later section of this chapter.

Negotiations. The postwar record of limiting and controlling armaments offers little promise that negotiation alone is the route to security. As noted above, arms control has a role to play; but we cannot ask too much of it. Many of the leading proponents of arms control have finally come to recognize this.[18]

It must be acknowledged that arms control negotiations are the product of an adversarial relationship that, if it changes at all, will change only over a long period of time. Nuclear weapons will be with us for the foreseeable future. East–West competition and hostility are also likely to persist for many decades. Thus, arms control is likely to be most effective at the margins in moderating this competition (e.g. in agreements like the INF Treaty and the Partial Test Ban Treaty). And, somewhat paradoxically, in order to have successful negotiations we will still need military forces for bargaining purposes.

Even significant reductions of atomic stockpiles cannot reduce the dangers of a nuclear war; indeed, some reductions could increase the possibility of war. For example, reducing the number of strategic missile launchers without at the same time reducing the ratio of warheads to launchers or somehow making the remaining launchers less vulnerable (e.g. through mobility or active defense) could increase crisis instability by making a first strike appear more attractive. Still, major reductions in nuclear arms could alter the political environment favorably if they are perceived to be equitable and stabilizing. The problem, however, is finding the ever-elusive political will – on both sides – to move toward such reductions in an equitable, balanced, and therefore stabilizing fashion. In the absence of such a long-range and complex arms control plan, the best prospect for negotiations is to work incrementally to enhance stability (i.e. to lessen the risk of war).[19] Mutual reduction of MIRVed missiles could be one step. Supplementary measures, including confidence-building arrangements (such as joint crisis management centers or on-site verification procedures) could be another step to mitigate somewhat the risk of miscalculation in a crisis.[20]

Unilateral initiatives such as a nuclear freeze or a NATO no-first-use policy, however appealing, do not solve our security problems and could lead to increased risks if the Soviets fail to reciprocate.

The conventional alternative. Public fear of nuclear war understandably creates pressure to reduce reliance on nuclear weapons. One way to alleviate such fear and concern would be to replace the nuclear arsenal with conventional weapons. Examples are highly accurate precision-guided weapons and cluster bombs, tailored for special effects against armor or airfield runways. Modern conventional weapons, to be sure, are also highly destructive; but, unlike nuclear weapons, they do not pose the threat of a conflict that could destroy large segments of societies. Some advocates of this approach make the additional point that increasingly advanced nonnuclear weapons technologies can find and destroy targets as effectively as nuclear weapons and with less collateral damage. As a result, conventional weapons could replace nuclear ones in some roles.[21]

There are a number of drawbacks, however, with the conventional alternative. One is cost. One well-known plan for conventional modernization, developed by General Bernard Rogers, the former Supreme Allied Commander Europe, calls for an average annual real increase of 4 percent in defense spending by each NATO member, to be sustained over a six-year period. Another plan, formulated by a group of prominent European and American specialists, requires a similar spending level.[22] In 1977 NATO agreed to increase defense spending by 3 percent annually in real terms; however, most of the member states have failed to meet even this modest goal.[23]

Another problem with this alternative, in the European view, is that by relying on conventional forces – which are seen as more "usable" – the threshold of deterrence may be lowered. As already noted, the European preference is to rely primarily on strategic deterrence and the threat of prompt nuclear escalation in order to avoid any type of conflict. Some of our European allies believe that more formidable conventional forces may appear provocative to the Soviets in that such forces are seen as more "usable," thereby jeopardizing West European relations with their neighbors to the east. Some Europeans oppose even modifying NATO doctrine toward a marginally more offensive orientation (e.g. Deep Strike) for precisely this reason.

A third drawback is the Soviet response. While the Soviets are prepared to make some reductions in nuclear weapons, there is no evidence that they will abandon nuclear deterrence in the foreseeable future. So long as the Soviets retain their nuclear forces, it is doubtful that the United States and NATO could disregard the nuclear unit of military currency possessed by the Soviet Union. The conventional alternative – however desirable – is not a real alternative. Some conventional modernization is desirable and feasible, but conventional forces cannot be expected to replace nuclear forces in deterring nuclear attack.

Finite deterrence. There are influential schools and sub-schools of thought that oppose the current thrust of official U.S. strategy. In this view, the only role that nuclear weapons should play is to deter the use of nuclear weapons by others, thereby suggesting that there is no warfighting role for these armaments. Rather, it is assumed that once the threshold between conventional and nuclear weapons is crossed, escalation to a general exchange (i.e. homeland-to-homeland, *with cities as targets*) is inevitable. In terms of force structure, this view stresses the need to maintain the survivability of retaliatory forces in order to assure a prompt and massive response. Endurance is not necessary because the war will be over quickly. A large residual force is not necessary either, for the main targets of retaliation are cities, and

358

the ability to destroy a limited number of cities should be enough to deter.

There are several problems with this approach. One is moral – the threat to hold innocent civilians hostage in urban areas. This consideration is important, but for now I leave this debate to my colleagues in the fields of philosophy and ethics. A fundamental shortcoming of this view from a strategic perspective is that it relates the degree of danger to the size of the arsenals. This is a tenuous proposition. Indeed, it can be argued that small arsenals, particularly if they are vulnerable, are more unstable than large ones. With small arsenals the potential payoff and thus the potential risk from cheating is greater. Furthermore, a limited force may offer an increased temptation to use it preemptively before it can be destroyed. Finally, if the United States were to adopt a finite deterrent force, we could be subject to pressures from smaller nuclear powers, and new incentives might be created for nuclear proliferation.

There is, moreover, an immediate credibility problem. Could a U.S. strategic force with, for example, 2,000 warheads[24] serve as a deterrent to a limited Soviet aggression in Europe, where theater nuclear weapons have been largely if not altogether eliminated? It seems unlikely, and such a posture would be self-deterring, for with such numbers there are few choices available save escalating to large attacks on cities. If deterrence failed, a principal option with a Finite Deterrence force would be a massive retaliatory strike. This would constitute an invitation for a Soviet response in kind and could therefore involve mutual devastation. Therefore, a U.S. response would lack credibility. Extended deterrence would exist only in name. Moreover, if the West moved toward a Finite Deterrence policy it would probably be unable to compensate for the reduction in nuclear strength with increased conventional forces, for reasons just discussed.

The Finite Deterrence force Feiveson describes illustratively would be made up entirely of single-warhead ICBMs and SLBMs and some bombers.[25] Such a force would be highly vulnerable to technological advances, such as ballistic missile defenses, ASW (anti-submarine warfare), or highly accurate missiles capable of disarming the United States. More important, how would we achieve these reductions: unilaterally or through negotiation? How would this be verified? As outlined above, any transition to Finite Deterrence without a much higher level of political trust between the superpowers is likely to increase rather than diminish tensions. While it is indeed laudable to hope for such reductions, this alternative offers little to responsible officials who must manage strategy in light of a heavily armed adversary and allies in need of our protection and reassurances.

Offensive force buildup. The goal of this alternative would be to try to close the gap, described above, between the objectives of U.S. strategy and our current and projected capabilities by pursuing essentially the same offensive programs as today, but extending and accelerating them. To narrow this gap would first require a significantly improved C^3I system with enhanced endurance and flexibility. It would also require the acquisition of greater numbers of offensive delivery systems: e.g. MX (in a reliable basing mode), a Midgetman missile on mobile and hardened launchers, the D-5 SLBM, cruise missiles, and the B-1 and Stealth bombers. This program would also increase the number of warheads in the U.S. arsenal, especially those capable of destroying hardened targets.[26] This buildup might also include substantial NATO conventional modernization, in order to widen our span of options in a crisis.

A major problem with this program is, again, cost. At a time when defense budgets are being reduced it would be difficult to gain the political support – domestic and allied – for a large across-the-board military buildup of this type. If the West really believed that it was confronted with an ever-growing threat posed by an expansionist Soviet Union, there might be political support to finance such an endeavor; but we know that there is no such consensus in the United States or within NATO today.

If the United States started on an offensive arms buildup, it would inevitably lead to disregard of the already fragile existing arms control regime (i.e. the SALT II Treaty, non-binding but still essentially adhered to). Such action could appear provocative to the Soviets, who might see in it a U.S. quest for military superiority. If tensions increase it could lead to a military confrontation or, at minimum, an even greater Soviet offensive buildup. Indeed, since the Soviets at present already have many more open production lines, their ability to counter any U.S. buildup is greater than our ability to catch up. These are some of the problems the United States faces in attempting to narrow the strategy/capabilities gap. Of course, a buildup of defensive arms would also be costly and could be perceived by the Soviets as provocative – or so they might contend. The point I wish to make here is that a continuing buildup of offensive arms also presents problems.

Technological solutions. Many Americans have a strong faith that technology can solve the formidable problems of our time. In this tradition, what President Reagan proposed in March 1983 as the solution to the threat of nuclear war was a defensive system capable of rendering ballistic missiles "impotent and obsolete." Reagan called on the scientific community, which gave us nuclear weapons, to give us a nonnuclear defensive counter. The Reagan proposal was rooted in the fundamental belief that such an effort was a moral obligation: Innocent civilians should no longer be held hostage to the threat of nuclear war. In addition, as defenses became more effective it would become obvious that offensive forces were a poor investment, and negotiated reductions in offensive forces would be more feasible. This view contends that defense is the correct route to effective arms control.[27]

Yet President Reagan's "vision" requires gigantic scientific and technical progress that for the foreseeable future remains beyond our grasp. If this remains the case, nuclear weapons will be a central component of any strategy for a long time. Moreover, even if SDI is largely successful, it will not provide defense against all types of delivery vehicles that can carry nuclear weapons. At some point it will be necessary to supplement SDI with other appropriate defenses (e.g.

air defenses) or to augment conventional capabilities that can meet lower-level threats.

Aside from the difficulty of translating research concepts into mass-produced weapons systems, there is the problem of cost. It is unlikely that we could afford to sustain the expenditures necessary to provide for this type of system over an extended period of time. In the meantime, such expenditures would cut into resources for offensive nuclear and general-purpose forces. For the most part, the supporters of Reagan's SDI proposal have not thoroughly addressed these questions. Nor have they fully explored the implications – near- and long-term – of defensive systems for extended deterrence. For example, the deployment of strategic defenses could "decouple" the U.S. guarantee to defend Western Europe. Even the prospect of such a deployment some time in the future has already created some serious political strains within the NATO alliance. The quest for a "full-up" defense raises many questions about its feasibility and about its impact on East–West and intra–NATO relations. Yet these uncertainties should not lead to the abandonment of SDI *research*. Defenses need not be perfect to have strategic utility. Incremental incorporation of defenses can bolster our security and perhaps, over a long period of time, eventually achieve President Reagan's objective.

Evolution to offensive–defensive mix. While the prospect of a deployable and nearly leakproof defense seems very distant, Reagan's initiative did provide the impetus for a renewed examination of the role that active and passive defenses could play in U.S. strategy. As I explain further below, even less-than-perfect intermediate defenses can strengthen deterrence.[28] Indeed, current U.S. strategy already suggests a role for such defenses. The concept of a countervailing strategy that seeks to deny an adversary confidence in achieving his military objectives clearly would include a role for defenses. For example, in order to enhance the credibility of limited options, U.S. forces kept in reserve need to be protected from retaliation. Furthermore, active defenses can play a decisive role in protecting critical C^3I assets, whose survivability is essential for our ability to manage any type of nuclear conflict.

This alternative reflects the view that U.S.–Soviet geopolitical competition is a continuing phenomenon, which will not be altered substantially by negotiation in the foreseeable future. It also acknowledges that nuclear weapons are here to stay. Neither technology nor negotiation is likely to alter this fact. Even if SDI is "successful" it will not provide defense against all types of nuclear weapons systems. Thus, deterrence is also here to stay, for it cannot be replaced entirely either.

The rest of this chapter describes how less-than-perfect defenses can work to strengthen deterrence and assist in achieving our security objectives. It essentially states the case for a strategy that includes such defenses.

STRATEGIC DEFENSE

Role, objectives, benefits

Since the late 1960s, the Soviets have markedly improved their strategic and theater offensive capabilities, both nuclear and conventional. They have deployed extensive passive defenses and air defenses and have also actively pursued research in ballistic missile defense systems.[29] The Soviets have therefore moved effectively to reduce the United States' ability to achieve its strategic objectives – deterrence of a range of threats, reassurance of allies, escalation control, damage limitation, and war termination.

In addition, Soviet strategy places emphasis on the value of preemptive attack and surprise, with strikes aimed at military targets rather than retaliatory strikes aimed at industry and cities. Soviet forces reflect the pursuit of damage-limiting objectives as these were defined by the United States in the 1960s. This was accomplished by heavy investment in prompt counterforce and defense capabilities rather than through a strategy of escalation control as now envisioned in the U.S. posture. Soviet defensive activities seek to protect governmental and societal assets, with particular emphasis on continuity of government.

Given these developments, the requirements necessary to maintain deterrence have changed, as President Reagan stated in his 1983 address. Our present posture still serves as a powerful deterrent. However, when one considers the current Soviet posture along with likely future developments, U.S. capabilities to counter this buildup need to be augmented in some important way. It is not clear that reliance on offensive forces alone will suffice to meet U.S. security objectives.

The incremental incorporation of intermediate, less-than-perfect defenses in U.S. strategy would work to offset Soviet gains. The principal rationale for deployment of some level of active defenses against ballistic missiles is that they will reinforce deterrence. Intercepting some portion of the attacking force makes the enemy's calculations of the attack outcome more complicated. He could not be certain how many warheads would reach their targets and thus which targets his attack would destroy. High uncertainty about the outcome of an attack will act as a deterrent for the enemy. Moreover, defenses will raise the cost of attacking, thereby placing the onus for escalation on the Soviet Union.

I am not arguing that defenses should supplant offensive forces or that the mechanism of denial should replace the threat of retaliation as a deterrent. Defenses of this sort would supplement offenses as a deterrent. The problem with relying on offenses only is that the implementation of the retaliatory threat is not cost-free – far from it – and this is well known to everyone: adversaries, allies, and our own public. Thus, such a threat is not credible unless the nation's most vital interests are at stake. Specifically, it is becoming less and less credible in extending deterrence to third parties.

Limited defenses help extended deterrence in two ways. First, they reduce the confidence that the Soviets would have of achieving calculable results from a first strike, and thus they make such a strike less likely. Second, they could make it at least somewhat more credible to the Soviets (who will assume the defense works better than it probably will) that the United States would initiate the use of nuclear weapons in support of an ally, because we would have some protection against Soviet retaliation. With partial defenses, we might not have very much confidence in our ability to limit damage; but one has to ask how it looks to the Soviets – who, after all, are the ones we are trying to deter. With no defenses at all, extended deterrence does not look very credible any more. With some defenses it at least looks more credible, and as our defenses grow in capability so should the credibility of extended deterrence.

A nuclear war remains most unlikely, but calculations about war outcomes affect perceptions and the actions of states in peacetime. As things now stand, if the Soviet Union decided to strike U.S. forces – and, again, Soviet doctrine emphasizes the value of preemptive surprise attacks – they would meet with virtually no resistance and should have little uncertainty about the results of the attack save for failures in their own systems (for which they can compensate). After a Soviet countermilitary strike the United States, having lost a significant portion of its force, would face a serious dilemma. On the one hand it could choose to try to respond in kind with an attack that would cause heavy collateral damage and might have little military effect, since Soviet high-value military forces would either have been used or would be, in the aftermath of attack, unlocatable. This result would be due to degradation of U.S. C^3I and the likely mobility of Soviet residual forces. In addition, even the limited present-day Soviet ABM capability could serve to blunt if not deter the – probably "ragged" – U.S. retaliation. On the other hand, the United States could choose not to respond, conceding victory to the aggressor.

The deployment of limited active defenses would make such an attack less likely in the first place. Furthermore, such deployment is perfectly consistent with our traditional nuclear strategy, enhancing the denial component of deterrence while working to preserve retaliatory forces. A carefully blended mix of offensive and defensive forces will reinforce deterrence rather than replace it. Intermediate defenses can also support U.S. damage-limiting objectives, even if in an imperfect manner. If a war does occur, some defenses are better than none. If the capability exists to limit damage, would it be a responsible policy for the U.S. government not to deploy it?

At this juncture it is not possible to define a future offense/defense mix precisely; one can give only an impressionistic view. The future mix will depend on how SDI technologies develop, how the Soviets respond to SDI, and what progress, if any, can be made in arms control. However, we envision defenses that are less than perfect and offenses that are reduced from today's levels, either through negotiated arms control or through unilateral action in response to the rising cost of penetrating defenses. The process of moving toward a more balanced offense/defense mix will take many years, if not decades, to accomplish. Thus, a decade from now offensive forces are still likely to predominate in the mix. Two decades hence, defenses could begin to play a dominant role; if so, offenses may well be reduced further.

The current emphasis in SDI research is to design nonnuclear kill mechanisms to destroy incoming missiles at some point during their trajectory, which is usually divided into boost-phase, post-boost, midcourse, and terminal stages of flight. Each layer of defense poses a different problem to the attacker. From the standpoint of the defender, the earlier the missile is destroyed the better, to preclude the release of penetration aids designed to confuse the defender with decoys that mask the location of the armed warhead. Early interception, however, is the most demanding phase of defense. The ABM systems of the 1960s were unable to limit damage or even complicate an attack, owing to technical limitations, which meant that they could be relatively easily overwhelmed by the attacker. Today's technology offers opportunities in the next ten to fifteen years for creating limited layered defenses.[30] Such defenses should be seen not as defending specific targets but rather as providing several layers of protection, simultaneously defending several military targets or military targets and collocated population.[31]

The most recent research also suggests that boost and post-boost interception would depend heavily on the development of space-based sensors and weapons possessing the ability to track, assess, and destroy warheads quickly. These are the elements that the supporters of the Reagan vision are counting on to provide a "near-perfect" defense.

Intermediate defenses can add to the complexity and cost of the attacker's plans without reaching nearly this level of capability. Deterrence can be enhanced by the creation of one or more layers of defense (even if that defense is "leaky") and by the possibility of preferential, ambiguously arrayed defenses that leave the attacker unsure as to what is defended and to what level. He will get some warheads through these defenses, but he cannot have in advance any confidence in being able to neutralize most of the targets high on his priority list. Thus, he is more likely to be deterred from an attack even in a serious crisis. The destruction of a few targets will not meet Soviet objectives. And if the Soviets choose to limit themselves to a restricted target set, defenses might, as the Hoffman Panel analysis suggests, "require a level of force inconsistent with limiting the level of violence, while depleting the attacker's inventory for other tasks."[32] This prospect could serve as a powerful deterrent to the contemplation of an initial attack.

As mentioned above, intermediate defenses support the U.S. objective of extended deterrence as well. They would improve the credibility of our limited options policy and NATO's first-use option, a credibility that is already eroding because of Soviet force developments such as tactical missile defenses, which are not constrained by the ABM Treaty. A NATO defense against tactical missiles (ATBM) could be a useful first step to counter the rapidly growing Soviet nuclear and conventional ballistic missile threat to Europe. Defense of key NATO installations against these missiles is a natural extension of already approved plans to defend against

Leon Sloss

aircraft attack utilizing the Patriot air defense system. Future steps, such as possibly extending a U.S. space-based defense to Europe to intercept intermediate-range missiles (before they reenter the atmosphere) can work to mitigate Soviet efforts to erode extended deterrence and NATO's limited options.

Problems and costs

The incorporation of intermediate defenses is bound to raise strategic, political, technical, and financial questions. This section addresses the most prominent criticisms of an intermediate SDI.[33]

One of the most frequent criticisms of SDI has to do with the cost, particularly the opportunity cost, of an SDI program. At a time when the defense budget is declining, budgetary aspects are an important consideration. There are several points to be made. First, no one knows today what the outlays for SDI will be. This will depend a great deal on what kind of SDI is deployed and over what period of time.[34] But under any circumstances SDI deployment will be very expensive – at least tens and in some cases hundreds of billions of dollars. However, deployment will occur over a period of many years, which will attenuate (though by no means eliminate) the fiscal impact of the program. Finally, it is likely that other defense programs will be affected by SDI deployment, but it is impossible at this point to predict which programs will be affected or how. Whether an SDI program is "worth the cost" depends precisely on what the program consists of, how well it works, how expensive it is, and the extent to which it impacts on other programs. None of these factors can be determined with any precision now. They should and undoubtedly will be important determinants of future decisions on SDI.

Another frequent criticism relates to arms control. Critics charge that SDI will inevitably lead to a breakdown of the ABM Treaty, which is viewed as a major constraint on a new arms race in defensive weapons and as the centerpiece of an arms control regime devoted to the preservation of mutual deterrence. While there is some question as to how much the ABM Treaty constrains the Soviets, the critics are correct in asserting that the treaty would have to be modified, unilaterally or by negotiation, to allow for the testing and eventually the deployment of advanced defenses. But would SDI lead to a new arms race? Not necessarily. Defenses may lead to new forms of arms competition, but it is not clear what form this competition will take or whether it will replicate the dangerous trends of the current race, which sees the Soviets consolidating advantages, particularly in hard-target kill capabilities and in the sort of defenses – those at the tactical ballistic level – that are not prohibited by the ABM Treaty.

Furthermore, if defenses become truly cost-effective for the role they are intended to play, then at some point it will cease to make sense to try to overwhelm the defenses. If they do not become cost-effective, we should not deploy them. It may take some time to find out whether or not defenses will provide positive cost–benefit ratios. In the meantime we could have some competition, but it appears that we have that already. The question is whether the competition that may be stimulated by defenses is going to be more or less harmful to stability and U.S. interests than the competition we would have without defenses. The answer is not apparent but is not clearly in the negative. If the Soviets are forced to deploy penetration aids or to design fast-burn boosters, they will not be creating more destructive power but, rather, utilizing some of their throw-weight to overcome defenses. If they simply try to increase the number of warheads (which they could do with their large missiles), they are probably choosing the wrong solution if the defense has a boost-phase capability, for that will make more warheads vulnerable to each successful intercept in the boost phase. However, both sides will be limited on what they can spend on armaments, so a major effort to build defenses and to respond to the other side's defenses will likely come at the expense of something else. What is the "something else"? Unless we know what the alternatives facing the United States and the Soviet Union are, it is hard to evaluate this issue. In sum, new forms of arms competition are not necessarily bad. If one assumes that competition is inherent in the U.S.–Soviet relationship, then it becomes necessary to contemplate what new forms might emerge and whether they are really worse than what we have now.

Another criticism of defenses relates to their impact on extended deterrence. Initially, the United States' allies reacted adversely to SDI.[35] But by late 1985 and early 1986 some changes had occurred, especially when the British formally agreed to participate in the SDI research program. This agreement has been followed by similar ones with Germany, Italy, Japan, and Israel. Despite these official commitments, legitimate questions remain: Would SDI lead to a strategic environment where the United States is so secure that it no longer feels compelled to extend deterrence, thereby "decoupling" the U.S. guarantee to our allies? If SDI renders ballistic missiles "impotent and obsolete," what are the implications for the investments that the French and British governments have made and will continue to make in order to upgrade their nuclear deterrent forces? Will SDI lead to a new arms race with the Soviet Union that creates greater international tensions, reduces Western security, and jeopardizes European relations with the Soviet bloc? If a theater-based SDI is pursued by the Europeans, how much will it cost, and would the United States agree to share sensitive technologies with its allies? Will the SDI program exacerbate antidefense and antinuclear sentiments that could create dangerous political divisions within European countries? How great will be the resources that SDI would divert from other defense programs, such as conventional forces? Finally, how credible is SDI, given past U.S. initiatives that have either failed or increased intra-NATO tensions, such as the Multilateral Force, the Enhanced Radiation Warhead, and Intermediate Nuclear Force plans?

These are serious questions. Yet what is remarkably evident from these questions is that a very wide spectrum of defensive systems is under discussion, including tactical, intermediate, and population defense. This suggests that the

United States does not have and therefore has not been able to present to its allies a clear rationale for the purposes and ultimate direction of the SDI program. Before the United States can demonstrate to its allies the benefits of an intermediate SDI, it must establish objectives and coherence for the SDI research and development program, which has yet to focus on specific systems.

Despite a seeming lack of coherence, many NATO governments are beginning to recognize that the Soviet missile threat to Europe is large and expanding. In addition, the Soviets are developing an ever-improving air defense system with anti-tactical-missile capabilities. For these reasons, defenses cannot be ignored when considering the European military balance.

In any event, there are no easy answers to the above questions. The SDI program, as currently envisioned, will have a fundamental impact on the strategic relationship between the superpowers and therefore on the U.S. relationship with NATO. The United States has attempted to reassure its allies that defenses will neither decouple the U.S. guarantee nor cut off the Europeans from the benefits (strategic and technological) that SDI might yield. The Reagan Administration rightly protested the notion that SDI could lead the United States to a "Fortress America" posture. Indeed, it emphasized that defenses will be used to strengthen extended deterrence. This goal is consistent with the objectives of an intermediate defense and must be further stressed.

Another point that has to be emphasized is that the Soviets have been conducting SDI-type research for some time; they are not just responding to the U.S. SDI program. Thus, we should not assume that U.S. restraint will bring about similar Soviet restraint. The continuation of Soviet activities (both defensive and offensive) is moving us toward a point where NATO's capacity to execute limited options or a flexible response will be critically eroded.

Yet another area of concern is that the development of defenses could be destabilizing, especially in the transition period. Intermediate defenses, it is argued, "work much better if an adversary's force has previously been damaged in a counterforce strike, intensifying incentives for preemption in a crisis."[36] But assessments of stability often proceed from different assumptions about national defense and nuclear strategy. In a Finite Deterrence or MAD view, defenses are deemed inherently destabilizing because they threaten to reduce the opponent's ability to destroy cities – the central feature of the assured destruction retaliatory strike. If one rejects this view, as the U.S. government has for over twenty years, defenses can be viewed in a more positive light. Intermediate defenses could improve crisis stability by reducing the Soviets' confidence in their ability to strike U.S. forces – strategic or conventional. Defenses could reduce the growing Soviet advantages in strategic offensive and defensive forces; and, from the standpoint of political perceptions and resolve, defenses can increase Western confidence in our deterrent and enhance our ability to resist Soviet political pressures and intimidation.

With regard to transition to a U.S.–Soviet strategic regime embodying intermediate defenses, two general possibilities exist. One is that if the United States is seen as determined to proceed with an SDI program that appears to be making progress, the Soviets could engage in even more strenuous efforts to try to disrupt the program. This would of course place additional strain on superpower relations. On the other hand, as has been previously noted, the Soviets already have a strong commitment to defenses. They may come to accept the need to adjust to a world in which both sides will have defensive systems.[37]

Finally, a strategy including both offensive and defensive forces (or defenses in combination with other measures) can enhance stability by reducing the pre-launch vulnerability of offensive forces. Stability will be further increased if, to quote from the Hoffman Panel, "defenses avoid high vulnerability, [are] robust in the face of enemy technical or tactical countermeasures, and . . . compete favorably in cost terms with expansion of the Soviet offensive force."[38] The Reagan Administration, as evidenced by the statements of Ambassador Paul

Nitze, supported these important and demanding criteria, which SDI will have to respond to in order to be viable: Defenses will have to be survivable and cost-effective at the margin. If overwhelming them through increased offenses is cheaper than adding to the defense, then the whole exercise may prove to be futile. It should be noted that Nitze made this argument in relation to the ultimate goal of a "near-perfect" defensive system. If the objective is instead to strengthen deterrence by a mix of offensive and defensive forces, the criteria could become more flexible.

This last point raises another criticism of SDI touched on above: its financial cost. The Reagan Administration originally requested $26 billion for Fiscal 1985–89 for research to investigate a future decision whether to develop and deploy defenses.[39] However, Congress has substantially cut the administration's requests for funding. In an era of budgetary restrictions, economic considerations must be closely monitored. Yet, while we know the research and development of strategic defenses will be costly, even the advocates of SDI admit that we cannot accurately calculate how much money would be spent. The cost will depend heavily on the program's objectives. Moreover, as already pointed out, the expenditures will be spread out over many years.

Congressional oversight will be an important check on ensuring procurement of cost-efficient defenses. To date, Congress has reduced every SDI budget request while allowing the Strategic Defense Initiative Organization (SDIO) to distribute the cuts as it sees fit. Finally, costs have to be related to benefits. If strategic defenses do enhance deterrence in the future while simultaneously lowering the level of nuclear risk, they could prove to be well worth the expense in terms of our strategic and security objectives.

CONCLUSION: THE CASE FOR DEPLOYING STRATEGIC DEFENSES

One theme has been emphasized throughout this essay: A strategy that incorporates defenses is not a panacea, but neither is a strategy without defenses. Given Soviet strategic preferences and existing programs, a world without any defenses is illusory. There remain many uncertainties and lingering concerns about the impact of defenses. However, a strategy that carefully incorporates a mix of offensive and defensive forces is better than what we have at present, and also better than the other more or less plausible options outlined above. I do not intend to repeat the shortcomings encountered with each alternative. Suffice it to say there are no panaceas. Extreme solutions – be they Finite Deterrence or a population defense – do not present realistic options to those responsible for national security, given the state of today's technical or strategic environment.

The strategy advocated above would be achieved through an evolutionary process, permitting the effects of defenses on deterrence and stability to be examined and evaluated on a step-by-step basis as we proceed. The ultimate test of these defenses is whether they are able to stabilize deterrence and reduce the risks of war by making the prospect of attack less likely. These are goals that we all can share.

NOTES

1. These goals are reiterated in Caspar W. Weinberger, *Annual Report to the Congress for Fiscal 1986* (Washington: U.S. Government Printing Office, 1985), pp. 13, 25.
2. On this subject, see William C. Potter, "Nuclear Proliferation: U.S.–Soviet Cooperation," *Washington Quarterly* 8 (Winter 1985), 141–54.
3. For an examination of the origins and development of the concept of nuclear deterrence, see Lawrence Freedman, *The Evolution of Nuclear Strategy* (New York: St. Martin's, 1981). The most important American statements on the concept of deterrence include: Bernard Brodie, *Strategy in the Missile Age* (Princeton: Princeton University Press, 1959); Herman Kahn, *On Thermonuclear War* (Princeton: Princeton University Press, 1960); William W. Kaufmann, ed., *Military Policy and National Security* (Princeton: Princeton University Press, 1956), pp. 12–38; Henry A. Kissinger, *Nuclear Weapons and Foreign Policy* (New

York: Harper & Row, 1957); Thomas C. Schelling, *The Strategy of Conflict* (Cambridge, Mass.: Harvard University Press, 1960); Thomas C. Schelling, *Arms and Influence* (New Haven: Yale University Press, 1966); Glenn H. Snyder, *Deterrence and Defense: Toward a Theory of National Security* (Princeton: Princeton University Press, 1961); and Albert Wohlstetter, "The Delicate Balance of Terror," *Foreign Affairs* 37 (January 1959), 211–34. For a critique of deterrence theory, see (inter alia) Philip Green, *Deadly Logic: The Theory of Nuclear Deterrence* (Columbus: Ohio State University Press, 1966); Robert Jervis, "Deterrence Theory Revisited," *World Politics* 31 (January 1979), 289–324; and Colin S. Gray, *Strategic Studies: A Critical Assessment* (Westport, Conn.: Greenwood, 1982).

4. Not included in this list, but nevertheless important, are various economic policies.

5. For a history of the evolution of current strategy, see Leon Sloss and Marc Dean Millot, "U.S. Nuclear Strategy in Evolution," *Strategic Review* 12, no. 1 (Winter 1984), 19–28; Colin S. Gray, *Nuclear Strategy and Strategic Planning* (Philadelphia: Foreign Policy Research Institute, 1984), esp. ch. 3; and Henry S. Rowen, "The Evolution of Strategic Doctrine," in Laurence Martin, ed., *Strategic Thought in the Nuclear Age* (Baltimore: Johns Hopkins University Press, 1979), pp. 136–41.

6. Weinberger, *Annual Report 1986*, pp. 25–32.

7. See Senate Foreign Relations Committee, *Nuclear War Strategy* (Washington: U.S. Government Printing Office, 1981) (proceedings of Top Secret hearing on PD-59, held September 16, 1980), pp. 8–9.

8. While command and control is a primary target, it may not be attacked in a limited strike in order to leave open the possibility of negotiating a cease-fire. Industry, of course, remains a target but is thought of more as a target of last resort.

9. Weinberger, *Annual Report 1986*, p. 27.

10. For an overview and discussion of the divergence between U.S. and European strategic thinking, see Gregory Treverton, *Nuclear Weapons in Europe*, Adelphi Paper No. 168 (London: International Institute of Strategic Studies, 1981); and Marsha McGraw Olive and Jeffrey D. Porro, ed., *Nuclear Weapons in Europe: Modernization and Limitation* (Lexington, Mass.: Lexington Books, 1983), esp. ch. 3–5. See also Michael Howard's

insightful and important article "Reassurance and Deterrence," *Foreign Affairs* 61 (Winter 1982–83), 309–24.

11. The extent of the Soviet buildup is catalogued in John M. Collins, *American and Soviet Military Trends Since the Cuban Missile Crisis* (Washington: Georgetown Center for Strategic and International Studies, 1978).

12. The theoretical underpinnings of this view are reflected in such writings as Leon V. Sigal, "Rethinking the Unthinkable," *Foreign Policy* 34 (Spring 1979), 35–51; Robert Jervis, "Why Nuclear Superiority Doesn't Matter," *Political Science Quarterly* 94 (Winter 1979–80), 617–33; Spurgeon M. Keeny, Jr., and Wolfgang K. H. Panofsky, "MAD versus NUTS," *Foreign Affairs* 60 (Winter 1981–82), 287–304; and Robert Jervis, "MAD is the Best Possible Deterrent," *Bulletin of the Atomic Scientists* 40 (March 1985), 43–50.

13. Soviet nuclear doctrine is discussed in, inter alia, Robert P. Berman and John C. Baker, *Soviet Strategic Forces: Requirements and Responses* (Washington: Brookings Institution, 1982), pp. 27–37; Donald W. Hanson, "Is Soviet Doctrine Superior?" *International Security* 7, no. 3 (Winter 1982–83), 61–83; Notra Trulock III, "Weapons of Mass Destruction in Soviet Strategy," paper presented at Conference on Soviet Military Strategy in Europe, sponsored by Boston Foreign Affairs Group and Royal United Services Institute, Oxfordshire, England, September 24–25, 1984 (unpublished); and U.S. Department of Defense, *Soviet Military Power* (Washington: U.S. Government Printing Office, 1985).

14. The costs of strategic forces were less than 15 percent of the FY 85 defense budget; see Statement by Caspar W. Weinberger before Senate Armed Services Committee in conjunction with FY 85 Budget for the Department of Defense, February 1, 1984, p. 13.

15. For example, Gray, *Nuclear Strategy and Strategic Planning*; Alan J. Vick, "Post-Attack Strategic Command and Control Survival: Options for the Future," *Orbis* 29, no. 1 (Spring 1985), 95–117; and Bruce G. Blair, *Strategic Command and Control: Redefining the Nuclear Threat* (Washington: Brookings Institution, 1985).

16. See Samuel T. Cohen and Joseph D. Douglass, Jr., "Selective Targeting and Soviet Deception," *Armed Forces Journal International* 121, no. 2 (September 1983), 95–101.

17. Weinberger, *Annual Report 1986*, pp. 216–20.
18. For example, Harold Brown and Lynn E. Davis, "Nuclear Arms Control: Where Do We Stand?" *Foreign Affairs* 62 (Summer 1984), 1145–60.
19. See, for example, the approach advocated in the *Report of the President's Commission on Strategic Forces* (Scowcroft Commission), April 1983.
20. William Langer Ury and Richard Smoke, *Beyond the Hotline: Controlling a Nuclear Crisis* (A Report to the U.S. Arms Control and Disarmament Agency by the Nuclear Negotiation Project, Harvard Law School, 1985); and Graham T. Allison, Albert Carnesale, and Joseph S. Nye, Jr., ed., *Hawks, Doves, and Owls: An Agenda for Avoiding Nuclear War* (New York: W. W. Norton, 1985).
21. See, for example, Carl Builder, *Strategic Conflict Without Nuclear Weapons* (Santa Monica, Calif.: RAND Corporation, April 1983), R-2980-FF-RC. For a further assessment, see *New Technology and Western Security Policy*, Adelphi Papers Nos. 197–99 (London: International Institute for Strategic Studies, 1984).
22. Bernard W. Rogers, "The Atlantic Alliance: Prescriptions for a Difficult Decade," *Foreign Affairs* 60 (Summer 1982), 1145–65; Rogers, "Greater Flexibility for NATO's Flexible Response," *Strategic Review* 11 (Spring 1983), 11–19; and European Security Study, *Strengthening Conventional Deterrence in Europe* (New York: St. Martin's, 1983).
23. Only five countries (the United States, Great Britain, Italy, the Netherlands, Luxembourg) achieved real increases in the first year of operation. Six achieved it in 1980, but only the United States and Luxembourg appear on both lists. See Roger L. L. Facer, *Conventional Forces and the NATO Strategy of Flexible Response* (Santa Monica, Calif.: RAND Corporation, January 1985), R-3209-FF, p. 44. According to the U.S. government, this trend persisted through 1983. See U.S. Department of Defense, *Report on Allied Contributions to the Common Defense* (Washington: U.S. Government Printing Office, March 1983).
24. Harold A. Feiveson, Richard H. Ullman, and Frank von Hippel, "Reducing U.S. and Soviet Nuclear Arsenals," *Bulletin of the Atomic Scientists* 41 (August 1985), 144–50.
25. Harold A. Feiveson, "Finite Deterrence," Chapter 6 of this volume.
26. This modernization plan was essentially formulated by the

Leon Sloss

Carter Administration and later embraced by the Reagan Administration. However, only cruise missiles have been deployed in significant numbers; MX and B-1 are slowly being phased in, while Midgetman, the D-5, and Stealth are in various phases of development. For an analysis of the offensive buildup, see Congressional Budget Office, *Modernizing U.S. Strategic Offensive Forces: The Administration's Program and Alternatives* (Washington: U.S. Government Printing Office, May 1983), esp. pp. 1–27.

27. This view is reflected in various official statements, including President Reagan's address of March 23, 1983; the presidential White Paper on SDI (January 1985); and an administration Fact Sheet on SDI (June 1, 1985).

28. This view is reflected in the 1983 "Hoffman Panel" study prepared for the Department of Defense. See Future Security Strategy Study (Fred S. Hoffman, study director), *Ballistic Missile Defense and U.S. National Security: Summary Report* (October 1983); rpt. in Steven E. Miller and Stephen Van Evera, ed., *The Star Wars Controversy: An "International Security" Reader* (Princeton: Princeton University Press, 1986).

29. Ibid.; and Albert Carnesale, "Special Supplement: The Strategic Defense Initiative," in George Hudson and Joseph Kruzel, ed., *American Defense Annual, 1985–86* (Lexington, Mass.: Lexington Books, 1985).

30. See Hoffman Panel *Report*, passim; and the technical discussion in another report prepared for the U.S. government by the "Fletcher Panel": Defense Technologies Study (James C. Fletcher, director), *Defense Against Ballistic Missiles: An Assessment of Technologies and Policy Implications* (April 1983); rpt. in Miller and Van Evera, *The Star Wars Controversy*.

31. Fred S. Hoffman, "The SDI in U.S. Nuclear Strategy," *International Security* 10, no. 1 (Summer 1985), 13–24, at 20; rpt. in Miller and Van Evera, *The Star Wars Controversy*, 3–14.

32. Hoffman Panel *Report*, p. 10.

33. For a balanced discussion that highlights the problems and costs of SDI (and provides useful citations), consult Carnesale. Also see the more critical discussion in the July–August 1984 issue of *Arms Control Today* 14, no. 6, and in Charles L. Glaser, "Do We Want the Missile Defenses We Can Build?" *International Security* 10, no. 1 (Summer 1985), 25–57; rpt. in Miller and Van Evera, *The Star Wars Controversy*, pp. 98–130.

34. The most comprehensive public study of SDI costs so far is Barry M. Blechman and Victor A. Utgoff, "The Fiscal and Economic Implications of Strategic Defenses," SAIS Papers in International Affairs No. 12 (Boulder, Colo.: Westview, September 1986). In this paper the authors postulate several SDI programs, each of which would have different fiscal and economic implications.

35. See John Newhouse, "The Diplomatic Round," *The New Yorker*, July 22, 1985, pp. 37–45.

36. Hoffman, "SDI in U.S. Nuclear Strategy," p. 21.

37. For a discussion of possible Soviet countermeasures, see Thomas Krebs, "Moscow's Many Problems in Countering a U.S. Strategic Defense System," *Heritage Foundation Backgrounder No. 454*, September 17, 1985.

38. Hoffman Panel *Report*, p. 12.

39. See Department of Defense, *Report to the Congress on the Strategic Defense Initiative 1985*, p. C-24.

Chapter 9

Morality, the SDI, and limited nuclear war

Steven Lee

> Defense is moral; offense is immoral.
> *Alexei Kosygin*

Ballistic missile defenses such as those envisioned under the Strategic Defense Initiative (SDI) are proposed mechanisms for limiting a nuclear war through the interception of ballistic missile warheads. A nuclear war involving a nation with such defensive systems would be, in some sense of the word, a "limited" nuclear war. A moral evaluation of the SDI can best proceed by considering the nature and extent of the limitations that the SDI defenses would impose on nuclear war. The moral advantages that are claimed for the SDI are a consequence of its potential war-limiting capacity. The strategic novelty of the SDI is the new way it promises to limit nuclear war, and an understanding of this is crucial for the moral evaluation.

Limited war, as understood here, is a war that is substantially less destructive than it would have been had the participants not exercised certain restraints or intervened in certain ways in order to limit the level of damage. Limited war is usually seen in terms of restraints that each side exercises in the damage it does to the other side, especially to its civilian population. But I will broaden the notion to include limitations resulting from active interventions as well, thereby including defenses as a war-limiting mechanism. The overall destructiveness of war creates, of course, a general moral interest in its being limited and in the development of capacities for its limitation. But a war does not become morally acceptable merely because it is limited in some way, nor does it become morally preferable to deploy defenses merely because they would limit a war.

The strategic novelty of the SDI is that it represents a new, potentially more active form of intervention, or damage limitation, to limit the damage done to the United States in a nuclear war. Heretofore, the only form of active damage limitation (as distinguished from passive measures such as civil defense) available against Soviet ballistic missile warheads has been counterforce offensive capability, the ability to destroy Soviet ballistic missiles before they can be launched. Apart from intervention, the only way that the United States can limit damage to itself in a nuclear war is to get the Soviet Union to exercise restraint in its nuclear attacks. This would be achieved through a form of nuclear deterrence in war, as distinguished from the deterrence of war itself. Nuclear retaliation can be threatened not only to avoid war altogether, but also to limit a war in progress. Defenses and retaliatory nuclear deterrence represent contrasting mechanisms for limiting a nuclear war. But defenses may play a deterrent role as well, as we shall see.

SDI defenses would have morally relevant consequences in addition to damage limitation. Thus, a moral evaluation of the SDI should consider more than its damage-limitation capability alone. SDI defenses would become part of, and would help to shape, a broader military policy, and the SDI must be morally evaluated in the context of this broader policy.[1] For example, one argument asserts that the government ought to deploy defenses because of its general moral obligation to protect its citizens. But such an argument errs in failing to consider the moral relevance of the broader policy context of SDI deployments. One's obligation to provide defense for others may not extend to making defensive preparations that have morally unacceptable features.[2] For example, if there is a significant possibility that children in a home where there is a handgun will get hold of it and do themselves or others harm, this is relevant to the moral evaluation of the homeowner's possessing a handgun. The obligation of a family member to defend other members does not by itself determine the moral status of handgun ownership. Such an obligation may not justify preparations for its exercise that create a serious risk of harm to others.

The SDI is, at this point, a research and development program directed at creating the technology required for the interception and destruction of ballistic missiles and their warheads in flight. The development of such technology is, of course, a separate undertaking from its deployment in defensive systems. Our concern here is the moral evaluation of the deployment of SDI defenses, and not, strictly speaking, of the SDI itself.[3] Proponents of the SDI often complain that criticisms of the program are misdirected, since the SDI is only a research and development effort. But it has become clearer as the program has progressed that many of its supporters see the SDI as necessarily leading to whatever defensive deployments prove technologically feasible. They do not see a deployment decision as a separate policy matter. If the decision to continue with the SDI program is tantamount to a decision to deploy whatever defenses can be developed, then the moral unacceptability of deployment would probably entail the moral unacceptability of the SDI itself.

Because the SDI is still at the research stage, however, we do not know what defensive systems may be ultimately developed and deployed. But there are some basic features common to all defensive deployments envisioned under the SDI.[4] First, the deployments would seek to provide protection not just for military assets but for population centers as well. Second, the deployments would consist of several defensive systems in a layered arrangement. Included would be a "boost-phase" layer designed to destroy Soviet ballistic missiles in the early phase of their flight, a "midcourse" layer designed to destroy the warheads in their ballistic arc above the atmosphere, and a "terminal" layer designed to destroy the warheads as they fall through the atmosphere to their targets. Third, exotic directed-energy technologies, such as lasers and particle beams, would be employed if practicable. These three features are closely connected, since significant population defense seems possible only if missiles can be intercepted in the boost phase, and exotic-technology systems may be necessary for this.[5] It is in the proposed boost-phase layer that the SDI differs from the U.S. ballistic missile defense program of two decades ago. Since significant population protection would be possible only with an effective boost-phase layer, this difference is of great moral and strategic importance, and it is a major assumption of a moral evaluation of the SDI that SDI deployments would include a boost-phase layer.

A more important area of controversy is the goal for the defenses in terms of their effectiveness. How limited a nuclear war – that is, how much damage limitation–would the defenses make possible? Are they to be designed to intercept *all* ballistic missiles and their warheads launched against the United States, to provide a leakproof defensive shield over the entire nation? This is the goal President Reagan apparently set forth when he proposed what became the SDI, calling upon the American scientific community "to give us the means of rendering these nuclear weapons impotent and obsolete."[6] Or would it be acceptable to have something less, defenses that could intercept a substantial portion but not all of the nuclear warheads in a large-scale Soviet attack? This is the more modest goal that many proponents of the SDI have argued the United States should adopt (or settle for) – not limiting completely the damage from a nuclear attack, but limiting the damage to some extent. There turns out to be a great moral (as well as strategic) difference between these goals, and the argument must divide accordingly. I shall refer to SDI defenses that would achieve the goal of a leakproof defense against ballistic missile warheads as "SDI-1," and to those that would achieve an at least moderately effective leaky defense as "SDI-2."

Two principal moral arguments have been offered for the SDI. First, it is argued that the policy of nuclear deterrence is morally unacceptable and that SDI defenses would remove this basic moral problem with current U.S. policy by replacing nuclear deterrence. Second, it is argued that even if SDI defenses could not replace nuclear deterrence, the damage limitation they would provide could make their deployment morally preferable. The first argument applies to SDI-1, while the second applies to SDI-2. The overall moral status of the SDI turns on the soundness of these two arguments.

Before assessing these arguments, however, two assumptions behind the present study should be mentioned. First, I assume that it is technologically possible to build at least moderately effective SDI defenses, including a boost-phase layer. This may not be so,[7] in which case neither SDI-1 nor SDI-2 is possible, and a moral examination of them would be of little practical interest. Second, I assume here that the primary purpose of the SDI is the defensive one of replacing nuclear deterrence or providing a capacity for damage limitation. If there is some other main purpose, a moral examination of the SDI would have to take it into account. One possibility is that the SDI is meant to recreate for the United States the kind of absolute nuclear superiority it enjoyed over the Soviet Union in the 1950s, so that the United States could practice not mere deterrence but "compellence," seeking not only to deter Soviet aggression but also to extract concessions from the Soviet Union through nuclear blackmail. Another possibility is that the SDI is primarily meant to advance military high technology in general, providing the United States with an advantage over the Soviet Union across a broad military front. But even if the SDI has one of these other purposes, a moral examination of the program in terms of its stated defensive purpose could serve, if the results are negative, to strip the program of its public rationale and so require that it be defended for what it really is.

Steven Lee

THE SDI AND THE MORAL ACCEPTABILITY OF
NUCLEAR DETERRENCE

Let us consider the argument that the SDI would remove the basic moral problem of current U.S. policy by replacing nuclear deterrence. An SDI-1 leakproof defensive shield, presupposed by this argument, would be radical in moral as well as strategic terms. It would be strategically radical because it would undo the nuclear revolution, eliminating the condition of mutual vulnerability that has been a fundamental military reality since at least the early 1960s. Nuclear deterrence has rested on the fact that the Soviet and American societies are each vulnerable to destruction by the nuclear weapons of the other, and on the hope and belief that this would lead each side not to aggress against the vital interests of the other. Mutual vulnerability (sometimes referred to as "mutual assured destruction" or "MAD"), understood not as a policy but as a fact inherent in the nature of existing weapons systems, makes nuclear war, in practical terms, potentially unlimited in its destructiveness. SDI-1 defenses would eliminate the condition of mutual vulnerability by eliminating the ability of Soviet ballistic missile warheads to destroy American society.

SDI-1 defenses would be radical in moral terms because they would avoid the unprecedented moral consequences of the condition of mutual vulnerability. Mutual vulnerability gives rise to moral paradox.[8] It is of the greatest moral importance to prevent the destruction of one's society, and in a situation in which one's opponent has an assured destruction capacity it seems that this can be accomplished only by threatening the opponent with societal destruction. But such a threat is morally impermissible, since it is directed against innocent persons. It is in violation of the Just War principle of discrimination and is a form of hostage-holding.[9] So the continuation and the abandonment of nuclear deterrence are both morally required[10] – a paradox that seems as permanent as the condition of mutual vulnerability.

This paradox represents the basic moral problem of cur-

386

rent policy based on nuclear deterrence. Solving this problem requires eliminating the condition of mutual vulnerability. This is precisely what SDI-1 defenses promise. They would eliminate U.S. vulnerability to Soviet ballistic missile attack.[11] They would not, of course, eliminate Soviet vulnerability to nuclear attack by the United States, but the United States, no longer threatened by Soviet ballistic missiles, could then choose not to threaten the Soviet Union with nuclear weapons. The defenses would have replaced nuclear deterrence.[12] Free of the moral paradox, the United States could abandon nuclear deterrence. Clearly, though, SDI-1 defenses would not by themselves solve the moral problem of current policy. The solution requires that the United States free Soviet society, not American society, from the threat of nuclear attack.[13] Deployment of SDI-1 defenses would not be the abandonment of nuclear deterrence; that would require an additional policy choice. Ending U.S. vulnerability would solve the moral problem of current policy only if it led the United States to abandon nuclear deterrence.

But the United States almost certainly would not abandon nuclear deterrence.[14] For one thing, leakproof SDI-1 defenses would not by themselves eliminate the Soviet nuclear threat to the United States. These systems would have to be augmented so that the United States would be protected not only from ballistic missile warheads, the sole concern of SDI defenses, but also from nuclear weapons delivered in other ways, such as by bomber or cruise missile. But even if the SDI-1 defenses could be augmented to provide complete protection against all Soviet nuclear weapons, however delivered, there are still good reasons why the United States would not abandon nuclear deterrence. First, American leaders would never be sufficiently sure that the defenses would work perfectly to trust them completely, because the defenses could not be fully tested prior to war. Prudence would require that American leaders regard the United States as vulnerable even if it were in fact invulnerable. Second, American leaders could never be confident that the defensive shield would work perfectly against a future Soviet offensive threat, and they should expect that it would not. The offensive threat is unlikely to be permanently suppressed. Methods of defeating the defenses would eventually be developed, bringing the United States again under the threat of Soviet nuclear weapons.[15] So, even with a leakproof shield in place, neither the present nor the future invulnerability of the shield could be prudently counted on. Thus the United States could not be expected to abandon nuclear deterrence.

But the claim that the United States would not abandon nuclear deterrence does not imply that it should not do so. Perhaps the moral advantage of leakproof defenses is that they would permit the choice to abandon nuclear deterrence, even if that choice is not likely. But this criticism misunderstands the argument. A reasonable belief that the United States was vulnerable to nuclear attack would remain even with the deployment of leakproof defenses, and so the United States would have the same reason for practicing nuclear deterrence that it now has. The moral problem of current policy is not merely that the policy is morally unacceptable and ought to be abandoned – that is only the half of it. If that were the entire problem, the United States could choose to solve it today by abandoning nuclear deterrence. The other half of the problem – what makes it a paradox – is that the Soviet nuclear threat makes nuclear deterrence seem the only way to avoid the morally (and prudentially) unacceptable consequences of a Soviet nuclear attack. Because SDI-1 defenses, even when augmented to cover other means of delivery, could not provide grounds against a reasonable belief that the United States was vulnerable to a Soviet nuclear threat, they would not allow the solution of the moral problem.

Whatever Soviet nuclear threat remained after the United States deployed augmented SDI-1 defenses would, however, be a lesser threat than currently exists. The Soviet Union would not be able to do nearly as much damage to the United States with nuclear weapons as it now can. A lesser Soviet threat would presumably allow a lesser U.S. retaliatory threat to deter it. This would seem at least to ameliorate the moral problem of current policy. The U.S. nuclear threat would pose less of a risk to the hostages it holds. It seems, then, that SDI-1 defenses would allow some moral improvement, and hence that the first moral argument for the SDI goes through, albeit in a weaker form than originally stated.

There are two responses to this. First, according to the moral logic of the situation, mere amelioration cannot count as a satisfactory solution. While it is in some sense morally better to lessen the risk to one's hostages, it remains morally unacceptable to hold them hostage. The morally appropriate solution is not to lessen the risk to them, but to let them go. Second, however, it may well be false that the U.S. nuclear threat would be lessened with the deployment of SDI-1 defenses. For the magnitude of the threat is the product of two factors: the amount of harm that is threatened, and the likelihood that the threat will be carried out. With the deployment of SDI-1 defenses, the United States may choose to decrease the first factor, but the second factor may well increase. Nuclear war may become more likely than it now is once the defenses become leaky, as they almost certainly would because of advances in offensive technology. Leaky defenses are SDI-2 defenses, and SDI-2 defenses would probably increase the likelihood of war, as we shall see in the next section. In any case, the SDI does not have the moral advantage of solving (or allowing the solution of) the moral problem of current policy.

But whatever their moral status, SDI-1 defenses appear to face fatal practical problems. The SDI-1 goal of a leakproof defense cannot be achieved in the foreseeable future.[16] The large number of nuclear warheads in the Soviet arsenal, all of which the defenses might have to destroy in a very short period of time, along with the cumulative effect of a variety of countermeasures the Soviet Union is likely to take against the U.S. defenses, would seem to make leakproof defense an impossibly difficult task. The form of limited nuclear war promised by SDI-1 defenses – complete damage limitation – not only fails to solve the moral problem of current policy: It is also not feasible. Whatever moral case is to be made for the SDI, then, must be made in terms of SDI-2. Indeed, the infeasibility of SDI-1 is so apparent that anyone seriously criticizing SDI-1 might justly be accused of setting up a straw man, were it not that one of the principal moral arguments offered by supporters of the SDI assumes it feasibility.

Since the first moral argument for the SDI has failed, we must turn our attention to the second. According to the second argument, the damage-limitation capabilities of SDI defenses would make their deployment morally preferable even if the protection they provide would not be complete. If a nuclear war comes it is better to save some lives, even if we cannot save them all.

THE SDI AND THE MORALLY PREFERABLE POLICY

SDI defenses would limit nuclear war through damage limitation. Damage limitation, as a form of harm avoidance, is of moral value. The first moral argument for the SDI did not appeal directly to the moral value of damage limitation, but to an alleged consequence of the capacity for complete damage limitation, the ability of leakproof defenses to replace nuclear deterrence. Even though SDI defenses could not replace nuclear deterrence, however, they could still provide some damage limitation. The second argument, then, is that having some capacity for damage limitation is morally preferable to having none. But this is true only if other things are equal, and they may not be. This is where the context of SDI deployments becomes important. Judgments of moral preferability are all-things-considered judgments. If SDI defenses are considered by themselves, deploying them might well appear to be morally preferable to not deploying them.[17] But when the defenses are considered in their context of deployment, the moral implications of the resulting military policy must be considered as well. Because defenses cannot remove the Soviet nuclear threat, the context for their deployment would be a policy of nuclear deterrence.[18] Indeed, President Reagan was called to account for publicly raising moral doubts about nuclear deterrence, and thereby undercutting its perceived legitimacy, when the United States is unable to abandon the policy.[19]

Proponents of the SDI argue that the deployment of SDI-2 defenses would better deter war, that the defenses would enhance deterrence.[20] This strategic argument is also a moral argument, although it is not usually presented as such.[21] Since the avoidance of war is of significant moral value, the argument that SDI-2 defenses would enhance the deterrence of war is an additional moral argument for the SDI. In strategic terms, the capacity for damage limitation is regarded as a *means* to enhance deterrence, and hence better to avoid war. We must examine the claim that there is a means–end relation between damage limitation and war avoidance.

War avoidance might, of course, be seen as a form of damage limitation more broadly understood, since the avoidance of war limits completely the damage that would have occurred had war not been avoided. The common moral currency of war avoidance and damage limitation is the avoidance of harm, and especially the saving of lives. (In terms of damage limitation, the avoidance of war is the equivalent of genuinely leakproof defenses.) But there are good reasons, in addition to respect for standard usage, for keeping the notions of war avoidance and damage limitation distinct and not conflating them under their common moral denominator of harm avoidance. First, the argument that SDI-2 defenses would enhance deterrence depends on the claim that there is a means–end relation between a capacity for damage limitation and war avoidance. Second, a proper account of the argument that the obligation of leaders to protect their citizens justifies acquiring a damage-limitation capacity appears to require that the notions be kept distinct.

Third, damage limitation and war avoidance differ in moral weight.[22] Given the great destructive power of nuclear weapons, even a nuclear war limited by SDI-2 defenses could involve catastrophic damage to the United States. The principal moral measure of damage limitation is lives saved, but the effectiveness of SDI-2 defenses in saving lives would be generally much less than their effectiveness in intercepting warheads, especially when cities are the target. There is a rapidly diminishing marginal "utility" of destruction for successive nuclear detonations on a city, because of the great destructive power of each detonation. The defenses would have to intercept a very high proportion of the many Soviet warheads aimed at American cities to achieve any significant level of damage limitation measured in terms of lives saved.[23] The number of lives saved if there is a war might be large in absolute terms, but not large relative to the number lost in the war. Avoiding war has a much greater potential for saving American lives than does limiting a war's damage through SDI-2 defenses. In addition, avoiding war saves the lives of Soviet as well as American citizens. So war avoidance is more important morally than damage limitation, and it may aid moral understanding to keep the two notions distinct.

Comparing war avoidance and damage limitation in terms of life-saving potential is, of course, unnecessary if SDI-2 defenses would enhance deterrence, for then the defenses could only save lives. But if SDI-2 defenses would weaken rather than enhance deterrence, the likelihood of war would be increased and the defenses represent a potential loss of life as well. Then this comparison would become crucial to the overall moral assessment of SDI-2. If SDI-2 defenses would increase the likelihood of war, their life-losing potential would have to be morally weighed against the life-saving potential of their capacity for damage limitation. There are other factors morally relevant to the all-things-considered judgment of whether or not the deployment of SDI-2 defenses is morally preferable. Some of these are additional matters of damage limitation, such as a concern to protect the United States from a small number of nuclear warheads launched accidentally by the Soviet Union or deliberately by some third country. Some are concerns of other sorts, such as the economic costs of the SDI program in the face of pressing social needs. But although these other factors are morally important, they pale in comparison with what may be at stake in terms of significant shifts in the likelihood of war. The overall moral assessment of the SDI will depend crucially on the question of war avoidance, and thus on the soundness of the argument that SDI-2 defenses would enhance deterrence.

Arguments that SDI-2 defenses would enhance deterrence most frequently claim that these defenses would increase Soviet uncertainty about the outcome of a nuclear attack on the United States and would raise the "threshold" for such an attack. Leon Sloss argues as follows:

> The principal rationale for deployment of some . . . active defenses against ballistic missiles is that they will reinforce deterrence. . . . the enemy's calculations of the attack outcome [become] more complicated. . . . [since he] could not be certain how many warheads would reach their targets. . . . High uncertainty about the outcome of an attack will act as a deterrent for the enemy. Moreover, defenses will raise the cost of attacking, thereby placing the onus for escalation on the Soviet Union.[24]

The argument seems to be this. The Soviet Union would be less likely to attack the United States with nuclear weapons if Soviet leaders could not be so certain of the results of that attack or if the cost of that attack to them (the threshold for the attack), in terms of military resources expended, was higher. SDI-2 defenses would bring this about, and so would lessen the likelihood of war. The capacity for damage limitation would create a greater uncertainty about the outcome of an attack and raise the threshold, becoming in this way a means to war avoidance.

In examining this argument it is important to consider the strategic concerns that underlie it. Increasing the uncertainty of outcome and the cost of a Soviet nuclear attack is irrelevant in the case of an attack meant to destroy American society, since the condition of mutual vulnerability guarantees the outcome of such an attack, and the cost in terms of the number of warheads is irrelevant. The kind of Soviet attack the defenses would discourage, according to this argument, is a limited counterforce attack aimed at U.S. nuclear forces. This shows that the kind of damage limitation that is seen by proponents of SDI-2 as a means to war avoidance is not primarily the saving of lives (the morally relevant form of damage limitation), but the saving of military hardware. Discouraging a limited Soviet counterforce attack is seen as a valuable war-avoidance measure, because such an attack is viewed as the most likely way for a nuclear war to start.

The need to strengthen deterrence to discourage limited Soviet nuclear attacks is often tied to two military disadvantages that the United States is alleged to suffer in relation to the Soviet Union. The first disadvantage is a result of the U.S. policy of extended deterrence, the doctrine of using nuclear threats to deter Soviet conventional aggression, especially in Europe. It is argued that the ability of the United States to meet the special demands that extended deterrence places on its military capabilities has been undercut by the Soviet achievement of nuclear parity with the United States. SDI-2 defenses are seen as a way to satisfy these special demands despite nuclear parity.[25] Second, over the past fifteen years the Soviet Union has greatly increased both the number and the accuracy of its ballistic missile warheads, and this is thought to have undercut the effectiveness of deterrence. It is argued, for example, that the Soviet Union can now threaten to destroy virtually all American land-based ballistic missiles in a first strike (creating a "window of vulnerability") and thus has the United States at a military disadvantage. SDI-2 defenses are seen as solving this strategic problem, thereby restoring the effectiveness of nuclear deterrence.[26]

The claim that SDI-2 defenses would be a response to the problems of extended deterrence and missile vulnerability shows the link in the minds of strategists between these defenses and the official U.S. nuclear doctrine of countervailing strategy, as well as its stronger variant, nuclear warfighting strategy – both of which are also seen as a response to these problems.[27] Under countervailing strategy, the United States seeks the capability to match the Soviet Union at any potential level of military conflict, including nuclear conflict. Under nuclear warfighting strategy, the United States seeks the capability to fight a nuclear war with the Soviet Union and "prevail." To put it roughly, the contrast between these two doctrines is that countervailing strategy seeks to deter the Soviet Union by convincing Soviet leaders that they could not win a war at any level, while nuclear warfighting strategy seeks to deter the Soviet Union by convincing Soviet leaders not only that they could not win a war at any level but that the United States could, with the result that the United States can credibly threaten to initiate the use of nuclear weapons to deter low-level Soviet aggression. Both of these doctrines rely on extensive counterforce targeting of nuclear warheads to make possible the kind of limited nuclear war that they require the United States to be able to fight.

Both strategies see a major role for SDI-2 defenses.[28] Such defenses are seen as increasing the United States' ability to match the Soviet Union at any potential level of conflict and to prevail in any nuclear war that may occur. The connection between SDI-2 defenses and these strategies shows that the perceived usefulness of the defenses goes beyond helping to discourage a Soviet first strike. The defenses are meant to contribute to a capacity to fight a limited nuclear war, which means that they are expected to help provide deterrence in war as well as deterrence of war. Thus, the defenses are meant to deter not only a Soviet first strike but also a Soviet second, third, or fourth strike. If a nuclear war is to be limited in such a way that the United States could be said to have "prevailed," then early in the conflict (which it is assumed will begin with limited nuclear strikes), the Soviet Union must refrain from escalating the conflict further, and this requires that Soviet retaliatory strikes, as well as Soviet first strikes, be discouraged. In any case, it is important to recognize that the context of SDI-2 deployments – the military policy of which SDI-2 defenses would become a part – is a form of countervailing or nuclear warfighting strategy. It is this kind of nuclear deterrence that SDI-2 defenses would be meant to enhance.

The relation between the SDI and the notion of limited nuclear war can now be made clearer. War may be limited by restraint or by intervention: Restraint may be achieved by deterrence in war, intervention by defenses. Given the condition of mutual vulnerability, the only hope, if any, for significantly limiting nuclear war (as well as for avoiding it) has rested on restraint induced by deterrence. The original promise of the SDI was that it would revolutionize the military situation by the extent to which it could limit nuclear war through intervention, providing complete damage limitation. The United States could, by itself, prevent any damage to itself in a nuclear war, making Soviet restraint irrelevant. This would allow the United States to abandon nuclear deterrence. But with the recognition of the failure of the first moral argument for the SDI and the infeasibility of SDI-1, the promise of damage limitation has faded. SDI-2 defenses could not by themselves directly prevent the destruction of American society by a large-scale Soviet nuclear attack, so for this form of damage limitation the United States must, as always, rely on encouraging Soviet restraint through deterrence. But defenses are seen as contributing to deterrence in war, lessening the likelihood of Soviet escalation, as well as providing a better deterrent of war. This shift in perspective on how SDI defenses would contribute to limiting nuclear war is a shift from seeing the SDI as something special to seeing it as just another implement of counterforce warfare. The SDI is, in effect, simply one more weapons system designed to contribute to the goal of a countervailing or nuclear warfighting strategy, which is both deterrence in war and deterrence of war. The question is whether SDI-2 defenses would make nuclear deterrence a better deterrent of war.

The argument that SDI-2 defenses would make nuclear deterrence more effective in deterring war is, as we have seen, based on the premise that they would create Soviet uncertainty about the results of a nuclear attack on the United States and would raise the threshold for such an attack. There are three lines of criticism of this argument. First, the argument makes assumptions that may be false. Second, there is good reason to regard the premise of the argument as false. Third, the premise is insufficient to establish the conclusion.

First, the argument makes two assumptions that may be challenged. One is that there is not already sufficient Soviet uncertainty about the results of a limited nuclear attack on the United States, and a high enough threshold for such an attack, to insure a more-than-adequate level of deterrence effectiveness.[29] A number of factors creating uncertainties about the results of a limited Soviet nuclear attack already exist, such as the possibility that the United States might launch its missiles on warning of an attack. In addition, the threshold for an effective Soviet limited counterforce attack is now probably quite high, given the large number of counterforce targets in the United States. This may already be sufficient to deter the Soviet Union from a limited nuclear attack, so that any additional uncertainty or any further raising of the threshold would be redundant. Another questionable assumption is that there are no easier and less costly ways than deploying SDI-2 defenses to create greater uncertainty and to raise the threshold further. Passive measures to lessen the vulnerability of American land-based missiles, such as making them mobile or increasing the hardness of their silos, might increase uncertainty and raise the threshold as much as the defenses would, and such measures would be far easier and less costly to implement.

According to the second line of criticism, there is good reason to regard the premise of the argument as false. Doubts about the premise may be raised by introducing the notion of "attack price," which can be used as a quantitative measure of the degree of effectiveness of defenses.[30] The attack price is, roughly, the number of warheads that would have to be launched at a target to achieve a high level of assurance of its destruction. Due to existing uncertainties in the performance of weapons, hardened military targets already generally have an attack price greater than one. SDI-2 defenses would simply increase the attack price: The more effective the defenses, the greater the increase. In other words, the situation now is that x warheads (the attack price) launched at some target yield y percent certainty (say, 90 percent) of the target's destruction. The deployment of SDI-2 defenses

397

would result in some of these warheads being intercepted, so that if x were held constant y would fall. To bring y back up to its original value one could simply increase x, the amount of increase being a function of how effective the defenses are. This is paying the higher attack price.

This means that defenses would have a substantial effect on the uncertainty of an attack outcome only if the higher attack price they exact were not paid. If the price were paid, a nation should be about as certain of the results of its attack on defended targets as it is of the results of an attack on undefended targets.[31] Given that the Soviet Union already has a very large number of nuclear warheads and could easily increase this number substantially, it should be able to pay the increased attack price exacted by SDI-2 defenses for a limited attack. If so, SDI-2 defenses would not significantly increase Soviet uncertainty about the outcome of a limited nuclear attack on the United States. It is doubtful, of course, that the Soviet leaders would know precisely, or perhaps even roughly, how effective United States defenses were; but such knowledge on their part need not be assumed, for all they need do is assume the worst in their estimate of the defenses' effectiveness and be prepared to pay the attack price required by this estimate. Uncertainty about the defenses' effectiveness would not by itself, then, lead to uncertainty about the outcome of the attack.

If the claim that SDI-2 defenses would raise the cost or the threshold of a Soviet nuclear attack is understood in the way necessary to support the argument, it is probably false. Assuming that the Soviet Union is able to pay the increased attack price, it seems that the increase in the number of warheads required to pay that price would not by itself do much to discourage the attack, given the importance the Soviets must place on the attack to risk it in the first place. What might discourage the attack would be an increase in the amount of extra damage done by the attack, especially to populations, beyond the counterforce damage inherent in achieving the attack's objectives. For an increase in the extra damage is more likely to lead to a stronger U.S. response and so to an unwanted escalation in the conflict. But the larger number of warheads used is unlikely to produce a significant increase in the extra damage done, at least so far as immediate damage goes, since many of the additional warheads will be intercepted by the defenses and any that get through will detonate on counterforce targets already destroyed. Thus, an attack against defended targets paying the increased attack price would be unlikely to do much more immediate damage than an attack against undefended targets, and so would do little to increase the risks of escalation.[32] If the higher cost or threshold of attack refers merely to the number of warheads used, the premise of the argument does not support the conclusion; and if it refers to damage done in the attack, the premise appears to be false.

The third line of criticism is that the premise, even if true, does not provide sufficient support for the conclusion that SDI-2 defenses would reduce the likelihood of war. This is because the argument ignores the ways in which SDI-2 defenses would tend to increase the likelihood of war. One way would result from the vigorous arms race they would be likely to initiate.[33] The Soviet Union can, as we have seen, avoid being put at a strategic disadvantage from SDI-2 defenses if it has the ability to pay the increased attack price exacted by the defenses. To ensure themselves this ability, Soviet leaders would almost certainly undertake an offensive weapons buildup. This would be in addition to their efforts to deploy their own defenses of the SDI-2 type, efforts they would very likely initiate or accelerate in response to U.S. defensive deployments.[34] The United States would feel compelled to respond with more offensive forces, and so forth. Neither side could trust its own defenses enough, in the midst of their development and deployment, to allow itself to fall behind in offensive forces. This arms race would likely be more vigorous than the arms race has been heretofore, because each side would be doubly driven to offensive increases – by both the offensive and the defensive advances of the other side.

This new arms race would likely no longer be restrained by arms control agreements. The deployment of SDI-2 defenses would mean the abandonment of the 1972 Anti-Ballistic-Missile Treaty limiting ballistic missile defenses, the treaty regarded as the cornerstone of the current arms control regime, and its loss would probably signal the end of that regime.[35] One of the strongest motivations behind the ABM Treaty was the avoidance of an unrestrained arms race.[36] The value of arms control agreements is that they make the arms competition more predictable than it would otherwise be, even if the agreements do not actually reduce the levels of armaments. Unpredictability in an arms race increases the likelihood of war, for each side tends to fear that the other may achieve some breakthrough that would give the other a decisive military advantage. Such fear would increase mutual suspicions and may make each side more prone to risk-taking behavior in an effort to avoid or offset the military disadvantage it may believe the other is about to impose on it.

Proponents of SDI-2, while generally recognizing the dangers in a new arms race, have disputed that such defenses would lead to an arms race, arguing that the defenses would lead instead to a reduction in Soviet offensive forces because U.S. defenses would lessen the value of such forces.[37] This argument assumes that the defenses would be cost-effective in comparison with the Soviet offensive increases that would be needed to offset them, for only then would the military value of the offensive forces be lessened by the defenses. This point has been made by Paul Nitze, and marginal cost-effectiveness has become known as one of the "Nitze criteria" for the deployment of defenses:

> New defensive systems . . . must be cheap enough to add additional defensive capability so that the other side has no incentive to add additional offensive capability to overcome the defense. If this criterion is not met, the defensive systems could encourage a proliferation of countermeasures and additional offensive weapons to overcome deployed defenses instead of a redirection of effort from offense to defense.[38]

SDI-2 defenses, however, are unlikely to lead in this way to a reduction in Soviet offensive forces.[39] First, given the technological difficulties facing the development of SDI-2 defenses and the necessary complexity of the deployed defensive systems in comparison with the relative simplicity and known reliability of offensive systems, it is hard to imagine that the defenses would prove to be cost-effective. Nor is it simply a matter of deciding not to deploy the defenses if they prove not to be cost-effective. For it may not be known until they have been deployed whether they would be cost-effective, and once they have been developed at great expense there may be great pressure for their deployment in any case. But even if the defenses were cost-effective when deployed, and could be seen to be so, they might still spur a Soviet offensive buildup, either because the Soviet leaders would believe that the cost-effectiveness of the defenses could be nullified by technological advances or because they place so much importance on their offensive deterrent threat that they would seek to maintain it despite the cost advantage of the defenses.

A second way in which SDI-2 defenses would make war more likely is a consequence of their potential to provide extensive population defense and the effect this would have on the chances for war in a situation of political or military crisis between the United States and the Soviet Union. This is a version of the general problem of avoiding war in a crisis.[40] Deterrence by threat of retaliation depends on a potential attacker's being deterred by the belief that attacking and receiving retaliation would leave him worse off than not attacking. Choosing not to attack normally leaves the one side in a state of peace with the other, and even a bad peace is clearly preferable to suffering retaliatory nuclear damage. The question, then, for each side is *whether attacking would leave it better off than continuing in a state of peace,* and with mutual, credible retaliatory threats neither side would believe that it would. So neither side has an incentive to attack, and this makes mutual deterrence a stable condition in which the deliberate initiation of war is unlikely.

Steven Lee

But in a crisis the psychological basis of deterrence begins to shift, for each side then begins to consider the possibility that there might be no resolution of the crisis short of war, and expects the other side to be having similar thoughts. If each side comes to believe that war may occur, it cannot continue to assume that the alternative to its not attacking is no war, for the other side may attack first. Each side must ask itself whether the other, believing that war may occur anyway, would choose to attack first. The other side might do so if it believed that this would yield a relative advantage. The question for each side thus becomes *whether the other side's attacking first and receiving retaliation would leave it better off than being attacked first* – a very different question. In a crisis, if the answer is Yes, war is more likely. For then the one side, fearing the other side's attack, would have a strong incentive to seize the initiative and strike first in what it would regard as a preemptive attack. It might do so in the belief, or merely the hope, that it would thereby achieve a relative advantage of its own, avoiding some of the damage to itself that would come if the other side struck first. On the other hand, if neither side believes that the other could achieve a relative advantage from attacking first, each is less likely to believe that the other is going to attack, and so each is more likely to wait out the crisis without starting a war.

A crisis can lead the first side to attribute to the second the belief that war is coming. The danger arises when the first side attributes to the second the additional belief that there would be a relative advantage in its striking first. Such an advantage is a function of how the second side's nuclear weapons are targeted. Weapons aimed at military targets – that is, counterforce weapons – may provide such an advantage, because a first strike with them could lessen the amount of damage that the other side is able to inflict. So if either side has extensive counterforce capabilities, the other might attribute to it the belief that it would be better off attacking first and receiving retaliation than being attacked first. This is especially the case when a single missile can carry several independently targeted warheads, as the missiles of the United

States and the Soviet Union now can, for then the advantage of striking first is magnified.

But so long as each side is able to destroy the other in retaliation after receiving a first strike, which is the condition of mutual vulnerability, it is unlikely that either side will attribute to the other the belief that it would be better off attacking first. The destruction of a society, like the death of an individual, is a kind of absolute loss that overwhelms any apparent relative advantage from taking an action that leads to it. If, however, the first side acquired, or was perceived to have acquired, the ability to remove by a first strike the second's ability to destroy the first's society, then the first side could achieve, or would be perceived as being able to achieve, a real relative advantage from attacking first. The second side might then, in a crisis, attribute to the first the belief that the first would be better off doing so. The problem is that very effective defenses with some ability to defend populations, when deployed in conjunction with an extensive counterforce capacity (as they would be under a countervailing or nuclear warfighting strategy), could create such a capability, or at least the perception of one.

How would this work? With its extensive counterforce capacity, the United States might in a first strike destroy a large portion of Soviet strategic nuclear forces. If the United States also had very effective defenses, it might be able to intercept almost all of the few surviving warheads fired in retaliation, leaving the Soviet Union unable to destroy American society.[41] Under such conditions, the Soviet Union might in a crisis be strongly tempted to launch a preemptive attack out of fear that the United States was about to attack and in the hope of limiting, at least somewhat, the damage to itself. In this way, deploying very effective defenses might significantly set back the cause of war avoidance.

There are three counterarguments that might be raised against the criticism that SDI-2 defenses would increase the likelihood of war in a crisis. The first counterargument would accept the claim that very effective defenses could increase the likelihood of a Soviet attack in a crisis, but would argue that this would not increase the overall likelihood of a Soviet attack because the resulting deterrence policy would also decrease the likelihood of crises arising. Indeed, one of the virtues claimed for countervailing and nuclear warfighting strategies, which the defenses would be meant to enhance, is that they more effectively deter small-scale Soviet aggression, thereby keeping crises from arising. It is, of course, not enough that the likelihood of crises arising simply be lowered; it must be lowered enough at least to offset the increase in the likelihood that a crisis would lead to war. And there are good reasons to hold that the likelihood of crises arising cannot be sufficiently lowered by SDI-2 defenses. First, crises need not arise from deliberate Soviet aggression; they can easily arise from factors beyond the control of either nation, such as conflict in the Third World. The likelihood of such crises arising presumably would not be affected by the defenses. Second, SDI-2 defenses may actually have the opposite tendency from the one claimed, for one result of the arms race that is a likely outcome of the deployment of these defenses, as we saw above, would be a greater level of mutual suspicion, and this would make crises more likely to arise.[42]

The second counterargument would reject the claim that very effective defenses would increase the likelihood of a Soviet attack in a crisis. According to this criticism, a necessary condition for such an increase is the vulnerability of U.S. offensive forces, but very effective defenses would ensure that U.S. offensive forces would be largely invulnerable.[43] If these forces were largely invulnerable, Soviet leaders would perceive that a preemptive attack on their part could gain no relative advantage, so they would not launch such an attack in a crisis even if they believed that a United States attack was imminent. A preemptive attack requires a perception of relative advantage – that is, a damage-limitation rationale – and if the other side's offensive weapons are largely invulnerable it can have no such rationale.

The argument is, first, that the same defenses that in a crisis might make Soviet leaders fear an imminent U.S. attack would make a Soviet attempt to preempt such an attack futile, and, second, that a preemptive attack would not be launched if it was going to be futile. Each of these claims can be called into question. As for the second, it is not necessarily the case that an objectively futile preemptive attack would not be launched. In a crisis atmosphere, there might be a stronger tendency than usual toward irrationality. Soviet leaders might, contrary to the evidence, simply refuse to believe that U.S. offensive forces are largely invulnerable. Given the psychological pressures at work in a crisis, they may engage in wishful thinking. Believing that the United States was about to attack, they might preempt the attack out of sheer desperation. A crisis is likely to put decision makers in a frame of mind quite different from that of the careful calculators of prudential advantage they might otherwise be. Fearing an imminent attack, they would not necessarily refrain from an objectively futile action. Such fear might, of course, invoke an irrational response of the opposite sort, paralysis of will. But since it may also invoke an act of desperation, the futility of preemption could not guarantee that it would not occur.

But there is also reason to doubt that SDI-2 defenses could make the offensive forces sufficiently invulnerable for a Soviet preemptive attack to be futile. The attack-price argument presented earlier shows that defenses make the targets they protect invulnerable only if the other side is unable to pay the increased attack price. The Soviet Union, with its large nuclear arsenal, may thus perceive a damage-limitation rationale for a preemptive attack despite the defenses. The force of this point is increased by the fact that U.S. offensive forces suffer from the vulnerability of their command and control network.[44] There are a small number of targets whose destruction might cripple the offensive forces, and the increased attack price on a small number of targets could be easily paid by the Soviet Union. So in a crisis, Soviet leaders would have some reason not to regard U.S. offensive forces as invulnerable.

But the most important reason why a Soviet preemptive attack would probably not be futile is the likely vulnerability of the SDI-2 defenses themselves.[45] If the defenses serve to protect the offensive forces, the vulnerability of the defenses will result in the vulnerability of the offensive forces.[46] The danger in vulnerable defenses is recognized by Paul Nitze: "The technologies must produce defensive systems that are survivable; if not, the defenses would themselves be tempting targets for a first strike."[47] Invulnerability has become known as the other "Nitze criterion" for the deployment of defenses. But certain characteristics of SDI-2 defenses would make the defenses easier to attack than to defend. First, major components of the defenses, especially the boost-phase system, would be in earth orbit and operating over Soviet territory, and as such would be easy to attack. Second, each defensive system would involve a complex interactive set of data-gathering, data-assessing, and "fighting" components, and disabling any one of these components may seriously weaken the whole system. These characteristics would make the invulnerability of the defenses very hard to achieve. But, more important, these characteristics would provide a basis for a reasonable Soviet belief that the SDI-2 defenses, and hence U.S. offensive forces, were not invulnerable. This belief would give the Soviet Union a damage-limitation rationale for attacking first in a crisis.

The third counterargument would maintain that the defenses the Soviet Union would deploy in response to U.S. defenses would ensure that war would not become more likely in a crisis. War becomes more likely only if the Soviet Union is tempted to attack preemptively as a result of the belief that the United States could by a first strike avoid the retaliatory destruction of American society, and Soviet defenses would guarantee that a U.S. first strike could not destroy a sufficient portion of Soviet offensive forces to accomplish this. The vulnerability-making characteristics of defenses of the SDI type, however, blunt the force of this response. These characteristics may lead both sides to believe that the other's defenses are vulnerable even if they are not, and they may lead to the defenses becoming vulnerable through simple technological advances. So Soviet leaders might, in a crisis, believe that the United States believed that Soviet defenses were vulnerable, which would lead them to believe that the United States would perceive a real relative advantage from striking first. Thus, the temptation to attack preemptively would not disappear. This suggests that the possession of very effective defenses by both sides, which might seem to be a very good situation, might turn out to be a very bad one. For if the defenses were vulnerable, or were perceived to be, each side might believe that both sides had the ability to avoid by a first strike the destruction of their society. The pressure to strike first in a crisis would then be great.

One further point should be raised about the likelihood of war in a crisis. The population-protecting potential of SDI defenses might increase the likelihood of a Soviet attack in a crisis, even if the defenses were not very effective.[48] SDI-2 defenses might make it seem that the United States was working toward extensive population defense, even if it were not, and even if such a defense were technologically infeasible. Because SDI defenses would involve a boost-phase system, they could not be unambiguously designed not to protect population, since at the boost phase one cannot tell where the warheads are aimed. Hence, a nation deploying defenses of the SDI type would appear to a suspicious opponent to be seeking extensive population protection, which is what is required to avoid the destruction of one's society in a retaliatory strike. If the Soviet Union believed that the United States was working toward extensive population defense, this might also increase the likelihood that it would initiate war in a crisis. Soviet leaders might fear the significant strategic advantage they expected the United States soon to acquire, and they might believe that an attack on the United States before it had this advantage would be the only way to avoid it. This would provide some incentive for an attack. In the context of a crisis, this incentive, in addition to the general increase in suspicion the crisis would generate, might significantly increase the likelihood that the Soviet Union would attack.

Taken together, these three criticisms seem to defeat the argument that SDI-2 defenses would reduce the likelihood of war. The criticisms show not only that there is no reason to accept this conclusion, since the premise on which it is based is probably false, but that there is strong reason to regard the conclusion as false, since the vigorous arms race likely to result and the increased potential for a Soviet preemptive attack in a crisis would together substantially increase the likelihood of war.[49] The capacity of SDI-2 defenses for damage limitation is not, as proponents of the SDI argue, a means to war avoidance; it would have instead the opposite result, an increase in the likelihood of war.

The judgment of whether it is morally preferable to deploy SDI-2 defenses – that is, whether it is morally preferable to have a nuclear deterrence policy with SDI-2 defenses or one without – requires, as mentioned earlier, that the increase in the likelihood of war upon deployment of the defenses be weighed against their expected capacity for wartime damage limitation. Given the earlier argument that war avoidance is of greater moral importance than damage limitation, it is clear how this comparison comes out: Since avoiding war is a more effective way of saving lives than limiting the damage in a war, the moral disadvantage of SDI-2 defenses outweighs their moral advantage.[50] It is morally preferable not to deploy SDI-2 defenses.

What if a capacity for damage limitation is seen as part of a special obligation the U.S. government has toward American citizens to provide protection for them?[51] As the fulfillment of an obligation, damage limitation would carry greater moral weight, perhaps enough to override the concern about the expected increase in likelihood of war. But to equate a capacity for damage limitation with the provision of protection construes "protection" too narrowly. Avoiding war is also a way of providing protection. Thus, a judgment about what satisfies this special obligation requires the same weighing of war avoidance against damage limitation as does the straight judgment of moral preferability. To argue that the U.S. government's obligation to provide for the defense of the American people requires it to deploy defenses is to equivocate on the term "defense." "Defense" in the former sense implies keeping people from harm without specifying means, while in the latter sense it refers to a specific means of keeping them from harm.

It must be admitted, of course, that the claims made above about the likelihood of war are rough and ready. Claims about the consequences of alternative policy options in the area of nuclear weapons policy, as in other areas of public policy, cannot be made precise and generally involve competing speculative judgments about likelihoods. Granting this inevitable limitation, however, the arguments presented provide strong backing for the claim that SDI-2 defenses would significantly increase the likelihood of war. The arguments discussed here sketch, so to speak, a possible SDI world – that is, one of the ways the world might be if SDI defenses were deployed – and it is a world to which our world is morally preferable. Objections to these arguments could be cast in terms of alternative possible SDI worlds that would be morally preferable to our own.

In one such world, the United States and the Soviet Union negotiate the transition to a military relationship in which both sides have defenses and neither side has offensive forces. In this world, both sides abandon nuclear deterrence, so the moral problem of nuclear deterrence is solved and the likelihood of nuclear war has been virtually eliminated. Another possible SDI world is one in which U.S. deployment of defenses is accompanied by a severe reduction in U.S. offensive forces. In this world, the likelihood of war would be much less despite the defenses, because there would be no arms race and less chance that the Soviet Union would believe that the United States could avoid the destruction of its society through a first strike. Moreover, if the few nuclear weapons the United States had remaining were aimed at isolated Soviet military targets, there would be little threat to Soviet populations, so the moral problem of nuclear deterrence might be solved as well.

Proponents of the SDI would argue that deployment of defenses is the route to these morally preferable worlds. Indeed, they are possible SDI worlds. But the question is: Are these worlds more likely to come about than the morally nonpreferable world sketched above? They are not, because each would require an unprecedented level of cooperation between the United States and the Soviet Union in a situation in which weapons deployments are bound to raise suspicions. The agreements envisioned in the first world go far beyond anything that the two nations have been able to accomplish to date. The second world would also require extensive cooperation, since as a matter of domestic politics it is hard to imagine that the United States could severely cut its offensive forces unless the Soviet Union reciprocated with offensive force cuts of its own. Though such a level of cooperation is not impossible, it is far beyond what the history of the American–Soviet relationship leads one to expect. Cooperation must, of course, be sought, but it cannot be counted on to avoid the morally nonpreferable world likely to result from the deployment of SDI-2 defenses. Though these alternative SDI worlds are morally preferable to the present world, and though the deployment of SDI-2 defenses might bring them about, such a deployment is not itself morally preferable, because it is more likely to bring about a world morally worse than the present one.

The two moral arguments for the SDI fail. The SDI cannot replace nuclear deterrence, so it cannot help us to escape the moral paradox of nuclear deterrence. Nuclear deterrence will remain a moral problem whether or not defenses are deployed. Nor does the damage-limitation capacity of SDI defenses provide a sufficient moral argument in their favor, given the increase in the likelihood of war that would result. SDI defenses should not be deployed in conjunction with our current policy of nuclear deterrence. Practicing such a policy without SDI defenses is morally preferable to practicing it with SDI defenses. Because the moral problem of nuclear deterrence remains, however, it does not follow that practicing nuclear deterrence is morally preferable to not practicing nuclear deterrence. A moral examination of the SDI shows that defenses will not help solve the moral problem of nuclear deterrence. For this, other approaches will be necessary.[52]

Morality, the SDI, and limited nuclear war

NOTES

1. On the moral importance of viewing SDI defenses in the context of their deployment, see Henry Shue, "Morality of Offense Determines Morality of Defense," *Philosophical Forum* 18, no. 1 (Fall 1986), 8–14; rpt. in Douglas P. Lackey, ed., *Ethics and Strategic Defense: American Philosophers Debate Star Wars and the Future of Nuclear Defense* (Belmont, Calif.: Wadsworth, 1989), pp. 84–90.

2. For a similar argument, see Gregory Kavka, "A Critique of Pure Defense," *Journal of Philosophy* 83, no. 11 (November 1986), 625–33; rpt. in Lackey, *Ethics and Strategic Defense*, pp. 91–98.

3. Is there reason for morally favoring research and development if deployment proves to be morally unacceptable? One reason might be to seek to deter the Soviet Union from deployment of defenses by a credible threat of rapid U.S. deployment. But the current size of the SDI program is more likely to stimulate than to deter Soviet defensive efforts, and Soviet deployment could be more effectively prevented through a mutual ban on the testing and deployment of defenses.

4. For a discussion of the proposed SDI systems, see Stephen Weiner, "Systems and Technology," in Ashton Carter and David Schwartz, ed., *Ballistic Missile Defense*, (Washington: Brookings Institution, 1984), pp. 49–97.

5. Because so much more research is needed into exotic technologies, recent calls for early SDI deployments have proposed that nonexotic technologies be used in all layers, including the boost-phase layer.

6. Reagan's March 1983 speech proposing an accelerated development of strategic defenses, which became the SDI program, is reprinted, among other places, in *Daedalus* 114, no. 3 (Summer 1985), 369–71. The quotation is from p. 371.

7. For a general discussion of the potential effectiveness of SDI defenses, see Office of Technology Assessment, *Strategic Defenses* (Princeton: Princeton University Press, 1986), ch. 8, and Union of Concerned Scientists, *The Fallacy of Star Wars* (New York: Random House, 1984), ch. 7.

8. The moral paradox of nuclear deterrence is discussed by Gregory Kavka in "Some Paradoxes of Deterrence," *Journal of Philosophy* 75 (June 1978), 285–302, and by me in "Morality and

411

Steven Lee

Paradoxical Deterrence," *Social Philosophy and Policy* 3, no. 1 (Autumn 1985), 136–53.

9. I discuss nuclear deterrence as a form of hostage holding in "The Morality of Nuclear Deterrence: Hostage-Holding and Consequences," *Ethics* 95, no. 3 (April 1985), 549–66.

10. It has been argued that a form of nuclear deterrence based exclusively on counterforce targeting could avoid the moral paradox. See, for example, Albert Wohlstetter, "Bishops, Statesmen, and Other Strategists on the Bombing of Innocents," *Commentary* 75, no. 6 (June 1983), pp. 15–35. For some criticisms of this argument, see my "Morality and Paradoxical Deterrence."

11. Vulnerability, in the phrase "mutual vulnerability," refers to the inability of the United States or the Soviet Union unilaterally to avoid the destruction of its society in the event of nuclear war. Such destruction would require a number of nuclear detonations. But the United States would regard itself as vulnerable, in a stronger sense, if *any* Soviet nuclear weapons could be detonated on its territory, especially on its cities. SDI-1 defenses promise to remove U.S. vulnerability in both senses. It seems clear that unless the United States escaped vulnerability in the stronger sense, it would regard the Soviet nuclear threat as needing to be countered with a U.S. nuclear threat.

12. To put it differently, the defenses would provide the United States with a new, morally acceptable form of deterrence – deterrence by threat of denial, rather than deterrence by threat of retaliatory punishment. Leakproof defenses would deny the Soviet Union the military gain from an attack, rather than punishing it by doing harm to its population and military forces in nuclear retaliation. The distinction between deterrence by threat of denial and deterrence by threat of punishment is drawn by Glenn Snyder, *Deterrence and Defense: Toward a Theory of National Security* (Princeton: Princeton University Press, 1961), pp. 14–16.

13. This point is made in Shue, "Morality of Offense Determines Morality of Defense," p. 14.

14. A similar argument is offered by Jonathan Schonsheck, "Philosophical Scrutiny in the Strategic 'Defence' Initiatives," *Journal of Applied Philosophy* 3, no. 2 (1986), 164.

15. See Charles L. Glaser, "Why Even Good Defenses May Be Bad," *International Security* 9, no. 2 (Fall 1984), 92–123, at 97–

99; rpt. in Steven E. Miller and Stephen Van Evera, ed., *The Star Wars Controversy: An "International Security" Reader* (Princeton: Princeton University Press, 1986), pp. 25–56.

16. This judgment is affirmed by James Schlesinger, "Rhetoric and Realities in the Star Wars Debate," *International Security* 10, no. 1 (Summer 1985), 3–12, at 5 (rpt. in Miller and Van Evera, *The Star Wars Controversy*, pp. 15–24), and in Office of Technology Assessment, *Strategic Defenses*, p. 33. According to Ashton Carter, "most knowledgeable observers" agree that "the prospect that BMD [ballistic missile defense] will thwart the mutual hostage relationship . . . is so remote as to be of no practical interest" ("Introduction to the BMD Question," in Carter and Schwartz, *Ballistic Missile Defense*, p. 11). Colin Gray, a strong supporter of the SDI, admits: "Strategic defense, in the future as in the past, will never be beyond successful challenge" (ibid., p. 405). A good discussion of the feasibility problems of SDI-1 defenses is to be found in Peter Zimmerman, "Pork Bellies and the SDI," *Foreign Policy* 63 (Summer 1986), 76–87.

17. But see Douglas Lackey, "Moral Principles and Strategic Defense," *Philosophical Forum* 18, no. 1 (Fall 1986), 2–3; rpt. in Lackey, *Ethics and Strategic Defense*, pp. 72–78.

18. An indication of this is that the U.S. military has already been moving to merge its offensive and prospective defensive forces under a single nuclear war plan and command structure. See "U.S. Studies Plan to Integrate Nuclear Arms with a Missile Shield," *New York Times*, May 29, 1985, p. A8.

19. See, for example, Schlesinger, "Rhetoric and Realities in the Star Wars Debate," pp. 5–6.

20. The argument that SDI defenses would enhance deterrence is made in virtually all pro-SDI writings. See, for example, Casper Weinberger, Report to Congress, 4 February 1985, rpt. in *Daedalus* 114, no. 3 (Summer 1985), 373–77. Proponents of the SDI argue that these defenses would also enhance deterrence *in* war, as will be seen below.

21. One who presents the strategic argument as also a moral argument is Colin Gray, in "Strategic Defense, Deterrence, and the Prospects for Peace," *Ethics* 95, no. 3 (April 1985), 659–72.

22. See Gregory Kavka, "Space War Ethics," *Ethics* 95, no. 3 (April 1985), 675.

23. See Ashton Carter, "BMD Applications: Performance and

Limitations," in Carter and Schwartz, *Ballistic Missile Defense*,
pp. 102–3, and Office of Technology Assessment, *Strategic
Defenses*, pp. 285–89.

24. Leon Sloss, "The Case for Deploying Strategic Defenses,"
Chapter 8 of this volume.

25. Keith Payne, *Strategic Defense: "Star Wars" in Perspective* (Lan-
ham, Md.: Hamilton, 1986), pp. 212–18. Fred S. Hoffman,
"The SDI in U.S. Nuclear Strategy," *International Security* 10,
no. 1 (Summer 1985), 13–24, at 15 (rpt. in Miller and Van
Evera, *The Star Wars Controversy*, pp. 3–14).

26. Zbigniew Brzezinski, "Mutual Strategic Security and Strategic
Defense," Zbigniew Brzezinski et al., ed., *Promise or Peril*
(Washington: Ethics and Public Policy Center, 1986), pp. 56–
66.

27. These doctrines are discussed in Office of Technology Assessment, *Strategic Defenses*, pp. 76–86.

28. Ibid., pp. 87–89; Leon Sloss, "The Strategist's Perspective,"
in Carter and Schwartz, *Ballistic Missile Defense*, pp. 39–43.

29. Charles Glaser, "Do We Want the Missile Defenses We Can
Build?" *International Security* 10, no. 1 (Summer 1985), 25–57,
at 36–37 (rpt. in Miller and Van Evera, *The Star Wars Controversy*, pp. 98–130).

30. Carter, "BMD Applications," pp. 103, 111–13.

31. Glaser, "Do We Want the Missile Defenses We Can Build?"
p. 36.

32. Ibid., p. 34.

33. This is referred to as the problem of arms-race instability. For
a general discussion of SDI-2 defenses and arms-race stability,
see Union of Concerned Scientists, *The Fallacy of Star Wars*,
pp. 154–59; and Office of Technology Assessment, *Strategic
Defenses*, pp. 128–32.

34. Some believe that the Soviet Union is sure to deploy extensive
defenses of the SDI-2 type whether the United States deploys
them or not. But the Soviet Union seems eager to negotiate a
mutual ban on space-based missile defenses, so the United
States can probably preclude the Soviet deployment by bargaining away its own option to deploy.

35. Union of Concerned Scientists, *The Fallacy of Star Wars*, p. 168.

36. See Robert McNamara, *Blundering into Disaster: Surviving the
First Century of the Nuclear Age* (New York: Pantheon, 1986),
pp. 55–59. Kosygin's remark quoted in the epigraph of this

article was an outburst in response to McNamara's pointing out to him that the deployment of defenses would lead to a vigorous arms race (ibid., p. 57).

37. Keith Payne and Colin Gray, "Nuclear Policy and the Defensive Transition," *Foreign Affairs* 62, no. 4 (Spring 1984), 839.

38. Paul Nitze, "On the Road to a More Stable Peace," United States Department of State, Bureau of Public Affairs, Current Policy No. 657, p. 2.

39. Schlesinger, "Rhetoric and Realities in the Star Wars Debate," pp. 7–8; Glaser, "Do We Want the Missile Defenses We Can Build?" pp. 37–40.

40. When the likelihood of war in a crisis is increased, this is referred to as crisis instability. For a general discussion of crisis stability and a view on how it would be affected by SDI-2 defenses, see Office of Technology Assessment, *Strategic Defenses*, pp. 113–14, 119–28; and Sidney D. Drell et al., "Preserving the ABM Treaty: A Critique of the Reagan Strategic Defense Initiative," *International Security* 9, no. 2 (Fall 1984), 51–91, at 80–81 (rpt. in Miller and Van Evera, *The Star Wars Controversy*, pp. 57–97, at 86–87).

41. Earlier it was claimed that SDI defenses could not eliminate the vulnerability of American society to Soviet attack. The point here is that very effective SDI-2 defenses might eliminate the vulnerability of American society *in conjunction with an extensive counterforce first strike* – or at least appear to be able to do so. (The counterforce first strike would, in Glaser's phrase, become the "pre-boost-phase" layer of defense.)

42. Glaser, "Do We Want the Missile Defenses We Can Build?" p. 52.

43. Glaser, "Why Even Good Defenses May Be Bad," pp. 107–8; Hoffman, "The SDI in U.S. Nuclear Strategy," p. 22.

44. For a general discussion of the vulnerability of the command and control network, see Bruce Blair, *Strategic Command and Control: Redefining the Nuclear Threat* (Washington: Brookings Institution, 1985).

45. The vulnerability of SDI-2 defenses is often discussed as part of an overall assessment of their technological feasibility, specifically that part which concerns the effect of Soviet countermeasures. See, for example, Union of Concerned Scientists, *The Fallacy of Star Wars*, pp. 115–25, 137–40, 144–46.

46. The basic assumption in this part of the argument is that the

Steven Lee

defenses are very effective, and it may seem that defenses could not be very effective if they were vulnerable. But it is best to keep judgments of effectiveness and vulnerability separate, since the impact of the vulnerability of defenses on their performance depends in part on whether the other side strikes first.

47. Nitze, "On the Road to a More Stable Peace," p. 2.
48. See Schlesinger, "Rhetoric and Realities in the Star Wars Debate," p. 10.
49. If the defenses were very effective, the premise might not be false, since the Soviet Union might not be able to pay the increased attack price. But the more effective the defenses, the more the likelihood of war would be increased because of the potential for Soviet preemptive attack in a crisis.
50. As we have seen, it is claimed that SDI-2 defenses could limit a nuclear war in a second way – by serving as a deterrent in war. But the judgment that war avoidance is of greater moral importance still stands, since the basic truth remains that any nuclear war would almost certainly involve a very large loss of life. In addition, there are serious doubts about how effective deterrence in war could be, given the obstacles to keeping a nuclear war limited.
51. Colin Gray claims that "the U.S. government has a moral obligation to make what provision it is able to for the saving of American lives – an absolute value": "Strategic Defense, Deterrence, and the Prospects for Peace," p. 660.
52. This article is republished, with minor editorial changes, from *Philosophy & Public Affairs* 17, no. 1 (Winter 1988), 15–43, with permission of Princeton University Press. Copyright © 1988 Princeton University Press. This article was written in 1986–87 while I was a Rockefeller Fellow at the Institute for Philosophy and Public Policy at the University of Maryland, and I would like to thank the Institute and its staff for the support and stimulation they provided, and also to thank the many others who contributed to my thinking on these issues during that time.

Index

ABM Treaty, *see* Anti-Ballistic Missile (ABM) Treaty
abolition of war, 15–20, 24, 42, 286
abortion, 266
accuracy, 103, 258, 259
  improved, 99–100, 264
  in World War II, 244, 246–7
action
  intention and, 179, 182–3, 184–5, 187, 189–90
  moral life and, 207
  psychological orientation toward, 182–3, 187, 190–2
Active Defense, 296, 299–301, 303, 304, 311, 322
  and add-on strategy, 302
  in U.S. strategy, 362–3, 364, 365–6
add-on strategy, 302
Adenauer, Konrad, 312, 313
aerial bombing, 8, 233, 235
  in World War I, 235–9, 241–2
affordability, of conventionalization, 306–8; *see also* cost(s)
Afghanistan, 122, 137, 163
Afheldt, Eckart, 326
Afheldt, Horst, 314–15, 316, 317, 330
agent(s)
  character of, 185
  as moral being, 189–91, 192, 193, 196, 207–8
  orientation to evil, 206
  relations between, 197–216
air defenses, 323–4, 368
  Soviet Union, 355, 363, 371
  U.S., 350
air force(s), 257–8
  future, 323
AirLand Battle doctrine, 304–6
  fire element of, 306, 307
air raids, counterforce, 236
air warfare
  in Korean War, 249
  in Middle East wars, 251
  kill ratio in, 324
  in World War I, 239–44
  in World War II, 244–8, 256
air warfare theory, 242–3
Allen, Malcolm, 326
alliances, U.S., 344–8
allies, 52
  deterring nuclear attacks on, 2–3
  and finite deterrence, 280–3
  and Nuclear Protectionism, 130–1
  U.S. commitment to security of, 10, 347–8, 350–1, 355, 362, 370, 371
  see also extended deterrence
Alternative Defense, 324–5
  evolution of, 311–13
  implementation and response, 335–7
  NATO and, 333–5
  philosophy and history of, 308–17
  public support for, 328–33
analogy(ies), avoidance of, in moral hypocrisy, 265–6
answering in kind, 336
  NATO policy of, 310, 328, 330
anti-aircraft umbrella, 306

Index

anti-ballistic-missile (ABM) weapons/
 systems, 227, 254, 350, 353, 354,
 365, 366
Anti-Ballistic Missile (ABM) Treaty,
 350, 353, 367, 400
 effect of SDI on, 368–9
antitank guided weapons (ATGWs),
 314
Arab-Israeli War, 299
area bombing, 244–5
area defense, 314–15, 318, 321, 322
 air forces and, 323
 Alternative Defense and, 325, 326
armored and mechanized formations,
 300, 301, 303–5, 312–13
arms control, 52, 154, 329, 366
 and defense programs, 352–3
 effectiveness of, 356–7
 Nuclear Protectionism and, 152–4
 strategic defenses in, 119
arms control agreements, 138, 353, 400
arms control negotiations, 332, 348
arms control regime, 361, 368–9
arms race, 62–3, 97, 98, 99, 185, 213,
 290, 336
 defenses and, 368–70
 dynamics of, 310
 SDI and, 399–401, 408
arms reductions, 1–2, 8, 43–4, 216,
 356–7
arsenals, size of, and finite deterrence,
 359; *see also* Nuclear arsenals
art of war, 305–6
artillery rockets, precision-guided, 314–
 15
assured destruction, 8, 120–1, 122, 129,
 167, 352
 abandonment of, 212–13
 capacity for, 73, 212–13
 and credibility, 61
 defense of, 7–8
 overkill beyond, 271–3
 required level of, 100
 and second-strike capability, 18
 standard of, 56–7, 78
 in U.S. policy, 255
 see also mutual assured destruction
 (MAD)
assured destruction strategy, 152
 morality of, 124
attack assessment systems, 354
attack price, 11, 397–9, 405
attrition, 301–3, 311
autonomous effects, 183, 184

B-1B bomber, 144, 360
balance, 329, 330, 331, 335
 stability dependent on, 310, 311
balance of forces, 97–8
balance of terror, 18, 19–20, 57, 271,
 289
Ball, Desmond, 285
ballistic missile defenses, 359–60, 363,
 381, 384
ballistic missiles, 274, 275, 278
barrage attacks, 278
Battle of Verdun, 252
Benn, Stanley, 187
Betts, Richard K., 37
Biedenkopf, Kurt, 328
blitzkrieg, 296–7
blockades, 7–8, 233, 234, 238–9, 240,
 242, 247, 248, 262
bluff (bluffing), 57, 123, 179, 180, 181,
 230
Boeker, Egbert, 322
Bonin, Bogislaw von, 312–13, 328
Bonin Plan, 313, 329
Brezhnev, Leonid, 138
Brodie, Bernard, 119
Brossollet, Guy, 314
Brown, Harold, 44, 168, 349
Bundeswehr University (Munich), 317,
 335–6
Bundy, McGeorge, 5, 68, 120, 171, 182,
 283
burden sharing, 324
 two-pillar concept of, 334–5

C^{3}I (command, control, communications and intelligence) systems,
 302, 349, 360, 365
 survivability of, 354, 362–3
camouflage, 319–20, 325
Canby, Steven, 322
capability(ies), 88, 115
 as deterrent, 73–5, 76, 120–1
casualty estimates, 271–2
 in counterforce attacks, 281–3
Catholic bishops (U.S.), critique of U.S.
 nuclear policy, 6, 7, 117, 125–7,
 200–1, 264, 269
Catholic Church, 331; *see also* Catholic
 bishops
cease-fire, 78–9, 80, 82–3, 85, 176
Central Europe, threat scenarios, 293–8
China, 186, 274, 283
Christian Conservatives (political party,
 West Germany), 331

Index

conventional deterrence (*continued*)
 in NATO policy, 328
 structural change in, 334
conventional force reduction, 2, 9, 334
 symmetrical, 138
conventional forces, 9, 119, 130, 133,
 351
conventional modernization, NATO,
 360
conventional war, 3, 17, 130, 215
 counterforce strategies in, 175
 likelihood of, 165
conventionalization, 294
 NATO's approach to, 299–308, 310,
 325–6
cooperation, 185–6, 410
 mutual vulnerability and, 18–19, 43
Corbett, Sir Julian, 238, 251
Corcoran, Ed, 321
corruption
 conditional intention and, 183–93
 consequentialist justification of, 195
 effects and connections of, 191–2
cost(s)
 of conventional deterrence, 358
 of defense, 101
 of offensive buildup, 360–1
 and retaliation, 364
 and SDI, 362, 368–73
cost-benefit ratio
 and Alternative Defense, 324–7
 and defenses, 369–70
cost-effectiveness
 of SDI, 401
 technology in, 317
counterconcentration, 314–15, 326
counterforce, 8, 31, 212, 279, 285
 and demands of superiority, 31–3
 distinct from countervalue, 232–3,
 235–9, 241, 242, 245–6, 247–53,
 254–5, 259–60, 262, 267–9
 modest, 4, 5–6, 7, 174–5, 178, 212–
 14, 258–61
 preemptive, 36, 102
 and proportionate risk, 26–31
 and proportionate threat, 21–6
 see also finite counterforce
counterforce attacks
 casualty estimates in, 281–3, 282f
 as damage limitation, 30
counterforce capability, 32–3, 70, 101,
 144, 149
 ambitious, 61, 62, 63–4, 97
 in damage limitation, 384

 in finite deterrence, 279–83
 first-strike, 98, 99
 modest, 97, 102
 of Soviet Union, 363
 survivable, 249
counterforce strategy, 6, 7–8, 124
 in U.S. policy, 167, 168
counterforce targets, 273, 276, 397
counterforce warfare, 55, 56
 costs/benefits of, 84–5
 and credibility, 59, 60–1
 damage limitation by, 82–4, 85–6,
 88–9, 90, 91, 93, 97, 99–100, 102,
 103, 175–6, 286–7
 force reduction through, 67
 as proper response to nuclear attack,
 74, 77, 78–96
 SDI as implement of, 11, 396
 second-strike, 85–9, 90, 96, 98, 99,
 100, 101, 103
counterforce weapons, 269, 273, 276–9,
 402
 deep reductions in, 274, 276–9, 290
counter-military/political retaliatory attacks, 116, 128–9
countervailing strategy, 4–5, 6, 10, 24,
 124, 362
 criticism of, 42–3, 117–18, 144, 152
 and damage limitation, 30–1
 effectiveness of, 24, 25
 implementation of, 37
 logic of, 115–16
 mutual, 38, 43–4
 in Nuclear Protectionism, 153
 problems with, 31–3
 and preemption, 42
 and proportionate risk, 26–31
 SDI and, 11, 394–5, 396, 403, 404
 and stability, 152–3
 superiority of, 38–40, 41–2
countervalue, 7–8, 16, 84
 distinct from counterforce, 232–3,
 235–9, 241, 242, 245–6, 247–53,
 254–5, 259–60, 262, 267–9
 in prevention/termination of war,
 267–8
 separable possibility of, 233–5
countervalue targeting, 230, 240, 261,
 262
credible response options, 115, 116
credibility, 13, 98, 103, 229
 of countervailing strategy, 32
 damage limitation and, 97
 defenses in, 367

Index

with finite deterrence, 359
and mutual vulnerability, 21–5
of nuclear threats, 121
proportionality and, 23–4
of retaliation, 364
of SDI, 370
credibility problem, 102, 303
in existential deterrence, 69–70, 72–3
in MAD, 52, 54, 55–6, 57, 58, 64–5, 73
in NUTS, 58–9, 60–2, 64–5, 73
crisis(es), 75, 83, 213, 214
existential deterrence and, 69–71, 72
response to, 83
SDI and likelihood or war in, 401–8
temptation to shoot first in, 298
crisis bargaining, 354
crisis management, 357
crisis prevention, 404
crisis stability
defenses in, 372
force reductions in, 290, 293
cruise missiles, 257, 275, 360
Cuban Missile Crisis, 34
cultural standards, and prevention of war, 264–5
Czechoslovakia, 163, 171, 297, 298, 304

damage, counterforce, 398–9
damage limitation, 5, 6, 29–31, 55, 98
in conventional posture, 294
in counterforce warfare, 82–4, 85–6, 88–9, 90, 91, 97, 99–100, 102, 103, 175–6, 286–7
in countervailing strategies, 30–1
defenses in, 101, 350
in deterrence, 98, 124, 347
in existentialism, 77–81, 103
first strike and, 145
incapability of, in NATO nuclear posture, 309
intermediate defenses in, 366
in MAD and NUTS, 59–60
moral value of, 11, 391–2, 394
in Nuclear Protectionism, 133
in preemption, 36, 404, 405
in relation to war avoidance, 391–4, 408
through SDI, 212, 382, 384–5, 389–90, 396, 408–10
in Soviet strategy, 363
target coverage requirements for, 278
technology in, 154
in U.S. policy, 254–5

damage-limiting capabilities, 116, 136, 149
deployment of, 150
in extended deterrence, 280–1
in Nuclear Protectionism, 153
damage-limiting strategy, 276
criticisms of, 144, 152
morality of, 118, 124
Nuclear Protectionism as, 128–9
Danish navy, 324
decapitation strike, 148–9, 349
decision making, 202
in nuclear war, 183, 188
rational, 171
uncertainty in, 182
declaratory policy, 52, 168, 182
in finite counterforce principles, 102
decoupling, 362, 371
Deep Strike, 298–9, 301–3, 306, 315, 325, 328, 358
defense, 55, 56, 259
alternative form of conventional, 9–10
in arms control, 361
in deterrence, 27, 116, 361–2
finite counterforce and, 100–1
fire-oriented, 299–301, 302
force reduction through, 67
good offense as, 27, 29
just, 126
preemptive strike as, 36–7
in U.S. strategy, 347
see also Active Defense; Alternative Defense; passive defense
defense budgets, 294, 306, 360, 368
defense capability, of Soviet Union, 363–4
defense planning, West Germany, 335–6
defense policy, politics of, 102–3
defense spending
of NATO, 357
and social policy, 107–8
defense technologies, 116
defenses, 88, 212, 254, 361
active, 346, 350 (see also Active Defense)
and arms race, 369–70
cooperation in, 18, 19
cost-effectiveness of, 369–70
and counterforce warfare, 61
in deterrence, 10–11, 382, 390–410
effectiveness of, 384–5
in finite deterrence, 287–8

421

Index

defenses (*continued*)
  intermediate, 367–73
  layered, 366–7, 383–4
  "leaky," 367
  less-than-perfect, 363–73
  and likelihood of nuclear war, 389,
    392–3, 399–410
  methods of defeating, 388
  moral consequences of, 382–3
  Nitze criteria for deployment of, 400
  vulnerability of, 405–7
  as war-limiting mechanism, 382
defensive defense, 314
  response to, 335
defensive posture, 317, 318
defensive strategy, of Soviet Union,
  138–9
defensivity, 312–13
demographic crisis, 295, 317, 319, 325
denial, 9, 313; *see also* deterrence by
  denial
denial by attrition, 304, 311
destabilization, 144
  defenses in, 371–2
deterrence, 2–4, 6–7
  abandonment of, 210–16, 409–10
  alternatives to, 227, 228
  assured destruction as bedrock of,
    271
  conventional warfare in, 215 (*see also*
    conventional deterrence)
  and corruption, 194
  criticisms of, 13
  and damage limitation, 98, 124, 347
  as defense, 27
  defenses in, 10–11, 367, 374, 382,
    390–410
  destabilization of, 71–2
  existence of weapons in, 67–8, 73
  of finite deterrence, 279–83
  forms of, 2, 3
  immorality of, 183–202, 212
  incoherence in, 15
  internalist critique of, 165–71, 179–83
  logic of, 149, 265–7
  MAD as, 53–8
  and likelihood of war, 164
  means/ends in, 15–20
  and moral use of nuclear weapons,
    115–62
  morality of, 6–7, 228, 254, 262–8, 385
  objections to, 163
  rationales for, 1
  reduced role of, 293–4

  refusal to face reality of, 228, 239,
    248–58, 262–3, 266–7, 268–9
  renunciation of, 52
  replaced by SDI, 385, 386–90
  requirements for, 364
  resolve in, 115, 118–24, 129, 134
  standard of, 99
  strengthening of, 10
  success of, 62
  understanding of, 103
  in U.S. strategy, 347, 387–8
  see also extended deterrence; finite
    deterrence; immoral deterrence;
    strategic nuclear deterrence
deterrence by denial, 10, 23–4, 31, 33,
  43, 116, 325, 364, 365
  shift from, to deterrence by punish-
    ment, 228, 241, 250
deterrence by punishment, 24, 228,
  229, 241, 242, 248–53, 325, 326
  candor in, 253–6
deterrence capability, 115
  and deterrence failure, 283–6
deterrence failure, 5, 8–9, 36, 73, 77,
  116–17, 152, 166–7
  deterrence following, 60
  fighting back after, 41–2
  and finite deterrence, 283–9
  historical, 149–50
  and justification of nuclear weapons
    use, 6
  likelihood of, 212, 214
  morality of nuclear weapons use fol-
    lowing, 165–6
  NATO policy and, 333
  response to, 57–8, 83–4, 181–2
  "deterrence only" stance, 117, 122–3,
    352
deterrence policy, 163, 213
  government-citizen relation and,
    200–2
  immorality of, 179–80
deterrence theory, 25, 143, 153
  moral paradox of, 227
  targeting in, 170
deterrence threshold, 358
deterrent intention, 186, 187
  abandoning, 214
"Devil's Bargains and the Real World"
  (Lewis), 193
DGB (German All-Union Congress,
  332
Dick, C. J., 297
diplomacy, in U.S. strategy, 348

Index

disarmament, 119–20, 200–2, 210–16, 227, 269, 330
  deterrent threats in, 286
  in reduction of counterforce capabilities, 273
  and strategic defense, 288–9
  see also unilateral (nuclear) disarmament
disarmament talks, 329
discrimination (principle), 29–30, 166, 169, 172–3, 177, 386
disengagement, from immoral policies, 7, 202–5, 206–7, 208–10, 212–16
disproportionality, 20, 26
distance (relation), 197–9
distinctions, arbitrary, 266
doctrinal development, 299–300, 310–11
Doctrine of Deterrence by Denial, 24
Doctrine of Flexible Response, 24
Donnelly, C. N., 297
double effect (principle), 93–4, 95, 177–8
Douhet, Giulio, 239–40, 241, 242, 256
Dresden, 246
Dummett, Michael, 195–6
Dutch navy, 324

early warning systems, 350
East Germany, *see* German Democratic Republic (GDR)
economic warfare, 234
Economist, The, 323
Eden, Anthony, 169
Einstein, Albert, 16
ends
  good, 94
  in prevention of war, 15
  see also means/ends relation
endurance, in U.S. strategy, 353–5, 358, 360
Enhanced Radiation Warhead, 370
escalation, 57, 70, 82
  in conventional conflict, 327
  in easy stages, 71
  inevitability of, 358
escalation control, 349, 350, 363
escalation risk, 83, 117, 120, 126, 129, 170, 171, 294, 303, 325, 345, 346
  attack price and, 399
  justification of, 135–6
  in maneuver warfare, 305
  NATO policy and, 310
  unacceptable, 123–4

ESECS panel (European Security Study), 301, 302
ESECS II, 306–7
ethical analysis, 2, 3–4
Europe
  conventional defenses, 215
  defense of, 230, 293–342
  limited nuclear war in, 170–1
  and Nuclear Protectionism, 134–5
  in superpower confrontation, 282–3, 334, 351
  see also NATO
European Defense Initiative (EDI), 298–9, 328
European Study Group on Alternative Security Policy, 9
Europeanization (NATO), 334–5
evidence condition, in preemption, 34, 35, 38
evil, 209–10
  corruption and, 191, 192
  disentanglement from, 203
  moral choice in, 197
  orientation to, 190, 192, 206
Evolution of Nuclear Strategy, The (Freedman), 1
existential deterrence (existentialism), 5, 6, 8–9, 53, 65–73, 74, 75, 76, 81, 89–90, 98, 101, 120–2, 182, 213, 216, 283
  and damage limitation, 78
  and MAD and NUTS, 52
  objections to, 69–73
extended deterrence, 2–3, 71–2, 170, 175, 348, 350–1
  crises in, 75
  defensive systems for, 362
  effect of defenses on, 370–1
  in finite deterrence, 8, 280–3, 359
  intermediate defenses in, 367–8
  limited defenses and, 364–5
  MAD in, 229–30
  SDI and, 394–5
extrication (problem), 6–7
  immoral deterrence and, 163–225
extrication strategies, 201–2, 203, 204, 206–7, 208–10, 212–16

Falkenhayn (German commander), 252
fallout, 56, 63–4, 92, 95
  global, 131
  reduction of, 99, 100
Federal Republic of Germany, 9, 186, 283, 318, 370

423

Index

Index

Index

Index

433

Index

435